In the Shadow of the Prophet

In the Shadow

Milton Viorst

of the Prophet

The Struggle
for the Soul of Islam

A Member of the Perseus Books Group

Copyright © 2001 by Westview Press, A Member of the Perseus Books Group

Westview Press books are available at special discounts for bulk purchases in the United States by corporations, institutions, and other organizations. For more information, please contact the Special Markets Department at The Perseus Books Group, 11 Cambridge Center, Cambridge MA 02142, or call (617) 252-5298.

Published in 2001 in the United States of America by Westview Press, 5500 Central Avenue, Boulder, Colorado 80301–2877, and in the United Kingdom by Westview Press, 12 Hid's Copse Road, Cumnor Hill, Oxford OX2 9JJ

Find us on the World Wide Web at www.westviewpress.com

A CIP catalog record is available for this book from the Library of Congress.
ISBN 0-8133-3902-2
Originally an Anchor Book, published by Doubleday, a division of Bantam Doubleday Dell Publishing Group, Inc.
1540 Broadway, New York, New York 10036

The paper used in this publication meets the requirements of the American National Standard for Permanence of Paper for Printed Library Materials Z39.48–1984.

10   9   8   7   6   5   4   3   2   1

This book is dedicated to
men whose friendship,
generosity of spirit and commitment to a better world
have inspired me.

Leonard Boudin, François Coulet, Sol Price, Joe Rauh,
Ben Spock, Izzy Stone, Merle Thorpe, Harold Willens

Contents

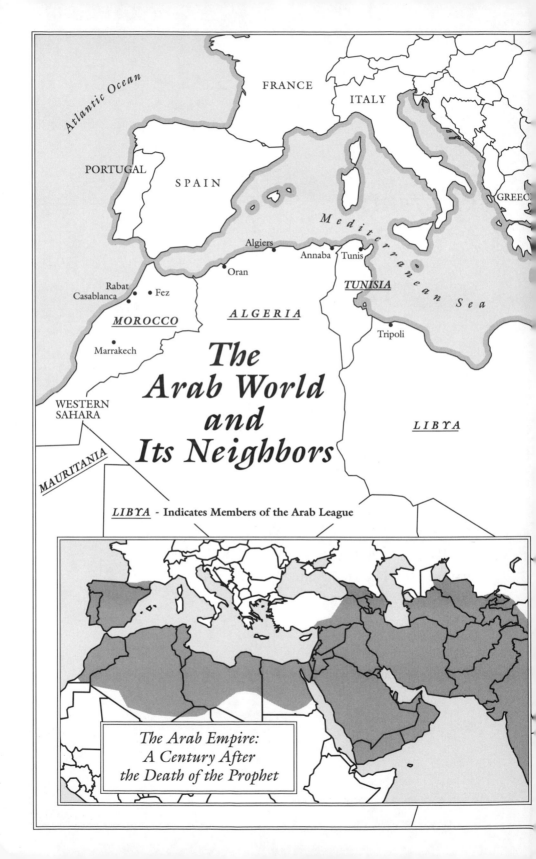

The Arab World and Its Neighbors

LIBYA - Indicates Members of the Arab League

The Arab Empire:
A Century After
the Death of the Prophet

Foreword

THIS IS NOT a prescriptive book. As a writer, I would be more comfortable if it were. Over the course of some twenty-five years of work and study, I have acquired a fondness for the Arabs and an esteem for their civilization. And so, as the world changes, I am troubled that the Arabs, both politically and economically, are falling increasingly behind other societies. This is not my observation alone; most Arabs share it. But I must leave to them the quest for a formula to reverse the course.

This book is an exploration into what, after a dazzling beginning, went amiss in Arab society. It abjures the Western clamor against terrorism, as well as Arab claims that all would be well if only the West were less imperious. These subjects, whatever their merits, I abdicate to others. This book aspires to strip off the exterior layers to get to the heart of Arab culture, the body of conventional Islamic belief. It is there that the current problem surely lies. Certainly, the struggle for the soul of Islam that is being waged throughout the Arab world is not just religious; it is about politics in the widest sense.

The analysis may trouble some readers. Since to raise questions about religion, particularly the religion of others, is a delicate matter, it troubles me too. But I believe readers can approach an understanding of one of the world's major civilizations only by recognizing the religious values that underlie it. To convey that understanding, within the context of the Arabs' painful religious struggles, is the goal of this book.

I am grateful to many people of the Islamic faith who have shared their wisdom and observations on this subject with me. I have found them throughout the Middle East, as well as in the United States and Europe. More than a few are identified in the text, but they are only a fraction of the total number. I could not have written this book without their wisdom and candor.

I want also to thank those who examined the manuscript, in whole or in part, saving me from many errors. I express my particular appreciation to Francis E. Peters of New York University, among our country's great Islamic scholars, who read major segments of the text. I also want to thank Leonard Beerman, Namir Jawdat and, especially, Nicholas Viorst, my son, an excellent editor. I am grateful for the help of Adnan Abu Odeh and Musa Keilani in Amman, Said Aburish in London, Sadiq al-Azm in Damascus, Tahsin Bashir in Cairo, Gilles Delafon, Olivier Roy and Brahim Younessi in Paris, Shihab Jamjoom in Riyadh, Alireza Haghighi in Tehran, Youssef Nacib in Algiers and Hafez el-Nager in Khartoum. I was well served by the dedication of the staff of the Middle East Institute Library, notably Betsy Folkins.

I thank James Hoge for publishing major excerpts of the book in *Foreign Affairs*. I also thank my agent, Andrew Wylie, for his faith in the book. And I especially thank my wife, Judith, who was, as always, unfailingly helpful and unremittingly supportive.

In the Shadow of the Prophet

1

Through the Damascus Gate

ONE EVENING in the fall of 1993, I passed beneath the arch of the Damascus Gate in Jerusalem and rediscovered the cobblestone labyrinth of the Old City. It was a few weeks after the signing of the Oslo Accord, by which the Jews and Arabs of Palestine seemed to signal that their long struggle might be coming to an end. The Old City's shops, after the years of strife known as the *intifada,* had at last reopened. Display windows were brightly lit. Merchants summoned passersby to examine their wares.

I loved the Old City, and had wandered through its narrow streets countless times before. But as I browsed to the left and right, an observation came to mind that I had not made before. How different, I thought, were the products offered by the Arab and Jewish store-keepers. Most of the Arab shops had identical olivewood camels for sale, beautifully carved by native craftsmen; the Jewish shops peddled dazzling jewelry, freshly designed, obviously fabricated in state-of-the-art workshops.

The notion occurred to me that evening, and has remained with me since, that the two products summarized, in simple but tangible terms, the cultural difference between the Middle East and the West. The wooden camels, emblem of the bedouin roots to which so many Arabs remain attached, were a reminder of the resistance to change that strongly pervades Arab culture. The silver necklaces—many far less pleasing to my eye than the camels—testified to the innovativeness, as well as the glitz, that the Jews who settled in Israel brought with them from the West.

My epiphany did not signal the superiority of one of these cultures over the other. People are partial to the system of values they know best, but no objective standards exist to judge either of these two as morally preeminent. The difference represented by the products was functional. But, as such, the difference seemed to me to bear heavily on the relative position of West and Middle East in today's world.

The camels, I believe, bespeak the deep attachment of Arab culture to a heritage that has been transmitted largely intact over countless generations. The jewelry encapsules the greater readiness of Westerners to subject their practices to constant review, experimentation, modification.

I would argue that this difference, in large part, explains why the West is rich and the Arab world poor. Commerce, rightly or wrongly, rewards initiative. Moreover, in an age of global economics, when the returns more than ever go to those who move smartly to stay ahead of the competition, the gap between the two cultures is growing steadily wider.

The numbers underline the trend. The 1995 Unified Arab Economic Report, published by a consortium of pan-Arab organizations, reports per capita income among the Arabs at about $2,000 annually—a seventh that of Israel, a tenth that of the United States.

Even the $2,000 represents a distortion, however, since it includes income from oil, which was concentrated in rather few hands, in a few Arab countries. Take out the oil revenue—the product not of entrepreneurship but of geological good fortune—and per capita income was substantially lower.

But more ominous than the level of income itself was the trend. Income in the Arab world had fallen by more than 20 percent since 1980, a period during which income throughout the West steadily rose.

The report showed that the total domestic product of the Arab world since 1980 grew at about 1 percent annually. Population, meanwhile, increased at triple that rate, from 165 million to 245 million. Exports, investment, productivity and the management of infrastructure and natural resources slipped further behind the more prosperous societies, while oil prices, declining in recent years, showed long-term signs of falling even further.

In Saudi Arabia and its Gulf neighbors, oil reserves assure the preservation of acceptable living standards. But in other Arab states the combination of stagnant growth and a soaring number of mouths to feed creates an increasing strain on the fabric of the society. The pressure is felt most immediately on food supplies but it also encompasses institutions like schools and hospitals. This strain is steadily eroding Arab morale, as well as the material level of Arab life.[1]

Wealth, of course, is not the only measure of Arab status. A thousand years ago the Arabs dazzled the world with their military prowess, no less than with their intellectual and artistic attainments. Western culture offered no match for Arab achievements, and Arab civilization seemed assured of a preeminent future. Yet today, the Arab ranking in these same fields is painfully low. Arabs are not insensitive to the gap and look back to their days of grandeur with nostalgia, and discontent.

Some Arabs claim the West attained its superiority by virtue of its long head start in technological and economic development. The claim helps relieve them of responsibility for their failures and, more important, permits them to dream that they will someday catch up. But it also leaves them without an explanation for Japan's leap ahead, or for the economic upsurge elsewhere in Asia that has more recently left the Middle East far behind.

Not many decades ago the entire Pacific rim was as poor as the Middle East, and observers made little distinction between the promise of the two regions. I have an Egyptian friend who remembers his grandfather telling him that all of Cairo rejoiced in Japan's military victory over Russia in 1905, taking it to mean that the East, including the Arab world, was bringing the era of Western superiority to an end. Japan did, and now the Koreans, the Chinese, the Thais and even the long-lagging Filipinos are approaching Western levels of prosperity. The Arabs, however, are not.

Indeed, what Arabs find at home is economic lethargy and social stagnation. The energy, the daring, the entrepreneurial spirit that suddenly appeared in Pacific societies remain largely absent in the Middle East. The Arab world seems weighed down by pessimism over its future, if not outright despair.

Unfortunately, the rest of the world seems indifferent to this condition. The headlines in the international press that deal with the Middle East point instead to the violence and terrorism that are made out to be the region's chief product.

In Lebanon, Egypt and Algeria many thousands have been killed in recent years in savage civil strife. Middle East governments are suspects in the blowing up of Western airliners, causing hundreds of deaths. Suicide bombings by Palestinians in Israel have become commonplace. Syria, Libya, Iraq and Sudan are on a list prepared by the State Department of countries whose governments sponsor terrorism. The signs say to Westerners that terror, like poverty, is intrinsic to the Middle East.

The observation is, at best, shortsighted. The West's wars in this century were the deadliest in all history. Western streets are far more dangerous than the Middle East's, and crime, heavily related to the drug trade, takes more victims than all the Middle East's terrorists combined.

Recently I came across an article which offered evidence that terror is not uniquely Middle Eastern at all. "As the 19th century ended," wrote Walter Laqueur in *Foreign Affairs,* "it seemed no one [in the West] was safe from terrorist attack." In citing just the luminaries, he noted that French President Sadi Carnot was assassinated in 1894, Spanish Prime Minister Antonio Canovas and Austrian Empress Elizabeth in 1897, Italian King Umberto I in 1900 and U.S. President William McKinley in 1901.

"If in the year 1900 the leaders of the main industrial powers had assembled," Laqueur wrote, "most of them would have insisted on giving terrorism top priority on their agenda, as President Clinton did at the Group of Seven meeting after the June [1996] bombing of the U.S. military compound in Dhahran, Saudi Arabia. From this perspective, the recent upsurge of terrorist activity is not particularly threatening."[2]

The West's focus on Middle East terrorism is much too narrow. Terrorism is a serious problem, one that requires constant vigilance. But terrorism is a symptom of ailments that the social lens must be widened to include.

Arab weakness leaves few diplomatic or military options to achieve the society's external goals. Internally, Arabs see their social cohesion eroding as they fail to deal with the pressures of population and poverty. They feel that the international community treats them with disdain. Terrorism is the cry of a society in disarray, a society which acknowledges that it has lost its bearings.

The problem posed by Arab society—to itself, as well as to outsiders—has much broader implications than terrorism. I refer back to my earlier metaphor in noting that, in a world of rising prosperity, the Arabs will not overcome the barriers that confine them by carving olivewood camels.

The difficulty that Arab society experiences in adapting to a rapidly changing universe leaves it poised to become a permanent underclass. Terror will be one of the ways that it reacts. War—waged with cheap weapons of mass destruction—may be another. The flight of the hungry and unemployed has already begun, with substantial and growing Muslim communities taking refuge in Europe and the United States. Clearly, the problems of Arab society are spilling over into the West, and are unlikely to stop at any time soon. But the problem is only indirectly the West's. Its consequences are becoming global. And if there is to be a solution, it is in the hands of the Arabs alone.

· II ·

EARLY in the seventh century the Prophet Muhammad, claiming direct guidance from God, led an Arab army in spreading a monotheistic faith called Islam—literally, "submission" to God—throughout the Arabian peninsula. After his death in A.D. 632, his followers continued his work and, in a dozen years, their armies had shattered the old Roman Empire, conquering Syria, Palestine, Egypt and Iraq. In a second surge a few decades later, Arab armies occupied the coast of North Africa as far as the Atlantic Ocean. These conquered lands—where 100 million people speak Arabic and practice Islam—make up the Arab world today.

The empire established by Muhammad's heirs extended far beyond the Arab boundaries, however. Persia was an early conquest, and its culture contributed powerfully to Arab civilization. Much of India and Central Asia followed. Legions under Islam's flag subdued Spain and penetrated into France, though their occupation proved transitory. Later, missionaries converted major segments of Southeast Asia and the African coasts. Even today, Muhammad's faith finds new converts, extending the perimeter of what believers call Dar al-Islam, the Islamic world.

Globally, Muslims—literally, "those who submit" to God—are estimated at about a billion people. Islam covers societies as diverse as Nigeria and Afghanistan and the Maldive Islands, each of which expresses the faith in terms set by its own historical experience. Malaysia and Indonesia, for example, embraced Islam only in the fifteenth century, through the intermediation of Arab traders, and have since retained much of their native culture. Islam is a mansion of many diverse rooms.

But, while Islam has no central authority and accepts all believers as equal, the Arab world remains the heartland of its orthodoxy. All Muslims pray in Arabic and recognize the singularity of the Quran, an Arabic book. It was the Arabs, in Islam's first centuries, who shaped an inchoate body of Islamic commandments, the Prophet's heritage, into the powerful religious and legal creed, the *shari'a,* that remains today the core of the Muslim faith. Today, only Arabs are born to the tongue in which God addressed the Prophet, and the great institutions of

Islamic learning are still Arab. Islam defines the Arabs' civilization more than it does any other.

In many years of travel in the Middle East, it became apparent to me that Islam's impact on everyday life there is far greater than is Christianity's in the West. The Arab world today recalls historians' descriptions of Christian Europe, deeply immersed in religion, in the early Middle Ages. You feel Islam not just in the mosques but in the streets, the schools, the marketplaces. You see it in the dress of the women, hear it in the call of the muezzin. The degree to which Western society is permeated by Christianity is arguable; one can have no doubt that Arab society is profoundly permeated by Islam.

That does not mean that all Muslims, or even most, engage faithfully in religious practice. A substantial number ignore Quranic strictures by skipping prayers or drinking whiskey or failing to make the pilgrimage to Mecca. Piety in Islamic society, as in the West, may now be more the exception than the rule.

But Islam, like other religions, is more than a system for worshiping God. A faith imposes moral imperatives that have a far greater impact than ritual on the society to which it belongs. Religious values imperceptibly invade thought, speech and behavior. In the Arab world, Islam is the body of values, the moral imperatives, that lie at the foundation of the civilization.

The civilization is a sturdy one. Algerians boast, for example, that during France's 130-year occupation, Christian missionaries, though they worked under the aegis of the colonial government, made almost no converts. Throughout its history the Arab world has been repeatedly devastated by foreign invaders. For most of the past millennium its people have suffered the indignity of foreign rule. Arab culture has been subjected to foreign influences from ancient Greece to modern Europe. Notwithstanding all of these incursions, the Arab world has made few compromises with non-Muslim civilizations, retaining its Islamic integrity intact.

That is the positive side. Many Arabs, recognizing how enriching foreign contributions can be to a civilization, lament that theirs had absorbed so little. Islam, unlike Judaism and Christianity, did not reach maturity under foreign rule; it created its own civilization. Until modern times, even its conquerors were mostly Muslim; those who were not Muslims often became converts to Islam. Arab intellectuals—particularly those exposed to Western critical traditions—contend that Islam, as a closed society, deprived Muslims of the intellectual diversity they needed to compete with the outside world.

Many critics blame the Arabs' rigid orthodoxy that was forged from the Quran and Muhammad's personal guidance a thousand years ago. Fatima Mernissi, an Arab feminist, argues in *Beyond the Veil* that it is orthodoxy's perpetuation of the subjugation of women that accounts for the society's economic and social underdevelopment. Her interpretation may be tendentious, but orthodoxy, in its social imperatives, surely proved better at preserving solidarity than inspiring dynamism and originality. Demanding unquestioning submission to God and Islamic law, orthodoxy kept dissidence at bay, stifling individuality and creativity, qualities that Arabs had once demonstrated in abundance.

This orthodoxy is today the *Weltanschauung* of the Arab world. It plays the role that, in the West, Christianity played until religion's intellectual monopoly was broken by the secular ideals of the Renaissance. In the Arab world, where secularism has had little impact, Islam alone provides the guideposts of human conduct. It is embedded in the pores of the society. The last time that orthodoxy was seriously threatened by the assaults of reason—as we shall see in Chapter 5— was a millennium ago. Over the ensuing centuries, orthodoxy has successfully preserved Islam from meaningful change.

Westerners were given a lesson in orthodoxy's power when Iran's Ayatollah Khomeini in 1989 issued a *fatwa*—an order based on Islamic law—condemning to death the Muslim writer Salman Rushdie. Khomeini declared that Rushdie, in his novel *The Satanic Verses,* had defamed the Prophet, a capital offense.

Though many Arab intellectuals were embarrassed, few protested. Some were intimidated at the prospect of retaliation by religious extremists; others submitted to social pressure. But most accepted the orthodox position that, admirable as the right to free expression may be, those who insult God or the Prophet are subject to the death penalty under the law of Islam.

Islamic law constitutes the bedrock of Muslim belief. Few Muslims over history have challenged it. But in the twentieth century it appears that the bedrock may be shifting, that Muslims have begun a reexamination of their faith. It is hard to gauge how deeply the reexamination has penetrated the great body of believers. At the least, it can be said that this reexamination is having a major impact on the intellectual class, where social change normally begins.

At its present stage, the review of Islam does not suggest a reordering of values of the magnitude that the Renaissance imposed on Christianity. The reexamination is in the realm of interpretation that does not place the fundamental premises of the faith in jeopardy. Still, Muslims are asking questions.

The review of Islam began, for the most part, in the Arab community. It then moved on to Muslims outside—in Afghanistan and Turkey and Malaysia—where the Arab agenda tends to echo. As the twentieth century closes, the disputes have grown more stormy. One might say that the Arabs, who for nearly a millennium had few debates over their *Weltanschauung,* are unable to defer them any longer.

The reexamination is probably happening now because the twentieth century is different from the previous ten centuries in Arab history. Historians place the Arabs' apogee in about 950, after which there was steady decline. In the sixteenth century most of the Arab patrimony was overrun by the Ottoman Turks and reduced to neglected provinces. At that time, the Arabs, as instigators of events, dropped out of history.

They returned only after World War I, when the Ottoman Empire fell, though they were still far from controlling their own destiny. Their lands fell into the hands of the victorious Europeans, who divided them into twenty-one states, placing most under colonial rule. By mid-century, nearly all the Arab states had regained their independence, but they have continued to thrash about, seeking to make the transition to modern times.

Malek Bennabi, an Algerian thinker, is among the many Arabs who have addressed the issue of Arab society's failure to build strong economic and social institutions.[3] Arab nationalists, he wrote in 1970, condemn colonialism for their enduring backwardness. Though the charge may contain some truth, he said, it is basically a smoke screen for what is an Arab responsibility. Severe as the trauma of colonialism, both Turkish and European, undoubtedly was, Ottoman influence has all but disappeared from the Arab world, and the impact of Western rule diminishes notably each year. How long, Bennabi asked, can the Turks and the Europeans be blamed for the region's laggard condition?

Neither Ottomans nor Westerners ever ruled Yemen, Bennabi pointed out, but no Arab country is more backward, which suggests that colonialism may have little to do with the problem. Algeria, Bennabi's homeland, has a very different society from, say, Saudi Arabia's. The Arab countries are diverse in their geography, their natural resources, their historical experiences. What they have in common, Bennabi maintained, is underdevelopment—and Islam.

Is there, he asked, a correlation between the two? It is time for the Arabs, he wrote, to stop blaming outsiders for their dilemma. The real explanation for their impotence, he argued, lies within their own minds. These minds have been shaped around Islamic values. If the

Arabs are to restore their grandeur, he argued, they must begin by looking into themselves for the obstacles to growth that reside in the core of Islam.

Bennabi acquired followers who in time enlisted in the Islamic movement that, in the 1990s, challenged Algeria's secular regime. But within the movement were several factions, engaged in the disputes that characterize twentieth-century Islam. The debate was ostensibly over the meaning of Islamic texts. But the prize—as is so often true in religious disputes—was political power. All the Algerian factions acknowledged that Arab society was in sorry condition. Each contested for power on the grounds that its particular interpretation of Islam—and its interpretation alone—promised to transform the Arab destiny.

In a book called *Sandcastles*, published a few years ago, I examined some of the themes of Arab underdevelopment. But *Sandcastles*, chiefly concerned with Arab politics, contained only a glance at the contending doctrines within Islam. Since then my studies—and the criticisms of some readers—have persuaded me that, without my going more deeply into Islam myself, it is impossible to convey an understanding of the Arabs today, politically or otherwise. This book is the product of these studies. It is an examination of the doctrines of Islam, of the conflict among Muslims over the interpretation of these doctrines, and of the impact of the conflict on contemporary Arab society.

In the chapters entitled "The Prophet and the Book" and "Making the *Shari'a*," I examine the foundation of Islamic belief, how it has been shaped since the era of Muhammad and how it has become the hub of debate over the Arab future. In reports from the field, I explore the four Arab countries—Egypt, Sudan, Saudi Arabia and Algeria—where the conflicts over interpretation have become the most tumultuous.

In addition, the book contains a chapter on Islam in Iran, the most important of the non-Arabic countries in shaping the faith among the Arabs. And it has a chapter on Islam in France, host to the first—but surely not the last—major Muslim community within a Christian society. It concludes with a chapter on Jordan, where the Hashemite monarchy seems to offer Islam options that are not available in more orthodox states.

The struggle among Muslims for the soul of Islam is surely a difficult subject for most Westerners. The framework is unfamiliar. Most readers know few of the names and little of the history which lies at the foundation of this struggle. Since there are fine studies of Islamic history and doctrine for those interested in going further, I have tried to limit the technical information in the book to what is necessary to make its argument.

But because we in the West have ignored Islam for so long, I would urge readers to make the effort. The West, I believe, cannot function in indifference to the ideas that drive the Arab world. The stakes are too high. Whoever wins the factional struggle within Islam will acquire a great prize. At the least, the winner will determine the shape that relations take, in the short term and the long, between the Islamic world and the West.

· III ·

INEVITABLY, one begins the study of Islam with the Quran, the central text of the faith. Literally translated as "recitation," the Quran is the collection of revelations made in Arabic to Muhammad beginning about A.D. 610. Considered the literal word of God, the Quran—to be examined in detail in Chapter 3—is treated as holy, legally supreme and irrefutable. In omitting answers to many of the questions of daily life, however, it required a complementary source of authority. Because most Muslims also consider themselves people devoted to custom, they specifically sought that complementary source in the conduct of Muhammad and his immediate followers, those known as the *rashidun*, the "rightly-guided" caliphs.

The customs they adopted as law are called the *sunna*, which can be translated as "the way." How they came to adopt it is explored in Chapter 5. Those who recognize the preeminence of its rules are referred to as Sunnis. No deviation from the precedents of the Prophet is authorized to Sunnis; innovation—*bid'a* in Arabic—is regarded as heresy. The overwhelming majority of the Muslims in the Middle East are Sunnis. This book is principally about them.

Islam's largest schismatic sect are the Shi'ites, who heed, in addition to the Quran, a different source of authority from the Sunnis. Shi'ites are the dominant sect in Iran and are a majority in Iraq, but make up only about 10 percent of Muslims worldwide. The Sunni-Shi'ite schism is examined in Chapter 5 and Iranian Shi'ism, a major influence on the Arabs, in Chapter 6. The conflict on which this book dwells, however, is between the rival schools of interpretation among Sunnis, since the winner will determine the future of the Arab world.*

---

* Students of Islam are aware that there are four rival schools of jurisprudence, called *madhabs*, which account for modest regional variations in Islamic law. I mention this to avoid confusion. These schools are not the book's concern.

Sunnism's doctrines, the mainstream of Islamic belief, trace back to the establishment of the *shari'a,* Islamic law, in the tenth century. The term "orthodox"—defined by Webster as "correct doctrine, especially religious doctrine"—has been identified historically with Judaism and Christianity. Only in the twentieth century did Islam have to deal seriously with dissent—from (to use contemporary political vernacular) "modernism" on the left and "fundamentalism" on the right. Within this context, "orthodoxy" is an accurate designation for the Islamic mainstream.

Orthodoxy, while acknowledging underdevelopment, has never worried much about Muslim society. Deeply conservative, it is committed to safeguarding Islamic practice—social and economic as well as ritual—without change. Orthodoxy does not compare Islamic society with the outside world. It sees the Islamic community as separate and unique. The interest of its leaders, known as the *ulama,* lies in preserving the status quo, which they defend against attacks from both flanks.

Modernists and fundamentalists, more willing to measure their society against outside cultures, are disturbed by what they find. Resenting the West's intellectual and material preeminence, they position themselves in opposition. Orthodoxy, as they see it, is a barrier to restoring the vigor of Islamic civilization.

Though modernism proposes to bring Islamic culture to the level of competition with the world's prosperous societies, modernists make clear that, if they must choose between sacrificing prosperity or the essence of Islam, they will give up prosperity. Fundamentalists go much further. Though they claim that a return to the values of seventh-century Islam will restore Muslim culture's competitiveness, are they, in reality, revealing a willingness to abdicate competing? Are they saying, deep down, that catching up with the West is hopeless? Fundamentalists are determined to have Islamic culture follow its own rules, but in doing so they seem to acknowledge that the contest with the West is permanently lost.

The three models—orthodoxy, modernism, fundamentalism—thus have different visions of Islam. Yet, in examining them closely, it becomes very clear that they hold in common certain basic values. These values make up Islam's social foundations.

All three accept the priority of preserving the faith from the assaults of the godless. Their common adversary is secularism, a body of thought and practice which they associate with the West. Secularism, which warrants society to go about its business without reference to

God, makes Muslims as uncomfortable today as it probably made most Christians five hundred years ago.

Many Muslims contend that secularism would not exist were it not for the West. Islamic governments, however, perform the same secular duties as Western governments—policing the streets, collecting taxes, regulating commerce, conducting diplomacy, waging war. The governments of the Arab world generally render homage to Islam, and may even follow some provisions of the *shari'a*. But Muslims have never clearly defined Islamic government, and over the centuries have generally permitted their states to perform their normal duties without formally acknowledging their secular nature.

But as if secularism were not sin enough, most Muslims see it as an invitation to atheism, an even greater abomination. Believers give high priority to beating back secularist beachheads through which atheism might enter. Orthodoxy, modernism and fundamentalism all hold that the best defense against atheism is a state governed by the *shari'a*. But that is theory. In practice, they are in serious disagreement on what the *shari'a* would demand of such a state.

Similarly, Muslims accept the tenet that Islam is a total "way of life," while disputing what that means. Most take it to require rejection of the separation of state and religion. It also suggests the centrality to Muslims of living in an Islamic community and measuring all conduct on God's scales. In the end, differences over an Islamic "way of life" may reduce to competing strategies for keeping God at the center of the culture.

It is no surprise that each of the combatants in the current struggle claims to uphold the "real Islam," insisting that its rivals misunderstand God's word. Skilled at Islamic argumentation, they conduct much of their combat in the arena of theology. But all acknowledge that they are also political movements, and they do not deny that the stakes in this three-cornered conflict have at least as much to do with power as with faith.

The *ulama* (singular: *alim*) are the chief purveyors of Islamic orthodoxy. They are Islam's highest-ranking officials. Their title, which translates as "the learned," comes from the Arab word *ilm*, meaning "knowledge."

The *ulama* are not clergy; they are jurists. Sunni Islam, which has no Vatican-like central authority, also has no formal ecclesiastic bodies. That is not surprising. In a faith in which conduct is more important than spirituality, it makes sense that the highest authorities are jurists rather than priests.

But the *ulama* are as close as Islam gets to clergy and, in fact, they resemble rabbis, in being an elite trained to exercise moral authority through interpretation of religious law.[4] History made them the guardians of Islamic law, a role that is by nature conservative, and the orthodoxy they defend is the expression of that historical role.

Today's *ulama* have not strayed from the Islamic vision that their predecessors defined, in crafting the *shari'a,* a thousand years ago. They accept the centrality of the Quran, which, having been imparted directly by God, provides mankind with divine guidance. Complemented by the *sunna,* it makes up the *shari'a,* which contains all the wisdom that the society requires. Bennabi, the Algerian thinker, laments that the notion "Islam is a perfect religion" has been transformed over time to "We are Muslims; therefore, we are perfect." Convinced of Islam's perfection, the Islamic establishment rejects any legal revisions to accommodate either new learning or new needs, much less human reason.

This concept teaches Muslims that all *bid'a,* religious innovation, is human presumption. One Islamic thinker notes wryly that, when Islamic believers debate, they score highest with accusations of *bid'a.* The ban on *bid'a* renders all non-Islamic learning suspect. The *ulama* see literacy itself as tempting the masses from God's truth. In much of the Arab world the *ulama* have been persuaded only very reluctantly to accept the teaching of science and mathematics. Muslim orthodoxy would prefer to confine learning to the holy scriptures, to avoid undermining the faith.

It is true that Judaism and Christianity, as revealed religions, share Islam's aversion to theological change. But Islam extends the interdiction to society as a whole, a power the other two lost long ago. This power imposes a reticence toward initiating change that lies near the core of the culture's economic and social underdevelopment.

The *ulama,* it can be noted, are not reticent about using contemporary gadgets—printing press, television, radio, video and audio cassettes—to promote their ideology. Cassettes have become hugely popular in disseminating the sermons of popular preachers. Governments in all Islamic countries have put the airwaves at the service of the *ulama* to propagate the faith.

But, as the scholar Fazlur Rahman reminds us, the *ulama* distinguish between technology and technological principles. Principles are *bid'a,* says Rahman, on the grounds that Islam already has all those it needs. The *ulama* argue, he says, that new principles sow "doubt and disruption in the Muslim mind."[5]

In one major area, the *ulama* have allowed an amendment to creep into orthodoxy. Muslims, from Islam's earliest days, were bound by the Prophet's precedent to wage *jihad,* "holy war" to promote the faith. The very name given to the non-Islamic world—Dar al-Harb, the "domain of war"—reaffirmed this duty. But over the centuries the *ulama* have softened the duty, thereby enabling Islam to coexist with its diverse neighbors.

The reason for the shift is not documented, but chances are it was meant to please prudent rulers, who knew better than to wage war without respite. And so the *ulama* redefined *jihad* into an *inner* struggle against godlessness. *Jihad,* though still a duty, no longer requires Muslims—either rulers or ruled—to be ready at any time to pick up the sword to spread the faith.

The shift on *jihad* throws light on the relationship of the *ulama* with Islam's secular rulers. As Islam's standard-bearers, the *ulama* claimed the authority to bestow legitimacy, whether to leader or to policy, and neither caliphs nor kings could ignore them. Their direct jurisdiction was limited to public education, but in time, they became handmaidens to power, a role that historically enhanced despotism. At the same time, the relationship has ensured their own survival as Islam's most entrenched institution.

The *ulama* have never denied tolerating the Islamic imperfections of the ruling classes. They have argued that these accommodations are a barrier against the excesses of secular power, particularly the oppression of the masses. More important, they said, their authority safeguarded the state's Islamic character. The *ulama* were slower to admit that their deals assured their own absorption into the very establishment that they were pledged to curb.

Over time, the *ulama* did win the gratitude of the masses. But just as often they sacrificed the masses, shaping their doctrinal interpretations to serve the interests of the state. Since orthodoxy's acquisition of rivals from the left and the right in the twentieth century, this reputation for compromise has proven costly to them.

The partisans of both modernism and fundamentalism argue that the *ulama* can no longer be trusted to watch over the interests of Islam. In demanding curbs, they call for a reexamination of orthodox doctrine and a reform of how Islam is run. On both fronts, they are attacking a thousand years of Islamic practice.

Not surprisingly, criticisms of the *ulama* promote strife—at levels varying from generally respectful discourse in Morocco to bloody civil war in neighboring Algeria. Even staid Saudi Arabia has been unable to steer clear of conflict between the *ulama* and radical reformers. Profiting from their ties to the institutions of state, the *ulama* in most countries have retained their preeminence. Yet the orthodoxy they uphold has never been so besieged.

· IV ·

ISLAM'S MODERNIST MOVEMENT dates from the turn of the present century, when an Egyptian *alim* named Muhammad Abduh called on his society to rise to the challenge of the West. Napoleon had landed in Alexandria one hundred years before, effortlessly brushing aside the Egyptian army to demonstrate the West's superiority in technology and organization. By the end of the nineteenth century, the British ruled in Cairo. Abduh was deeply distressed that the Islamic world had fallen so far behind in the age-old rivalry with the West.

In the century after Napoleon, Muslims had learned a great deal about the West. They mastered Western languages. Thousands of their students attended Western universities. They adjusted their laws and their institutions of state to emulate European practice. Yet Arab society had gained little ground. In Egypt's cities, in fact, the Muslim population had become an underclass, as thousands of Europeans arrived to colonize the natives.

Abduh was not prepared to concede a central point that many Muslims believed: that the West's superiority was the product of its secular nature. A pious man, he considered secularism a value that Arabs must reject. Islamic society, he believed, must catch up to the West without sacrificing its Islamic character.

The blame for Islam's failure, Abduh believed, lay in the *ulama*'s grip on the society. Only by transforming orthodoxy, he contended, could Muslims create a culture that was dynamic and modern, while still fully Islamic.[6]

Muslims were mistaken to reject Western ideas simply because they were non-Islamic, Abduh said. Departing from the conventional view of Islam as perfect, he maintained that it was no embarrassment for Muslims to learn from the West. Abduh argued that Western ideas and methods could be adopted selectively, enriching Muslim life without adulterating it with secularism.*

It was daring for Abduh to serve as Egypt's Grand Mufti, the state's

---

* Malek Bennabi, in *Le Problème des idées, dans le monde musulman*, p. 102, observes sardonically that Western culture "presents itself in the eyes of each Muslim in the personage of Satan. . . . When Satan says that two and two make four, Muslims will say that it is not true because Satan says it. On the other hand, if a voice believed to be authentic says that two and two make three, Muslims accept its truth because this authentic voice has told it to them."

authorized interpreter of Islamic law, while attacking the *ulama*. He had credibility, as a member of the *ulama* himself, that could command an influential audience. Abduh reproached orthodoxy for perpetuating intellectual lethargy in the society. He proposed to peel away what he considered the layers of spurious doctrine that over centuries had become encrusted in Islam.

Theologically, Abduh rejected the orthodox notion that the faith demanded a literal reading of the Quran and the Sunna. In its place, he articulated a belief that a spiritual understanding of the scriptures was the key to God's truth.

Abduh accepted the traditional tenet that Islam reached its golden age during the lifetime of the Prophet and the *rashidun*. He did not, however, share the orthodox ideal—since adopted as the centerpiece of fundamentalism—that Muslim society must aspire to re-create this golden age. Islamic salvation does not lie in nostalgia, he said. In establishing a modern society, he argued, it was enough to attain the level of *spirituality* set by the Islamic leadership during the prophetic era.

To reach this level, he wrote, the *shari'a* should be revised to fuse human reason to Quranic ethics. He was particularly committed to incorporating reason into Islam as an instrument for attaining truth. Without reason, he argued, there was no prospect for reviving Islamic society.

Abduh knew, of course, that, ten centuries before, orthodoxy had defeated precisely this argument, raised by a body of dissident theologians called Mu'tazilites, who are discussed further in Chapter 5. Orthodoxy decreed then that it was heresy to go beyond the authority of the Quran and the Prophet to invite reason into Islam. Abduh pleaded with the *ulama* to reform this view but, considering themselves bound by the ruling of their predecessors, they were unwilling to reexamine it.

Abduh also tried to make his modernist ideas attractive to Egyptians by fusing them with nationalism. In politicizing Islam, he set an important precedent. But the masses did not let their anticolonialist sentiments sway them. Their ancestors had supported the *ulama* against the Mu'tazilites in the ninth century; they themselves showed little interest in Abduh in the nineteenth. Shaped in Islamic schools, living within the traditional culture, they endorsed the orthodox contention that Abduh's proposals were *bid'a*.

Part of Abduh's problem lay in his nature: he was a thinker rather than an orator or an organizer. Though he had some success in promoting reforms in Islamic schooling, the *ulama* managed to block most of his program. As for Egypt's political leaders, they saw no advantage to jeopardizing their historical alliance with the *ulama,* or provoking the British, and so did not come around to his side.

Islamic modernism never became a popular movement, and Abduh, though much esteemed, has not been widely emulated. His following, both in Egypt and throughout the Arab world, has chiefly been among a Westernized elite. Even today, most Islamic modernists are products of a Western education. Yet modernism's appeal has been strong enough to survive since Abduh's day, and in our own time is even enjoying a revival.

But the Muslim masses, from what the evidence shows, have not participated in the revival. It is not that they are indifferent to the grimness of their existence, or insensitive to the backwardness of their world. Rather, they have not been comfortable with modernism. When willing to turn away from orthodoxy, as many seem to be, they have answered far more positively to the summons of Islamic fundamentalism.

· V ·

HISTORIANS may one day denominate the late twentieth century as the age of fundamentalism. Movements characterized as fundamentalist have established themselves among both Catholics and Protestants in the West, among Jews in Israel and among Hindus in India, as well as among Muslims in the Middle East. Though the immediate circumstances surrounding their rise vary, no one can say for sure that the causes are not somehow interrelated. Future historians will have a better perspective. In our own time, we can at least try to ask the right questions.

Has the Enlightenment, with its worship of reason, run its course, leaving behind a sense of emptiness that can be filled only by primitive faith? Do the masses feel that technology has made them increasingly powerless, persuading them to turn for relief to an exigent God? Has modern society so depersonalized human affairs that mankind requires stringent religious practice to give meaning to life?

If the answer to these questions is yes, then humanity has changed direction from the secularizing process on which it embarked some five hundred years ago, when European thinkers began undermining the rigors of the Church-dominated society. If this is so, then one can surmise that the world is only at the beginning of the change. Furthermore, as waves of history go, there may not be much that anyone can do to reverse the course.

We see signs of a transformation of values in the influence that Christian, Jewish and Hindu fundamentalisms have recently had on the politics of their nations. The impact may be transitory or not. But in Islam, fundamentalism has had an even greater impact than elsewhere, and it seems unlikely to fade away very soon.

The explanation for fundamentalism's impact on Islamic culture may be that, well before the current wave began and long before it acquired a name, Muslims already had the most fundamentalist of religions. Islam never made the accommodations that Christianity and Judaism reached centuries ago with great secularizing movements. Over the centuries, Islam stayed close to its historical and spiritual roots. When things went wrong, Muslims instinctively turned back to these roots. Fundamentalism did not have far to travel to challenge Islamic orthodoxy.

Islamic fundamentalism's proximity to the religious mainstream—in contrast to the distance of Islamic modernism—puts Muslims at ease with its message. Muslims who value political and social stability—and that probably includes most—are not much upset by fundamentalism. To the Arabs, fundamentalism exudes the familiarity of old mosques. In the years since independence the Arab world has largely repudiated—like a body whose immune system rejects foreign objects—both socialism and democracy, foreign ideas. But fundamentalism has remained on the agenda, not only among the Arabs but among Muslims everywhere.

Clearly, most Muslims feel less threatened by their fundamentalism than most Christians and Jews feel by theirs. If fundamentalism is to win out among any of the "Abrahamic" faiths—Judaism, Christianity and Islam are all said to descend from the patriarch Abraham—it will surely have its first triumph in Islam.

Before going further, let us try to define fundamentalism. The term, born in the West, only recently came to be applied to an ideological wing of Islam. It was first attached to a small movement of American Protestants who, early in the twentieth century, rejected the liberal ideas that they regarded as an encroachment on traditional Christian thought. Their aim was to restore the faith to its original purity, as measured by a literal reading of the scriptures. Some scholars question whether the term retains its validity in the cultural leap into Islam.

In a series of essays entitled *Islamic Fundamentalism Reconsidered*,[7] the Syrian philosopher Sadiq Al-Azm argues that it makes the leap very well. The English term "fundamentalist," he writes, has an Arabic analogue, *usuli*. The translation is derived from the Protestant experience but is now routinely used by both friends and foes of the fundamentalist movement. *Usuli*—from the root *usul,* meaning "basics" or "foundations"—is faithfully rendered back into English as "fundamentalist."

But its accuracy is more than linguistic. The term, Al-Azm writes, describes a religious vision that applies equally well to Christianity and Islam. The vision calls for a return to the seminal texts of the faith to reestablish a "fundamental" bond with God. In Islam, the process goes a step beyond scripture to call on believers to emulate the life led by Muhammad and his Companions, but the concept remains the same.

This vision has deep roots in Islam, Al-Azm says. Only the term is new to the Islamic experience, and that is because the vision was not distinguishable from mainstream Islam before the present era. Once it acquired a political identity, however, the movement needed a name, and "fundamentalism," Al-Azm says, suited it well.

Fundamentalism, the political movement, started in Egypt in 1928, a few years after Turkey's President Ataturk abolished the caliphate. For seven centuries the Ottoman sultans had claimed the office of caliph, successor to the Prophet Muhammad. The caliph was not a cleric, however. The powers he asserted were more on the order of the chief executive of the Islamic community. Though the caliphate's authority had oscillated hugely over the years, its symbolism had cemented that community together. When Ataturk replaced the Ottoman Empire with a secular republic, ending the caliphate, Muslims everywhere felt a blow.*

"To appreciate the stunning impact of the abolition of the caliphate," writes Al-Azm, "the Western reader should try to imagine what would have happened had the Italian nationalists in 1870 abolished the Papacy." Al-Azm may be inaccurate in comparing institutions, but the impact he describes on Muslims was no doubt profound.

The blow fell as Egypt, the bellwether Arab state, was passing through a period of rapid change. Britain's colonial administrators, backed by Egypt's nationalists, were determined to renovate the society. Abduh's Islamic modernism had sapped the authority of historic

---

* Muslim believers, whether inside or outside Turkey, have never forgiven Ataturk, as illustrated in a *New York Times* story on May 18, 1997, which described a video secretly made at a Quranic school in Istanbul. The video, the *Times* wrote, "showed students lining up to file past and spit on a bust of Mustafa Kemal Ataturk, the revered leader who transformed Turkey from an Islamic to a secular state three-quarters of a century ago. 'I swear by Allah,' the students vowed in unison, 'to strive to create a state based on religion and Islamic law in Turkey and to devote myself to the war against Mustafa Kemal atheism.' "

institutions. Many Egyptians saw the foundations of their society eroding. The lesson that Islamic history taught most Egyptians was that the time was ripe to reassert ancient values.

Hassan al-Banna, a charismatic schoolteacher from Ismailiyya, seized the moment—discussed in greater detail in Chapter 2—to found the Muslim Brotherhood, promising Egyptians the caliphate's restoration. But al-Banna's real target was secularism. The Ottoman caliphate, as he saw it, was no more than an Islamic cover for secular despotism. The new caliphate, he promised, would govern strictly according to the *shari'a*, integrating Islam into every aspect of Muslim life.

Al-Banna saw secularist plots everywhere. The Ottoman caliphs, having succumbed to secularism, had opened the door to Napoleon. The Ottoman *ulama* had bowed to the Western secularists who came to rule Egypt, and to the Muslim political class that served them. Egypt's kings were colonialism's accomplices in imposing secular political institutions and legal codes. The result was an Egypt brought to its knees by the secularization of its national life.

By the 1940s the Muslim Brotherhood had shifted its priority from reviving the caliphate, which proved politically unattainable, to establishing a state that would restore the Islamic purity of the Prophet's era. Rejecting the *ulama*'s benign interpretation of *jihad*, it returned to the historic meaning, declaring that every Muslim had the duty to wage war in Islam's behalf. The Brotherhood initiated a campaign of violence against the authorities, proclaiming as its ultimate goal the restoration of the strength that had once made the Arabs the envy of the known world.

Al-Banna built, ironically, on the strategic groundwork that had been laid by Muhammad Abduh. He followed Abduh's lead in alerting believers to the dangers of secularism. He emulated Abduh in linking Islam to popular anticolonialism. He echoed Abduh's attacks on orthodoxy and the *ulama*. Some have speculated that, without Abduh the modernist, al-Banna the fundamentalist would not have existed.

The parallels between the two must not be overdrawn, however. Abduh had left al-Banna no precedent in the use of violence, which became the Brotherhood's routine practice and enduring heritage. Abduh, moreover, had done little to organize his followers; the fiery al-Banna not only recruited energetically but imposed on his followers a rigorous discipline. To this day, no movement exists to propagate Abduh's ideas, while the Brotherhood has a presence as an organization in every Islamic country, with many thousands of adherents.

Still, in challenging the *ulama* as the keeper of Islamic orthodoxy, Abduh and al-Banna were both looking for those responsible for the humiliation that Western imperialism had inflicted on the Arabs. For centuries Egypt had been ruled by Muslim tyrants; now it was occupied by a power that was both foreign and Christian. Moreover, the *ulama* had cooperated with all of them. Abduh and al-Banna agreed that a purified Islam must reassert control, starting by reforming, if not replacing, an *ulama* that over the ages had gone corrupt.

Al-Banna's quarrel with orthodoxy was more bureaucratic than theological. Fundamentalism and the *ulama* did not much differ on ideology; both endorsed the goal of an Islamic state modeled on the Prophet's era. Al-Banna's grievance against the *ulama* was that, as establishmentarians, they had sold out the goal. Muslims could count on the Brotherhood, once in power, he argued, to begin building the Islamic state without compromise.

Al-Banna, of course, was also the enemy of Abduh's modernism. Abduh had proposed to defeat the West by coopting its ideas; al-Banna urged the rejection of all the West represented. Abduh regarded Islam's historical repudiation of reason as a profound mistake; al-Banna accepted only a literal reading of the scriptures as the route to Islamic truth. Abduh's proposals were modeled on the age of science, al-Banna's on the age of prophecy.

Al-Banna and the *ulama*, in contrast to the modernists, were contemptuous of democracy. Both argued that, since Islam holds God to be sovereign, man has no right to make law. The Quran and the *shari'a*, they said, provide Muslims with all the laws they need. They agreed that freedom of conscience—unknown even in the West before the sixteenth century—was tantamount to condoning error, if not heresy. The two judged democracy, in sanctioning deviation from the *shari'a*, as defiance of God's authority.

By the same logic, they regarded elections as non-Islamic. They disavowed even those political parties that promoted an Islamic state, explaining that their existence conceded moral equivalence to secular parties. Yet both the *ulama* and the Brotherhood spun theories in support of elections. The *ulama* were willing to accept elections when they buttressed existing authority; the Brotherhood when they promoted its own power. Some fundamentalists declared openly that once an Islamic state was elected to rule, no further elections would be held, a principle sometimes called, half facetiously, "one man, one vote, one time." God, they argued, would not allow Islam to provide a vehicle for the restoration of secularism.

Whatever the two have in common, however, the *ulama* has consistently supported official efforts to crush fundamentalism. Upset by modernist ideology, they often reveal a soft spot for fundamentalist thinking. But they also recognize fundamentalism as a threat to the established governments in which they hold a place of eminence. The oppression exercised by Arab governments has not crushed fundamentalism, however. On the contrary, it continues to thrive.

· VI ·

IN 1979 THE SOVIET UNION launched a major invasion of its mountainous neighbor Afghanistan, a Muslim society ruled by a Communist Party that had come to power in a coup the year before. Moscow's primary objective was to shore up a friendly government on its southern flank against a rising Islamic insurgency. Its collateral goal was to replace a traditional Islamic culture with modern socialism. The paradoxical result was to bring to power the world's most fundamentalist regime, confirming the deepest fears of both Muslim and non-Muslim foes of today's fundamentalist movement.

Over a decade of fighting, the insurgents—called *mujahideen,* "makers of holy war"—inflicted defeats on the Soviets until they finally limped home. The *mujahideen* victory led inexorably to the collapse of the Soviet Union two years later.

The Afghan insurgency was the first to be driven by Islamic ideology since the Mahdi—discussed in greater length in Chapter 4—rose up against Anglo-Egyptian rule in Sudan a century before. The Muslims who in the ensuing years took up arms against foreign occupiers—in Syria in the 1920s and Algeria in the 1950s, for example—had identified themselves chiefly as secular nationalists. The Afghan *mujahideen* exploited the Islamic link to nationalism that Abduh had forged and al-Banna later refined to wage a successful *jihad,* a remarkable war of liberation.

Under the influence of the Muslim Brotherhood, Islamic militancy had become popular during the 1970s on Afghanistan's campuses. When the Communists made their coup, tribal and ethnic leaders were ready to counterattack; the Brotherhood's indoctrination had given them ideological cohesion. Saudi Arabia backed the insurgency with money, Pakistan with training facilities, the American CIA with arms. Meanwhile, the Brotherhood promoted the insurgency throughout the Islamic world, enlisting young Muslim zealots as volunteers. The longer the war lasted, furthermore, the more radical—the more fundamentalist—the *mujahideen* became.

Instead of an Islamic state, however, victory over the Soviet Union triggered a resumption of the tribal conflicts that were long integral to Afghan society. The anti-Soviet war evolved into a civil war, creating social chaos. Out of this chaos emerged a faction called Taliban, dominated by youths whose common bond was the loss of homes and families during the fighting. Taliban—which translates as "religious students—was even more extreme in its Islamic militancy than the preceding cadres of leaders.

In September 1996, after a twenty-two-month siege, Taliban captured the Afghan capital of Kabul.[8] Violating international covenants, its fighters invaded the United Nations compound where Najibullah, the former Communist President, had taken asylum. Transported to a gallows, Najibullah was castrated, tortured and shot, and his body was left to hang in public view. After the execution, even Taliban acknowledged that such behavior was "un-Islamic."

Taliban then proceeded to establish a secretive six-man council of clerics to reshape the life of Afghanistan. The policy the council adopted was to expunge all practices inconsistent with the Quran and the Sunna. It issued decrees requiring men to give up shaving, on the grounds that Muslims had the duty to grow beards. It required women to cease work outside the home and don the *chaderi,* a full-length gown with a tightly woven mask that covered the face. Not only were violators imprisoned, Taliban soldiers also beat up women they found on the streets wearing improper dress.

Further decrees of the ruling council commanded the closing of movie houses, the banning of all music and the shutting down of the local television station. Stereos and cameras were smashed, and non-Islamic books were confiscated. The council even banned paper bags, on the grounds that recycled paper might include pages of the Quran.

"These are big sins," said Mullah Muhammad Hassan in an interview. "We take our lead from our Holy Prophet, Peace be Upon Him, and whatever he prohibits, we prohibit. We cannot say that this or that is permitted because it is allowed in Egypt or Saudi Arabia or Iran. We have studied many religious books and in all of them, the things we have prohibited are prohibited.

"So while we may say that what these countries do is their business, just as what we do is ours, we also say that nothing they say or do can allow them to escape from the basic fact: They are permitting things that are prohibited in Islam."

Mullah—the title means "religious scholar"—Hassan was a grizzled war veteran, older than most Taliban fighters. Born in an Afghan village about 1950, he was schooled in a madrasah, an austere religious institute where learning consisted largely of memorizing passages from the Quran. Seriously wounded in 1988 in an attack on a Soviet base, he lived with a crude steel shaft that served as an artificial leg. After Taliban's victory, he became governor of a province and a senior policy maker.

"Of course, we realize that people need some entertainment," Mullah Hassan said. "We tell them to go to the parks and see the flowers. From this, they will absorb the essence of Islam."

Taliban enforces the *shari'a* more rigorously than do the Islamic states of Sudan and Iran. Citing Islamic law, it routinely amputates hands and feet for theft, stones adulterers to death and flogs drinkers and sellers of alcohol. In keeping with the Quran, it leaves the execution of murderers to the families of victims. But, as Hassan admitted, it is in a quandary over what to do about homosexuality.

"According to the Quran, homosexuality is a great sin," he said. "But the *shari'a* does not specify a punishment and our religious scholars are not agreed on the correct response. Some say we should take these sinners to a high roof and throw them down, while others say we should dig a hole beside a wall, bury them, then push the wall down on top of them."

Until the disagreement is resolved, the mullah said, Taliban has settled for blackening offenders' faces and making them stand for long hours in public places. He said he was confident that such shaming would put an end to homosexuality in Afghanistan.

It is discouraging to moderate Muslims that Mullah Hassan, the fundamentalist ideologue, is in power, while the Tunisian Rashid Ghannoushi, having dedicated his adult life to promoting a modernist Islam, has been banished from his homeland.

Ghannoushi was in exile when I met him in the mid-1990s. His party—Ennahdha, meaning "renaissance"—had been declared illegal at home, forcing its remnants underground. In Tunisia, Ghannoushi's version of Islam was squeezed between a secular autocracy and a rising tide of fundamentalism.

Early one summer morning Ghannoushi and I had breakfast together in a pleasant restaurant in London's West End. I had many times seen Ghannoushi's look; it was the melancholy look of political exiles. In his mid-fifties, he appeared much older. He wore an inexpensive blue suit without a tie. His posture was lax. His eyes were watery and his graying beard was unkempt.

"I can't be in Tunisia, where I want to be," were the first words he said to me. "I have much work to do at home."

I had expected Ghannoushi to speak in French, the language in which he once studied philosophy at the Sorbonne, but he insisted firmly on using English. I was aware that he had dedicated his life to freeing Tunisia of the influence of France, its colonial ruler for three fourths of a century. His preference for English, which he spoke haltingly, was obviously political, not linguistic.

"I can't be in Tunisia because it's a dictatorship," he said. "The government calls me an extremist. It says my party is fanatic. Sure, extremism exists within the Islamic movement, but in Tunisia it is marginal. We are the party of moderation. It is the government that is extremist."

Ghannoushi, described currently as a disciple of Abduh, was not always seen that way. In the 1970s, when he first became prominent, Tunisia's official policy was to promote Western secular values. French was the language of government and higher education. Women were not permitted to cover their hair and workers were urged to ignore the Islamic fast of Ramadan. Ghannoushi, a preacher who drew large crowds to mosques in working-class districts, was known then as a follower of the Muslim Brotherhood, delivering radical messages, promoting al-Banna's vision of an Islamic state.

His outlook changed in 1978, after soldiers savagely crushed a general strike of Tunisia's trade unions. Until then he had kept his distance from the trade unions, antagonized by their Marxist ideas. The army's brutality made him aware of how little social relevance traditional Islamic doctrine contained. "I wondered how our students felt," he said, "studying Islamic philosophy when it offered them a bunch of dead issues having nothing to do with the problems of today."[9]

After the suppression of the strike, Ghannoushi said, he recognized that a link to trade unions could enrich Islam, promoting activism in behalf of the poor and oppressed. He began speaking out on workers' rights, jobs, wages and poverty and political participation. He also called for a living Islam to supplant the "museum Islam" that had once preoccupied him and still preoccupied the *ulama*.

Arguing against Islamic orthodoxy, Ghannoushi acquired a major following among students and workers. He also won over women by championing a set of rights unknown to the *shari'a*.

In 1981, Ghannoushi was allowed to form a political party, ultimately to become Ennahdha, which challenged the state's French-oriented secularism. Though the party was never fully legalized, twice he led it into secular elections, in which he won enough votes to disturb the government.

Though Ghannoushi distanced himself from both the Muslim

Brotherhood and Iran's Islamic revolution, arguing for a Tunisian solution to Tunisia's problems, it did not help his standing with the government. Nor did it make a difference that, in contrast to both, he declared Tunisia's Islamic movement to be nonviolent. In 1981, Ghannoushi was imprisoned, and was released only during a new round of rioting three years later.

In 1987, Ghannoushi was arrested again, on charges of sedition, which carried the death penalty. This time, popular protests brought down the government, but the regime that replaced it, while granting a few concessions to the Islamic movement, made none to Ghannoushi or his party. The government's first election was so thoroughly rigged, in fact, that the opposition did not win a single seat. When Tunisians protested, the government explained that mixing religion and politics was so volatile that the country had no real choice but to remain secular.

"In opposition, we have chosen an intellectual route, appealing to the hearts and minds of our people," Ghannoushi told me. "Since we have the weaker hand, we have declined to counter official violence with our own. Patience is the only available posture. Still, if I were in Tunisia now, I'd have to choose between being underground, which is where Ennahdha is, or in prison."

Ghannoushi said that Ennahdha, far from demanding Islamic rule, was ready to share power within a secular framework. Its current priorities, he said, are free elections and public liberties and, given the anarchism of the political system, establishing the rule of law. There will be time later, he said, to consider the issue of *which* law. Insistence by Ennahdha now on an Islamic state, governed by the *shari'a*, he said, was premature.

"Reformers must be sensitive to time. They can't treat Islam as if it is outside history," Ghannoushi continued. "The Islamic movement, as a social phenomenon, must constantly develop and transform itself. Historically, the process moves from radicalism to pragmatism, which is inevitable as the Islamic movement reacts with real life. It is what happened to us in Tunisia.

"It is true, as Muslims say, that solutions to all problems are in the Quran. But to discover many of them requires exertion of the intellect. In Tunisia, we learned that Islam emerges out of an interaction of idealism and reality. This is not a sacrifice of principle. It is the implementation of ideals within the context of the real world."

Ghannoushi credits Abduh with restoring the bond between the Muslim mind and history. Abduh, he said, reunited "the Quran with life, after the two had been separated during the long era of Muslim decline."[10] Thanks to Abduh, he said, "the Quran has become again, as God ordained it, a light which guides its reader to what he ought and ought not to do in real life."

Ghannoushi reproaches the *ulama* for "drowning Muslims in linguistic researches and historical legends." He defines fundamentalists as believers, "that they have the truth, that they are the only ones who have it and can impose it on others." He faults fundamentalism for being guided by "models from the age of decline." Its mentality, he said, "is afflicted with what resembles paralysis in understanding reality. . . . Societies have evolved while fundamentalists have not."

Islam, he said, can profit from "realistic fundamentalism," not from an ideology linked to the "community's legacy of decay."

"It is true," Ghannoushi said, "that Islamic texts are not like plastic, capable of being shaped into anything we want. Muslims cannot, for example, legalize homosexuality or liquor or adultery. If only one Muslim were left in a world of homosexuals, a believer would still have to oppose homosexuality.

"But Islam does not have a mechanism of enforcement. Unlike Christianity, it does not have institutions to make decisions that bind the faithful. It is a religion based on each Muslim's reading of its texts. The examination of the texts must never cease, and the meanings that emerge will change with circumstances. Islam makes room for different opinions."

Ghannoushi's claim that each Muslim has the power to shape the faith for himself is the position of a committed reformer. Most members of the Muslim community would probably reject Mullah Hassan's rigidities. But few, I suspect, would accept Ghannoushi's principle that in Islam there is a right view and a wrong view on only a few specific issues, and on the others a believer is responsible for establishing God's truth for himself. Even without rigorous clerical institutions, not many Muslims would embrace Ghannoushi's pluralist definition of the faith.

Ghannoushi's admirers argue that he is seeking to liberate the Muslim spirit without violating the boundaries of Islam. Some compare him to the medieval Christian scholastics, who bent their minds to reconciling religious ideas with science. Clearly, he is trying to validate internal criticism in a faith that has long been intolerant of every departure from the *ulama*-established norm.

At this stage of his life Ghannoushi sees himself as Abduh's heir in trying to prepare Muslims for the intellectual combat that can restore Islamic society to the front rank of world civilization. As Abduh's disciple, he is unquestionably a believer. Yet, as a modernist Muslim, he has been targeted for attack not just by a secular state but by orthodox and fundamentalist Muslims. In the struggle for who rules Islam, the modernists are underdogs. Islamic history teaches us that the odds heavily favor traditionalist beliefs.

2

The Murder of Farag Foda

AT TWILIGHT on the seventh of June 1992, Dr. Farag Foda stood on the sidewalk outside his office in Heliopolis, a middle-class suburb north of downtown Cairo. Two young men approached him on a motorcycle and, on reaching close range, fired with automatic weapons. Foda, struck by several bullets, died in a nearby hospital the next day, leaving a wife and four children. His son Ahmad, a teenager who had stopped by to join his father for the drive home, was wounded by stray bullets but recovered.

When the murder occurred, Foda was leaving the office of a political society called, in translation, Enlightenment. He had founded it a few years before to advance his life's work. Enlightenment promoted the right of Egyptians to dissent from conventional Islamic belief, and particularly to challenge the dogmas of Islamic fundamentalism.

Gama'a Islamiyya ("Islamic Group"), a terrorist organization committed to suppressing heresy and establishing an Islamic state, claimed credit for the killing. In sweeps over the next few days, the police arrested a member of the Gama'a organization as a suspect, along with hundreds of Gama'a sympathizers.

Foda was Islamic extremism's most prominent victim since the assassination of Anwar Sadat, Egypt's President, in 1981. In the years after Foda's death, extremists have killed hundreds more Egyptians, many of them police, as well as dozens of foreign visitors. Foda, a challenger of conventional Islamic dogma, had been targeted as a heretic. Other lives were taken more casually, on the theory that civil disorder would bring down Egypt's regime, hastening the establishment of an Islamic state.

Gama'a's headquarters was in Asyut, a provincial capital of some

400,000 on the Upper Nile, about two hundred miles south of Cairo. The city's population had doubled and redoubled in recent decades, with rural migrants in search of a better life arriving from the surrounding countryside. Most were never integrated into the city's stagnant economy, much less its urban culture. Tens of thousands of students, drawn to Asyut's sprawling, overcrowded university, were frustrated by an education that failed to serve their middle-class aspirations. Egyptian social scientists recognized in Asyut the combustive elements that made it a center of radical fundamentalism.

From its underground offices in Asyut, Gama'a proclaimed proudly that, in killing Foda, it had enforced the Islamic law on apostasy. It cited an opinion issued by the *ulama* of Al-Azhar—not a *fatwa,* a compulsory religious decree—which proclaimed that Foda's beliefs were at odds with Islam. The authority on which the opinion was based was the Quranic verse that the Ayatollah Khomeini had cited in 1989 in passing the death sentence on the writer Salman Rushdie. Gama'a stated that, in killing Foda, it was following the *shari'a.* "Al-Azhar ruled that he reneged on Islam . . . ," Gama'a declared. "Killing Farag Foda was our Islamic duty."

Foda's murder was recognized as a milestone in the struggle over whose doctrine rules Islam. Egypt is the principal battlefield in that struggle. The largest and most powerful of the Arab states, it is recognized as a model for the Arab world. Intellectual hub of Arab civilization, it is the seat of Al-Azhar, the mosque/university which serves as the voice of Islamic orthodoxy. In Egypt, Muhammad Abduh and Hassan al-Banna crafted the doctrines which put orthodoxy on the defensive. Nowhere is Islam more deeply rooted. As Egypt goes, most Muslims would say, so go the Arabs from the Atlantic to the Gulf.

Yet Egyptians have historically been the most infatuated of the Arabs by the ways of the West. Napoleon introduced Europe to Egypt in 1798. In the ensuing century, thousands of Egyptians were educated at the Sorbonne. Khedive Ismail, who ruled over Egypt when the Suez Canal was cut, declared in 1863, "My country is no longer in Africa. It is in Europe." Egypt's indigenous population is a tenth Christian; its literature and art are heavily influenced by Europe.

Foda's blood—like Sadat's—underlined the division between the Egypt that faces Mecca and the Egypt that faces Europe. It is a metaphor for the struggle being waged throughout the Arab world for the soul of Islam. Though the struggle is largely conducted in religious terms, the stakes are much higher. It pits those prepared to march into the twentieth century against those who dream of a return to the prophetic era.

By coincidence, on the day I arrived in Cairo to look into Foda's murder, Islamic extremists armed with knives attacked Naguib Mahfouz, Egypt's Nobel laureate in literature. As Egypt's preeminent secular artist, Mahfouz brought to Egypt's culture a global recognition that evoked great popular pride. But secular culture was precisely what fundamentalists had vowed to crush. Because Mahfouz was beloved for his shyness and modesty, the fundamentalists' criticisms of him did not resonate widely. Most Egyptians felt the assault on Mahfouz personally, and to the relief of nearly all, he survived. But Foda, incendiary in letters and in life, exercised no comparable claim on Egypt's emotions.

Farag Foda, like Mahfouz, was a nonpracticing Muslim. Islam has traditionally tolerated such members of its community. But Mahfouz was quiet about his impiety; Foda boasted of it. An agronomist by profession, he worked as a consultant to private companies and international organizations. He was also a professor of agriculture at Cairo University. Warned by police that he had been placed by extremists on a "hit list," Foda had declined the offer of a bodyguard.

Egyptians recall Foda as a mountainous man, well over six feet tall, weighing in the range of three hundred pounds. His large head, usually wrapped in tinted glasses, was bald. His personality, like his body, was outsized; his presence dominated a room. He had a hearty appetite, drank copiously, loved women, laughed raucously and was an enthusiast of good music and soccer. His friends described him as romantic, even quixotic in his willingness to fight losing battles in support of his convictions. He was full of jokes, typically heavy with sarcasm, many of them told at his own expense. When informed that he was third on the zealots' hit list, he lamented wryly that he would have been first if only he had been better at his work.

There was truth in this irony, for Foda recognized that, whatever the fundamentalists' interest in him, he was not a household name among ordinary Egyptians. He had been an outspoken critic of Islamic orthodoxy since the 1970s, but his impact did not extend beyond intellectual circles. Officials in charge of Egyptian radio and television did not invite him to broadcast his provocative ideas. For a time he was active in the Wafd, a party with a long history of struggle for Egypt's independence, but he withdrew in 1984 when it abandoned its secular past to make an expedient alliance with the Muslim Brotherhood. He then declined a bid to join Tegamma, a leftist party, on the grounds that his beliefs were neither left nor right.

Twice Foda ran as an independent candidate for parliament from Shobra, a shabby working-class district of Cairo, and was defeated.

Later he filed papers to form his own political party but the government denied him the required license. When he took the matter to court, he was granted, as a compromise, permission to establish Enlightenment as a "cultural" association "to fight sectarian strife." While continuing the legal battle to found a party, Foda wrote books to promote his views and published articles in obscure political journals.

Most of the members of Foda's Enlightenment were not Muslims at all but Copts, Egypt's native Christians. Early in the seventh century, all Egyptians were Christian; when Islam came, most converted. The Copts are descended from those who did not. Throughout Egypt's history, Muslims and Copts had lived amicably as neighbors, but fundamentalism's rise had exposed the Copts to growing harassment, which the government did little to discourage. Foda was the Copts' indefatigable defender.

"Say that the country is now for Muslims only," Foda once told an audience, "and I, a Muslim, will put my finger in your eyes. Egypt belongs to all Egyptians. Egypt was Egyptian before Christianity, and it will be Egyptian after Islam."

In 1991, Foda was invited to become a regular contributor to *October*, a popular journal of politics and the arts. Though state-owned (most Egyptian publications were nationalized in the 1950s, under the totalitarian regime of Gamal Abdel Nasser), the magazine does not hew to an official line. Its editor told me he hired Foda to bring a fresh voice and unconventional thinking to the magazine. Foda's columns exposed his views to a widening circle of readers and made him something of a luminary in Cairo's spirited literary world. But they still brought him little in the way of public acclaim, even from secular intellectuals.

Many Egyptian intellectuals shared Foda's concerns about fundamentalism but, while admiring his courage, declined conspicuously to make commitments of their own. Like Foda, they recognized a danger in the fiery sermons denouncing secularism that were routinely delivered on Fridays in Egypt's mosques. Well before Al-Azhar's pronouncement on Foda's apostasy, the radical Sheikh Omar Abdel-Rahman—later convicted of the bombing of the World Trade Center in New York—called Foda a heretic and a blasphemer, and Abdel-Rahman was not the only one. Instead of fighting back, secular intellectuals—lawyers, professors, journalists, businessmen—decided it was too risky to identify themselves publicly with Foda's positions.

In January 1992, Foda was invited to speak at Cairo's annual International Book Fair, which presented him with a rare opportunity to make his case to a large audience. In general, Egyptians dislike roiling political waters in public confrontations, and the book fair had always been a stodgy event. But in 1992 the sponsors decided to break precedent by organizing an open debate on the question of "Egypt Between a Religious and Secular State." Foda was to share the platform with Islamic thinkers ranging from Al-Azhar *ulama* to Muslim Brothers to Islamic modernists. As the debate was organized, it was Foda on one side and Islam on the other. It was his opportunity to take on all of them.

The book fair's organizers had expected a large crowd; they had not figured on 20,000, most of whom were fundamentalists responding to a call from their leaders. The crowd filled the halls and spilled over onto the fairgrounds, where loudspeakers were installed to accommodate it.

The Islamic dress worn by most of the audience—robed men, veiled women—was a proclamation of allegiance. At one moment the proceedings were abruptly interrupted when thousands dropped to their knees—a show of force as well as piety—to recite prayers. But hundreds of security men patrolled the aisles, and the long afternoon passed without adverse incident.

Not surprisingly, spectators retain different recollections of the debate. Most described a dignified encounter, in which the speakers expressed themselves courteously and the audience listened respectfully. Foda softened his usual sarcasm and his opponents forswore overwrought invocations of the faith. In the end, it was said, neither speakers nor listeners shifted position, and the contest seemed to be without winners.

But among strong Islamic believers, many recalled Foda as offensive, if not heretical. That was certainly true of two young listeners, robed and bearded, who several months later would be Farag Foda's assassins.

· II ·

IN ADDITION to his Ph.D. in agronomy, Farag Foda had acquired, on his own, an exceptional knowledge of Islam, the use of which irritated his Islamic antagonists. Muslims tend in general to be indifferent to analyses of their faith produced by Western scholars, no matter how critical; they respond differently to the commentary of other Muslims. Few scholars in the Islamic community have ever subjected their faith to the kind of rigorous scrutiny that Western scholarship routinely applies to Christianity and Judaism. Islam, among Muslims, is a body of doctrine that believers are expected to accept unquestioningly, without checking for flaws. Foda rejected such a limitation.

Foda took satisfaction in meeting his foes on their own religious turf. He knew that to challenge them with arguments drawn from secular ideologies or modern science would be pointless. But he could confound them, he knew, by citations from Islamic theology and history.

Believers responded by calling him an atheist, or a non-Muslim. Foda expressed indignation, real or feigned, insisting that, even if nonpracticing, he was a Muslim in good standing. His sister wore a *hejab,* he said, and his children went to Muslim schools. The evidence did not impress them. His opponents still berated him for using his knowledge to impious ends.

It was typical of Foda that, rather than seek to split his opponents with arguments on which they differed among themselves, he would attack doctrines on which all of them agreed. One of his favorite objects of attack was the *rashidun,* the Prophet's successors, the four "rightly-guided" caliphs who governed the community of the faithful from A.D. 632 to 661. Tradition holds that the era was the moral apogee of Islamic history.

The four—Abu Bakr, Omar, Uthman and Ali—had been, while Muhammad was alive, his faithful servants and friends. Muslims maintain that all four were personally modest and pious, and as leaders were motivated not by political but by spiritual concerns. Among Arabs, the *rashidun* are regarded as models of compassion. They are said to have shown, before Islamic government was corrupted by worldly men, how glorious religious rule can be.

Foda's version of the era, published in book form in 1985, is called, in translation, *Before the Fall.* The interpretation he offered was permeated with contempt for the veneration that typically surrounds Muslim accounts. For readers used to Muslim apology, his narration was profoundly shocking. But Foda liked to shock. He writes:

> Dear reader, we come to the realization of an awesome, yet well-known fact: three of the first four caliphs were assassinated. One was killed by a Magian youth, and two were killed by radical Muslims. . . .
>
> You may agree with me, dear reader, that the impact of this calamity is somewhat softened by the fact that the first caliph did escape assassination and died in bed of natural causes. I am referring, of course, to Abu Bakr. But, dear reader, you will be dismayed like me when you learn that that remains an unconfirmed fact. According to some accounts, Abu Bakr and a

friend were eating a favorite dish, when the friend was reported to say, "Eat no more from this dish, O Caliph. It is poisoned. You and I will die on the same day." Abu Bakr stopped eating from the dish, but the two men were not well after that, and they died on the same day at the end of the year.

Thus we have the certainty of knowing that three of the first caliphs were assassinated, and we suspect that the fourth suffered the same fate. All this happened in less than three decades after the Prophet's death, during the lifetime of his contemporaries, during the most radiant days of Islam, during those days that are the closest to the faith and the principles of the religion. . . .

In writing these florid sentences, Foda surely knew how troublesome they would be to most of his readers, and with more than a touch of scorn addressed their anxieties.

It behooves me to pause here briefly and ask myself before the reader asks me, "And what was the purpose of the foregoing exposition?" In fact, I can almost sense the question turn into a statement accusing me of trying to focus on the darker side of the events of this great period. But I swear to the reader that that had never crossed my mind. On the contrary, what I want to do is to create some kind of balance so that the reader can acquire an understanding of Islam comparable to mine.

I want the reader to understand Islam from a politician's and intellectual's perspective more than that of a clergyman. I want him to reach an understanding of Islam that is based on a fundamental principle: that Islam was not revealed to angels but rather to human beings like ourselves. . . . The closer the *rashidun* get to our own hearts and lives, the better we can understand them; we can understand them better than we can if we were to overstate our accounts of their deeds, associate them with extraordinary sacred qualities or attribute miracles and fables to their lives. . . .

An ideal society, a city of virtue, has never been achieved in the entire history of the Islamic caliphate, not even in the most radiant days of Islam. Therefore, those who tell inexperienced young people that establishing a religious government would turn all of society into a heaven on earth where affection and tranquillity prevail; where citizens feel secure; where rulers feel safe; and where individuals would be free of all evil intentions and evil tendencies are merely depicting a dream that has nothing to do with reality. Those people are describing a fantasy that is far removed from historical facts and has nothing to do with human nature.

At this point, Foda aimed his wrath directly at the fundamentalists, along with their theological allies in the *ulama,* whom he saw as promoters of the impudent claim of possessing special access to God. Foda could not contain his outrage at their purporting to know what God wanted, and particularly at their assertion that God would punish Muslims who failed to support their goal of an Islamic state.

> Those people tell us that if we were to change our ways and apply the laws of God, our misfortune would turn into good fortune and our poverty would turn into wealth. We should refute them by saying that the laws of Islam ought to be applied because one wants to apply them, and not because one wants to use them to obtain riches.
>
> If our defeat in 1967 were a manifestation of divine wrath, as they claim, what do they say about Israel's victory? Was it a demonstration of God's pleasure with the Israelis? If the decline in our country's standard of living were a sign of God's displeasure with us for departing from His laws, how can we explain the rise of the standard of living in Western countries? We must tell these people that what is happening to us is the product of the government's failure to follow the best course.
>
> To put it briefly, the shortcomings of government and the application of Islamic law are two separate issues.

Foda was unalterably opposed to the application of Islamic law in Egypt. Though Western judicial practices had long before been incorporated into Egypt's legal system, the *shari'a* remained dominant in several areas of the law, particularly family matters. Independent *shari'a* courts continued to exist, their judgments enforced by the state.

The fundamentalists, however, were not content with partial success. In 1980 their pressure had led President Sadat to order Egypt's constitution amended to designate Islam as the "religion of state" and the *shari'a* as "the only source of legislation." But that was still not enough. The fundamentalists complained of the government's failure to implement the amendments and demanded the restoration of Islamic law *in toto*. Foda argued that a state which was governed by the *shari'a* would be harmful not just to Egyptians but to Islam itself.

Foda reached into Islamic history to make his case. Without specific endorsement in the Quran, Muslims have historically held that faith and politics were a single domain. Caliphs over the centuries justified their absolutist style by claiming to follow the Prophet's precedent. The Muslim state, as a result, never developed a theory of the responsibility of citizenship; in fact, it never developed a concept of citizenship at all. Foda argued that the Muslim state exploited Islam to justify whatever actions it took, without regard for the interests of the governed.

Oppressive states, most scholars agree, have imbued Muslims with the habit of looking on government with fear and contempt. Foda argued that, historically, the only restraint on government was the *ulama,* an argument the clerics themselves conventionally made. Foda contended the *ulama*'s goal was to keep rulers to the strict observance of Islamic law, through which was threaded Quranic ideals of social justice. The *ulama,* he said, showed Islam's humane face. Their services proved that, far from collaborating with temporal power, Islam was a beneficent rival.

In the Islamic state that fundamentalists envisage, Foda said, the *ulama* would share in government, if not actually rule. Such an arrangement would target them for the reproaches that inevitably accompany misgovernment. This is precisely what has happened in Khomeini's Islamic state. Islam would be richer, Foda insisted, if it remained free of the state, to offer its criticism to the rulers and its compassion to the faithful.

A Muslim, in the following paragraphs, would find Foda a critic of Islamic orthodoxy but not a man disdainful of Islam. On the contrary, Foda's words can be read as those of a thoughtful, discerning believer.

There is quite a big difference between the Islamic religion and an Islamic state. Criticizing an Islamic state does not mean deviating from Islam. One may find much to say about or object to in an Islamic state, even in its greatest days. But one can only bow reverentially, adoringly and faithfully when one talks about the Islamic faith.

This was true in the days of the rightly-guided caliphs, and it was even more true in subsequent caliphates, which actually made the first assertions of religious government. Proponents of religious government proclaimed then that their state showed the true face of Islam. And yet, they were the ones who sanctioned mindless killing and rampant injustice. They were the ones who engaged in practices that were not pursued even by the pre-Islamic pagans.

Foda marshaled his powers of reason to castigate doctrinal orthodoxy, while rendering homage to Islam itself.

A distinction must be drawn between the Islamic religion and the Islamic state. Islam draws from a divine message, but an Islamic state is a worldly institution. In His divine message (the Quran), God revealed precepts to regulate the affairs of the world, but He left other matters for people themselves to regulate. God provides people with the general principles to follow but leaves it up to them to decide upon matters that change with time. This shows God's mercy for people who know more about the affairs of their world than their ancestors did. . . .

I reject any notion that religion should be ignored. Religion is desirable because it is one of the foundations upon which conscience is formed in society. All of us are pleased to memorize the Quran. All of us like to listen to verses from the Quran in the media and rejoice in celebrating religious occasions. All of us like to see clergymen being recognized, respected and honored. But religion should be separated from politics. There is a difference between Islam and Muslims. Islam is sacred and divine, but Muslims are fallible because they are human and worldly, and this is something that cannot be altered.

By identifying the evils of the state as political, you will be preserving the beauty, glory, awesomeness and sanctity of religion. Separating the two issues of religion and politics would be merciful to Islam and to Muslims.

Fundamentalists, of course, disagreed with Foda's interpretations of Islamic history and the holy texts, dismissing him as an atheist. They also refused to engage him in argument. If Foda believed he could provoke them into rethinking their positions, he was naive. The extremists among them found it easier to kill him than to refute him.

· III ·

SHEIKH MUHAMMAD AL-GHAZALI, a distinguished theologian trained at Al-Azhar, testified for the defense at the Foda murder trial. The youth arrested near the scene of the crime was Abdul-Shafi Ahmad Ramadan, the defendant. The government had brought him before a military tribunal, where it could count on the application of harsher standards of justice than in a civilian court, and where there was no appeal of the punishment. The prosecution had asked for pronouncement of the death penalty.

Ghazali, nearly eighty, had once belonged to the Muslim Brothers, but as the years passed he acquired a reputation for moderation in his scholarship. He never, however, went beyond the strict limits of orthodoxy, particularly on the issue of apostasy. "Can Islam be asked to grant life to apostates," he once asked rhetorically, "so that they may participate in its death?" The defense lawyers called him to testify on orthodoxy's view of apostates.

Ghazali testified that Ramadan, a member of Gama'a Islamiyya, had performed his Islamic duty in killing Foda, who had revealed his apostasy in opposing the establishment of an Islamic state, in rejecting the *shari'a* as the law of the land and in challenging the unity of religion and the government. Islam requires that an apostate be given ample time to reflect and repent, Ghazali said, but if he persists in error, the *shari'a* demands his execution.

Ghazali bowed to the imperatives of public order in saying that, in his judgment, "to avoid anarchy, the judicial system and not the masses should carry out such punishment." His personal preference, he added without explaining, would have been to consign Foda to a lifetime in prison.

Nonetheless, he said, Islamic law requires that "if the state fails to do this [carry out a death sentence] and someone takes it upon himself to kill an apostate, then he is considered to have done what the government should have done." Asked whether there was a penalty for killing an apostate, Ghazali answered: "I remember no such penalty in Islam."

Coming from within Al-Azhar, an institution close to the state, such a declaration embarrassed the regime. Osama el-Baz, a senior adviser to President Hosni Mubarak, challenging Ghazali, told the press that "the consensus of scholars on this point is as follows: that no citizen can take the law into his own hands, for any purpose." As punishment, the government canceled Ghazali's regular radio and television broadcasts. But it desisted conspicuously from demanding that Al-Azhar's *ulama* issue an official rebuttal.

The episode dramatized the Egyptian government's dilemma in dealing with an institution which purported to speak in behalf of God. History had imparted huge power to Al-Azhar, which it often used in political battles. Al-Azhar's support in the struggle against fundamentalist militants was important to Mubarak. The government had no intention of jeopardizing this support by taking on Ghazali.

The Mosque of Al-Azhar has been the hub of Egypt's Islamic culture since A.D. 970, when it was erected by the Fatimids, a dynasty whose seat was in Tunis, shortly after they captured Cairo. The mosque was designed to equal any in the rival cities of Damascus and Baghdad. It was also a school of Islamic law and theology. Its name means "most shining." Historians believe the name refers to the brilliant lights with which the mosque was illuminated during the evening celebration of religious feasts.

Adjacent to the famous Khan al-Khalili bazaar, Al-Azhar became the hinge of a quarter that, to this day, is Cairo's liveliest. It served the Fatimids until the twelfth century, when Cairo was seized by Saladin, who founded his own dynasty during his successful campaigns against the Crusaders. Since then, regimes have come and gone, but Al-Azhar has remained a monument to Egypt's dedication to Islamic orthodoxy.

In a major historical study, Bayard Dodge tells us that Al-Azhar's authority reached its peak under the Mamluks, slaves who had been brought from Turkey in the thirteenth century as official bodyguards and who wound up ruling Egypt, off and on, for five hundred years. Usually illiterate themselves, the Mamluk despots enjoyed the prestige of their alliance with the venerated mosque.

Financed by wealthy Muslims, Al-Azhar became an intellectual as well as a religious center. Its resident scholars codified Arabic, while its graduates spread its influence throughout the Arab world. Al-Azhar also served as a shrine for the pious, a hostel for pilgrims, a refuge for the poor. Under the Mamluks, it reached for the first time beyond Islamic knowledge to teach the sciences and other worldly matters, making it the Middle East's preeminent educational institution.

It was during Mamluk rule that the *ulama* of Al-Azhar emerged as the people's champion. Historians generally back Foda's assertion that Al-Azhar, in keeping its distance from tyrants, helped preserve Islam's appeal to the masses. Even after the Ottomans took Cairo in the sixteenth century, the Mamluks retained effective control over local matters. But by then the West had placed the Ottomans on the defensive, and Al-Azhar's intellectual influence was embarked on its steady decline.

Al-Azhar resisted with vigor the secular ideas that the West brought to Egypt in the nineteenth century. An English observer, noting courses offered on alchemy and astrology, commented of the faculty: "To say that the earth revolves around the sun they consider absolute heresy." Save for the pilgrimage to Mecca, Al-Azhar scholars rarely ventured beyond the bounds of Cairo. Their library was poor, and non-Islamic research nonexistent.

The brilliant thinkers that Al-Azhar routinely produced searched diligently for Islamic responses to the widening intellectual gap with the West. But few, if any of them, reached beyond the limits of orthodoxy. To this day, Al-Azhar trains religious scholars in Islamic doctrine, without confronting the intellectual challenge of the West head-on. Living on religious credentials, Al-Azhar long ago ceased to be a center of worldly wisdom.

Under the absolutism of Gamal Abdel Nasser, who ruled Egypt from 1952 to 1970, Al-Azhar lost much of its autonomy over religious opinions. Nasser initiated reforms giving Al-Azhar departments of agriculture, pharmacology and medicine. But his interest in Egypt's institutions was limited to the service they could render to the state. The curriculum reforms that Nasser instituted did little to enhance Al-Azhar's intellectual standing.

Nasser's successor, Anwar Sadat, continued the practice of using Al-Azhar for political ends. One of the *ulama*'s famous opinions endorsed his controversial initiative on making peace with Israel. Sadat's successor, Hosni Mubarak, arranged a new compact, under which Al-Azhar agreed to support the state's campaign against Islamic extremism. In return, he agreed to restore Al-Azhar's autonomy and not meddle in its Quranic judgments.

Ghazali presented Mubarak with a dilemma. Ghazali's defense of Foda's assassin was a clear challenge to the enforcement of law and order. In the end, however, Mubarak was loyal to the compact, remaining silent in response to the provocation.

To more liberal Egyptians, Ghazali's testimony proved the triumph within Al-Azhar of Wahhabism, an austere version of fundamentalism that was promoted by Saudi Arabia. Openhanded with their money, the Saudis had in recent years invited hundreds of Al-Azhar's teachers and administrators to well-paying posts at Saudi universities. In all, some 5 million Egyptians, profiting from the oil boom, had spent time working in Saudi Arabia, and it was said that many returned home thinking like Wahhabis, rejecting Egypt's traditional tolerance. Many Egyptians took Ghazali's words as evidence that Al-Azhar was now a Wahhabi outpost.

Evidence for this contention lay in Al-Azhar's increasing use of its powers to stifle Egyptian literature and art. With Mubarak's approval, Al-Azhar banned books, including the Mahfouz masterpiece, *The Children of Gebalawi*. In 1991 it promoted the arrest of a minor novelist on charges of "offending and degrading religion in a way which jeopardizes national unity." It was behind the prosecution of Youssef Shaheen, director of a popular film said to have violated the *shari'a* by depicting real characters from the Quranic era. It routinely tried to remove books from the shelves of the Cairo Book Fair.

In 1994, at the UN population conference in Cairo, Sheikh Gad al-Haq Ali Gad al-Haq, Al-Azhar's octogenarian senior cleric, declared that Islam opposed family planning, at the very time the government was making a major show of its programs to contain Egypt's birth rate. A month later the same sheikh issued a ruling—to the shame of most Egyptians—that Islam supported female circumcision, a practice more realistically called genital mutilation.

"If girls are not circumcised as the Prophet said," declared Gad al-Haq, as if there were a record that the Prophet had said it, "they will be subjected to situations which will lead them to immorality and corruption."*

In 1996, Gad al-Haq initiated a campaign to reverse Egypt's easygoing observance of the monthlong Ramadan fast. In a step to Islamize law enforcement, he demanded official punishment of any Muslim caught eating or drinking in public during the holiday.

Sheikh Muhammad Tantawi had tried to soften Al-Azhar's Wahhabi-style message. In an effort to impose some limits, Mubarak, after Gad al-Haq's death in 1996, named Tantawi to the leadership of Al-Azhar. The Islamic establishment has not been happy with the appointment. Tantawi had been dean of Islamic studies at Al-Azhar and later the Mufti of the Republic, an official position charged with issuing interpretations of Islamic law. He and Gad al-Haq, as twin pillars of institutional Islam in Egypt, had repeatedly clashed over the duties of the Muslim faithful.

Tantawi has consistently supported Mubarak's campaign against Islamic extremism. But, unlike much of the *ulama,* he has also spoken out strongly in behalf of equal rights for Copts. He has backed the state on family planning and the issuance of interest-bearing bonds, which the Quran's ban on interest makes a touchy issue. He has pledged to donate his organs for transplants, challenging orthodoxy's contention that the human body belongs to God. He has defied Egypt's rising anti-Israeli sentiment by condemning fundamentalist bombings in the Jewish state. Tantawi even stood next to Mubarak—an act of courage for both men—at Farag Foda's funeral.

Tantawi, when still the mufti, received me one afternoon at the Dar al-Ifta, the "House of Religious Advice," a new, two-story white building which stands beside a highway ringing Cairo. During a visit several years earlier, I found him temporarily quartered in a dingy apartment in a high-rise housing development. The new office was spacious, curtained and air-conditioned. Wearing the same white turban with a red crown, he looked more distinguished now, sitting in a green plush easy chair, next to a desk decorated with panels that matched the décor of the walls.

In our talk, Tantawi was conservative in upholding the interests of the Islamic establishment. He vigorously defended Al-Azhar's claim—

* In June 1997 an Egyptian court overturned a ban announced the year before by the Ministry of Health on the practice of female circumcision. Human rights advocates protested. On the other hand, Sheikh Youssef al-Badri, a prominent member of the *ulama* and author of *The Guide to Hell,* declared: "This is a return to Islam." In December 1997, the Egyptian Supreme Court reversed the lower court ruling, reinstating the ban, though it was unclear how rigorous enforcement was likely to be.

hotly disputed by both fundamentalists and modernists—to be the only authoritative interpreter of Islam. "It is a terrible mistake for some people to talk religion without knowing about religion," he said. "Ask the wrong people about religion, and you will get the wrong answers." Tantawi endorsed the need for scriptural reinterpretation, as long as it was undertaken by the *ulama,* Islamic scholars like himself.

"The Muslim Brothers," he said, "are ignorant of the real nature of Islam. They are misled blindly by the views of their leaders, who want fame and recognition and high positions.

"Hassan al-Banna was a pious man, who aimed to restore Islamic law to Egypt in small steps. He was unwilling to resort to force. He understood that the rules of heaven can be implemented only by preparing Egyptians, especially the youth, through education and the spread of social justice. But the concern of the current leaders is not the dissemination of Islamic morality and the imposition of the *shari'a*. It is to remove Egypt's present regime and place themselves in power."

When I asked him about Ghazali's pronouncement on Foda's murderer, he avoided direct criticism of his fellow cleric. It was not that Tantawi dissembled; his presence at Foda's funeral had spoken for itself. But, prior to reaching a condemnation, he engaged in a lengthy analysis endorsing a degree of religious pluralism that, to me, recalled the Tunisian, Rashid Ghannoushi, more than conventional Al-Azhar scholars.

"There are several levels of religious questions," Tantawi said. "There is one on which the whole *ulama* speak with a single voice. We all agree there is only one God. We all agree on the five daily prayers, on fasting during the month of Ramadan, on paying the *zakat,* Islamic taxes, and on going on the *hajj,* the pilgrimage to Mecca. We may differ on details, like whether the faithful must wash only the hands, or both the hands and face, before prayers. But we agree on the basic issue.

"Then there is a level of question, both theological and political, on which human minds can differ. It is like a man who has several children; each has its own mind and the right to his own opinion. There are many opinions surrounding the *shari'a*. I believe that Egypt's law should be the *shari'a,* but there are good Muslims who believe otherwise. No Muslim, however, is permitted to express his convictions regarding the *shari'a* through aggression. Muslims who disagree must engage in dialogue; they must listen to one another. Under no circumstances can Islam resolve its differences through killing."

Tantawi's oblique reproach, and his tolerance of multiple interpretations of Islam, contrasted sharply with the message I received a few days later from Dr. Abdelfattah El-Shikh, president of Al-Azhar University. El-Shikh, in our talk, dutifully followed the Al-Azhar line in opposing Islamic violence. But on other matters his words seemed stuck in thousand-year-old Islamic texts. My sense was that, within the bounds of Islamic orthodoxy, Tantawi's tolerance was the exception, El-Shikh's rigidity the rule.

I visited El-Shikh at the university's new campus in Nasser City, a half-hour drive from downtown Cairo, near the parade grounds on which Sadat was gunned down. It was several miles beyond the ancient, crumbling buildings of the old campus, adjacent to the mosque, itself a badly weathered shrine where beggars take shelter. The new campus had been reclaimed from the desert only a few years before and its academic buildings, still unstained by swirling sand, were a blinding white. The trees planted along the avenues were too young to provide shade.

El-Shikh told me he had received degrees in Islamic law from Al-Azhar schools, then worked for some years in Saudi Arabia. He had a bald head, a small mustache and a trim physique, as if he worked out in a gym. He wore a Western suit with a shirt and tie. A computer and a telephone, up-to-date touches, sat on his desk.

"The basic task of Al-Azhar University," El-Shikh told me, "is to teach students correct Islam. Students hear opinions from all sides—from their parents, from newspapers and television, from politicians—on what is correct Islam. Not everyone who reads the Quran can understand it. Years of study are required. I'll admit that, like any scientific theory, there are different approaches to Islam. Opinions differ, for example, on how to conduct ablutions before prayer. We expose students to all these different opinions, but we tell them which ones are correct.

"You have to remember that the Prophet was succeeded by the *rashidun,* the 'rightly-guided' caliphs, and grouped around them were the Prophet's followers, all of whom knew him personally. They had access to the Prophet's authority and were able to interpret the Quran very accurately. Their experience was passed on to disciples for the several generations that followed the Prophet's death. After that, the knowledge faded away. No one will ever again have the wisdom that came directly from the Prophet.

"Now there are modernists who claim the right to interpret the Quran in their own way. We understand that they are trying to be relevant. But when they try to introduce new interpretations, they inevitably are shallow. The new ideas will never be equal to the old ones. Furthermore, any fresh interpretations of the Quran are by nature harmful to Islam. Here at Al-Azhar we ask our scholars only to transmit correct ideas.

"Even scholars who have studied all their lives frequently have to refer back to the first interpreters, whose ability was unique. I'm not saying that the Quran is closed to ongoing interpretation. But what person has the qualifications to challenge the traditional interpretations? Such qualifications do not exist. The Prophet's companions were very cautious, very modest. They knew that if they mistakenly interpreted God's views, they would be carrying this sin to the day of judgment.

"Sometimes a person, even a scholar, makes an error and can come back to correct it. But if you interpret the Quran without the knowledge to do it faithfully, then you sin by conveying the wrong ideas to the people. And no matter how much you study, if you persist in your misinterpretation, you are an infidel."

El-Shikh spoke willingly of Farag Foda. He called Foda a "leftist," and said that all leftists were Islam's enemies. He acknowledged, however, that "Foda had not reached the point where he deserved to die," since he had not been given an opportunity to repent. Had Foda repented, El-Shikh said, he would have been forgiven; otherwise, the state would have no choice but to execute him.

El-Shikh knew, of course, that Foda was a man so committed to his beliefs that he was unlikely to repent. It was a fine theological point. El-Shikh was saying that, so long as procedures were followed, Islam had no objection to Foda's execution.

As an Islamic scholar, Nasr Hamid Abuzeid was in a very different category from El-Shikh. Abuzeid described El-Shikh as "one of those Al-Azhar people who respects only what was said ten or twelve centuries ago." Such people, he said, believe the Arabs can rely totally on the Quran—without learning from the West, without creative thinking of their own, without challenging age-old practices—to emerge from stagnation. Abuzeid told me he considered such thinking disastrous.

Abuzeid was an associate professor in the Arabic department at Cairo University when I met him. Cairo University was founded during the colonial period as a secular challenger to Al-Azhar; its name then was King Fuad University. Al-Azhar's adoption in the 1950s of secular disciplines did not lessen Cairo University's top rank. It is generally agreed, however, that in recent times, Cairo University's atmosphere has become increasingly Islamic and its training less rigorous.

In 1992, Abuzeid found himself in trouble because his techniques for interpreting the Quran offended the university's powerful Islamic establishment. In a series of books Abuzeid had examined aspects of Islam using such modern critical tools as linguistics, semiotics, rhetoric and deconstructionism. The books were well regarded in the academic world and earned him invitations to lecture at universities in America, Europe and Japan.

Eligible for promotion to full professor, Abuzeid appeared before an academic committee led by Sheikh Abdul Sabour Shaheen, an Islamic scholar trained at Al-Azhar. Shaheen was the head of an autonomous college within Cairo University, where Islam was supposed to be studied as an academic discipline. Under Shaheen's leadership, however, the college was said to have become as orthodox as Al-Azhar itself. Shaheen not only vetoed the promotion but declared Abuzeid's work to be anti-Islamic.

Since then Abuzeid's life has been in turmoil. He began receiving death threats in the mail and denunciations as an apostate on Cairo's streets and in its mosques. The government posted a security guard outside his house.

Most upsetting, a suit was filed in Islamic court under the *shari'a,* whose provisions on family law have been incorporated into Egypt's legal system. The *shari'a* authorizes any Muslim to sue to dissolve the marriage of a heretic. The plaintiff, whom Abuzeid had never met, was a militant Islamic lawyer. He argued that Abuzeid's wife, Ibtihal Yunis, a university professor of French, must be divorced to be saved from her husband's heresy. Going a step further, Sheikh Gad al-Haq, in behalf of Al-Azhar, called on the government to execute Abuzeid if he did not renounce his heresy.

After a tumultuous hearing, repeatedly interrupted by the shouting of the adversaries, the judge refused the divorce. But the plaintiff, financed by unidentified sources, filed an appeal.

While the appeal was being considered, I met with Abuzeid on the Cairo University campus, which is in Dokki, a lush suburb on the western side of the Nile. The grounds at midday swarmed with young people of both genders, some in Islamic dress but most in sweaters and jeans. Polite, good-humored students directed me to the Faculty of Arts, which on the outside looked like any academic building on an American campus. Inside, however, the unswept stairways and peeling paint were unmistakable signs of an institution that had for too long been overcrowded and undermaintained.

Abuzeid had no office of his own. I located him in a smoke-filled faculty lounge, from which we adjourned to a vacant classroom down the hall. He was a small, rotund man, with the pleasant brown face and curly hair associated with generations of Egyptian peasants. He told me his father, a village grocer in the Nile delta, died when he was a teenager, and that he took a job as an electronics technician to help support the family.

After attending high school at night, Abuzeid said, he attained his dream of studying Arabic at Cairo University. An excellent student, he applied for a faculty position on graduation. He hoped, he said, to be a professor at the university for the rest of his life.

"Al-Azhar," he said, in explaining the research that had caused him so much trouble, "does not differentiate between the Quran, Islam's original text, and the interpretation that the *ulama* makes of it. The Muslim Brothers take that position too.

"Both hold the text and the interpretation to be equally sanctified, which means that they have made human thought as holy as God's. Orthodoxy has become a defense of its own ideas, rejecting critical examination. I've studied the texts, applying modern academic techniques, to try to humanize them.

"I applied these techniques to both the Quran and the interpretations. Muslims believe that the Quran is God's words, not man's. God, however, spoke in Arabic, a human language. We don't know God's words in eternity. We know his thoughts only through language, our language, at the time He expressed them. I have tried to study the Quran, looking at metaphors and myth, for its richness of meaning.

"The Quran is the greatest book in Arabic, and it opens the door to our history and culture, to literary criticism and linguistics. The Quran was also twenty years in the making, and I'm trying to grasp how it changed over that period. For the orthodox, that effort alone is enough to make my work taboo."

Abuzeid described himself as a practicing Muslim, doing work that was fully consistent with Islam. Far from being a challenge to the Quran, his research, he said, was an attempt to open it to greater understanding. But as an innovation, different from what had been done in the past, the *ulama* perceived his work as a threat to their control over the scriptures, and thus an attack on their power. That was enough to provoke a counterattack, he said, in the form of an accusation of apostasy.

Abuzeid, whose soft manner veiled his underlying intensity, had no apology for using Western academic techniques. He defended Western culture, in fact, and expressed impatience with those Muslims who argue that Islamic civilization is sufficient into itself, without need of infusions from outside.

"If we Muslims are to get out of the crisis in which we are living today," he said, "we have to reach out. Our Arab ancestors saw what the Greeks, the Persians, the Indians had to offer, and drew from them. It's that amalgam that made the earliest Islamic culture. We should be proud of how our civilization was formed, reaching far outside Arab borders. Other civilizations have deepened our understanding of our own.

"But for hundreds of years we have kept our minds closed. If we are to overcome our stagnation, we have to stop repeating ourselves, as our society has been doing for a thousand years. We must reopen our doors to other influences.

"I'm discouraged to hear some of my students take the Muslim Brothers' line. Many of them are very fanatic. I don't ask them to agree with me, only that they think for themselves, but they won't. I try to refer them to Naguib Mahfouz, who has given Egypt fifty years of his creative and secular thinking. Though every Egyptian has come under his influence, many of my students disparage him. Meanwhile, Cairo University is evolving into a copy of Al-Azhar. The chances of emerging from training here with a critical mind are growing less and less each year."

One evening I sat down in the press room of the Egyptian television building to talk about Abuzeid with Sheikh Abdul Sabour Shaheen, his chief antagonist. Shaheen not only holds a university post but is the *imam*—the leader of the Friday prayer—of a mosque. He had come for our meeting from a studio several floors above, in which he had taped some of his sermons for broadcast over Egypt's official TV channel.

Shaheen arrived two hours late, the result of a taping that ran longer than expected. From what I knew of his beliefs, I assumed he would be wearing robes and a turban. That was a mistake. His dress—expensive brown suit, snappy green tie—was European. His small beard was carefully groomed. Far from contrite at keeping me waiting, he conveyed the sense that I was fortunate to be in his presence. He seemed by his manner to be a man who never apologized for anything.

"I read his research material," he said, barely containing his contempt for Abuzeid. "I found fault with his methodology, with his prejudices and with his orientalist sources, including his Shi'ite view of the Quran. He also expressed Sufi opinions from the Andalusian period, which are contrary to the truth.

"What is worse, the man is a total liar, violating the essence of both Islamic thought and Islamic history. That was the assessment of his work that I conveyed to the university council, which accepted my judgment. The fact is that this man is not an Islamic scholar but a Marxist, and I saw through him at once."

Then Shaheen's voice rose, and the words came more quickly.

"His problem is that he does not understand the Quran. In fact, he understands nothing. I asked him during his appearance before the board what his specialty was. He answered vaguely, 'I am a critic of the Quran.' He criticizes the Quran! The Quran is the word of God; it is above criticism! This man has a pathological mentality. We should have put him directly into an insane asylum. This man is an ass.

"Anyone who says he is a critic of the Quran is a *kafir*, an unbeliever. Maybe he knows some rhetoric or philosophy, something about metaphor. But he understands nothing about the Quran. Everyone has the right to write what he wants, but once he enters into the scholarly community, he submits himself to its judgment, and the scholarly community knows what the Quran is. If he wants to criticize the Quran, he can be Voltaire, but he cannot improve on the word of God, even in style. I have studied the Quran from every angle, and I cannot find a single fault with the style of God. What this man does is pure atheism."

Soon after I left Cairo, Abuzeid's divorce case became a *cause célèbre*, known to virtually every Egyptian. The attention Abuzeid received from the press only inflamed the extremists. Their harassment interfered with his work, and the death threats came in ever greater profusion. Foda's example made clear that his antagonists had to be taken seriously.

Finally Abuzeid and his wife accepted an invitation from a European university and left Egypt. While he awaited the outcome of the appeal, he and I occasionally spoke by phone. He was optimistic. Then, in August 1996, Egypt's highest court upheld the apostasy judgment and the couple was declared divorced.

The defendant, said the court, had "mocked the Prophet." According to the judge's opinion, Abuzeid "says apostasy must be proven beyond the shadow of a doubt. But this is wrong. Islam is a complete system and is not fragmented. One cannot believe in some aspects of it and deny others. . . . One may not refrain from prayer or paying alms or going on the pilgrimage. If one knowingly denies these things, then this person is a heretic."

Abuzeid, the court continued, "is an apostate because he showed himself to be a heretic after having professed his faith. His claim of reinterpretation [of the Quran] is refuted, because interpretation does not permit a Muslim to depart from the *shari'a*. Interpretation has controls and criteria provided by scholars. It does not depart from God's path and what God has explicitly forbidden. . . . It is God's right to separate a couple because of the apostasy of one of the spouses."[1]

Abuzeid was shocked, but so was Egypt's intellectual community. The ruling surprised even many fundamentalists. It was an embarrassing reversion to medieval religious justice, and on its face was beyond the government's power to overturn. The ruling made clear to Abuzeid and his wife that they could no longer return home. They have since lived unhappily in Europe as exiles.*

· IV ·

THE MUSLIM BROTHERHOOD, the flagship of fundamentalism in the Arab world, is best understood within the context of its founding in Egypt nearly seventy years ago. After the Ottoman caliphate fell, Christian armies occupied much of the Arab world. Egypt's government, nominally led by a hereditary monarch, was subservient to Britain's colonial authority. The energy that Al-Azhar once applied to safeguarding Muslims had been diverted into supporting the monarchy and splitting the hairs of Islamic legalisms.

The era after World War I was the first in which a generation of Egyptians—or, at least, Egyptian males—had grown to adulthood knowing how to read. Though reading had not *educated* this generation, it offered a vehicle for understanding the Quran without clerical intercession. Literacy was a further threat to the authority of Al-Azhar. It also prepared young Muslims for a role in public affairs as patriots and religious activists.

Hassan al-Banna, founder of the Brotherhood, was born in 1906 in the Nile delta, son of a minor sheikh who had been educated at Al-Azhar. From childhood, he was recognized as intellectually gifted and charismatic. According to Richard P. Mitchell,[2] the preeminent historian of the Brotherhood, al-Banna also possessed unique powers of oratory. Mitchell quotes an acolyte on first hearing al-Banna speak: "One hundred minutes passed, and he collected the hearts of the

* Apparently buoyed by the Abuzeid decision, a group of Al-Azhar scholars brought a case in 1997 to have Hassan Hanafi, a professor of Islamic studies, dismissed from Cairo University, alleging that his writings insulted Islam. Like Abuzeid, Hanafi, known for his modernist tendencies, was accused of apostasy.

Muslims in the palms of his hands . . . and shook them as he willed. The speech ended, and he returned to his listeners their hearts . . . except for mine, which remained in his hand."

As a boy, al-Banna attended Islamic schools, and at sixteen moved to Cairo to study religious doctrine. There he encountered young men like himself, antagonistic to colonial rule, convinced they had no need of the Islamic establishment. Most of them had village roots and looked with disfavor on secularism, Cairo University, literary salons and a political system that they believed, despite its anticolonial ideology, served to undermine the Islamic way of life. Al-Banna was soon a leader among them.

In 1927 al-Banna received an appointment as a teacher in an elementary school in Ismailiyya in the Suez Canal Zone, where Egyptian workers lived dismal lives in slums, performing the menial labor that kept the canal in operation. Al-Banna quickly understood the mix of class and political resentment felt by these men toward the colonial regime. Within a year he had founded a society which he described as a "brotherhood in the service of Islam." The identity of its membership made plain that, from the start, the Muslim Brotherhood was the product of both religious and economic discontent.

The response of the Muslim underclass to al-Banna's appeal was understandable. His success in proselytizing among the urban middle classes and professionals is harder to explain. The answer may lie in the technological and economic changes that were buffeting Egypt's social structure, and in the incompetence of a government that made no distinction among victims. The whole society seemed mired in insecurity. Al-Banna's genius lay in comforting the needy of all classes with a promise of Islamic resurrection.

Calling himself the Supreme Guide, al-Banna demanded, and received, unlimited personal dedication. "His mastery over his followers," a disciple wrote, "was complete and inclusive, almost approaching sorcery." The results were prodigious. When the Brotherhood moved its headquarters to Cairo in 1932 it had already enlisted tens of thousands of supporters in every Egyptian province. Within a few years its adherents numbered in the millions, in branches throughout the Arab world.

Al-Banna's plan was first to banish the British, then to purge Egypt of all non-Islamic influence. In one of his few comprehensive statements on the nature of Islam, he described it as "all inclusive, encompassing the affairs of the people in this world and the hereafter . . . an ideology and a ritual, a home and a nationality, a religion and a state, a spirit and work, a book and a sword." Al-Banna's Islamic system, embracing every aspect of life, would leave no room for the corrupting ideas infiltrating the society from the West.

Al-Banna envisaged the Brotherhood as the avant-garde of a spiritual awakening, manifest in a rigorous puritanism, which would transform Islam one Muslim at a time. But it would bring about a renaissance that would lift all of Muslim society. Al-Banna was not interested in nominal conversions. To him, the only real believer was a total believer, willing to make a full commitment to his own ambitious ideals.

Though researchers have found no evidence that al-Banna ever specifically commanded the use of violence, a revolutionary aura hovered over his organization. The total dedication that he demanded led readily to the establishment of a "secret apparatus" within the Brotherhood, made up of paramilitary groups that talked of *jihad* and the use of strong-arm tactics.

While the Brotherhood's propaganda focused on its mosque-centered education and welfare programs, its identity in the public mind was increasingly linked to the "secret apparatus." Its first targets for assassination were the British; they were followed by Egyptian officials who collaborated with the occupation. Even without hard evidence, no one doubted that the killers did their deeds with al-Banna's full knowledge.

By the late 1930s killings by Muslim Brothers had become common. During World War II, Egypt's help to Britain in defeating Germany provoked the Brotherhood into open conflict against the government; but despite the assaults of British and Egyptian security forces, al-Banna brought the organization into the postwar era intact. As war in Palestine loomed, he proceeded to build his own army, proclaiming the intention of the Brotherhood to wage a *jihad* against Zionism.

The Brotherhood initiated the Arab military challenge to the founding of Israel, sending volunteer contingents to fight alongside the local Arabs. Its efforts sparked the Arab governments, which had hitherto shown little interest in Palestine, into sending armies of their own. Al-Banna's men fought courageously but in vain. He called their defeat God's sign of displeasure with the Arabs for abandoning the *shari'a*.

Late in 1948 the Brotherhood launched its program to overthrow the Egyptian state. Before police forces were able to respond, it had conducted a series of spectacular assassinations of public officials. Banning the Brotherhood, the government mobilized. Six weeks after the Prime Minister was killed, al-Banna himself was murdered, presumably by the police as an act of retaliation.

In 1952, three years after al-Banna's death, Gamal Abdel Nasser conducted the coup d'état that transformed Egypt. As early as 1940, al-Banna had met with Nasser's associate, Anwar Sadat, then a young lieutenant, to discuss the prospect of political collaboration. From 1950 to 1952, Brotherhood figures conspired directly with members of the Free Officers, Nasser's secret association.

When the coup came, however, Nasser was strong enough on his own, and excluded the Brotherhood from participation. Despite the snubbing, the Brotherhood was convinced it had earned a share in the exercise of power. But its members had no more in common with Nasser than with the parliamentary regime. Nasser's vision for Egypt was more Marxist than Muslim. And so, after a brief truce, al-Banna's heirs resumed their violence against the regime, culminating in an attempt on the life of Nasser himself.

Nasser's response was, for him, typically brutal. Six Brothers were executed, and thousands were imprisoned and tortured. The Brotherhood was forced to go underground, but the repression continued. It did not relent until Nasser's death in 1970.

Nasser's success against Britain also exacted costs from the Brotherhood. As a foe of the monarchy's cooperation with the British, the Brotherhood had long been linked to nationalism. Then, in 1954, Nasser drove the British out of Egypt, breaking the link. Al-Banna had made no plans for Britain's absence as an enemy, nor had he anticipated an Egypt ruled solely by Egyptians.

Sayyid Qutb, a disciple of al-Banna, provided the doctrine for adapting to the new conditions. Al-Banna's contemporary, Qutb had once been more liberal in interpreting Islam. But the brutalization he suffered in Nasser's prisons profoundly embittered him toward secular rule. Qutb ratcheted up sanctions for the violence that the Brotherhood already practiced. He argued that the goal of an Islamic state was sacred enough to justify whatever blood had to be shed. Fundamentalists adopted Qutb's belief to enlarge their commitment to *jihad*.

In *Signposts,* a book written in prison, Qutb called Nasser's state *jahili* (the noun is *jahiliyya*), a Quranic term used to describe the paganism that existed in seventh-century Arabia prior to the era of the Prophet. He also compared Nasser to Ataturk, the man who secularized Turkey and abolished the caliphate. A *jahili* state in our own time, Qutb said, was one that failed to fully enforce the *shari'a*. Qutb's vision may be summed up in the following excerpt:

In any time and place, human beings face a clear-cut choice: either to observe the Law of God in its entirety or to apply laws of one sort or another laid down by man. In the latter case, they are in a state of *jahiliyya*. Man is at the crossroads and that is the choice: Islam or *jahiliyya*. Modern-style *jahiliyya* in the industrialized societies of Europe and America is essentially similar to the old-time *jahiliyya* in pagan and nomadic Arabia. For in both systems, man is under the dominion of man rather than of God.[3]

Qutb dismissed much that was tolerant in orthodox teaching. Orthodoxy, for example, held that Islam did not demand perfection of believers; it also taught that a sinful government was preferable to social disorder. Qutb argued that an imperfect Muslim was a sinner and that only a fully Islamic state was legitimate. Central to his thinking were the Prophet's holy wars to end *jahiliyya*. Muslims must emulate the Prophet, he said, and not shrink from force to establish an ideal Islamic state.

This was the doctrine cited by the gunman who assassinated Sadat. Qutb's heirs built on it to maintain that not only is the Egyptian state *jahili*, but so are the Copts, who had long lived at peace within Islamic society. Qutb's doctrine became an invitation to believers—some might even say a command—to become killers for the dream of re-creating the sinless state of the *rashidun*.

In 1966, Nasser had Qutb hanged, and Al-Azhar dutifully proscribed his work. The vast majority of Muslims today show no interest in his writings, subscribing instead to the traditional, limited definition of a Muslim as one who, however imperfect, surrenders to the will of God. Most believers, obviously, live in states that fall short of Islamic perfection. But the minority who are Qutb's spiritual heirs accept his ideals as truth and continue to claim the right to kill in God's name.

It is ironic that Sadat, years later, became Qutb's victim. Sadat referred to himself, in contrast to Nasser, as Egypt's "believing President," and in an early memoir defended the "murder and terrorism" used by the Brotherhood against Egyptian officials. Sadat released the militants whom Nasser had imprisoned and granted the Brotherhood unofficial recognition. He also built mosques, closed nightclubs, lauded the *shari'a* and imbued Egypt with a more Muslim look by encouraging women to wear the *hejab*.

The West's common observation that Sadat died in 1981 for making peace with Israel has surely been overstated. It was a factor. But his assassins, in gunning him down, shouted that they were killing Pharaoh, whom fundamentalists consider the ultimate *jahili* ruler. Sadat, as head of a secular state, was deemed an apostate; that was reason enough to kill him.

Sadat's murderers were convinced that his death would touch off a religious uprising. But even in Asyut, home of Foda's killers and Egypt's most volatile city, only small disorders followed. Though Sadat was not personally popular, Egyptians displayed almost no signs of support for his assassins.

Twenty-four defendants, most from Islamic Jihad, subsequently went on trial for Sadat's murder. Five died on the gallows. Among the acquitted was their spiritual leader, Sheikh Omar Abdel-Rahman, who the court decided had had no operational responsibilities. Egypt arrested him again in 1985 for issuing a call for the murder of Copts, and soon afterward he fled Egypt. In 1995 Abdel-Rahman was tried and convicted in the United States as the leader in the bombing of New York's World Trade Center. He is now serving a life sentence in an American prison.

After Sadat's assassination, Egyptians rallied behind the state, reaffirming the commitment to social order that for thousands of years had regulated life in the Nile Valley. In Cairo the normal rhythm of activity resumed. Gad al-Haq, renewing the *ulama*'s traditional bond with the secular authorities, issued a scholarly opinion denying Islamic validity to Qutb's views. Yet, as events would reveal, Qutb's vision had not been laid to rest.

· V ·

WERE EGYPTIANS ABLE to transform their homeland by making wishes, they would choose to be a modern country, enjoying prosperity and power. But if they had wishes, they would also choose to accompany this prosperity and power with the essentials of their Islamic heritage. Much as they would like both, however, Egyptians have historically faced the dilemma of choosing one or the other. The modern world has been dangled before them, correctly or not, as a goal that is attainable only at the sacrifice of their Islamic values.

Egyptians in the twentieth century have experimented with various secular doctrines—parliamentarism, socialism, Arab nationalism—in the search for prosperity and power. They have succeeded with none. Secularism's failures became an invitation to the fundamentalists, who have largely shifted popular attention back to the society's Islamic heritage. Their success has reversed a trend that began with Napoleon and lasted until our own time.

A century ago, Muhammad Abduh and other Muslim thinkers argued that Egyptians could have the package, and they examined ways to reconcile Western innovation with Islamic belief. It seemed only a matter of time before a formula would be found to permit an Islamic

Egypt to join the modern nations. But this never happened. The idea of a modernist Islam, incorporating Western lessons into an authentically Muslim system of values, survives. Squeezed between secularism on the one hand and orthodoxy, however, it has fallen on hard times.

Like the fundamentalists, the modernists assert the right to challenge the authority of Al-Azhar's orthodoxy. For decades the Muslim Brotherhood has promoted the notion that Al-Azhar had lost its historic claim to the last word in interpreting the faith. Abduh's school actually predated al-Banna's. But it was the Brotherhood, as a political force, that gave legitimacy to the expression of dissident—including modernist—Islamic views.

That is not to say that the Brotherhood broke the mold of orthodox thinking. It did not. The limits of Islamic criticism acceptable to the community are still not wide enough to accommodate Nasr Hamid Abuzeid, who pressed Islamic analysis to the edge, or Farag Foda, who pushed it over. The ideas of these dissidents have little popular following. Still, the Brotherhood—quite unintentionally, it might be said—has eased the way for modernist thinkers who envision an Islam that is less legalistic than Al-Azhar's and less aggressive than Islamic Jihad's, but which does not breach the immutable truths of the Quran and the *sunna*.

Some secularists contend that modernist Islam is an oxymoron. They argue that Islam is hopelessly inflexible, and that modernist Muslims delude themselves in saying that the faith can be reformed. Orthodox Muslims, on the other hand, argue that modernists are nothing but secularists in Islamic disguise. They deny that modernism has a place in Islam's lexicon.

Modernists, however, insist on defining themselves. In our own time they have shown considerable vigor in claiming for their interpretation of Islam a seat at the Muslim table.

Fahmy Howeidi, a columnist for Cairo's *Al-Ahram,* is among the more vigorous claimants. He is widely known as a defender of the Muslim Brotherhood, though he is consistent in condemning violence. He is committed to the idea of an Islamic state, but he insists that it be established and preserved by elections. Denounced by secularists as an apologist for fundamentalism and by traditionalists as a quasi-heretic, he says that what he articulates is an Islam adapted to our century, which he contends is as legitimate as the Islam practiced in any other century.

Born in 1937 in Cairo, Howeidi is the son of a Muslim Brother, and as a teenager served time for Islamic dissidence in Nasser's jails. After his release he took a law degree at Cairo University, and since 1958 has worked as a journalist. When Sadat barred the publication of his writing, he migrated to Kuwait and then to London, and returned home only in 1984. The first time I met him was in his handsome apartment in Heliopolis, decorated in the Islamic style, with small rugs, low tables and chairs of inlaid wood. The next time was in his bare-walled office in *Al-Ahram,* the newspaper which syndicates his influential opinions throughout the Arab world.

"We who are committed Muslims," Howeidi said, "feel we have a mission to build a society in a way that satisfies God. Egypt is a poor country, but economic development is not a goal in itself. When we won our independence, Egyptians felt we had achieved so much that we could ignore God. That was a mistake.

"We want to make a connection between the material and the spiritual worlds. We believe in the importance of the family, more than you do in the West. We believe in human rights, but we claim that they are already in the Quran. We believe that the Quran commands that men and women be equal, and that the contrary practice has passed into the Arab world today from pre-Islamic traditions. People of my school of thinking hold that the *shari'a* must be changed to reflect the real values of Islam."

Howeidi dismissed the fundamentalist aspiration of bringing back the age of the "rightly-guided" caliphs. Spokesmen of the Islamic movement who make such a claim, he said, are fooling the people, leading them down a road to catastrophe.

"We know you can't go back," he said. "These ideologues say the *shari'a* cannot be amended in any way. We reject that idea. Though man's relations with God cannot be changed, relations between people change according to place and time. The challenge that faces Islam is living in the modern world.

"The problem is how to get there. Al-Azhar is not dedicated to any reformulation of the *shari'a.* It is dominated by the government and not trusted by the people. Tragically, Islamic institutions in Egypt are not free. An *imam* here is not a teacher; he is a government mouthpiece. We believe that Egypt should have free religious institutions to study the needs of our time and revalidate Islamic law.

"But before we Muslims think about implementing the *shari'a,* we have to reacquire an understanding of the real message of Islam, which I sometimes think we have forgotten. Islamic government is not the issue; Islamic society is."

Howeidi blamed the international media for spreading an impression that all Muslims hold the same view: antagonistic to women,

Christians, the West. Much of the world, he lamented, believes the lies purveyed by the press about Islamic practices.

"I'm among those who want to bring more of Islam to Egypt, but through legal channels," he insisted. "If you get a majority in the parliament, you do it; if you don't, you wait until the next election. The extremist groups like Islamic Jihad don't accept elections or parliament or the West or democracy, and they are willing to change society by overthrowing the government. Our way is to persuade, to teach, to learn, to move gradually. We are against any kind of armed coup.

"It's not true that modernists and the extremists have the same Islamic goals. Their understanding of society is different from ours. We have a few crazy people in Islam who want to kill Naguib Mahfouz, but there are millions among us who do not. Most Muslim believers are broad-minded and peace-loving."

As he continued to talk, I heard a strong case being made for the commitment of many believers to democratic reforms. Howeidi spoke with moderation and tolerance. He showed only disdain for violence as a way of promoting the Islamic cause.

Then I asked him his view of the murder of Farag Foda. His answer left me wondering whether there might not be validity to the skeptics who claim that, at some levels, modernist and fundamentalist Islam are hardly distinguishable at all.

"Farag Foda killed himself," Howeidi said. "He was not killed because he was a secularist. We have lots of them in Egypt. Most intellectuals are secularists, and they are never attacked. But he kept writing articles that undermined the people's belief in Islam. Sometimes I think that he was working for the *mukhabarat,* the secret police. It's easy in Egypt to work undercover for the security services and get many benefits. Foda wrote for *October,* which is owned by the government. It's possible he was a secret agent in the official campaign against Islam.

"Personally, he was very amiable, joking and laughing, but he failed to calculate correctly. I differentiate between moderates and extremists among the secularists, just as I do among the Islamists. The moderates, as I understand them, want to isolate religion from politics. The extremists are against religion itself. We Muslims accept moderates and their right to differ with us. But Foda went beyond separating religion and the state, to violating Islam itself. He didn't understand the difference between criticizing and insulting. He went too far.

"I remember, several years ago, a man who wrote an article insulting the Prophet Muhammad was killed by someone who was not part of any extremist group. The killer simply felt that the writer had assaulted something holy, and he could not accept it. In the Eastern world, there is a belief that some things must be respected, never violated. Foda attacked this belief head-on.

"Both he and his killers were fanatics, and I can say that about both of them, even though he used a pen and they used guns."

Muhammad Selim Al-Awa, another Islamic modernist, disagreed with Howeidi on Foda. Awa talked to me in his office in Heliopolis, not far from where Foda was killed. A lawyer, Awa was known for taking on the defense of Muslim dissidents; in Egypt this can be dangerous for a lawyer. In 1994 the government arrested the attorneys for a band of armed extremists, and a lawyer named Abdul Harith Madani was detained and ultimately died, apparently under torture. More recently, Awa represented some Muslim Brothers whom the government prosecuted as part of an obvious campaign of intimidation.

"I condemned Foda's killing from the very first day," Awa said. "I listened to him at the book fair." He rattled off from memory a list of the controversial positions that Foda expressed there: *shari'a* is not applicable to modern times; Muslims have not lived Islam since the Prophet's era; politics should be independent of religion; Islam has much to learn from the West. "Foda seemed to me to be raising legitimate questions which Islamic thinkers have to address, especially those of us that advocate liberalism and democracy.

"Foda and I had profound differences, but when he was killed, Islam lost someone who was forcing us to think over concepts that are very fundamental to its self-definition. That is very healthy, and I felt a deep sorrow, because the idea of killing a man for his views is so arrogant, so inhuman."

Awa, born in Alexandria in 1942, told me he is a believer who prays daily and refrains from drink. He has been a law professor in Saudi Arabia and Bahrain, and is the author of a book, *On the Political System of the Islamic State,* in which he presents a comprehensive theory of Islamic governance.

In the book Awa makes his case for an Islamic state, which he defines simply as one that promotes conditions congenial to the practice of the faith. According to the Quran, he says, the state need take no particular form, not the rule of clerics as in Iran, least of all a caliphate, which was al-Banna's vision.

In Awa's view, the principal Islamic imperative is a *shura,* a body that insures popular participation—though not necessarily Western-style democracy—in decision making. Unlike most Muslims, he also contends that Islam requires equal rights and duties, both for men and women and for Muslims and non-Muslims.

But it seemed to me that Awa's most striking challenge to orthodox Islam lay in his commitment to freedom of thought. Awa told me he rejects the standard view that Islam forbids reappraisal of the holy texts, or otherwise places shackles on the mind. On the contrary, he says, as he reads the scriptures, Islam guarantees intellectual freedom as an inviolable human right. He goes even further to say that freedom of thought for a Muslim is a "commandment to implement."

"If we are to restore our place in the world as a Muslim civilization," Awa said, "we must not be afraid of an ongoing process of reinterpretation. We must work at it every day.

"We Muslims must have more than faith; we must also have innovation. We who are moderates are fighting on two fronts: against the seculars who want to Westernize us inside and out, and against the traditionalists who are frozen in the seventh century and don't want to move a millimeter. We can't forbid young Muslims to become fundamentalists, but we can offer them an Islam that is part of the mainstream of their lives."

Yet it is fair to note that Awa stopped short of attributing Western standards of free expression to Islam. Though troubled by Sheikh Ghazali's justification of Foda's murder, in his book he reaffirms the validity of Islamic limits on dissent. He rejects the execution of apostates, but believers who do not show proper respect for the scriptures, he writes, "should be detained and may, under certain conditions, be punished."

I was bewildered by how Awa would reconcile his limitation on free expression with his goals for a broad reinterpretation of Islam. I was also bewildered by the optimism with which he ended our talk. Awa stated not only that the fundamentalists lacked the power to overthrow the Egyptian state but that their ideas were in irreversible retreat.

"The fundamentalists are losing the war for the Muslim soul," he declared. "That's why they look for small victories in attacking Mahfouz or killing Foda.

"Our side is winning in the universities, the streets, the labor unions, the professional associations. The political establishment is suspicious of modernists like us, placing us indiscriminately under the same Islamic heading as the extremists. But ultimately we will persuade the Muslim world that our way leads to building a society of men and women who are deeply committed to religion, yet are creative and productive. We are laying the groundwork for a renaissance."

Rifaat Said, an avowed secularist whom I saw a few days later, dismissed Awa's optimism as good intentions, and spoke with unmistakable disdain of Howeidi. Though the Muslim Brothers participate in elections, he conceded to them no real commitment to democracy. The Islamic movement, he insisted, has no moderates, only extremists.

"Howeidi and the others," he said, "are a devil's tree, bearing bitter fruits." The Islamic movement, he continued, was strictly political, seeking power like all other movements, except that it tries to cover its deeds with the halo of God.

Said heads Tegamma, a left-wing, secular party with a Marxist past. After World War II, he told me, he had the choice, as a young man committed to radical change, of becoming a Muslim Brother or a Communist. Having chosen Communism, he said, he spent much of his adult life in Egyptian jails. Though he long ago lost his conviction that Communism was the way for Egypt, he said, he remains profoundly anti-Brotherhood. He once invited Foda to pursue his campaign for intellectual freedom within Tegamma, but Foda declined, saying the party was too sectarian. Still, Said said, Foda must be mourned as a martyr to a more liberal Egypt.

My meeting with Said took place at Tegamma's office, on a tiny street in downtown Cairo. Secular leaders, in protest of the attack on Mahfouz, had announced a demonstration that day against the fundamentalists. Fearing bloodshed, the government vetoed it, but the city was tense. "We in the Arab world have no tradition of peaceful protest," Said later observed to me. Tegamma's street happened to be where the heavily armed security units assembled, and to reach his office I had to thread my way through a phalanx of uniformed men. Police bodyguards were stationed in the anteroom of Said's office when I entered. Said himself wore a pistol in his belt.

Said told me he believed most Islamic moderates, and notably Howeidi, were hypocrites about their commitment to democracy and freedom. He said Howeidi's Islamic state would surely deny equality to other faiths. Moreover, Islamic rule, he said, would equate any criticism of government with a criticism of the Quran, Muhammad and the *sunna,* and so would suppress freedom of speech. The political freedom that democracy requires, he insisted, would inevitably be denied, even in a moderate Islamic state.

"Howeidi and his friends," Said said, "acknowledge that Islam recognizes only God as sovereign. They reconcile this belief with their democratic pledges by saying that individuals will rule, though they will rule in God's name. In Tegamma we think that, if democracy is to survive, governments, far from pretending to be sacred, must rule in the people's name."

In expressing his misgivings about Islamic modernists, Said echoed the pervasive distrust once heard in the non-Communist world of the Communist Party, of which he was once a member.

"The Islamists claim to support a multiparty system, with periodic rotation of power. But their words lead us to believe that, when they take over, they will call themselves the party of God and will designate all others as parties of the devil. Surely, they'll find that the Quran will not permit them to yield power to a party of the devil, whatever the voters might decide.

"They also claim that they now accept working within the framework of a secular regime—an 'atheist' regime, they call it—but they acknowledge that this is a temporary measure, until they come to power themselves. What they are saying—what they have sometimes said explicitly—is that they will support democracy while it serves as a means to achieve their goals. Then an Islamic state will take over, and that will be democracy's end."

· VI ·

IN THE YEARS after Sadat's murder, the bands of extremists that descended from al-Banna's "secret apparatus," motivated by Qutb's ideals, enhanced their capacity for violence. These groups were heavily concentrated around the radical mosques of cities like Asyut in Upper Egypt. Mamoun Fandy, an Egyptian scholar, finds their discontent rooted less in poverty and religion than in feelings of inferiority toward Cairo and a sense of neglect by the central government. Whatever the sources, the police in the late 1980s identified a handful of these bands, linked in a loose network, and placed them under surveillance.

The bands referred to themselves as *gama'at,* meaning "groups," a word that has a Quranic connotation, referring to the followers of the Prophet during the *jahiliyya* era. Today's groups are distinguished by nuances of ideology and tactics, but they are united in the violence they are prepared to use to overcome today's *jahiliyya,* which Egypt's government symbolizes to them.

The most dangerous groups on the police list were Islamic Jihad and Gama'a Islamiyya, the latter tied to Foda's killing. Though infiltrated, they had succeeded in eluding control over their operations. Both had recently been strengthened by the recruitment of "Afghans," hardened Arab veterans of the Islamic war against the Soviet Union in Afghanistan. They also raised their level of training, probably at secret facilities in Sudan and Libya, and acquired new arms from drug traffickers and from illegal traders.

To abridge legal formalities, security forces operated against these groups under an emergency law decreed after Sadat's assassination. It gave them broad powers to arrest and hold suspects without trial. It also authorized summary trials in military courts, with no right of appeal.

The suppression conducted under this law has been brutal, and probably has set limits on terrorism. But it has also triggered a chain reaction of retaliation and counterretaliation, reducing behavioral distinctions between the police and their prey. Ordinary Egyptians have increasingly adopted the posture of bystanders, alienated from both sides by the savagery.

Amnesty International, in a recent report, placed a heavy burden on the government for the country's unremitting violence. "Thousands of people, most of them members or sympathizers of banned Islamist militant groups," the report said, "were detained [last year] under state-of-emergency legislation. Many were held without charge or trial but hundreds of others, almost all civilians, received unfair trials before military courts. Torture of political detainees was routine. At least 61 people were sentenced to death and 43, including 13 sentenced in previous years, were executed. Dozens were killed by the security forces in circumstances suggesting that some had been extrajudicially executed."

But Amnesty acknowledged tit-for-tat transgressions. "Armed opposition groups," the report said, "were also responsible for grave human rights abuses." In the period covered, militants on several occasions attacked busloads of tourists, reasoning that by frightening away tourism they could cripple the government financially. "Dozens of civilians were deliberately killed in such bomb attacks," the report said. "Others, including foreign tourists and Copts, were victims of targeted killings."

In the Foda case, Abdul-Shafi Ahmad Ramadan, the gunman apprehended immediately after the crime, was said by the police to have confessed to the killing. Few Egyptians doubted the possibility of torture, but the court accepted the confession as evidence.

The government described Ramadan as a twenty-nine-year-old who, after dropping out of studies at a technical academy, worked as a fish seller. Ramadan joined Gama'a Islamiyya out of religious conviction, the government said, and rose to become the chief of a cell in one of Cairo's poorest districts.

The government laid out a rather complicated chain of events. Ramadan's superior in Gama'a, who was in prison himself as a suspect in the murder of the speaker of the parliament, ordered Foda's killing. The order was based on a *fatwa* from Gama'a's spiritual head, Sheikh Abdel-Rahman, who by then had fled Egypt for New York. Ramadan, the government stated, had been instructed to find a volunteer for the killing but decided to commit the crime himself. Ramadan identified Ashraf Sayyid Ibrahim as his accomplice in the act.

Ibrahim, the second suspect, remained at large for nearly a year after the shooting and was finally arrested during a roundup of suspects in the attempted assassination of Safwat el-Sherif, Egypt's Minister of Information. Gama'a claimed responsibility for this crime too. El-Sherif escaped with minor injuries but his driver and bodyguard were seriously wounded. Ibrahim became one of fourteen defendants tried in a military court on charges ranging from the attempted murder of el-Sherif to the bombing of tourist buses in the parking lot outside Cairo's Egyptian Museum.

Ibrahim's trial was covered by a French news agency, which reported that on opening day "the militants launched a violent verbal attack against Mubarak from their separate iron cages. 'We don't recognize Hosni Mubarak or his laws. We only recognize *shari'a*,' they shouted. Some defendants also charged that they had been tortured by the security forces." The judge adjourned the court after the outburst and, at the request of the military prosecutor, conducted the remainder of the trial in secret.

At the end of twelve days of proceedings, Ashraf Sayyid Ibrahim was sentenced to death for the attempted murder of the Information Minister. Five other defendants were also given the death penalty, while three received terms ranging from ten years to life. Five were acquitted. In view of his impending execution, Ibrahim was never charged in Foda's killing.

After the trial, Middle East Watch, an international human rights organization, protested to the government that the death sentences were in violation of standards established in United Nations resolutions. Mubarak, in ratifying the executions, responded dryly: "I refuse to allow human rights to become a slogan to protect terrorists." Early in July 1993, Ibrahim and his five codefendants were hanged in a military prison.

By this time Ramadan's trial was under way. About a year later I met with a young lawyer who had been on Ramadan's defense team. His name was Ali Ismail, and he lived along a narrow, unpaved, unlit alley in Imbaba, a district of Cairo where in December 1992 some seven hundred Islamic sympathizers were arrested during street demonstrations against police brutality. His office, barely large enough for his desk and law books, was on the ground floor of his tiny house. The family's living quarters were above. Ismail asked me, on entering, to take off my shoes, a custom generally reserved for mosques. Sitting in stockinged feet, we sipped soft drinks while we talked.

Ismail was born in 1962 in Sohag, a mid-size city on the Nile just south of Asyut. His father was a shopkeeper who, he said, imbued the home with Islamic conservatism. The third of seven children, he was the only one interested in learning, and in 1984 he graduated from Cairo University's law school. Since then, though he claimed to belong to no Islamic group, his practice has consisted of representing Islamic activists. Married and the father of four, he remarked in passing that "the Quran and the scriptures encourage you to have as many children as possible." Ismail spoke softly and smiled easily, revealing none of the fury associated with the extremist stereotype.

Asked to describe his client, Ismail said Ramadan had been an ordinary young man, though easily roused to anger and deeply passionate about Islam. He had earned a high school diploma and was married with two children. Oddly, Ismail said, he had never heard of Foda until he went with his friend Ibrahim to attend the now celebrated debate at the Cairo Book Fair.

Ramadan and Ibrahim, said Ismail, left the debate in a rage at Foda's impudence. Ismail described Ramadan as particularly upset by the mockery of the Islamic movement, which Foda called "loony," and removed from reality. Foda had also ridiculed the movement's favorite slogan, "Islam is the solution," calling it hollow and substanceless. Both young men, Ismail said, saw Foda as a heretic who deliberately inflicted pain on believing Muslims.

After the book fair Ramadan went back and read some of Foda's articles in *October*. What finally triggered his resolve to commit the murder, said Ismail, was the column that turned out to be Foda's last. It was dated June 7, 1992, the day he was shot. I found it in *October*'s files.

> Sex and sexual frustration are behind the acts of the Islamic groups [the article said]. True, their protest is political, and with abundant economic and social cause. Yet sex influences their thinking and behavior. . . .
>
> In one province in Upper Egypt, the Islamic group has deemed squash and eggplant to be unIslamic, because these vegetables could be stuffed,

and the act of stuffing them might remind people of sex. This is how their adolescent minds work.

I also heard that these Islamic groups decreed that it is unIslamic for a girl to undress in front of a dog. Surely, this is the thinking of someone driven mad by preoccupation with sex.

What can I say to those who are looking for a solution to Egypt's current divisions? I am acquainted with Islamists who reach the age of 40 without having had a normal heterosexual relationship. I know that our times are difficult. Yet I see the phantom of sex behind all of their strange behavior.

Ramadan was particularly incensed, Ismail said, in finding a suggestion that fundamentalists—having had no "normal heterosexual relationship"—practiced homosexuality, a heretical act. Many sociologists, it is true, maintain that in Islamic societies, which solemnly forbid premarital heterosexual relationships, homosexuality is common. Ramadan took very personally, Ismail said, Foda's insulting allusion to the practice.

Ismail acknowledged that both Ramadan and Ibrahim belonged to Gama'a Islamiyya but denied that, contrary to the government's claim, either was under orders to kill Foda. The crime was planned, he said, by the two of them alone. Ramadan was so convinced of its rightness that he rejected the advice of his lawyers to plead insanity. Both men had no doubt, he said, that Islam had commanded them to kill Foda as punishment for his attacks on the faith.

"We tried to persuade the court to permit Ramadan to retract his confession," Ismail continued, "contending that it was extracted by torture. The judge refused. So all we could do was hope to avoid the death penalty by showing mitigation.

"We made arguments based on both the civil code and Islamic law. Under the civil code, we submitted Foda's books and articles, and tapes of the debate at the book fair, which we claimed were provocative. Then the judge surprised us by granting permission to cite Islamic law, too, though it surely did not apply. So we called in Sheikh Ghazali to testify that under the *shari'a* it was proper to kill Foda, and that the government itself should have executed him. The judge listened carefully to these arguments, but in the end they did no good. Ramadan was found guilty and sentenced to death. He was hanged a few months later."

The legal team to which Ismail belonged was headed by Abdul Halim Mansour, one of Egypt's most celebrated trial lawyers. Mansour told me he had made a career of representing political dissidents.

Some, he said, were Communists; a few were centrist democrats; most were Islamists.

Thirty years before, Mansour told me, he had defended the Muslim Brothers against Nasser's efforts to stamp them out. Since then he had represented nearly every prominent extremist brought to trial, including Khalid Islambouli, Sadat's chief assassin. He even traveled to New York for the trial of Sayyid Nosair, who was accused of killing Meir Kahane, the radical rabbi, and he was on the team named to defend Sheikh Abdel-Rahman in the World Trade Center bombing, although he complained that he had been denied a visa to attend the trial. His current ambition, Mansour said, was to go to Israel to defend the Islamic extremists of Hamas.

Mansour, with a doctorate in criminal law from Cairo University, conveyed the impression of a modern man. He told me he regarded himself as a pure lawyer, willing to offer his services to the defense of any client. He is a strong partisan of human rights, he said, and to prove his point he cited several human rights organizations in which he was active, both in Egypt and abroad. But he personally defined himself by his commitment to Islam, he said, and he looked forward to the day when all of the Muslim world was ruled by the *shari'a*.

Mansour had instructed me to meet him in the Cairo courthouse, a grand building in the classical style, now a shabby relic of the colonial era. I made my way through its crowded halls to the lawyers' lounge, jammed with men drinking tea and smoking, where he had said he would be waiting. I was told that he had already left for the main courtroom, and I found him there in a pew, wearing the black robe of a British barrister, engaging in what seemed like idle talk with fellow lawyers, identically dressed.

The courtroom recalled a Daumier caricature. Off to the side of the bench was a large iron cage, inside which a dozen prisoners were seated; another two or three were standing, making earnest conversation with their attorneys through the heavy bars. Three fans whined overhead, keeping the heavy air moving through the crowded room. The din was deafening and Mansour, a man in his mid-sixties with close-cropped white hair, suggested we move to the judge's bench to escape it. While talking into each other's ear, we were repeatedly interrupted by what I took to be less renowned lawyers, all deferential, consulting him on their cases. He responded graciously to each one, before returning to me.

"Ramadan received a fair trial," Mansour said, describing to me the sequence much as Ali Ismail had a few days earlier. "The only thing I found objectionable was the one-step decision. It was in military court and, under the emergency law, there is no appeal. That's wrong. But the government sets the rules.

"If I had my way, Ramadan would have been tried under the *shari'a*. Then Foda would have been found guilty, and my client would have been acquitted. I certainly agreed with Sheikh Ghazali's testimony that a Muslim who insults God or denies the Quran deserves to be killed. But the judges speak with one voice in applying the government's law and, as a lawyer, I must work within that reality."

Friendly and engaging as Mansour was, his comment on Ghazali shocked me. I asked him if there was not a contradiction in his claim to be a supporter of human rights and his endorsement of Ghazali's defense of Foda's killing.

"In supporting the *shari'a*, I am not dismissing human rights," he replied amiably, with a kind of patience he might show in explaining the obvious to a foreigner. "Farag Foda surely has a human right to speak against the government or"—jabbing a finger demonstratively in my chest—"against you. But no one has a right to speak against God. We are the slaves of God. God has the right to sentence us to death for insults. If I deny my creator, how can I ask Him to let me live? There are no human rights against God."

Mansour and I spoke for half an hour, before the judge arrived to convene the court and the lawyers began pushing their way to the bench to make their clients' arguments.

It occurred to me as I headed for the door that four or five hundred years had probably passed since a lawyer in a Western courtroom had expressed a notion of justice which held that "God has a right to sentence us to death for insults." It was not God who sentenced Foda, of course; it was two young zealots who did the killing and on whom Mansour bestowed his approval. Yet Mansour, I knew, was a serious man and, though we disagreed, I could not dismiss his endorsement of execution for apostasy. His words were swirling in my Western head as I descended the stone stairs of the courthouse, crossed the busy avenue and hailed a taxi to return to my hotel.

· VII ·

AFTER NASSER'S DEATH in 1970, the battered remnants of the Muslim Brotherhood, emerging from prison, crafted a reformist program to replace their old revolutionary defiance. Succeeding al-Banna, now dead, were men of more moderate disposition, willing to lay Qutb's doctrines aside.

Whatever their secret dreams of revolution, they faced up to the reality that the state's coercive powers exceeded their own. They decided to let the extremists go their own way, and in 1981, Gama'a assassinated Sadat. But the Muslim Brothers chose to adopt a peaceful course for themselves. Having proclaimed a program of promoting the gradual Islamization of Egyptian society, they made a truce with the secular world. By the mid-1980s the Muslim Brothers had largely succeeded in rehabilitating their image.

Mubarak, though more detached from religion than his predecessor, continued the practice of tolerating the Brotherhood. He prosecuted Sadat's killers ruthlessly, and in the ensuing years set the security services in relentless pursuit of extremism. But he accepted the Brotherhood's new identity, permitting it a range of political activities. The Brotherhood reciprocated by repeatedly denouncing the extremists for their violence.

Yet Mubarak was innately more suspicious of the Brotherhood than Sadat had been. After a decade and a half in office he still refused to legalize it and, having tolerated its official publication for some years, he again proscribed it. Mubarak maintained an aggressive surveillance over the Brotherhood's activists, keeping them off balance with petty harassment.

Mubarak's policies, however, did not reflect a secular vision of his own. In fact, most Egyptians agree that Mubarak's policies reflected no vision at all. At first, what Egyptians perceived was a more modest, warmer man than Sadat, but this impression gradually faded. It was replaced by an impression of Mubarak as an improviser, incapable of conducting a long-term policy to improve the conditions of Egyptian life. His tough line on security only reflected his ambition to stay in power.

Al-Azhar, playing its historical role, enhanced Mubarak's legitimacy. Mubarak's repayment was to give Al-Azhar an unlimited platform for promoting its orthodox doctrines. The result was not what he had in mind. Whatever limits he placed on the Brotherhood, Mubarak found himself presiding over Egypt's creeping Islamization, precisely the Brotherhood's political program.

Mubarak's indulgence of Ghazali's defense of Ramadan was an example. Not only did Mubarak stand aside for whatever opinions the *ulama* issued, he also sanctioned orthodox practices, new to Egypt, that were clearly inspired by fundamentalism.

He tolerated the rising Islamic harassment of the Copts. He made little effort to halt Islamic infiltration of the schools. He was passive toward Al-Azhar's campaign to suppress secular art. He offered no support to the efforts of human rights organizations, both Egyptian and international, to protect secular intellectuals from Islamic violence—though he chastised these same organizations for spotlighting the abuses of his police.

Mubarak's reasoning seemed to be that, by identifying himself with orthodoxy, he could coopt his Islamic rivals. His critics pointed out that if social and political stability were his goal he would be better served by cleaning up corruption and suppressing the vested interests that kept the economy in a state of stagnation. Mubarak's Islamic tilt demoralized his natural constituency, the supporters of a modern state.

But Mubarak found Islamization easier to accept than reform. He did not succeed in coopting the Muslim Brotherhood or the Islamic extremist groups; he only encouraged them. In granting a free hand to Al-Azhar he gave legitimacy to the vision of an Islamic state. Islamization acquired credibility from Mubarak's course.

This credibility encouraged the Brotherhood to step up its campaign for power through elections. Sadat had once declared that Egypt would never permit a religious bloc to dominate the parliament. The extremists, ironically, also opposed Brotherhood participation in the political system, claiming that it implied Islam's endorsement of the *jahili* state. In its debates after Nasser's death, the Brotherhood finally decided to defy both. In going into elections, its goal was to make the state recognize the movement as a major popular force.

In 1976, six Muslim Brothers won seats in the parliament, having presented themselves as candidates under the banner of the Socialist Arab Party. In the 1984 election the Brotherhood allied with the Wafd, a party that had once stood for a rigorous separation of religion and the state; the alliance, which cost the Wafd the support of Farag Foda, won 57 seats, enough to give it a significant voice in the 450-seat body.

In 1988 the Brotherhood changed allies again, coalescing with the Labor Party to win—notwithstanding considerable government vote-rigging—32 seats. The results made the Brotherhood a partner in the parliament's largest opposition bloc and gave its Islamic program a prominent place on the public agenda.

"Hassan al-Banna wanted nothing more than a democratic system," said Mamoun al-Hudaibi, son of the Brotherhood's second leader, Hassan al-Hudaibi, in what to me seemed like revisionist history. "And so did my father.

"They knew that an Islamic state would not be easy to establish, and it would not come soon. But the Brotherhood never accused other believers of being non-Muslims or subscribed to the ideas of Qutb. We adopted our own way, a peaceful way. Now we think that maybe an Islamic state will come after thirty years, or fifty, depending on the circumstances. Meanwhile, our organization is not even ready for an Islamic state. So the republicanism that my father advocated remains our policy."

Like his father, Mamoun al-Hudaibi spent years in prison under Nasser. Born in 1921, he trained as a lawyer and, after his release, had a distinguished career as a judge, rising to the presidency of the prestigious Cairo court of appeals. When he retired, he was elected to parliament on the Brotherhood-Labor Party ticket. Hudaibi, who has the title of spokesman, is considered the head of the Brotherhood's majority wing.

Hudaibi and I met in the Brotherhood's headquarters, a dark and shabby suite on Souk Tewfikiyya Street in downtown Cairo. Along the sidewalks on both sides of the entrance was the *souk* for which the street is named, offering vegetables, live pigeons, hardware, carcasses of beef, clothing. Men drank coffee and smoked narghiles in dingy cafés tucked among small shops. From a nearby mosque, a muezzin summoned believers to prayer.

Hudaibi, who wore a well-pressed safari suit, was seated behind an ancient desk, in front of a grinding air conditioner. He had a bald head, a sparse white beard and a barrel chest, conveying an impression of strength. Though his style of speech was gruff, he delivered his ideas with self-mocking joviality. I found him, to my surprise, quite likable.

"Of course," Hudaibi replied, when I asked whether most Egyptians wanted to be ruled by the *shari'a*. His sardonic grin suggested, however, that we both knew he was lying. He then proceeded to offer me the Brotherhood's current line.

"Egypt is 95 percent Muslim,* so naturally the people want the *shari'a*. But we have no intention of forcing it upon the country. The Quran says, 'no force in religion,'** and we recognize that. The Brotherhood has said a thousand times that we condemn violence. It is not accepted by our religion. But neither is it acceptable that the government commits violence and the people cannot.

"Torture gave birth to the Islamic groups, and there is now a blood feud between them and the police. We say that the way to stop vio-

---

* Like most Islamists, he diminished the percentage of Copts, to make them seem like an inconsequential minority. Though there is no confirmed data, the accepted figure is at least 10 percent and perhaps as much as 20 percent.
** See discussion in Chapter 3, pp. 94–97.

lence in Egypt is to give the people a right to choose their own government, free of fraud and free of coercion. The people want to live as Muslims as much as possible, and the government is not permitting them to do so."

I asked Hudaibi to describe the *shari'a* that he envisages, and was astonished to hear phrases that sounded more modernist than orthodox. Far from dwelling on Islamic law's immutability, he spoke of adapting it to contemporary needs. He also cited the *shura*, the consultative body that chose Muhammad's successors, as the precedent for the Brotherhood's support of electoral democracy.

"We can't amend the *shari'a*," he said, "and some principles can't be changed. But we live in an age of technology, far removed from the Prophet's era. Our prayers can't say, 'God, come down and get rid of technology,' or 'God, tell us whom to vote for in the next election.' We have to live in our time."

Hudaibi emphasized that an Islamic society today required programs of action—in agriculture, medicine and industry, as well as in politics—that were not contemplated in the Quran. Change, however, does not discredit the Quran, he said. God gave humans free will, he insisted, and mankind must accept responsibility for making rules that serve both religion and social needs. "God," he said, "asks only that we use the rules well."

When I questioned Hudaibi about Foda, he distanced himself from Ghazali's endorsement of the assassins. He answered with a complaint that the Brotherhood had been denied as much access to the people as Foda, in the press and on platforms, had had. His complaint, obviously, was a metaphor for the government's distrust of the Islamic movement. Hudaibi took a similar line on the murder, not justifying the killers but blaming the government for igniting a chain of violence which led to the killing.

"We condemned the Foda attack, as we did the attack on Naguib Mahfouz," Hudaibi said. "But if the government shuts the doors to free expression, our people's only outlet is violence.

"I had a dialogue with Foda at the Cairo Book Fair. He said bad things against Islam, our Prophet and our Quran. He tried to be provocative, and our people were provoked. He was deviant, and so our youth were deviant in return. The young men who killed him had wrong thoughts, which we would gladly have tried to correct. But the violence in our society will stop only when the government gives us full freedom to proclaim our beliefs and stops using violence to suppress us."

Looked at in retrospect, Hudaibi's statements seemed to be based on a premise of two pugilists, government and Brotherhood, continuing the rather gentlemanly sparring that they had practiced for some years under rules that both accepted. Neither, during these years, seemed interested in a knockout. But unbeknownst to Hudaibi at the time we spoke, Mubarak was in the process of changing the rules, preparing to deliver a knockout blow. Though Mubarak never explained his reasons, the events that preceded the election of 1995 shed some light on his thinking.

The Brotherhood, buoyed by Mubarak's tolerance of Islamization, may itself have triggered the change in policy by the vigor with which it geared up for the election. Organizing and infiltrating, it had taken control of the student unions and faculty clubs at the major universities, as well as the professional associations of engineers, doctors, dentists, lawyers and teachers. In themselves, these victories were trivial. But in Egypt, where democracy is fragile and parties weak, elections in university and professional bodies are seen as bellwethers, and the government perceived a danger in the Brotherhood's triumphs.

Mubarak no doubt interpreted the Brotherhood's pledge to fight for parliamentary seats throughout all of Egypt as a threat to the government's dominance. He considered it tolerable for the Brotherhood to have a parliamentary bloc from which to propagandize for its program, but unacceptable for it to reach out to govern the state.

Was the Brotherhood preparing a surprise? Mubarak, no doubt alarmed by a civil war in Algeria that was provoked by the Islamic party's electoral victories (to be discussed in detail in Chapter 8), decided to transform the terms of the contest.

In January 1995, Mubarak's police arrested eighteen of the Brotherhood's leaders. Speaking for the organization, Hudaibi's initial response was mild; he seemed to dismiss the arrests as another round in the sparring match. But he soon changed his mind. In the following months there were waves of arrests and, though no official figures were disclosed, by September an estimated hundred or more leading Brotherhood members were in custody. Many of them were parliamentary candidates.

Over the years Brotherhood members had often been detained for a few days and later released. This time, to the Brotherhood's dismay, the detainees were put on trial on charges of violations of political and antiterrorist laws. Furthermore, the trials were conducted in military courts, which was unprecedented, since none of the defendants had been accused of a violent crime.

In November fifty-four defendants were found guilty and sentenced to long jail terms. The judges also ordered the closing of the headquarters on Souk Tewfikiyya Street, citing as grounds—grounds not used since Sadat's time—that the organization was illegal. A few days later the police carried out the order.

Mubarak's aim was no longer in dispute. He was not satisfied to harass the Brotherhood; he wanted to destroy it. No government since Nasser had claimed such an objective.

Shortly after the trial and a few days before the election, Minister of Interior Hassan el-Alfi presented the government's new line on the Brotherhood. In a newspaper interview,[4] Alfi claimed to have solid proof of the Brotherhood's links to Gama'a Islamiyya and Islamic Jihad. In collusion with the extremists, he said, the Brotherhood had become a front for violence. The Brotherhood had reverted back to its campaign of political assassination of the 1940s, he said, and in fact had become more dangerous in concealing its strategy.

"Some people want to distinguish between those who bear arms and those who do not," Alfi said, "but those who incite are more dangerous than those who bear arms. The Brotherhood raises donations and spends money on the families of people accused in cases of terrorism, murder and bombing. Is that charity? How can they make the claim to have no connections to the extremists? The Brotherhood is an illegal organization, not recognized under the law. Its leaders are extremely dangerous. They are trying to seize power by any means."

In the balloting for parliament on November 30, 1995, Egypt, never known for clean elections, surpassed itself in irregularities. Mubarak had barred international observers, claiming they would be an infringement on Egyptian sovereignty. But witnesses pieced together a picture of what had occurred.

The opposition candidates and their supporters who had been arrested were retained in jail on election day. In addition, hundreds of voting monitors for the opposition parties were arrested on election day. Without monitors, ballot boxes were torched or stuffed. Electoral registers were manipulated. State security forces and pro-government gangs intimidated voters. Though no figures were released, witnesses estimated that about fifty Egyptians were killed in unsuppressed violence.

After the runoff, when the results were announced, Mubarak's party had won 95 percent of the seats. The Muslim Brotherhood had won one. Though the Brotherhood had risen from the ashes before, many Egyptians believe that this time Mubarak may have succeeded in breaking it.

But suppressing the Brotherhood was not the same as defeating extremism. In April 1996 an extremist group murdered eighteen

Greek tourists, apparently believing they were Israelis, at a Cairo hotel. In November 1997, fifty-eight foreigners and four Egyptians were murdered by Islamic gunmen in Luxor in Upper Egypt.

Mubarak's electoral victory, moreover, contained no signs of enlarged public support. He may have succeeded, in fact, in uniting the opposition forces, non-Islamic and Islamic, by the contempt that he heaped on the electoral process. The result has been that, since election day, Mubarak's popular standing has grown steadily weaker.

As the Mubarak regime approaches the end of its second decade in office, it seems caught on the grindstone of Islamic politics. Mubarak has calculated, no doubt correctly, that Egypt cannot be governed without reference to Islam. He enlisted the support of orthodoxy, as Egypt's rulers have traditionally done, to buttress his legitimacy. But to most Egyptians, orthodoxy does not seem like the appropriate dogma for our time. The most dynamic segments of the Islamic community, both fundamentalists and modernists, seem to have had enough of orthodoxy. They want something else.

Mubarak faces a dilemma. Fundamentalism as an ideology of government is surely fantasy; modernism as a political force is painfully feeble. Mubarak, unlike the leaders of other societies, does not believe he can find legitimacy simply by running an honest and competent government, supported by popular participation. He has certainly never tried it. On the other hand, having tied his political fate to orthodoxy, he has not shown the leadership that would be needed to fuse an honest and competent government with Islamic principles.

Mubarak's failure is unlikely to make a revolution. Egyptians, whose patience seems limitless, have never made revolutions. But the change that Mubarak, ostensibly a modern man, once appeared capable of inspiring has not taken place. Moreover, the good will and high hopes from which he benefited on taking office have largely been squandered. Mired in Islamic debate, Egypt seems unlikely at any time soon to emerge into the modern society, with or without Islam, to which it aspires. On the contrary, it seems doomed to remain where it has been for too long, in an intellectual wilderness.

3

The Prophet
and the Book

MUHAMMAD THE PROPHET, Islam's central figure, was born and brought up in the bleak, sun-scorched town of Mecca in western Arabia. Though a town dweller all his life, he absorbed the austere culture of the nomads of the surrounding desert. It was a harsh culture, in which tribes fought tribes and, within them, clans fought clans. Survival demanded loyalty, discipline and vigilance. The society produced by these demands was hierarchical, conformist and resistant to change.

Muhammad would try to impose a new sense of order in Arabia. As a reformer, religious faith would be his weapon. But he was no revolutionary, and the set of beliefs he shaped were deeply imbued with the nomads' system of values.

Muhammad, born about A.D. 570, was an orphan. His father died before his birth, his mother when he was six years old. He was raised first in the home of his maternal grandfather and later was placed in the charge of an uncle, Abu Talib, his father's brother. Muhammad's family, the Hashims, were merchants. Though not rich, they belonged to Mecca's preeminent trading tribe, the Quraysh, who had come in from the desert several generations before. Muhammad was thus a marginal member, if not an outsider, in the elite that dominated the town and its commerce.

Little is recorded of Muhammad's childhood. But Mecca, with few diversions, could have afforded little pleasure to a boy. A contemporary wrote of it that "no waters flow . . . not a blade of grass on which to rest the eye . . . only merchants dwell there."[1]

Muhammad was no doubt a bright child. The Arab tradition which holds that he was illiterate is probably a calculated error, on which more will be said later. Destined to follow his forebears into commerce, he surely learned at least enough reading, writing and arithmetic to satisfy a trader's needs.

Muhammad's thinking was apparently also shaped by the arrival in Mecca each year of pilgrims from throughout Arabia. Mecca was a religious as well as a commercial hub, treated as sacred, for reasons lost to history, long before the arrival of Islam. Muhammad's contemporaries venerated trees, stones and wells that were believed to be inhabited by powerful spirits, most of them female. In Mecca the pilgrims prayed before the Ka'ba,* a shrine under Quraysh control, a crude structure which in Muhammad's day was already known as "God's House." It is said to have been surrounded by shrines to dozens of other gods and goddesses. This was the period that Muslims call *jahiliyya,* the age of paganism. Muhammad, as a witness to this idolatry, was obviously offended by it. It seems apparent that, at some point in his growing up, he vowed to supplant it with devotion to a single God.

Muhammad came to manhood during a lull in the warfare that had long raged in Arabia. Two rival empires to the north, Christian Byzantium and Zoroastrian Persia, were long-standing contestants for regional dominance. But decades of battle had exhausted them, and both had lost interest in the peninsula. In time the wars in Arabia would resume, but the attackers would be Muhammad's followers, seeking to establish their new faith, before turning their attention to Byzantine and Persian conquests.

In the meantime, however, peace had invited a resumption of caravan traffic, and Mecca was thriving. In its marketplace spices and leather from the south were exchanged for cloth and grain from the north. The prosperity no doubt brought with it a rise in caravan raids, an ancient practice among the local bedouins. In bad times the raids were directed against one another, in good times against pilgrims and traders. For the Meccans, the raids were a major nuisance, and it is plausible that Muhammad, the merchant, gave serious thought to how to put an end to them.

Some historians believe that Muhammad's era was also marked by an explosion in the bedouin population, stretching the desert's limited resources in food and water to the breaking point. Like the Quraysh before them, more and more tribes were leaving nomadism for urban life. But while the town tribes grew richer, the desert tribes were

---

* Today the Ka'ba is a large stone structure draped in a black cloth, a sanctuary of Islamic monotheism within the walls of Mecca's great mosque.

getting poorer, creating an atmosphere that called out for fundamental reforms.

Muhammad lived in the eye of this crisis, though he may not have understood it. He claimed rigorously that he was an ordinary man, obeying God's will, and there is no need to dispute him. But it is noteworthy that the reforms he promoted in God's name were, in many cases, linked to the problems that would have attracted the attention of a committed advocate of social change.

When he was twenty-five, Muhammad, by now an established trader, was hired to take command of a cargo of goods being transported by caravan to Syria. The goods were owned by Khadija, a wealthy merchant's widow and, in her own right, a prominent businesswoman. Muhammad's biographers say he performed his duties so well that, on his return, Khadija proposed that they marry.

The widow brought to the marriage wealth and social position, which served Muhammad well when he began to proselytize God's message. Though tradition holds that she was fifteen years his senior, some historians are dubious, on the grounds that she bore him seven children, unlikely for a woman already forty. Of the seven, all the boys died in infancy; four daughters survived to adulthood. From what is known of the marriage, Muhammad and Khadija, for the two decades until her death, enjoyed a happy, monogamous relationship.

Muhammad was about forty when he told Khadija that he was receiving revelations from God. He soon began disseminating these revelations around the town, urging Meccans to abandon Arabia's array of gods in favor of the one, omnipotent God. Khadija, extremely supportive, became his first convert, but few Meccans followed her lead.

Muhammad was shaken at the reaction of his fellow Quraysh. Not only were they indifferent to his message; they exercised their influence to turn other Meccans away. It is unclear whether this was because he was regarded as an eccentric, or was perceived by the Quraysh commercial elite as a threat to the wealth derived from the pagan worshipers during the pilgrimage. Muhammad spent ten frustrating years trying in vain to convert his native city to monotheism. His failure provided no clue that, within another decade, his message would sway all Arabia, then reverberate throughout the world.

Muhammad never provided much detail about his encounters with God but, according to Muslim tradition, while meditating alone in a cave or on a hilltop, he had visions in which he heard a voice. The speech was in Arabic. He was certain the words were God's. Some

Quranic passages suggest that God himself was speaking, others that it was the Angel Gabriel, serving as an intermediary.

Muhammad insisted that, after each encounter, he committed to memory the words that he had heard. What he later transmitted in Mecca, and subsequently in Medina, he declared, was not his personal interpretation, nor a paraphrase, and surely not his own opinions. The words were God's precisely.

Quran in Arabic means "recitation," in this case the recitation of God. Jews and Christians, while considering their scriptures holy, acknowledge many of them to be of human authorship. Islam holds the entire Quran to be a verbatim record of God's speech. To be a Muslim requires acceptance of God's authorship. Believers hold that the Quran, being God's words, is a perfect book.

Not surprisingly, skeptics throughout history have cast doubt on the Quran's source. The Quraysh were the first doubters, but the tribesmen of the Arabian desert were, at the start, equally unconvinced.

Outside Islam, the claim was never taken very seriously. Though Muhammad may have had visions, it was conventionally said, he offered no evidence of the involvement of God. Over the centuries of Islam's rivalry with Christianity, Muhammad's credibility was judged politically in the West. His veracity was consistently attacked by Western churchmen, kings and philosophers.

But even some believers raised questions. The story is told that after Khadija's death Muhammad appealed to God to permit him to contract more than the four marriages permitted to other Muslims. Good marriages, he contended, would promote the spread of the faith. When God consented, the young Aisha, Muhammad's favorite wife, quipped: "Your Lord hastens to do your pleasure."

Scholars point out that much of the Quran's content required no guidance from God. Muhammad's Arabia was already familiar with the idea of monotheism, if only from the Christian and Jewish tribes that inhabited the region. Many of the Quran's lessons replicate, though often in garbled form, the scriptures of the Christians and Jews, the "people of the book."

It is unlikely that Muhammad, who knew no foreign languages, had read any of these scriptures himself. But, as a merchant, he surely met members of these communities when they traded in the marketplace in Mecca. It is also likely that he did business with them elsewhere in Arabia, or even beyond.

Muslims explain scriptural similarities by saying that God repeated to Muhammad what He had earlier told the Christians and Jews.

Arabia was an oral society, and the Quran originated in talk. Muhammad, some say, had the revelations inscribed after concluding that a monotheistic faith, by its nature, needed a "book." The Quran treats Christians and Jews as the earthly authorities, with the power to verify God's message.

"If thou [Muhammad] art in doubt concerning that which We reveal to thee," the Quran says, "then question those [Christians and Jews] who read the scripture before thee" (10:95). It also says that "the Torah and the Gospels" foreshadow Muhammad's later appearance as prophet, though scholars have found no passages to confirm this assertion (7:157).

The Quran offers a record of Muhammad's frequent dealings with Christians and Jews. The thread of meaning in his encounters suggests that at first he regarded his mission as an updating of their monotheisms. Muhammad's God was, after all, the same God as theirs. Only much later, after the two refused to embrace his message, did he quite reluctantly distance himself from them.

Islamic orthodoxy maintains that Muhammad was illiterate. The claim is based on a Quranic verse (7:157) that describes him as *ummi,* a word normally translated as "unlettered." The word illustrates the linguistic difficulties that the Quran presents.

Scholars are unsure whether the sense of *ummi* is properly "illiterate" or "untaught," or whether it has a meaning that is unrelated to letters at all. One fanciful translator has even chosen to render it as "immaculate."[2] Some scholars believe that, in the context of Muhammad's middle-class upbringing and mercantile vocation, "unsophisticated" may be the most plausible rendering.

Orthodox Muslims see none of these definitions as pejorative. If Muhammad were unable to write, they reason, he is obviously innocent of the charges of the infidels that he, not God, is the author of the Quran. His illiteracy would be evidence that he was singled out to spread the word of God. *Ummi* provides proof that he was God's choice.

In fact, in the end, whether Muhammad could read and write scarcely matters. What counts is his credibility as the carrier of God's message. Muslims take Muhammad at his word. The divine origin of the Quran is the seed of Islamic belief. To believers, the Prophet's assertion of this truth cannot be denied.

From the beginning, the converts that Muhammad made were required to pronounce a vow, called the *shahada* ("bearing witness"). It declared: "There is no god but God and Muhammad is his Prophet." The vow distinguishes Muhammad's message from the basic beliefs of

Judaism and Christianity. The difference is not the centrality that the *shahada* imparts to God; it is in the proximity to divinity that it assigns to Muhammad.

Whatever the proximity, Muhammad maintained that he was a simple man who did not know why God chose him. He never asserted for himself the divinity ascribed to Christ. He claimed no capacity to perform miracles. Muhammad described himself as the last in the line of prophets that began with Abraham and included Moses and Jesus. In his view, every one of them, being mortal, fulfilled a mission and then died.

The Quran, nonetheless, makes very clear that God thought of Muhammad as much more than an ordinary mortal. "Obey God," it says, "and obey His apostle if you would be true believers" (8:1). In another verse, the text puts God and Muhammad on a single plane, saying: "Believe in God and his Messenger" (64:8).

These verses impart great authority to Muhammad. If Muslims could not emulate God, Who is divine, they could emulate the Prophet, a human. Indeed, the *shari'a,* Islamic law, is based on the precedents set by the Prophet in his lifetime. The power that early Muslims attributed to Muhammad to interpret the divine word governs orthodox belief today.

Muslims recognize that God now and then saw fit to put Muhammad in his place. God suggests in one verse that His apostle was overreaching, saying: "We have not sent you to watch over the people. Your sole duty is to bring home the message" (42:48). In another, God reproaches Muhammad with a reminder that, until his selection as messenger, "Thou knewest not what the Scripture was, nor what was the Faith" (42:52).

But, whatever failings God found, He bestowed on Muhammad increasingly heavy worldly burdens. Having begun as a merchant, Muhammad emerged out of the crowd by being selected as God's messenger and prophet. From there he became the political and spiritual leader of the Islamic community in Arabia. Having organized a powerful army, he assumed its command and set out to spread a new faith through an expanding empire.

Mortal though he was, Muhammad was hardly ordinary. Islamic doctrine treats him as a paragon, a leader in possession of wisdom conveyed to him by God, a nearly perfect human.

When he began preaching God's tidings, Muhammad's aspiration was apparently no more than to wean the Quraysh from idolatry. Only later did he reconceptualize his mission and embark deliberately on the propagation of a new faith.

· II ·

MUHAMMAD'S REVELATIONS, scholars agree, reached him intermittently over twenty years. According to his biographers, he passed them on as he received them, by word of mouth, often to crowds in the marketplace. His words were generally written down by professional scribes, who recorded them—paper not yet being available—on scraps of parchment or palm leaves or, it is said, on a camel's shoulder blade or rib.

The revelations were not collected and organized during Muhammad's lifetime. The Quran commands "the putting together thereof and the reading thereof" (74:17), which suggests an early intent to turn the communications into scripture. But the Prophet clearly had no sense of urgency. The evidence of his biographers suggests that when he died he was still having visions and did not regard the transmissions from God as finished.

Abu Bakr, Muhammad's immediate successor, first ordered the revelations assembled, and for a time competing collections circulated. Only twenty years after the Prophet's death did Uthman, the third caliph, appoint a commission to end the confusion; it produced what became a standard edition. Linguistic refinements continued, however, until the end of Islam's first century, when scholars finally agreed on a stabilized text. Earlier versions of the Quran were then discarded and have since disappeared.*

Muslim believers do not entertain the notion that the seemingly haphazard process by which God's pronouncements became Islam's holy book undermines the Quran's integrity. In Arabia's oral culture, they contend, such a process was quite normal.

The Quran, as it was received from Uthman, is composed of 114 "suras," each a group of verses. Every sura is said to be a separate revelation, though clearly mixing among them has occurred.

The suras are not presented chronologically. In so far as the Quran has structure at all, they appear in order of length, starting with the longest. Curiously, because God's earliest pronouncements were the briefest, in the text they appear last.

Muhammad's first revelation, in fact, is the 96th sura. "Read," it commands and, according to Muslim scholars, Muhammad replied three times that he was unable to read.[3]

---

* Shi'ism, which quarreled with Caliph Uthman, did not accept his edition and has since adopted one of their own, though the difference is mostly in details.

The sura continues: "In the name of thy Lord who createth man from a clot . . . Thy Lord is the most bounteous, who teacheth by the pen, teacheth man that which he knew not. Nay, but verily man is rebellious that he thinketh himself independent." It concludes: "Prostrate thyself and draw near."

Based on internal evidence, scholars have largely determined which suras were conveyed in Mecca and which in Medina. Those from Mecca, where Muhammad was grappling with the nature of God and the universe, tend to have a more metaphysical ring. Those from Medina, where he exercised political power, dwell more on worldly matters. The placement of some suras, of course, is still in dispute.

Islamic orthodoxy, however, refuses to recognize any hierarchy among suras. Muslim scholars have expended considerable energy in trying to chart chronology, yet maintain that they are indifferent to history. Whether a sura came from Mecca or Medina is of no importance, orthodoxy holds, since all God's commands are equally valid. Every word of the Quran is sacred, say Islamic jurists, whatever the order of His pronouncements.

In fact, attempts to read the Quran as a source of history have had little success. The text makes little reference to time or events or, apart from the Prophet's, to personalities. It has none of the tales of love, tragedy and adventure that the Bible contains. It offers rather few clues to the nature of its times. It consists, mostly, of divine assertions and admonitions.

Though believers regard the Quran as perfect, non-Muslims often disagree. Thomas Carlyle once said churlishly: "It is as toilsome reading as I ever undertook, a wearisome, confused jumble, crude, incondite."[4] An Islamic encyclopedia, an excellent source of information, comments on the Quran's literary virtues with commendable diffidence. To recognize the Quran's perfection, it says, "is not easy to a reader with some stylistic training and a certain amount of taste."[5]

The Arab view of the Quran is enhanced by a pride in the fact that, of the many languages in which God could have communicated, Arabic was His choice. "We have revealed it in Arabic, so that you may understand" (8:2), says the Quran.

But in the seventh century neither the vocabulary nor the system of transcription of Arabic was up to the religion's needs. Scholars know something of the language from the popular poetry that has come down from the era, and it is clear that a new language had to be created to transmit the Quran's complex ideas. The new language brought in foreign words, metaphor and simile, even pagan incantations. Secular scholars tend to credit Muhammad with bringing to Arabic, through the Quran, a new linguistic richness.

Even for those fluent in Arabic, however, the Quran is not an easy book to read. It speaks in a seventh-century context. It uses words whose meanings the centuries have radically transformed. Its style is a mix of poetry and prose. Scholars who have spent their lives studying it remain stumped by ambiguities, literary allusions and obscure references.

Notwithstanding the difficulties, however, the Quran is read by millions daily. For many Muslims, to be sure, the reading is perfunctory, pure ritual. Such practice is encouraged by the *ulama*, who contend that the Quran can be properly understood only with their intercession. Still, the popular attention the Quran receives is evidence that its content follows a direct path into the Muslim soul.

Yet, even in translation, the Quran contains rewards. Reading it, though arduous, is not beyond normal capacities. The subjects of its sentences, after all, are followed by predicates. If some verses are murky, others are very clear. A bit of informed commentary helps. But, even without it, a conscientious reader can capture much of both the spirit and the meaning of the text.

Translations of the Quran—which run three or four hundred pages in English—inevitably modify meanings. Available versions differ substantially in style. But the problems posed by translations may be no different, in substance, from those posed by the original. Translations of the Quran evoke the same disputes over meaning that readers so often encounter in the original Arabic.[6]

For some twelve centuries, during which Christianity and Islam were locked in combat, Western scholars took pains to discredit the Quran. Having adopted the line that Muhammad was a charlatan, they concluded that his book had to be a fraud.

Only a century or so ago did that convention shift. Western academies began treating organized religion—both Christian and non-Christian—as an intellectual discipline. Specialists emerged, studying Islam as fellow researchers studied the French Revolution or the properties of microbes. Their work, though sometimes ridiculed today as "Orientalism,"[7] represented a deliberate effort to rise above earlier cultural prejudices.

In the current century, Western scholars, with still more detachment, have sought to understand Islam on its own terms. They have virtually ceased to ask whether Muhammad heard the voice of God, recognizing that the question is likely to remain forever unresolved.

Accepting the Prophet as he perceived himself, they stipulate that he probably heard a voice and certainly believed it. Backing away from disparagement, their focus has shifted to the role he played in shaping Islamic civilization.

Unfortunately the examination into Muhammad and his age is sorely burdened by a penury of reliable data. The Quran, with all of its limitations, stands nearly alone as an original source for the prophetic era. Verifiable records and observations from the period are extremely rare; archaeology has added almost nothing.

Only well after Muhammad's death did believers begin to collect statements attributed to him, as well as observations from his contemporaries. From this data, some Muslims built a structure of Islamic law; others wrote biographies.

Not surprisingly, the sayings of the Prophet, as well as the biographies, contain unverified material, much of it slanted to favor one faction or another in sectarian disputes. Like the Christian gospels, they are heavily apologetic. This data, though falling short of modern standards of historiography, remains the raw material for the studies of the Prophet's age.

Muslim scholarship has contributed disappointingly little to these studies. The view of the Quran as the precise word of God remains a barrier to its critical analysis. Muslim orthodoxy exercises a powerful restraint on any scrutiny that hints at modifying an idealized vision of the Prophet and his era.

Orthodox thinking, moreover, is shaped by an unusual doctrine adopted in the early days of Islam. The doctrine holds that the Quran was "not created" but has existed for all time. It argues that Muhammad, at a time chosen by God, simply transmitted to the Arabs a message that was, like God Himself, eternal. That God spoke in Arabic only underlined the Arabs' special responsibility to preserve the message in its purity.

In the ninth century, two hundred years after Muhammad's death, the Mu'tazilites, a body of dissident theologians, challenged this doctrine. Their challenge's political implications—described further in Chapter 5—were extremely disturbing to those with a vested interest in orthodoxy.

The Mu'tazilites denied that the Quran had existed for all time and maintained that God, in response to specific circumstances on earth, had "created" it. From this, they concluded that, as circumstances changed, He would have further pronouncements to make. Meanwhile, they argued, man could determine, by the exercise of reason, moral conduct in matters which God had not addressed. The

Mu'tazilites thus gave man a measure of free will and control over his future that orthodoxy denied.

Orthodox Islam, after a tumultuous battle, emerged triumphant over Mu'tazilism. The result was the reaffirmation of the dogma that, since God's work was complete, doctrine was immutable. Immutability, as scholars know, does not easily yield to examination. The victory placed a heavy burden on Muslims today who conduct critical studies into their own history or beliefs.

Only a few brave Muslim scholars, like Nasr Abuzeid, cross the barrier to analyze the background and content of the Quran, and of Islam. The penalties imposed on Abuzeid by Egypt's Islamic establishment are reminders of the difficulties faced by Muslims who violate intellectual conventions.

The Abuzeid incident illustrates how fear places a lid on scriptural criticism. Orthodoxy fears the changes that scrutiny of the Islamic past may produce; Islamic scholars fear the reprisals their studies will elicit. These fears explain the void in theological and historical analysis that only Westerners, often with their own misgivings, are generally prepared to fill.

Secular scholars—most of them Westerners—insist there is no disrespect in their treating the Quran as a historical document. They examine the text for subtle changes in voice or viewpoint, or for insight into the life of the times. Among their hypotheses are that more than one hand was involved in the Quran's preparation, that the Prophet himself had not finished when he died and that parts of the text were lost or perhaps even suppressed. Such hypotheses are barred to those who subscribe to orthodoxy's position that the Quran is a perfect book.

An example of the questions which intrigue secular scholars is the Quran's focus on commerce. "It is no sin," says the text, "that ye seek the bounty of your lord by trading" (2:198).

The Quran assures merchants that fulfilling their holy duties takes hardly any time at all. "When the call is heard for the prayer on the day of congregation [Friday at noon], hasten into remembrance of Allah and leave your trading. . . . And when the prayer is ended, then disperse in the land and seek of Allah's bounty, and remember Allah much, that ye may be successful" (62:9–10).

Some experts see in these verses Muhammad's search for a rapprochement with his Quraysh antagonists. It suggests that he may have meant the Quran not just as a moral but as a political document. To orthodoxy, a scholar's interest in Muhammad's dealings in Mecca's marketplace appears sacrilegious. But, as the Christian and Jewish experience suggests, scholarly interest is hardly likely to undermine religious belief.

In the end, the Quran's credibility, like that of the Torah and the gospels, is established not by scholarly analysis but by the faith that resides in the minds of believers. By that measure, Islam has demonstrated its sturdiness for nearly fourteen centuries. Yet this sturdiness has not dispelled orthodoxy's concern that, under the assaults of science, Islam will wither.

To make their case, orthodox Muslims argue that, since the Renaissance, science has severely weakened the orthodoxies of Christianity and Judaism. Though both religions thrive, their relationship with their believers and with the external world has been radically transformed. Orthodox Muslims say they are determined to prevent such transformation from happening in Islam.

Modernist Muslims rebut them by arguing that, while science has weakened Christian and Jewish orthodoxy, Western *society* has never been stronger. Most Muslims recognize as much. Many would even say they are uninterested in a more powerful society if its cost is to weaken faith. Few dispute, however, that Islamic civilization—except in spiritual terms—is not now the equal of the civilizations of either the Christians or the Jews.

The current struggle within Islam—recapitulating struggles other faiths have experienced, or experience still—addresses the issue of the price that a renewed society will ask of Islam.

Orthodoxy argues that Muslim society should hold the line against the assaults of non-Islamic knowledge, so to remain undefiled. Fundamentalism maintains that Islam must not only reject non-Islamic knowledge but look more critically into itself to return to a more virtuous era. Modernism holds that Islamic society must risk admitting some non-Islamic knowledge into its body of belief so that it can rebuild along more solid lines.

But conflict over interpretation is hardly new. Muhammad was barely in his grave when Muslims began arguing over how best to extend God's will into uncharted terrain. It took about three centuries of theological dispute for an orthodoxy to be established—that is, for one faction's interpretation to triumph over those of its rivals. But, as Christianity and Judaism show, such triumphs are never permanent. If, as some say, such struggles are a sign of vigor, Islam today is more vigorous than it has been in a thousand years.

· III ·

THE QURAN'S dominant vision is that God, an all-powerful deity, presides indefatigably over the fate of mankind. To acknowledge as much is Islam's first commandment. The term "Islam" means "submission"; Muslim translates as "one who has submitted" to God's will. Abd Allah, a proud common name, means "slave of God," implying liberation from all earthly temptation.[8]

Some find this vision grim. The noted British scholar H. A. R. Gibb argues that Islam is so deeply imbued with fear that the Muslim is left no room for frivolity. Visitors to Islamic countries will find something familiar in the observation.

In *jahiliyya,* the notion of a god who reigns over other gods was common. The Quran repudiated *jahiliyya* with the claim that other gods do not exist. "There is no god but God," says the Quran, "the originator of the heavens and the earth. When He decreeth a thing, He saith unto it only: Be! And it is" (2:17).

The Quran is pervaded by the notion that mankind's duty is to accept God's omnipotence. Indeed, in delivering His lessons, God is irritable toward those who, lacking faith, demand evidence of His powers. Yet, curiously, He does not reject their inquiries. He presents His case reasonably, suggesting that, while reassuring believers, He is also anxious to rebut skeptics.

"For people who think intelligently," the Quran says, "there are signs [of God's power] in the creation of the heavens and of the earth, in the alternation of night and day, in the ships which voyage on the seas to the profit of mankind, in the waters He sends down from the heavens giving life out of lifelessness to the earth, in the populating of the earth with every kind of living creature, in the hither and thither of the winds and clouds harnessed to his purposes between sky and land" (2:164).

In Muhammad's time, prominent among the skeptics of the Quran's revelations were Arabia's Jews and Christians. When Muhammad embarked on his mission, he thought of himself as sharing in their heritage and he expected to convert them to his cause. He never understood why they refused him, and his failure was obviously a source of enduring disappointment.

The Quran makes clear its respect, even awe, of the "people of the book." But God, we are told, became upset at their insistence that they did not need Muhammad to enter paradise. Having finally lost patience, God instructs His believers to "Fight against those who have been given the Scripture as believeth not in Allah" (9:29). In God's view, according to the Quran, Jews and Christians err not so much in rejecting Muhammad but in failing to understand their own faith.

The Jews, as God sees them, have become ingrates. "Remember," the Quran tells them, "when We delivered you from Pharaoh's folk, who were afflicting you with dreadful torment. . . . Even after that, your hearts were hardened and became as rocks" (2:49, 74).

The Christians fare scarcely better, having deviated over the dogma of Jesus's parentage. "Allah hath begotten [an offspring] . . . ," says the Quran of the Christian claim, "And lo! verily, they tell a lie" (37:152). From Muhammad's day to this, Islam has treated as heresy the idea of God's fathering a child. The divinity of Jesus, to Muslims, is a travesty of monotheism.

The God depicted by the Quran is not a single-minded autocrat. In one verse He is harsh and unyielding, in another benevolent and forgiving. He seems capricious in administering justice, applying coercion, showing mercy. His consistent concern is moral conduct, but He is presented in enough shades to justify a range of judgments, from strict disciplinarian to gentle mentor.

Active in shaping the course of life, God exercises His powers even more at death, when He determines where every man and woman will spend eternity. To a Muslim, the principal argument for submitting to God's will lies in the powers God exercises on the Last Day. In *jahiliyya,* the afterlife was inevitably cheerless and grim. Muhammad preached that submitting to God contained the prospect of enjoying the hereafter in paradise.

"Recognize," it says, "that the life of this world is indulgence in delusion, idle talk, and pageantry, and boasting among you, and rivalry over flaunted wealth and offspring. After a shower there is vegetation, the growth of which pleases the husbandman until, by and by, it dries up, turns yellow before your eyes and becomes straw. That is how it is with the vanities of this life, which is all illusion, but in the hereafter there is grievous punishment, and also God's forgiveness" (57:20).

The Quran's advocacy is powerful. The first test for eternity, the Quran says, is whether an individual has submitted to God's will. God makes no mistakes, it says. The Quran is tantalizing in pledging God's mercy to those who submit, and pitiless in assuring His wrath to those who do not.

"Men who surrender unto Allah, and women who surrender," says the Quran, "and men who believe and women who believe, and men who obey and women who obey . . .—Allah hath prepared for them forgiveness and vast reward" (33:35).

In some verses, however, God raises the bar, conditioning His rewards not just on submission but on behavior. These verses echo the old debate in Christianity on the comparative merits of faith and good works. The Quran says:

"Whoso doeth good works, whether male or female, and is a believer, such will enter paradise and they will not be wronged the dint of a date-stone" (4:124). And, "Those who believe and do good works, their Lord guideth them by their faith. Rivers will flow beneath them in the Gardens of Delight" (10:10).

The Quran often offers a reminder, and a warning, that earthly life is inconsequential compared to the hereafter.

The Quran is remarkably explicit in describing the paradise that awaits the virtuous. The vision seems a mockery of the harsh life of the desert that Muhammad's tribal contemporaries experienced. Paradise is patterned after what the desert is not.

"Shall I tell you what is better than all earthly desires? For those who keep from evil, there are with their Lord the Gardens of Paradise under which the rivers flow, where they will abide forever with pure companions and relish Allah's good will. For Allah looks after His servants, those who pray" (3:14–15).*

Heaven's tenants live in "Gardens enclosed and vineyards and maidens for companions, and a full cup" (78:32–34) among "rivers of water unpolluted and rivers of milk whereof the flavor changeth not, and rivers of wine delicious to the drinkers and rivers of clear-run honey; therein for them is every kind of fruit, with pardon from their Lord" (42:15).

Meanwhile, there is also hell, the Quran says, where "garments of fire will be cut out for them; boiling fluid will be poured down on their heads" (22:19). He also describes hell as "a home for the rebellious, [who] will abide therein for ages. Therein taste they neither coolness or any drink save boiling water and a paralysing cold, reward proportioned to their evil deeds. . . . So taste of that which ye have earned. No increase do We give you save of torment" (78:22–30).

Yet the Quran never quite makes up its mind on the human capacity for choice between heaven and hell. Islam is still locked in debate on the issue of free will versus determinism. While taking for granted God's omnipotence, the Quran leaves unresolved whether He imparted to men and women the freedom to select good over evil or

* Ben-Shemesh translation.

whether He, like a puppeteer, exercises His control over every act they perform.

"Whosoever will," it says, on the side of free will, "let him believe, and whosoever will, let him disbelieve. Lo! We have prepared for the disbelievers Fire" (18:30). In another verse, it speaks even more explicitly: "Of mankind are some who take unto themselves objects of worship which they set as rivals to Allah, loving them with a love like that which is the due of Allah only. . . . Oh, that those who do evil had but known, on the day when they behold the doom, that power belongeth wholly to Allah, and that Allah is severe in punishment" (2:165).

But on the predestinarian side, the Quran says, "If thy Lord willed, all who are on earth would have believed together. . . . It is not for any soul to believe save by the permission of Allah" (10:100). It also states: "Unto whosoever of you willeth to walk straight, ye will not, unless it be that Allah, the Lord of Creation, willeth" (81:27–29). Similarly, the Quran says, "Whosoever will may choose a way unto his Lord; yet will ye not unless Allah willeth. . . . He maketh whom He will to enter His mercy, and for evil-doers hath prepared a painful doom" (76:29–31).

Mutually contradictory, these verses present a whimsical God. The determinist verses tell us that who believes and who does not is God's choice. But we are also told that He decides an eternal destiny for them as if the choice were their own.

The ambiguity is troublesome. On the one hand, if God controls everything, what responsibility has mankind? On the other, unless mankind is free, of what logic are God's punishments and rewards? The Quran positions itself on both sides of the issue.

In Islam, as in Christianity, the debate between free will and determinism that has raged through the centuries is more than a theologian's quibble. A conviction that God scripts every move can only produce in mankind an impaired sense of personal responsibility. It breeds a gloomy judgment of human potential. It implies a hapless humanity, unable to mobilize its earthly resources to resolve its problems. It creates a willingness to accept, as God's will, conditions as they are. Of what service is human initiative, of what relevance personal exertion, of what help human decency, if God makes the calls?

In Christianity, the contest between the two visions has, under the long influence of secular thought, tipped in favor of free will. In Islam, the signs suggest that it is tipped the other way.[9]

Surely the sense that all is foreordained lies near the root of the fatalism that weighs so palpably on Islamic culture. Muslims acknowledge as much. It is hard to deny that determinism's pervasiveness in the Muslim mind has placed shackles on the earthly development of Islamic civilization.

Yet, whatever the thread of predestination that weaves through the text, the Quran exhorts believers to *choose* moral conduct.

No great knowledge of Jewish and Christian scriptures is needed to recognize a command that is barely distinguishable from the Golden Rule. God says in the Quran, "Wrong not, and ye shall not be wronged" (2:279). The everyday morality that the Quran commends does not differ significantly from the scriptural admonitions directed at Christians and Jews.

God, according to the Quran, urges "A kind word followed by forgiveness, [which] is better than almsgiving followed by injury. . . . Render not vain your almsgiving by reproach and injury, like him who spendeth his wealth only to be seen of men and believeth not in Allah and the Last Day" (2:263). And "Allah enjoineth justice and kindness, and giving to kinsfolk, and forbiddeth lewdness and abomination and wickedness" (16:90).

The Quran has praise for "those who preserve their chastity save with their wives . . . and those who keep their pledges and their covenant, and those who stand by their testimony and those who are attentive at their worship. These will dwell in Gardens, honored" (70:29–30). And it commands, "Confound not truth with falsehood, nor knowingly conceal the truth" (2:42).

The Quran often calls for financial generosity, and specifically cites the duty to tithe (*zakat*) for the poor (2:43). "Righteous is he," it says, ". . . who giveth his wealth for love of Him to kinsfolk and to orphans and the needy and the wayfarer and to those who ask. . . . Such are they who are sincere. Such are the God-fearing" (2:177). It even offers an incentive: "Those who give alms, both men and women, and lend unto Allah a goodly loan, it will be doubled for them, and theirs will be a rich reward" (57:18).

Echoing Judeo-Christian scriptures, the Quran calls on believers to share wealth with humility. It says: "If ye [the rich] publish your almsgiving it is well, but if ye hide and give it to the poor, it will be better for you and will atone for some of your ill-deeds. Allah is informed of what ye do" (2:271).

Some scholars have questioned whether the Quran actually introduced seventh-century Arabia to almsgiving, a practice the society may not have known. The frequent repetition carries the ring of something new. Mecca's merchant class may well have taken almsgiving as a burden that Muhammad was seeking to impose, like ending the pilgrimage. Some scholars ask whether the Quraysh saw charity as yet another of Muhammad's harebrained schemes.

In such admonitions it is possible to read the Quran as a charter for social justice. Many of the rules the Quran proclaims are aimed at the human condition. Indeed, it is reasonable to perceive the Quran's preoccupations with worldly conduct as reflecting Muhammad's efforts to create a more just social order.

In the Pickthall translation of the Quran, the "Index of Legislation"[10] cites nearly a hundred major rules to insure moral conduct. Some set terms for ritual behavior: prayer, the pilgrimage to Mecca, fasting during the holy month of Ramadan and desistence from certain foods, particularly pork. Others provide guidance on divorce and inheritance. But most deal with everyday human matters: adoption and adultery, cleanliness, the treatment of parents, widows and orphans, even sex during menstruation.

Probably the best known of the Quran's rules, at least to non-Muslims, is the ban on the consumption of alcohol, which is stated in conjunction with a ban on games of chance. Poets of the *jahiliyya* left behind descriptions of rampant drunkenness and gambling among Arabian tribesmen. It is fair to surmise that Muhammad was troubled by such behavior.

The Quran reveals some equivocation about how to deal with the drinking problem. These verses create a dilemma for Muslims, who deny Muhammad's hand in the text, yet dislike attributing uncertainty to God. Whoever was in charge, however, obviously engaged in considerable reflection before reaching a decision.

In one verse, God instructs the Prophet: "When they question thee about strong drink and games of chance, say: In both is a great sin, and some utility for men" (2:219). Clearly, a ban had not yet been decided. In fact, the Quran cites wine as one of the rewards of paradise, and even praises "the fruits of the date palm, and grapes" for providing both "strong drink and good nourishment" (16:67).

Secular scholars speculate that Muhammad, after trying to moderate drinking, ultimately recognized his failure. Finally, the Quran says decisively: "O ye who believe! Strong drink and games of chance and idols . . . are only an infamy of Satan's handiwork. Avoid them. . . . Satan desires to sow enmity and hatred among you with wine and games. . . . Abstain from them" (5:90). Thus was the ban on alcohol and gambling proclaimed.

One can also surmise that Muhammad had reservations about the customary laws which governed relations between the tribes. At their foundation was the *lex talionis,* the law of retaliation, based on a code of honor that moderns perceive as barbarous. But in setting specific limits on retaliatory violence, the Quran actually imposed restraints on the blood feuds that preceded it. The Quran did not abolish the *lex talionis* but defined a set of narrowing principles. Perhaps the most important of them held that Muslims, being brothers, could no longer kill one another. By such principles, Quranic law promoted more secure relationships in the desert.

"Whoso slayeth a believer deliberately," says the Quran, "his reward is Hell forever. . . . Allah hath cursed him and prepared for him an awful doom" (4:93). Yet the Quran, while promising "Hell forever," is oddly silent—deliberately silent, Muslims say—on an earthly penalty for murder. Islamic jurists have debated this absence for fourteen centuries.

In contrast, the Quran is quite specific in fixing compensation for mitigated killing. "He who hath killed a believer by mistake," it says, "must set free a believing slave, and pay the blood-money to the family of the slain . . ." (4:92).

Meanwhile, God, seemingly indifferent to the worldly penalties for murder, takes a quite contrasting view in punishments for adultery and theft. Secular experts have hypothesized that the explicit references to adultery and theft, like those to drinking and gambling, reflected Muhammad's concern with the pervasive laxity in Arabian society.

"The adulterer and the adulteress," the Quran says, "scourge ye each one of them with a hundred stripes. And let not pity for the twain withhold you from obedience to Allah. . . . And let a party of believers witness their punishment" (24:2). It also says: "As for the thief, both male and female, cut off their hands" (5:38).

Scholars are unsure how routinely these prescribed penalties (*hudud*) have been enforced over history. In our own time, they are being strictly applied by Taliban in Afghanistan and intermittently by the government of Saudi Arabia, but even fundamentalists debate their appropriateness. As unambiguously as God's voice enjoins them, however, it is hard for believers to ignore them.

It is also noteworthy that the Quran, like both the Old and the New Testament, did not abolish slavery. Muhammad obviously sought to soften the edges of a practice that was as integral to the culture as the *lex talionis.* Among the reforms the Quran commends are marriage with slaves (24:32) and kindness to slaves (4:36). While not requiring emancipation, the Quran, nonetheless, characterizes emancipating slaves as a virtue (2:177).

Inviting a rare glimpse into history, the Quran probably reveals something of the treatment of slaves in seventh-century Arabia in prohibiting what must have been a common practice.

"Force not your slave-girls to whoredom," it says, "that ye may seek enjoyment of the life of the world, if they would preserve their chastity." And in kindness to the victims, it adds, "And if you compel them, then after their compulsion, Lo!, Allah will be Forgiving and Merciful to them" (24:33).

The Quran is more direct about infanticide, which anthropologists tell us was another common desert practice. The tribes, faced with starvation, killed newborns, usually female, as a mechanism for keeping the population in balance with resources. For the same reason, infanticide was also common in medieval Europe.

The Quran seeks to bring the practice to an end, saying: "Slay not your children, fearing a fall to poverty. We shall provide for them and for you. Lo! the slaying of them is a great sin" (17:31). The ban can, in itself, be interpreted as a worthy moral injunction. But it also suggests a fear that, under the pressure of economic stringency, tribal behavior was descending into anarchy.

To say that the Quran is a men's document is not an overstatement. The Quran addresses men, rarely women. It holds men to a more rigorous standard of religious conduct. It is also solicitous of men's pleasures. Among its premises is the right of men to rule.

It instructs men, when women are fractious, to "Admonish them and banish them to beds apart, and scourge them" (4:34). It commends men to decent treatment of women but permits them, with scarcely more than a moral qualm, to dispose of wives who cease to please them: "If ye decide upon divorce, remember that Allah is hearer" (2:227).

"Men are in charge of women," says a much-quoted Quranic verse, "because Allah hath made the one of them to excel the other, and because they spend of their property for the support of women. So good women are obedient" (4:34).

Fatima Mernissi, a Moroccan sociologist and feminist, argues in a controversial book that Muhammad considered undisciplined women to be at the root of the social disorder in *jahiliyya*.

Society in *jahiliyya*, Mernissi contends, was matriarchal. Women, though lacking a formal status, were sexually free and took responsibility for their children. Arab men, she contends, deferred to women's sexual powers and had no family involvement.

Muhammad believed the system, in denying to men the assurance of passing on their wealth to their sons, was unduly weighted toward women. Islam, Mernissi says, transformed the balance. It required men to provide for their families, compensating them by creating a social system which guaranteed their dominance. It was a deliberate effort to build a patriarchal structure of social control by placing women under the rule of men.[11]

But Muhammad, as social reformer, also saw to it that women, having yielded their freedom, were accorded an official status. For the first time, Mernissi says, they were no longer tribal chattels, like sheep or camels. The Quran empowered them to testify at trials, though with half the evidentiary authority of men. It also provided them, if divorced, with limited rights of alimony, child custody and inheritance.

The Quran suggests that men were sullen about the reforms, in warning them: "Consort with [women] in kindness, for if ye hate them, it may happen that ye hate a thing wherein Allah hath placed much good" (4:19).

But while enhancing the status of women, the Quran's endorsement of polygamy also confirmed their social inferiority. The Quran's most controversial verse tells men: "Marry of the women who seem good to you, two, three or four; and if ye fear that ye cannot do justice to so many, then only one. . . . Thus it is more likely that ye will do justice" (4:3). This verse, more than any other, has set the tone of male-female relations throughout Islamic history.

Orthodoxy, seeing no equivocation, holds that the verse affirms man's option to take four wives. Reformers, in contrast, argue that the imperative to "do justice" is determinant, or at the very least powerfully cautionary. Scholars—and many ordinary Muslims—debate whether the verse is meant as an invitation to or a limitation upon polygamy.

The debate is further complicated by a verse in the same sura which warns, "Ye will not be able to deal equally between your wives, however much ye may wish to do so" (4:129).

Modernists argue that the verse, in recognizing the impossibility of a man's dealing "equally" with several wives, indirectly commands monogamy. Orthodoxy rejects this reading. Its interpretation is that God left each man as his own judge of his capacity—which it conventionally frames in sexual terms—for dealing "equally." Orthodoxy warrants the Muslim man to decide the number of his wives, up to four, assuring him of God's support of his decision.

In modern times, Quranic verses have also been at the center of debate on the dress of Muslim women. One verse says:

"Tell the believing women to lower their gaze and be modest, and not reveal their beauty, only that which is customarily exposed, and to draw their veils over their bosoms. Let them not reveal their adornment* save to their own husbands or fathers or husbands' fathers, or their sons or their husbands' sons, or their brothers or their brothers' sons or sisters' sons, or their women or their slaves, or male servants who lack vigor, or children who know naught of women's nakedness" (24:31).

In another verse the Quran commands: "O Prophet! Tell thy wives and thy daughters and the women of the believers to draw their cloaks close around them. That is more proper, so that they may be recognized and not annoyed" (34:59).

Scholars agree that Quranic reforms, including the dress codes, aimed to narrow the disabilities imposed by the desert culture on women, not to impose new ones. But by the time Arab armies spilled eastward from Arabia, Islam's reformist urge was largely exhausted and the Persian practice of secluding women, particularly those of the upper classes, was spreading into Arab culture. Scholars point out that the Quran says nothing of veils, the companion of seclusion, and demands at most that women dress modestly.

But orthodoxy, which has historically asserted guardianship over women, holds that God wants them fully covered. Early in the twentieth century Muslim feminists, emboldened by winds of liberation from the West, challenged this view, and women in much of the Arab world adopted Western dress. More recently, fundamentalist women have begun covering themselves again, using "Islamic" costumes as a statement of political allegiance.

Calling for greater modesty among women, fundamentalists are driving the debate today. Is covering the hair with a *hejab* a custom or a Quranic commandment? Can the Quran be interpreted to require the veil? Are gloves required when women shake the hand of a man? (Some say women must not shake men's hands at all.) Egypt's late Sheikh Gad al-Haq insisted that the Quran requires that women be circumcised. Like so much of religious debate, the citations are vaguely scriptural but the significance lies in the issue of whether males will continue to rule the society, a political question.

Politics are also at the root of what non-Muslims, particularly Westerners, have in our own era designated as "Islamic violence."

Violence, of course, has never been limited to Islam, or alien to it.

---

* In other translations this word, *zinat*, is rendered as "finery" and "faces." In standard Arabic, it means both natural beauty and artificial ornaments.

Jewish and Christian history have been equally bloody. From its beginning, Islam has been locked in competition, marked on all sides by cutthroat cruelty, with its monotheistic rivals. The three have also experienced recurring internal conflict, in which believers have dealt savagely with one another.

In fact, ambiguity toward violence characterizes all three faiths. Muslims, like Jews and Christians, find scriptural verses to authorize whatever position they wish to take. The Quran contains exhortations to both pacifism and the sword.

"There is no compulsion in religion" (2:256), the Quran says. The verse appears unequivocal. It is frequently quoted not just by those who are peacefully disposed but by others—like the Saudi monarchy—seeking to discredit challengers to their own powers and privileges. Muslims cite the verse as evidence that identifying Islam with violence is an error.

But a problem in the text arises after the renunciation of "compulsion." The following sentence states, "The right has been clearly distinguished from the false," which suggests an amendment. The two sentences together, while not fully clear, seem to declare that there is "no place for compulsion in religion," because Islam's truth is so obvious that violence is superfluous.

The verse as a whole might thus be read as an ideal, holding not that Islam bars compulsion but that God has no need of compulsion to spread His message. Indeed, the verse invites a reading which legitimizes violence toward those for whom "the right has—*not*—been clearly distinguished from the false."

Complicating the matter further is the injunction to *jihad* that pervades the Quran. Most Muslims today interpret *jihad* as a personal striving for holiness, though historically the term has also articulated a duty to wage "holy war." Some Muslim leaders use whatever definition suits their immediate fancy. It is not unknown for militant Arab leaders to urge foreigners to accept its pacific meaning, while gratifying followers at home by proclaiming an allegiance to armed struggle.

The Quran tells believers, "Ye should strive for the cause of Allah with your wealth and your lives" (42:11). To "strive" has the same linguistic root as the noun *jihad*.

"Whoso fighteth in the way of Allah," the Quran also says, "be he slain or be he victorious, on him We shall bestow a vast reward" (4:74). Elaborating on the idea of martyrdom, it adds, "Call not those who are slain in the way of Allah 'dead.' Nay, they are living, only ye perceive not" (2:154).

Again sanctioning violence, the Quran offers a waiver of the ban on murdering a Muslim. "Slay not the life which Allah hath made sacred," it says, "except for just cause" (6:152). But the text contains no definition of "just cause."

Muhammad himself illustrated the dual nature of *jihad*. Abandoning peaceful persuasion after leaving Mecca, he adopted warfare as his principal strategy for spreading the faith. The practice brought him many more converts; it also became part of the Islamic heritage. Still, the Quran's message is that God is averse to war, and endorses it only as a last resort.

"Fight in the way of Allah against those who fight against you," the Quran says, "but begin not hostilities. Allah loveth not aggressors" (2:190). More belligerently, it says: "Warfare is ordained for you, though it is hateful unto you; but it may happen that ye hate a thing which is good for you, and it may happen that ye love a thing which is bad for you. Allah knoweth, ye know not" (2:216).

But in yet another sura God sets strict limits on war: "O ye who believe, when ye go forth to fight in the way of Allah, be careful to discriminate, and say not to one who offereth you peace: 'Thou art not a believer' " (4:94). The verse was cited by the Al-Azhar *ulama* in 1979 in endorsing Egypt's peace treaty with Israel.

But if God has mixed feelings about shedding blood in the name of *jihad,* the same is not true about idolatry and apostasy. On idolatry, the Quran says, "Slay the idolators wherever you find them, and take them captives, and besiege them, and prepare for them an ambush" (9:5). Then, in Islamic fashion, it also offers freedom to those who repent or convert. As for apostates, God's words are even harsher.

"In this way," says the Quran, "shall Allah guide people who disbelieved after their belief and after they bore witness that the messenger is true and after clear proofs of Allah's sovereignty had come unto them. Allah guideth not wrongdoing folk. Their reward is that on them rests the curse of Allah and of angels and of men combined" (3:86–87).

Elsewhere God adds: "Whoso becometh a renegade and dieth in his disbelief: such are they whose works have fallen both in the world and the Hereafter. Such are rightful owners of the fire and will abide therein" (2:217).

Thus the Quran expresses God's feelings about apostasy. Yet, unlike adultery and theft, the text delivers to believers no instructions on how to punish it. On the contrary, the Quran places the apostate's punishment, as it does the murderer's, in the next world rather than in this one.

Did God intend by His promises of lasting torment a greater or a lesser penalty than death for the apostate? The Quran does not tell us. Muhammad, according to Islamic historians, never ordered an apostate's execution. After his death, however, his successors waged a two-year war against apostate tribes in Arabia. Based largely on the fierceness of the struggle, Islamic jurists have held apostasy to be punishable by death.[12]

Though Muslims over the centuries have questioned this penalty, it remains orthodox doctrine. Khomeini entertained no doubts when he ordered the execution of Salman Rushdie for writing a book. Al-Ghazali seemed very clear in testifying at the Foda trial that Islam contained no penalty for killing an apostate. As for Foda's murderers, they had no doubt of the rightness of their crime. In the present era, fundamentalists link the penalty for apostasy to their own justification of violence, contentious as the principle continues to be within Islamic law.

· IV ·

MUHAMMAD surely looked on himself as a failure in 619, the year he lost both Abu Talib, his uncle, and Khadija, his wife, the two people who were not only dearest to him but the strongest supporters of his mission. The Quraysh increasingly harassed him and his followers, excluding them from Mecca's commercial life. In some cases, Quraysh thugs even beat them. His mission seemed to be going nowhere. Muhammad's despair probably persuaded him that it was time to try something new.

The following year Muhammad became acquainted with several citizens of Yathrib, an oasis about 250 miles to the north, who had come to Mecca for the annual trade fair. The fair, run by the Quraysh, coincided with the popular pilgrimage to the Ka'ba.

The Yathrib people told Muhammad of ongoing disputes among the tribes in their town, some Jewish, others pagan. During the following year's pilgrimage Muhammad converted some members of the delegation and sent a few disciples back to Yathrib with them to preach his message. The year after, he was invited to Yathrib himself to mediate the differences between the squabbling tribes.

In June 622 the seventy members of Mecca's Muslim community, a few at a time, slipped secretly out of the town. The migration to Yathrib—the *hijra*—rejuvenated Muhammad's mission. It became the watershed of Islam. In *jahiliyya*, tribes kept no track of time; the *hijra* begins the Islamic calendar. It also became the occasion for discarding a pagan name; henceforth, Yathrib would be known as Medina, the City of the Prophet.

In converting Medina's pagans, Muhammad redefined his prophetic mission. In Mecca he had aspired to bring his own tribe to God; in Medina he made Muslims of other tribes, which signified a more comprehensive appeal. For the first time Muhammad appears to have recognized that his mission meant more than tribal redemption; he was creating a new religion, available to whoever would embrace it. In Medina, Islam became an Arab faith; within a few years it would be universal.

Muhammad, in making Muslims of the Medina tribesmen, did not attempt to expunge their tribal identity. It was a precedent he continued to practice. So deeply rooted was this identity that, in any event, the effort would probably have been futile.

Instead, Muhammad superimposed upon tribalism the concept of the *umma*, a community to which all Islamic believers belonged. The idea of the *umma* was not alien to *jahili* practice. The bedouins, as individuals, identified themselves within the context of their tribes. In becoming Muslims, they incorporated a faith into the tribe and the tribe into the Islamic community. Conversion was thus not so much a substitution of one belief for another as an enlargement of identity.

The Islamic concept created by the Prophet left little room within it for individuality. Islam, having no priesthood, in theory positioned Muslims in a direct relationship with God. But, in fact, this relationship passed—then and now—through the community. The Muslim can truly live his faith only within the embrace of the community. It is Islam's nature to blur private identity and to absorb the individual into the *umma*. The sense of the *umma* influences the consciousness of all Muslims to this day.*

As for how the community was to be ruled, God offered little guidance. The Quran says Muhammad was told in Medina that "Unto God belongeth the Sovereignty of the heavens and the earth" (5:40).** Islamic orthodoxy uses this verse to refute the idea that

---

* One might make a similar statement about Jews, though probably not about Christians. The scholar Bernard Lewis, in *Cultures in Conflict* p. 46, tells of a fifteenth-century Moroccan jurist who held that Muslims must flee Christian Spain, not merely because they could not live a truly Islamic life under infidel rule but, worse, because the greater the infidel's tolerance of Islam, the greater the danger of apostasy.

** Charles E. Butterworth points out in *The Annals*, November 1992, the similarity between this verse and the New Testament verse (Romans 13:1–2) which says, "There is no power but of God; the powers that be are ordained of God. Whosoever therefore resisteth the power resisteth the ordinance of God." Butterworth also recalls that in Matthew 22:21 Jesus says something quite different: "Render unto Caesar the things which are Caesar's, and unto God the things

political powers belong to man. The Quran vaguely links religion and the state by instructing Muslims to "Obey God and the Messenger and those in authority among you" (4:59). These verses, among the few that might be called political theory, do not provide much help in shaping a government.

Muhammad made God's sovereignty over the *umma* into the unifying element of a tribal confederation. He himself, treating his legitimacy as divinely sanctioned, became the *umma*'s leader. But the Quranic verses that authorized his absolutism passed none of his powers on to his successors. The Quran left no basis for building enduring ruling institutions.

Furthermore, even with divine powers, Muhammad had trouble establishing his hegemony in Medina. The Jewish tribes, on whose support he had counted, were not interested in his message. Some of the pagan tribes, though willing to embrace his monotheism, were unhappy with the strict rules that accompanied it. Once more faced with a barrier, Muhammad initiated a daring plan. As head of the Muslims, he summoned his followers to a war of conquest.

From his base in Medina, Muhammad sent out raiding parties, composed largely of faithful Meccans, to attack vulnerable caravans. The booty helped to support his congregation and finance further military actions. After two successful years of raiding, he felt strong enough to raise the stakes, recruiting Muslims from both Mecca and Medina to go after the annual Quraysh caravan coming from Syria laden with riches. His army engaged Meccan forces guarding the caravan at the wells of the oasis of Badr. The Muslims, though fewer in number, beat the Quraysh decisively.

The battle at Badr is celebrated as a great moment in Islamic history. Mosques, and sometimes children, are named for it. In our own time, the PLO's main fighting unit was called the Badr Brigade. The triumph was followed by a virtually uninterrupted succession of military victories.

Meanwhile, Muhammad consolidated his political power. In a few bloody encounters he drove the Jews out of Medina, the first step in their abandonment of Arabia. Having obtained God's approval, he negotiated politically favorable marriages—Muslim historians admit to nine—which enabled him to ally with major tribes. Other bedouins now flocked to him, many with the expectation of material reward. With plenty of men and the booty of his victories, Muhammad under-

---

which are God's." The latter concept is absent from the Quran, though the idea of separating church and state did not become current in the West until the Renaissance.

took more ambitious military campaigns. His successes ate at the Meccans' resolve.

In 630, leading an army that had grown to 10,000 men, Muhammad overcame faint resistance from the remnants of the Quraysh tribe and captured Mecca. His long campaign to win his native city had at last triumphed.

Muhammad, in victory, removed the idols from the Ka'ba and converted to Islam the remaining Quraysh in the town. Though the record suggests that in his early years he had been indifferent to the pilgrimages, he did not, as the merchants had feared, end them. On the contrary, Mecca, as a religious capital, changed little, simply shifting its identity from pagan to Islamic. Muhammad's decision to keep his political capital at Medina says to some believers—see the discussion in Chapter 9—that the separation of religion and the state may actually have been part of his plan.

Muhammad's capture of Mecca probably put an end to whatever link he still felt to the "people of the book." His armies had yet to confront Christianity but they had already defeated the Jews. Of more immediate importance, the religious inspiration he transmitted, linked to tribal organization, had made the Arabs into a major military power. Muhammad's armies were now ready to extend the *umma* to every point of the compass.

But in 632, two years after Mecca's capture and a decade after the *hijra,* Muhammad died. During his final illness he named Abu Bakr, his closest friend, to lead the community in prayer, a sign of his favor. Abu Bakr, a fellow Meccan, had been an early convert. He was also the father of Aisha, the wife Muhammad preferred above the others.

But neither the Prophet nor the Quran had made provision for the succession. The closest the Quran comes is to designate as the best of the believers those "who regulate their affairs by mutual counsel" (42:38). God commands Muhammad "to consult with them on the conduct of affairs" (3:159). These verses reaffirm the tribal tradition of high consultation (*shura*) for the resolution of communal problems. They are cited by modernists as God's endorsement of democracy, though most Muslims see in them, at best, a mandate to share political responsibility.

Muhammad's retainers did consult, however, and named Abu Bakr as caliph ("successor to the Prophet"). The following three caliphs were similarly selected. The four, together, are the *rashidun,* extolled by tradition for being "rightly-guided." They left behind a legend of their twenty-nine-year reign as the golden age of Islam.

But many Muslims objected to the succession process. Ali, Muhammad's cousin and husband of his daughter Fatima, presented his candidacy as a representative of the family. He and his supporters argued that only the Prophet's descendants could safeguard the piety of the office. Ali became the fourth caliph, but only after a dispute which initiated a permanent rift in Islam. To this day, Islamic culture has not adopted an outlook, much less a process, to assure a peaceful political succession.

At his death, Muhammad was the master of Hejaz, the western segment of Arabia, and was preparing to mop up what remained of opposition to his rule on the peninsula. A Muslim raiding party had already attacked a Christian town near the Dead Sea. Syria and Palestine beckoned, and before him lay the grander mission of carrying the faith directly to the heart of the infidel empires of Byzantium and Persia. Muhammad's bedouin tribes had frequently raided beyond the bounds of Arabia. Having established some permanent settlements there, they knew of its greener pastures.

Historians have speculated whether the growing stringency of desert life was not as responsible as the call of Islam for the Arabs bursting out of their homeland. Muhammad's reforms had probably ameliorated conditions only marginally, at best. Such injunctions as the ban on infanticide may, in fact, have made survival in the desert more fragile than before.

Evidence suggests that, for the bedouin soldiers, hunger was a major incentive to advancing northward. A Syrian poet in the ninth century wrote of the conquest:

> No, not for Paradise did thou the nomad life forsake;
> Rather, I believe, it was thy yearning after bread
>   and dates.[13]

Some scholars argue that Islam's spread in the years after the Prophet's death was as much a migration of the needy as conquest by the Muslim cavalry.

Before a foreign invasion, however, the Muslim armies had to deal with a series of uprisings by disaffected tribes at home. Called the *ridda* ("apostasy") in Arabic lore, the rebels aimed to restore the looser social controls of pre-Islamic society. In putting them down, the Muslim forces under the Prophet's successors confirmed the Islamization of Arabia.

The suppression of the *ridda* persuaded the caliphate without any doubt that it was easier to divert the tribes to foreign domains than to keep them under discipline at home. Despite Islam, the tribesmen continued the practice of raiding merchant caravans, as well as one another. In the course of the *ridda,* tribal contingents advanced to the edge of the Byzantine and Persian domains. The momentum carried them across the borders.

Raiding parties first entered the territory and, wherever they found the enemy weak, summoned bigger battalions. As they moved forward, they converted the border tribes, themselves ethnic Arabs long kept in line by imperial stipends. Without allegiance to either Persia or Byzantium, the local Arabs willingly enlisted in the cause of Islamic expansion.

The Muslims were good soldiers. Fighting on horses and camels, they ranged across the imperial landscape, striking by surprise. The Byzantine and Persian armies were larger, but were repeatedly defeated by superior leadership and fighting skills.

Barely a decade after Muhammad's death, the entire area known as the Fertile Crescent was in Muslim hands. Damascus and Jerusalem had become Arab cities. Persia's capital of Ctesiphon, along with much of the Persian heartland, had fallen to armies moving eastward. In the west, Egypt was captured and Muslim armies were moving across North Africa toward Spain.

Historians agree that the Arab occupation was, for the most part, benevolent. Muslim administrators imposed taxes on the conquered but did not force either the Quran or its language on them. Muslim commanders rarely quartered their troops in captured cities. Instead, they built new military towns—Kufa and Basra in Iraq, Fustat in Egypt, Qairawan in Tunisia. All would one day be great centers of Arab culture.

The military force that Muhammad had created transformed, with astonishing ease, the Mediterranean basin from the Atlantic Ocean to the Gulf. The Muslims established their dominance not only over a vast territory but over a wide array of races and cultures. The Prophet's bequest to the Arabs was more than the Quran and Islam. It was also the Arab patrimony, the expanse of land that his armies conquered and that makes up the Arab world today.

4

Sudan: The Islamic Experiment

WITHIN THE COMMUNITY of Arabs, Sudan is unique. While other countries may be slipping down a slope toward fundamentalism, Sudan has made the choice deliberately. It is the only Arab state in our age that has opted, albeit by coup d'état, for government by Islamic law.

By official admission, Sudan has yet to craft the institutions needed to realize Islam's ideals. In fact, the institutions thus far created bear a remarkable resemblance to military despotism. Yet Sudan's rulers maintain that the regime is on an authentic Islamic course, and they vow that, whatever the opposition, Islam will not be—as they like to say—"disestablished."

Sudan, it is often noted, may be a nation-state but it is not a nation. One of the world's poorest countries, it has 26 million inhabitants who speak a hundred different languages. The inhabitants are split into a multiplicity of ethnic groups, none more than a fraction of the total population. They are also separated by regional and tribal loyalties. Most divisive of all, the north, home of the majority, is culturally Arab, while the south shares in the civilization of black Africa.

Faced with this diversity, the regime, dominated by northerners, has decided—over the protests of the south—that only through Islam can the country be unified. It does not call on its citizens to worship according to Islam but, rather, to submit to Islam as political ideology. So, to make a nation, Sudan has embarked, almost vengefully, on Islamization.

The architect of this course is Hassan al-Turabi, a man of superior intellect and ineffable charm. At ease in both turban and tie, he articulates his goals as lucidly in English, which he speaks with the accent of the British aristocracy, as in Arabic, his native tongue. Since the coup, he has held no government position; his powers, though unmistakable, are unofficial. Turabi rules from a pedestal, a kind of philosopher-king.*

Admired by many Muslims, esteemed by non-Muslims, Turabi as thinker takes a flexible approach to Islamic doctrine. At home in the modern world, he promotes a modern, liberal Islam. But as ruler he is abhorred for the ruthlessness with which his minions follow his guidance. Turabi's governance, however liberal in ideology, is in execution a model of oriental despotism.

Born in eastern Sudan in 1932 of a family with a long history of Islamic learning, Turabi graduated from the faculty of law at the University of Khartoum in 1955. He received an M.A. in law in London and a doctorate—the first in Sudan, it is said—from the Sorbonne in Paris.

As a lecturer at the University of Khartoum in the mid-1960s, he founded the campus chapter of the Muslim Brotherhood, which in time he shaped into the political party known as the National Islamic Front (NIF). Since then he has used the NIF organization single-mindedly in his quest to establish a state of his own design.

Long before Islam rode to power on army tanks in 1989, Turabi took upon himself the responsibility for Sudan's transformation. He says Islam became his ideology because, without it, "Sudan has no identity, no direction." He calls his regime an "Islamic experiment," leading toward a new national consensus.

No doubt the concept of Islam that Turabi preaches—of which more will be said later—is, by Arab standards, open-minded and tolerant. Turabi himself, while rejecting any hint of Western liberal influence, says, "We do not advocate a very strict form of Islam." Few would dispute this assertion. But he perceives no contradiction in extolling a lenient Islam while pursuing a political zealotry backed by military power.

Turabi's proselytism has virtually isolated Sudan internationally. Washington has placed it on the list of countries abetting terrorism and maintains only minimal diplomatic relations. Its African neighbors charge it with meddling. In 1995, Sudan was accused of complicity in an assassination attempt against Egypt's President Mubarak. The

* In 1997, Turabi puzzled observers by accepting the post of speaker of the national assembly. There was much speculation on the meaning of the move, but his powers apparently remained unchanged.

United Nations regularly has censures of Sudan on its agenda, and the international human rights organizations routinely condemn it.

But Turabi calls the criticism unjust. Without denying his regime's harshness, he prefers to dwell on the future he envisages of an Islamic Sudan that is modern and prosperous on the one hand, while gentle and tolerant on the other.

Indeed, in a visit to Sudan, I saw many signs that Islamic practice is less strict than in the relatively easygoing Egypt, not to mention the highly austere Saudi Arabia, both neighbors.

I scarcely encountered the *hejab*, the head covering which makes Cairo's women forbidding, much less Saudi Arabia's full-face veil. The women of Khartoum, Sudan's capital, more often render homage to Islamic modesty in a "taupe," a brightly colored, almost form-fitting gown with a filmy head wrap that only partially covers the hair. Westerners find it quite alluring. I assume the Sudanese do, too.

Granted, the night life and the drinking that I recalled from a visit in the mid-1980s are gone. The coup has imposed a grim nighttime silence on the streets of Khartoum and on its more religious sister city, Omdurman. Still, the Sudanese seem more relaxed than other Arabs, and when they talk they do not seem much inhibited by the stern piety of the military regime.

Some Sudanese, of course, dislike the clement Islam preached by Turabi. Sheikh El-Hibr Youssef el-Daim, for example, told me Turabi was mistaken in claiming the right to soften the impact of orthodox scriptural interpretation. A traditionalist who currently heads Sudan's Muslim Brotherhood, el-Daim said, "Sudan is not his preserve to do what he likes about Islam." Sheikh Muhammed Hashem El-Hadiya, leader of the strict, Wahhabi-oriented Ansar Sunna sect, told me he objected to Turabi's liberal line on democracy and on the status of women, and particularly on Turabi's efforts to limit the powers of the Sudanese *ulama*.

Yet, among those I met, this point of view was an exception. Most of the Sudanese I encountered shared Turabi's preference for a genial, nonrigorous, individualist Islam. Such a preference, I was told, was more in keeping with Sudan's special experience within the flow of Islamic history.

The key to this experience lies in the fact that the Sudanese are not, ethnically, Arabs. As their dark skin attests, they are Africans, of diverse tribal stock. To be sure, Egyptian ethnicity is equally non-Arab. Egyptians, dominantly yellow-brown in complexion, are clearly a Nile people, who look much like the forebears pictured on the tombs of the pharaohs. Egyptian culture, however, evolved over the centuries into the Arab norm. Sudan, located at the Middle East's perimeter, developed a culture that is dramatically distant from this norm.

The difference between them can be traced back to the years after the death of the Prophet, when the bedouins storming out of Arabia defeated the armies of Byzantium and made camp along the Nile. After the conquest, Arabic became Egypt's common language, and in time most Egyptians converted from Christianity to Islam. For nearly fourteen hundred years Egypt has been an Arab society.

Sudan's history followed its own course. The Prophet's armies, after reaching the Nile, turned westward rather than upriver, to spread their culture and their religion across Africa's northern rim and then into Spain. Sudan was apparently too inaccessible and too poor to justify a major military campaign.

Sudan, in the centuries after Egypt's Islamization, was ignored by Arab forces, save for occasional raids, none of which achieved consequential results. Sudan succumbed to the Arabs a thousand years after Egypt, an interval that left it, psychologically as well as geographically, at the margin of Islam. Turabi himself calls his people "frontier Arabs."

The instrument of victory for Islamic civilization, moreover, was not military. Over the centuries Arab holy men, along with Arab merchants, infiltrated peacefully into Sudan. As their influence spread they displaced the native Christianity, while disrupting the established tribal order.

The holy men were missionaries who brought the Quran and the *shari'a* to Sudan, along with Arabic, the language needed to understand the scriptures' words. They came not just from Egypt but from Iraq, Arabia and North Africa. They set up schools, which taught both doctrine and literacy, the twin pillars of the culture. A few acquired considerable political influence among the tribes and were rewarded with great wealth in livestock and land.

These men, it is important to note, did not transmit the *ulama*'s orthodoxy, as proclaimed by Cairo's Al-Azhar. Their message was for the most part drawn from the tenets of Sufism, a dissidence dating back to Islam's early centuries. It was Sufi teaching which, over several generations, Islamized and Arabized Sudan. Notwithstanding the spread of this culture, however, Islam remains the religion of only two thirds of the Sudanese people, and Arabic the mother tongue of only half.

Late in the eighteenth century the last great wave of holy men descended upon Sudan and fanned out from the banks of the Nile deep into the countryside. Their proselytizing led in time to the founding of family dynasties, two of which were the Ansar and the Khatmiyya. Both would play a major role in the historical development of Sudan. In evolving into political parties, these dynasties illustrate how Sufism established its influence not just on Sudan's religious spirit but on its political life.

As a body of thought, Sufism emerged in reaction to the ritualism and legalism adopted by orthodoxy in the era after the Prophet. It did not seek to replace orthodoxy as much as to soften it. Throughout history it offered Muslims a complementary channel to Islamic truth. It was personal, emotional, mystical. To this day, Sufism, in contrast to orthodoxy, claims an attachment more to the love than to the fear of God.

Sufi worship took various forms, but its common elements tended to be pietism and austerity. Some scholars, in fact, think it had links with monastic Christianity, which followed a similar course of development during the same period. Though Sufism rejected monasticism, charismatic practitioners bonded with their followers into closely knit societies called *tariqas,* which even now are at the heart of Sufi religious and social practice.

Sufism, in Sudan and elsewhere, also embraced folk customs, including the veneration of saints and shrines, pagan practices that Islam had theoretically abolished. The *ulama,* emphasizing the *shari'a,* never quite came to terms with these practices. But Sufism, as a popular faith, has become so pervasive in Sudan that orthodoxy has largely given up trying to stamp it out.

Sudan puts its Sufi ways on display every Friday afternoon in a field in Omdurman, where Sufi dancers in colorful religious costumes whirl themselves into a dizzying ecstasy, their personal communion with God. In a city that has become painfully dull, these dances are the chief tourist attraction.

Sufism's presence is normally less dramatic. One evening I crossed the Nile in a cab to Omdurman to pay a call on the descendant of Ahmad ibn Idris al-Fasi, a famous Sufi sage who was born in Morocco about 1750. I met him in the Idrisi mosque, small and unadorned, and surrounded by a whitewashed wall. At the gate I was directed to an interior court, where I found Sheikh Idrisi—who in the daytime is Dr. Abdul Wahab El-Idrisi, an esteemed pediatrician trained in Cairo and London—chatting quietly with a half dozen friends.

Wearing white gowns and turbans, the men sat on chairs lined up along the perimeter of a nine-by-twelve Persian carpet that was spread on the hard clay soil. All were barefoot, their slippers arranged neatly at the carpet's edge. A few faded fluorescent bulbs attached to the clay-streaked walls cast the only light.

Sheikh Idrisi rose to greet me and in a soft voice offered me a seat. A young man arrived carrying teacups on a rectangular tray, one of which the sheikh passed to me. As I sat by silently, the conversation among the guests proceeded in desultory fashion. Then one by one the men rose, embraced the sheikh warmly, kissed his hand and quietly left. Finally, when only he and I remained, the sheikh invited me into an adjacent parlor to talk.

Sheikh Idrisi spoke with pride of his ancestors, whose portraits hung on the parlor walls. The Idrisis descended from the Prophet, he said, and are related to the dynasties of both Morocco and Libya. Ahmad ibn Idris al-Fasi, the founder, lived for seventeen years in Mecca, where he preached a mystical doctrine which his disciples spread throughout the Arab world. His descendants established an emirate in Arabia, which lasted until the Sauds absorbed it in 1930. Drawn by family ties to Sudan, the Idrisis early in this century founded a mosque in Omdurman. He himself, the sheikh said, serves north Sudan as a doctor, while at the same time leading the Idrisi order.

"We are a Sufi movement," said the sheikh, "which means that we concentrate on the individual believer, not the society as a whole, the end being to save a soul. We have some differences with more traditional Sufi movements. We believe, for example, that the soul unites with that of the Prophet after death. To some, this is heresy. But there are many strains within Sufism, from hermits to the most gregarious groups, and they all find reasons for their positions in the Quran and the Sunna.

"We Idrisis are not ascetics. We are a political as well as a religious movement, and we have strong support in the north, but we have not wanted to run in elections. In that sense, we are in the mainstream of the Sufis, who are more interested in the individual's relation to God than in who rules on earth. We believe that governments can do more harm than good to Islam, the principal task of which is to help people to rule over themselves, not others."

While we talked, Sheikh Idrisi was summoned to prayer by the muezzin calling over a loudspeaker from the minaret of the mosque. The sheikh excused himself graciously and, promising only a brief absence, asked me to remain. During his absence I sipped another cup of tea that a servant brought. Faithful to his word, Sheikh Idrisi returned a few minutes later.

"Turabi was originally a sincere Muslim," the sheikh said, "and so were the senior people around him. But much has changed since he took power, and we wonder whether he is still the ruler. His movement started by trying to Islamize the society, and now it wants to dominate everyone and everything, which puts it in conflict with a large proportion of the people.

"His government gives jobs only to its followers, and all others feel left out. At the medical school, where I was the dean, faculty appointments had to get approval of Turabi's party, and for that I resigned. Turabi's people are getting rich on contracts and buying big houses. In public, they don't drink, which is fine, but they violate Islam by lying to the people in all matters. Having made the coup, they're now afraid of losing power. We are surrounded by security measures. All Sufis agree that Islam should rule, but not misrule.

"I suppose someone will phone me in the morning to ask what you and I talked about this evening."

· II ·

BY FAR THE GRANDEST of the Sufis was Muhammad Ahmad ibn Abdallah, a pious mystic born in 1844 and known to history as the Mahdi, which in Arabic means "one who makes salvation." The term is often popularly translated as "Messiah."

Muhammad Ahmad, as the Sudanese call him, made Egypt the target of his zeal. Egypt invaded Sudan in the 1820s and imposed on it a harsh colonial rule. During the Egyptian years Sudan's Arabization was forcefully consummated. Many Sudanese still reproach Egypt, as the agent of Al-Azhar, for trying to stamp out Sufism in favor of Islamic orthodoxy. In 1881, Muhammad Ahmad launched a holy war, a *jihad,* to drive out the Egyptian occupier.[1]

Muhammad Ahmad, son of a boat builder from northern Sudan, was the sheikh of a small Sufi order that believed strongly in the coming of a *mahdi.* The Sufi doctrine of the *mahdi* held that from time to time a sanctified figure would appear to lead the *umma,* the Islamic community, in replacing an impious regime by a purified Islamic order. Muhammad Ahmad, in claiming the title of Mahdi, attracted thousands of supporters, many from along the Nile, even more from among the nomads of the western desert. He called them the Ansar—"helpers"—which was the name the Prophet had given to his followers in Mecca.

Seen retrospectively, Muhammad Ahmad was surely an early Sudanese nationalist. But in linking nationalism to a primitive Islam, and to hostility toward the *ulama,* he can also be seen as a precursor of modern fundamentalism. As Mahdi, Muhammad Ahmad conceived of himself as a successor to the Prophet. Like the Muslim Brotherhood's Hassan al-Banna a half century later, he aspired to the restoration of the faultless society that many Muslims believe existed only under the Prophet and the *rashidun*.

From 1881 to 1885 the Mahdi conducted his *jihad*. Not all of the Sudanese were with him. Tactically, however, he enjoyed the advantage of an Egyptian army that, though under British command, was underarmed and poorly led. Still, whatever Egypt's weaknesses, the succession of victories that the Mahdi's ragtag forces won on the battlefield was a remarkable feat.

The Mahdi's campaign reached a climax at Khartoum, where the British general, Charles George Gordon, commanded the Egyptian garrison. The Ansar waited until the annual Nile flood to cross on boats from Omdurman, a city which the Mahdi had founded as his capital. In a legendary battle the Ansar overran the defenders, killing Gordon himself on the steps of the governor general's palace.

The regime that the Mahdi proceeded to impose on Sudan—called by Sudanese the *Mahdiyya*—was, in theory, based on the *shari'a*. But in practice it was (like Turabi's) what its leader made it: autocratic, evangelical, egalitarian, puritanical. The Mahdi saw it as a step toward his ultimate goal, the universal triumph of Islam. In a famous letter he invited Queen Victoria herself to see the light and become a Muslim. His crusade, however, was cut short. On June 22, 1885, six months after his triumph over Gordon, Muhammad Ahmad died suddenly of typhus.

The *Mahdiyya* endured for thirteen more years. Convinced he was recapitulating the Prophet's life, the Mahdi had named his closest companions to succeed him, and even gave them titles linking them to the *rashidun*. But they were untutored in government and after his death they squabbled over power and spoils.

Faithful to the Mahdi's mission, his army continued pushing at Sudan's frontiers, but the money and organization required to wage foreign wars were absent, and the government had no idea how to correct its weaknesses. Its bedouin soldiers, unpaid and disillusioned, finally began to drift home, only to find crop failure and starvation. The *Mahdiyya*'s response was to invoke Islam, without making practical efforts to resolve the country's very real problems.

More ominously, European armies—this was the heyday of African colonialism—took positions encircling Sudan. In 1896 the British, having recently put down a revolt in Egypt, turned their attention to avenging Gordon. Invading from the north, they slowly but steadily advanced southward along the Nile. After a series of small battles they reached Omdurman, where they decimated the Mahdist army and crushed the regime.

Still the *Mahdiyya,* whatever its failings, must be seen as a heroic era in Sudan's, even in Islam's, history. A Muslim army had acquitted itself honorably against the technological superiority of the West. It is true that Britain remained in occupation—in theory, sharing authority under an Anglo-Egyptian condominium—until Sudan's decolonization in 1955. Nonetheless, the Sudanese had much in the *Mahdiyya* that was worthy of their pride.

And so I was surprised during my talks with Sudanese that I barely heard the *Mahdiyya* mentioned. It is my experience that Arabs are not bashful about discussing their moments of glory: the Saudis talk of their battles against the Turks, the Egyptians against the British, the Syrians against the French. So why, I wondered, did so few Sudanese boast about the *Mahdiyya?*

For the answer, I drove out one afternoon to the campus of the African International University, deep in the desert south of Khartoum. Established in the 1970s with funds from seven Arab countries, the university has a student body of black Africans, all of them Muslim. The language of instruction is Arabic; the curriculum is heavily Islamic.

Professor Hassan Makki met me in his office in the history department. Makki, who also lectured at the secular Khartoum University, has written widely on Muslim-Christian relations in Sudan. His *Sudan: The Christian Design* is very critical of the efforts of Christian missionaries to make converts in his country. He was also an expert on the *Mahdiyya.*

"Sudanese, in their personal and political relationships, have long historical memories," Makki said. "There's a class issue surrounding the *Mahdiyya* that remains with us today.

"In the Mahdi's time, the real strength of Islam was in the north-center of Sudan, along the Nile, which is where the early Sufi leaders settled. The inhabitants there regarded themselves, like the Egyptians, as descendants of the pharaohs. To them, other Sudanese were simple nomads. Long before Muhammad Ahmad, they believed in the concept of the *mahdi,* but they were certain that he would come from a distinguished family among themselves.

"Muhammad Ahmad's family was not very distinguished. He was a carpenter's son from Dongala, a Nile village. He came from the heartland of Sudanese Islam, but he was low class and his neighbors rejected him. And so he had to look elsewhere for support.

"Muhammad Ahmad left his village, just as the Prophet left Mecca.

He went to the west, where Islam was weak, recruiting ordinary people from the countryside and the desert. He organized them into the Ansar and gave them a consciousness of Sudan. He led them to power and founded Omdurman, which is still inhabited by the Ansar's descendants. He offered them a new identity, as defenders of the faith. Omdurman and the west are still centers of Mahdi sentiment. The rest of the country is not."

Hassan Makki said Turabi's family has a history, going back to Turabi's grandfather, of opposition to the Mahdi. Turabi's family were Nile Valley aristocrats, he said, convinced of their higher level of culture. They had ties both to Sufism and to orthodoxy, he said. Turabi himself was educated in both traditions.

While acknowledging Muhammad Ahmad's charisma, these families rejected his claim to be the Mahdi. They had no interest in making war against the Egyptians. More than that, Makki said, they were uncomfortable with the farmers and bedouins who were the backbone of the Mahdi's support.

"Turabi never won over the segments of the society that were with the Mahdi," Makki said. "His support is concentrated in Sudan's intellectual community, which is heavily from the Nile Valley. Today it is centered on Khartoum University, where Turabi built his movement on the base of the Muslim Brothers. His strongest followers are from the modern sector of the society—the army, the trade unions, the bureaucracy.

"Turabi's style is to make alliances, to avoid unnecessary conflict. His wife is from the Mahdi's family, which is not a coincidence. While the *Mahdiyya* was Sufi, his movement is orthodox, but he regularly says that he agrees with the program of the Mahdi's clan today to promote Islamic reform.

"I doubt that Turabi commands majority support in the country. He has almost no following in the rural areas, which are Sufi in their outlook. You don't encounter these people in Khartoum but they revere the *Mahdiyya,* not the present regime. Most of them, in fact, don't much like politics at all. They are more interested in their shrines and dances and religious ecstasy."

The current heir to the leadership of the Mahdist movement is Sadiq al-Mahdi, the great-grandson of Muhammad Ahmad. Sadiq—as he is called by most Sudanese—regards himself as a political man, without much interest in Sufi religious doctrines. He has quarreled with the family over his politicizing Mahdist institutions. The movement's religious wing do not accept Sadiq as their *imam,* their prayer leader.

Sadiq is head of the Umma Party, founded by his grandfather, Abdul-Rahman al-Mahdi, to serve as a Western-style instrument to promote the family's political interests. Sadiq's position makes him, after Turabi, Sudan's most influential political figure.

Born in 1936, Sadiq was educated in Khartoum and at Oxford. A politician for all of his adult life, he entered parliament at thirty and almost immediately became Prime Minister, a post he lost after a year. In 1969 he headed a government that was overthrown in a military coup, and he passed seven years in exile in England. As Prime Minister once more in 1986, he began Sudan's last experiment with parliamentary rule. Three years later he was overthrown by the army in Turabi's coup.

Sadiq and Turabi are brothers-in-law, Turabi being married to Sadiq's sister. Despite their political conflict, Sadiq described their personal relations as "correct." Both are partial to a liberal Islamic state. The difference between them is more of personality than of philosophy. Turabi, Sudanese say, is unscrupulous and cunning in promoting his political interests; Sadiq is without guile, lacking the killer instinct that is needed in Sudanese politics. Not surprisingly, Sadiq has been a consistent loser in the competition between them.

Indeed, Sudanese think of Sadiq as being too intellectual and too indecisive to be a real leader. That is not his only problem, however. Lacking Turabi's organizational skills, he never built up a wide popular following. In a society as fractured as Sudan's, he has been unable to extend his political support beyond the clans of the western desert that, more than a century ago, were his great-grandfather's most loyal followers.

"Correct" as their relations may be, Turabi imprisoned Sadiq for three years after the 1989 military coup. Following his release, Sadiq was repeatedly summoned by the police for interrogation. In 1995, during a campaign against its political critics, the government imprisoned him again for three months.

When not in prison, Sadiq has lived in his sumptuous home in Omdurman under police surveillance, with his movements restricted to greater Khartoum. When I saw him, it was clear that he did not live badly. In any other Arab country, Sadiq acknowledged to me, his fate would be far worse.

Plain-clothes policemen idled near the gate when I arrived at Sadiq's house for the appointment I made. The house is on a quiet street, a kilometer or so from the shrine that contains the Mahdi's remains. Standing behind a wall, within a well-watered garden that is bordered by palm trees, the house was grander than any other that I encountered in Sudan.

A servant showed me through the garden and into a thatch-roofed gazebo, designed to resemble a Sudanese country dwelling. It was furnished in contemporary *House and Garden* style. I was sitting in a stuffed armchair, sipping an iced fruit drink that the servant brought me, when Sadiq appeared, wearing an Islamic robe of light blue cotton. Tall and muscular, he displayed the crushed-nose face of a boxer, with a closely shaven head that accentuated his robustness. He keeps fit with tennis and polo, I was told, for which the Sudanese admire him. They also admire him for being the husband of several handsome wives.

"The *Mahdiyya* provided the missing link between Sufi Islam and the state," Sadiq said when I asked about the ongoing influence in Sudan of his family's history. His answers did not dispel his reputation for intellectuality. "Sufism was for hundreds of years seen as 'Islam minus the state.' The Mahdi restored the presence of the state to it, assuring to Islam a place in Sudan's body politic. Once Islam was introduced to the political system, it never came out. The British, always fearful of reigniting the *Mahdiyya*, never tampered with Islam during the occupation and, on independence, the mass political parties, except for the Communists, were all Islamic. It is impossible to imagine Sudanese politics today without the Islamic component."

Obviously identifying with the *Mahdiyya*, and taking pleasure in talking about it, Sadiq was sharp with his critics inside Turabi's camp. He called them the heirs of the Sudanese who turned their backs on the Mahdi in the last century. Now, he said with bitterness, they claim the right to rule the country.

But times are different, he said. Today's government does not face foreign enemies, much less a foreign occupation, as the *Mahdiyya* did. "Brazen imperialism is no more," he said, "the so-called 'scramble for Africa' is over." The challenge facing Sudan is to finish the task of unification that the Mahdi began. It has been badly mishandled, however, by the Turabi regime.

Sadiq was quick to cite his quarrels with Turabi over running an Islamic state. He said he believes, unlike Turabi, that Islam must be adopted by national consensus, not imposed by a single party with the power of the army behind it. "Coercion," he insisted, echoing the famous Quranic verse, "is not Islamic." Turabi's foisting of Islam on the country without the consent of its non-Muslim minority is intolerable. Though he himself favors Islamic rule, he said, the minority must be assured *a priori* that its rights will be preserved.

Sadiq acknowledged seeing eye to eye with Turabi that the *shari'a,* being anachronistic, must be revised. "Remember that it was the *Mahdiyya* that bequeathed to us freedom from the rigid schools of Islamic law," he said, blowing on the ashes of the Mahdi's feud with the *ulama.* "The *Mahdiyya* asserted that the only tenets binding on Muslims were linked to revelation, to the Quran. All the other rules, being man-made, were subject to review. That was a big leap in Islamic thinking. It unburdened Islam from the tyranny of outdated human formulations."

As an example of an outdated idea, Sadiq singled out the Islamic doctrine which holds all non-Muslim states to be enemies of Islam. It has needlessly made Sudan an enemy of the West, he contended, as well as of its neighbors. This tenet, having outlived its usefulness, must be revoked, he said. But he did not hold his brother-in-law responsible, blaming instead Turabi's party, the NIF, which he said was less tolerant than its leader.

Sadiq did not deny the shortcomings of his own political leadership, but he spoke with pride of his role in preserving the foundations of Sudanese democracy. The *Mahdiyya,* he admitted, was based on Islamic totalitarianism. In this sense, he said, Turabi's NIF, not his own party, is the *Mahdiyya*'s heir. The political heritage on which he draws, he said, comes from his grandfather, founder of the Umma Party, who sought to synthesize democracy with Islamic principles.

When he served as Prime Minister, the mission he adopted, he said, was to safeguard democracy's building blocks: a free press, neutrality of the civil service, autonomy of the university, noninterference in the trade unions, independence of the judiciary, integrity of the armed forces. Though his leadership failed, he said he had succeeded in keeping these ideals in the national agenda.

Sadiq said that as Prime Minister he tried to forge a modern state. He attempted to enlarge the constituency of the Umma Party, he said, but did not succeed in overcoming the religious and tribal loyalties on which Sudan's political organizations, including his own, were based. Inevitably, Sudan will evolve from a tribal to a national identity, he said. But Turabi, meanwhile, is discouraging this evolution by forcing a broad-brushed Islamization on the society.

"I can't prophesy but I'm confident that Sudan will get out of this dilemma," Sadiq said. "The opposition benefits from the government's unpopularity. Sudanese now recall my years in power with nostalgia. Though I can't imagine that I'll want to return to politics, I'm popular again. The problem is that Turabi's party has all of the institutions of the society in its hands, and the opposition is totally disorganized.

"The government promises free elections, but I doubt that it will ever hold them. Free elections would be contrary to their nature. The only way the government can survive elections is if they are cooked. I suppose that is what will happen. Without fraud and coercion, their game is undoubtedly up."

In December 1996, about a year after my meeting with him, Sadiq used the cover of the wedding of his daughter, which Turabi attended, to flee overland into Eritrea. At a press conference in Asmara a few days later, he repeated his aspirations to change Sudan's government by democratic means. But it was far from clear at the time what his political intentions were. Though his flight left the government plainly nervous, Sadiq has not succeeded since then in organizing a credible opposition to Turabi's regime.

· III ·

SUDAN ACQUIRED its present configuration—it is the largest nation in Africa, nearly a third the size of the continental United States—during the decades of the Egyptian colonization.

As occupier of Sudan, Egypt had direct political interests in the provinces adjacent to its borders, where the culture was very much like its own. This culture was Arab and Islamic on the one hand, and shaped by the Nile and the desert on the other.

Sudan's south, to which Egypt was largely indifferent, had none of these characteristics. Its culture was that of black Africa. Its terrain is savanna, its climate rainy. Its inhabitants practiced African religions and spoke African languages. In seizing the south, Egypt had only one concern: the slave trade.

Slave traders, mostly Muslims, had for centuries conducted raids into the African heartland from bases in the north of Sudan. Every year they transported thousands of captives to buyers in the Arab world and beyond. The Quran, though critical of slavery, does not ban it. Egypt was ready enough to take a share in the profits of slaving but it wanted more than money. Egypt's monarchs, hungry to conquer their Arab neighbors, used slaves in the early nineteenth century as manpower for their armies.

Only after mid-century were the Egyptians forced to curb their ambitions. Though Egypt may have been the strongest of the Arab states, Great Britain, reaching its imperial apogee, was far stronger. Already a major influence in Cairo, it was also the center of an international antislavery movement. Coerced by the British, Egypt in 1860 outlawed the slave trade in Sudan. It closed the slave market in Khartoum and began harassing the slave-trading tribes in the north. It failed, however, to stamp out slave-trading operations, keeping the south in a state of terror.

From a contemporary perspective, the Mahdi in 1881 made what looks like an unholy alliance with the slave traders. Both, for their own reasons, were indignant at the Egyptians. Gordon, the governor general in Khartoum, was not seen as their nemesis by chance. An ardent Christian, he was reviled by one ally for disrespecting Islam, by the other for his antislavery zeal. Killing him became a victory both for Islam and for the slave trade.

By the start of the twentieth century, however, the British were running Sudan, and conditions had changed dramatically. Britain not only suppressed the slave trade but applied a special status, called the "Closed Door," to Sudan's southern provinces. Replacing Arab administrators with blacks, they barred northerners from even entering the region. They turned over day-to-day government operations to tribal chiefs and authority for education and social services to Christian missionaries. They also encouraged the use of English among southerners and a revitalization of African tribal culture.

Northern Sudanese decried the policy as anti-Islamic and discriminatory, which it surely was. Indeed, while Islamic missionaries were excluded, Western missionaries converted a fourth of all southerners from their native religions to Christianity. Britain's motives in administering the Closed Door were not religious, however. Its long-term goal was to extend and consolidate its empire by attaching southern Sudan to its colonies in East Africa, buttressing its sovereignty in Africa from Cairo to the Cape. This design aggravated the already sharp differences between Sudan's Arab north and its African south.

What the British had not foreseen was imperialism's impending end. After World War I, nationalist fervor began to rise among the Arabs, Sudan's included. The allegiance that the southern Sudanese felt toward Britain was not nearly strong enough to stop it.

Sudan's nationalists were divided between the Mahdi's son (Sadiq's grandfather), who led the Umma Party in a campaign for full independence, and the Khatmiyya Party, which favored union with Egypt. Though rivals, both parties were Islamic. On the issue of the south, their nationalist and Islamic sentiments converged. Both held that the south should be absorbed, without a special status, into a sovereign Muslim Sudan.

With anticolonial feelings reaching a peak worldwide after World

War II, the British dismissed the south's pleas for protection. Submitting to Arab pressure, they dismantled the Closed Door and consented to the south's incorporation into an independent Sudan. The new Sudan, dominated by Arabs, rejected a federalism that would have given autonomy to the south. It went further to designate Arabic as the country's official language, and sent Arabs to seize the administrative posts in the south that had been lost to the blacks under Britain's colonial rule.

To southerners, independence meant replacement of a benevolent British colonialism by an Arab tyranny. What southerners heard in the proposals of the nationalist parties to establish a dominantly Arab state was tantamount to a call for revival of the slave trade. When the British left Sudan in 1956, an insurgency was already under way; it quickly grew into a full-scale civil war.

In 1969, with the civil war still raging, General Jaafar Nimieri seized power from Sadiq al-Mahdi's weak parliamentary regime. A secular despot, Nimieri sent Sadiq into exile, put Turabi in jail and granted to the south the autonomy that it sought. Nimieri's southern policy gave Sudan a decade or so of peace—its only peace since independence.

But in the early 1980s, with secularism under attack throughout the Arab world, Nimieri reversed course. He turned for support to the Islamists and named Turabi attorney general in his administration. In 1983 Nimieri decreed the "September laws," which imposed the *shari'a*—including the *hudud,* the amputation of the hand for theft—on the entire country. By then, the discovery of oil in the south had raised the stakes of the conflict. Army units from the south, hitherto loyal to Nimieri's regime, mutinied over the September decrees, reigniting the fighting. Since then the civil war has continued without respite, at a total cost of more than a million lives.

Sudanese from the north conventionally say that the war is not, as outsiders claim, between Islam and Christianity. They are right in arguing that it is a clash of incompatible cultures, which historical mischance placed under the same national flag. Religion is only one of many elements in the volatile mix.

Still, because the north has chosen to press its Islamic position so forcefully, religion is the most crucial of the elements. Sudan's Muslims, disclaiming culpability, like to blame the war on the British and their agents, the Christian missionaries, whose Closed Door practices prevented the south's cultural absorption. Their claim is based on the premise that the south's natural destiny is to become Islamic. That is a premise, however, that most southerners flatly reject.

As for Sudan's present policies, north and south, predictably, have conflicting perceptions. Northerners proclaim that the government, in waiving enforcement of some provisions of the *shari'a* in the south, could scarcely be more benign; its policy is based, they say, upon the Islamic tradition of religious tolerance. Southerners say the government treats them as *dhimmis,* a category of protected minorities, normally reserved for Jews and Christians, under Islamic law. *Dhimmis*, in Islam, are second-class citizens, a status that southerners have been unwilling to accept.

On arriving in Khartoum, I anticipated difficulty finding southerners willing to talk about their grievances. In its early days, and intermittently since, Turabi's regime had shamelessly intimidated dissenters, using torture and even execution. But the government during my visit was in one of its benign periods and, to my surprise, many southerners willingly unburdened themselves to me on their political discontents.

Khartoum, whatever the animosity of northerners, is heavily populated with southerners. Some made the journey long ago to take advantage of the capital's economic opportunities. But more numerous are the war refugees, who have fled the fighting to live in slums or horrid government camps. Demographers believe that southerners now make up a majority of Khartoum, swollen to some five or six million people. Their presence has Africanized the city in style and appearance.

International human rights organizations criticize the Sudanese government for failing to provide the refugees with suitable housing. Government officials deny negligence, claiming that the presence of so many southerners in Khartoum is proof enough of the state's benevolence. Both positions have some validity. But for the refugees, in large proportion Christian, reality is the persistent political and physical discomfort of their lives.

"The government is working for the Islamization and Arabization of the entire country," said Ezekiel Kutjok, reflecting the Christian position. A large man in his fifties with a dark, African face, Kutjok was born and raised in the south. President of the Sudan Council of Churches, he speaks in behalf of a half dozen Christian sects, denouncing what he calls the government's calculated anti-Christian policies. We met in the Council's offices, a converted home in a Khartoum suburb, outside of which soldiers lounged on the hood of a Jeep, eyeing whoever entered.

"I don't believe that Islamic tolerance exists," Kutjok said. "They want our children to wear Islamic clothes and learn the Islamic religion in school. They won't let us build churches in Khartoum, despite the huge inflow of Christians. They want the Quran to be our constitution, and they say they'll give us an exemption from parts of the *shari'a,* but it's not enough.

"Sudan is my country too. I want us all to be subject to the same law, but not Islamic law. Part of the problem is racism, even though it's not much discussed. But it's more religion than racism that divides us. Southern Christians believe that Turabi's people want to convert all of them to Islam."

Ghazi Salahuddin Al-Atabani, who is about forty and considered the government's leading intellectual, dismisses Kutjok's fears as ill placed. A religious man with family ties to the Idrisi and Khatmiyya orders, he told me that as a university student he had been an avid Turabi follower and was repeatedly jailed for Islamic activism. After graduation he went to England for a medical degree and a Ph.D. in endocrinology, and on returning home in 1985 became a university lecturer in medicine. Having resumed his involvement in Islamic politics, he said, he signed on after the coup in 1989 as an adviser to Sudan's President.

Atabani, a man of considerable personal elegance, talked with me in his ornately decorated office in the President's palace.

"The charge of forcible Islamization is smear propaganda," he said. "This government remembers with some bitterness the policies of the British, who discriminated against Muslims, but we don't hold Sudan's Christians to blame for them. We will not persecute any Christians, and the stories of persecution that you hear have been fabricated by a few individuals.

"The truth is that if Christians from the south feared persecution they would have fled to Christian countries, not to Khartoum and to north Sudan."

Atabani argued that the government's constitutional decrees treated all citizens equally, without reference to religion, color or ethnicity. The *shari'a* must be Sudan's source of legislation, he said, because the Muslim majority wants it that way. But he maintained that the regime not only waives "certain" *shari'a* provisions in the south but it respects much of the southerners' customary laws.

"This government," Atabani continued, "accepts an obligation to serve the pleasure of God, to which the secular model is oblivious. Fortunately, the Quran and the traditions of the Prophet have provided us with a loose garment that we can tailor to our own measurements. We are willing to elaborate a system of individual and communal rights for those who do not share our beliefs. But we will not accept the reductionist approach of secularism.

"We Muslims cannot accept the secular model, which requires the state to be neutral, or rather passive, toward religion. We feel compelled to offer something positive, linking the society to the inspiring and motivating power of faith and morality. Islam is the only cohesive element in our society, and we Sudanese need it as our term of reference. We do not want to slip into the fault of legalizing what displeases God."

The statements of Kutjok and Atabani reflect the sharp—some say irreconcilable—differences that exist in Sudan over the nature of the state.

The north thinks of Sudan as intrinsically Islamic, though it recognizes a need to treat southerners as exceptional. Southerners, however, refuse to be marginalized, holding that all religious practice in Sudan must be treated as equally valid. The northern view calls for the establishment of an Islamic state in which non-Muslims will be tolerated; the southern view is that the state must give preference to no religion. In short, the south rejects the north's premise that Sudan is an Islamic country.

It is true that both north and south render homage to the concept of regional autonomy, and endorse in principle the ideal of a federal charter. But defining such a system is another matter, and the debate is made more difficult by serious divisions within the leadership of both sides.

In Sudan, disputes within the ruling circles go well beyond ideology. Sudanese culture is defined by habits of loyalty to small groups, superseding obligation to the nation. Allegiances based on personalities, tribes and families—some historical, others expedient—are the norm. In the bargaining to end the north-south conflict, these loyalties are manifested in factional disputes without relation to ideology, often resulting in puzzling positions, which may change unpredictably.

Still, it is possible, through the haze, to discern mainstream positions. The southern leadership argues that federalism cannot work as long as the north's Islamic parties have a monopoly of power, and they demand a restructuring of the political system. An influential minority in the south, however, sees no point in restructuring at all, contending that both regions can have the freedom they seek only through separation.

The Muslims of the north reject the restructuring that the southerners want as heresy; as for secession, they regard it as treason. Yet they cannot reach agreement on the political and religious concessions that they are prepared to grant to the south in a federalist charter.

In 1989 Sadiq al-Mahdi's cabinet was about to offer the south a federal system that guaranteed full freedom of worship within the context of Islamic political and economic codes. Turabi's army officers stepped in at precisely that moment to conduct their coup d'état, and so the south never had the offer to consider. Few observers doubt that Turabi—though he has repeatedly denied it—acted to foreclose a deal based on religious freedom brokered by Sadiq.

Since Turabi's accession to power, the government has taken to calling the conflict not just a civil war but a *jihad,* raising the ideological stakes. On the other hand, it has elaborated a federalist plan based on what looks like an even wider devolution of power than Sadiq was planning to offer, and it boasts of having named southerners to many high government posts.

Southerners point out, however, that even under Turabi's plan they have been exempted from only 5 of 186 articles in the state's Islamic code. They say further that the official posts held by southerners carry only an illusion of authority. Most southerners maintain that Turabi has not improved on earlier federalizing proposals.

Perhaps most destructive in the north-south relationship is the mutual mistrust that has grown over the years of brutality and bloodshed. Added to the culture's innate factionalism, this mistrust has rendered rational negotiation all but impossible. The talks between the parties have been marked by dissembling, posturing and abrupt starts and stops. Neither side has tried to win the confidence of the other, and so the war has raged on.

· IV ·

THE COUP D'ÉTAT that overthrew Sadiq al-Mahdi's democratically elected government in 1989 was the third since Sudan's independence. Ineffectual at home and isolated abroad, the regime had little to commend it, and so the coup came as no surprise.

Many Sudanese had expected the army to seize power, as it had done twice before. Observers assumed that the leadership would come from the high-ranking professionals to whom authority had passed, down through the hierarchy, from the days of the British. These men had already signaled their dissatisfaction in complaints about the conduct of the war in the south.

But Sudan was surprised. The coup's perpetrators turned out to be a band of middle-level officers of strong Islamic orientation. Few Sudanese even knew them. All, however, were closely identified with—some say they were under the orders of—Hassan al-Turabi's National

Islamic Front. How the link between the two was established was unclear; likewise, who was in charge.

The head of the army group was a colonel named Omer al-Bashir, who promptly assumed the rank of lieutenant general and the title of head of state. Bashir was born in 1944 into a middle-class family in a small town on the Nile in northern Sudan. His tribe was known for its Islamic piety and, a century ago, for its dedication to the Mahdi. He had graduated from Sudan's military academy, attended staff schools abroad, trained as a parachutist and fought for several years on the battlefields of the south.

After the coup it became clear that Bashir, while deferential to Turabi, was more than a figurehead. In time, he won the admiration of most Sudanese for his simple virtues and soldierly resolve. He came to be regarded as direct, in contrast to the craftiness attributed to Turabi. Yet the Sudanese, north as well as south, have shown little loyalty to Bashir, either personally or politically.

I interviewed Bashir in the gingerbread castle on the Nile that Gordon built when he was governor general in the 1870s. The Sudanese still call it "Gordon's palace." Though a bit shabby for wear, the walls gleamed with a fresh coat of whitewash and the gardens were well tended and green. To reach the President's office, I climbed the very staircase on which Gordon is said to have been shot by the Mahdi's soldiers.

From the bright sunlight, I passed into an air-conditioned reception room with crystal chandeliers, where a young servant came by and offered me fruit juice and dried dates. Through the windows I scanned the broad waters of the Nile, fixing on the skyline of palm trees and minarets on the opposite shore.

Bashir was sitting behind a huge polished desk when I was ushered into his office. He was wearing a neatly pressed olive uniform with a name tag and parachutist's wings pinned to his chest. A man of middle size, with a stocky build, he seemed almost lost in the ballroom-size chamber. He had a round face; his bland features were set off by a well-trimmed beard and mustache.

A covey of retainers huddled around him and a television crew recorded our talk. That evening the tape ran silently on the nightly news show, nearly all of which was dedicated—as is characteristic of Middle Eastern despotisms—to showing off the stalwart leader at his work.

"Our principles for dealing with the south are quite reasonable," Bashir said when I asked about the prospects for settling the war. "Islam doesn't differentiate between the followers of diverse religions and cultures. It is possible for the adherents of all the different groups in the south to live together under an Islamic government without feeling prejudiced. Islam by its nature guarantees the rights of all peoples, in every aspect of life. The question southerners should answer is whether any of their rights have ever been denied because of the government's Islamic orientation. Their rights are embedded in Islam itself."

Bashir's words contained enough truth that he probably believed them. Since Muhammad's time, the Islamic occupation of conquered peoples has been generally benign, probably more benign than Western colonialism. What Bashir did not admit, however, was that the south considered itself coequal with the Muslim north and not a conquered province.

Bashir insisted that peace was his first priority, but he knew better than to predict that his policies would achieve it. Furthermore, he said, it is not the fault of his government that the war goes on. He blamed Sudanese dissidents, exiled in Cairo and supported by hostile Arab and African countries, for creating obstacles to a resolution. He also stated that, if London and Washington would stop meddling, the warring Sudanese would work out their differences on their own.

"Unfortunately," he continued, "there is also an anti-Islamic propaganda campaign going on, trying to strike fear into Christians and other groups. This campaign didn't start with the Christians but with our political rivals.

"These rivals are campaigning for their own power by citing our differences, which are not religious but political. The campaign started with the Communists. Now it comes from the Umma and the Khatmiyya parties, which are both Islamic. So maybe it's the leftists among them that have the loudest voice."

Bashir then lectured me on the commitment of his regime to bringing not just Islam but God to Sudanese society. His words persuaded me of the depth of his religious belief. A half hour earlier, on the staircase entering the presidential palace, I had crossed three dark-eyed, bearded men wearing black turbans and robes. Even they had a place in the vision that Bashir expressed.

"Before you arrived," he said, pointing at me, "I received a three-man delegation of Eritrean Copts. They came to Sudan as refugees during the war in Eritrea and we gave them asylum. As clergymen, they thanked me for providing the plot and a donation to build a new Coptic church. They understand that the *shari'a* is not just the application of Islamic law; it is a means of bringing the whole society closer to the spirit of God.

"Our government has brought Sudan a long way toward Islamization, but because we support all religions, not only Muslims but even non-Muslims now spend more time at prayer.

"We are also working for a society that doesn't have the diseases of secular societies—moral decadence, degeneration of the family, the growth of crime, the spread of extramarital sex and sexual diseases, like AIDS. We want a society in which people help each other, where the strong help the weak."

Bashir gave no hint of contemplating that the tyranny over which he presided might be an obstacle to realizing the Islamic goals he expressed. He also dismissed the possibility that the impact of Islamization on southerners might be prolonging the war. On the contrary, he insisted that, whatever the complaints at home or abroad, Sudan would persevere in the Islamic course on which it had embarked.

"We're now in the process of writing a constitution for the country," he said, "based on the principles of the Quran and the Sunna. The basic characteristics are already beginning to show up in our constitutional decrees, and they will be completed into a political system that will be ratified by an elected body.

"Not all groups agree on how we are interpreting the *shari'a*. We respect their opinions, since there is wide latitude for interpretation in Islam. We have chosen a moderate way, like the Quran itself, and so the *shari'a* in Sudan will be moderate.

"The constitutional dispute over what Islam requires lies in the area not of private life but of public affairs. Unfortunately there is no model in history for Islamic government. Fourteen centuries have gone by since the Prophet, and everyone now has his own image of an Islamic state. Some countries confuse traditions—like the suppression of women—with religion, but tradition is not Islam. We don't claim that we will implement Islam perfectly, but we intend to rise to the challenge."

Most Sudanese I met had no objections to the Islamic line that Bashir took. Like Turabi's, it was considered moderate, and among northerners, even those who were not especially devout said they could live with it. But few failed to note a major contrast between the tolerant talk and the oppressive practices. Many conceded that the brutality with which dissent was suppressed in the regime's first year or two had softened. With some irony, they noted that suppression was no worse in Sudan now than in Iraq or in other Arab despotisms.

Iraq also came up in another comparison. In both countries the ruling party—Sudan's NIF, Iraq's Ba'ath—had calculated very shrewdly how to attain total power, had pursued it ruthlessly and, after attaining it, was prepared to stop at nothing to hold on. Neither left much to chance. Though one was Islamic and the other secular, both blithely ignored the liberal principles present in their own ideology in favor of the practice of a relentless authoritarianism.

Even sophisticated Sudanese acknowledged ignorance about how the regime worked. None was sure of the relationship between Bashir and Turabi, though they noted that in the rare cases of public disagreement the army usually backed down. Most also noted that the NIF, not the army, commanded the skilled manpower needed to operate the machinery of the state and the society, suggesting Turabi's preeminence. Though Bashir signs the decrees, most Sudanese said they were not fooled. The consensus was that Turabi was the real architect of government policy and had the last word in implementing it.

Ann Moscly Lesch, a scholar who has done substantial research into Turabi's quest for power, maintains that the NIF deliberately began infiltrating the state bureaucracy and civil institutions well before the 1989 coup. Its designs led it to target first the judiciary, the security services and the armed forces, then the trade unions, the professional associations and the educational and communications systems. It infiltrated all of them with great deliberateness.[2]

When the coup came, these preparations enabled the NIF to capture the state's administrative apparatus almost without opposition. The NIF then fired thousands of key jobholders, whom it replaced by its own supporters. It acquired control of the economy by taking over banking, foreign trade and much of agricultural and industrial production. It also instituted a program of Islamic indoctrination that permeated the entire culture.

"We want people to be more religious, and we know television is an important instrument for that," said El-Tayyid Mustapha, who is the director of Sudanese TV. Born in 1943 in northern Sudan, a member of the same tribe as Bashir, he was educated in journalism at the University of Khartoum. A gentle man in a gown and turban, Mustapha talked with me in his windowless office in the state television's sprawling complex along the Nile in Omdurman.

"We use television," he said, "to mobilize people toward our goals, to get them to work hard, to cooperate with each other, to pray more often and to think positively of the government.

"But we're not strict, like Saudi TV, which does not allow singing. Though people think of me as a fundamentalist, I try to model myself after the Prophet Muhammad, who was moderate. When I had to make a decision on singing, I consulted the *ulama*, which said that if I could find support in the Quran and the Sunna, I could approve it. So now we allow singing, so long as it does not stimulate sexual feelings in either men or women.

"We also have a committee that selects songs for television. We even have some Christians on it, though those we've chosen feel the way we do about religion. The committee has stopped songs, for instance, that compare the breasts of women to oranges. Of course, we don't allow mixed dancing on television. We think dancing makes human beings like animals, and we're trying to uphold humanity. Life is preparation for the hereafter, and God should be obeyed, so why live like animals?

"Many of our TV productions now come from Egypt, and they are too liberal, too sexual. They keep people away from Islam and encourage them to lead a Western life. So we are producing more of our own TV dramas, and within a few years we hope to have 100 percent produced in Sudan, expressing our Muslim character."

The government also consolidated its power in the wake of the coup by ruthlessly crushing dissent. It executed twenty-eight army officers after a failed countercoup in April 1990. It neutralized the traditional Sufi parties, backbone of the electoral system, confiscating the wealth of the Khatmiyya and the Ansar orders. The action left Sadiq al-Mahdi and other prominent politicians without resources. Later the regime dissolved the Khatmiyya order altogether and took over Omdurman's Mahdist shrines, the heart of the Ansar.

Responding to strikes and public protests, the government arrested the leaders of the labor unions and abolished professional societies. It substituted an official body for the independent Sudan Human Rights Organization. It put down protests at Khartoum University with armed riot police, who shot and killed students; it also tightened its control of the campus by firing dozens of professors, and by periodic police sweeps aimed at the arrest of troublemakers.

"This university used to be the pride of Sudan," said Dr. Adlan el-Hardallu, a political science professor, in his shabby office on the campus. Dr. Hardallu, born in 1936, is the son of a sheikh from eastern Sudan and did graduate work in the United States and Germany. "Every prominent Sudanese was educated here. But the government denies the money to maintain its academic standards, while trying to Islamize its character.

"The books are out of date, the labs are a mess. The senior faculty are leaving, some voluntarily and some not, and their replacements are young Islamic ideologues. Academic freedom gets narrower. The university is still breathing but, if this government stays in power, I can't see much prospect for its future."

Hardallu told me that university elections in Sudan had long been a bellwether of Sudanese politics. He called them indicators of where the country was going. In the mid-1970s the Muslim Brothers took control of the student government, foreshadowing the NIF triumph, but in recent years students were drawing away from Islam. Partly to blame, Hardallu said, was the withdrawal of state subsidies, which angered students and made it difficult for them to stay in school. But young people were also fed up with Islamic rule, which was as hapless as the parliamentary regime in dealing with poverty and war.

"The new student opposition calls itself nonaligned," he said. "This means it is not Islamic, but neither is it anything else. The nonaligned movement may even be a majority, but it is still not a real challenge to the NIF.

"The student generation seems to have lost faith in Islam, as its fathers did in Communism and Nasserism, but parliamentary democracy and the old leaders have no attraction either. The students talk of a new leadership, free of racism, tribalism and sectarianism, but their ideas have not coalesced. These signs suggest trouble for the NIF, but not yet a real alternative."

The government has spoken often of impending parliamentary elections, which would legitimize the rule it was exercising. But the NIF never won more than 20 percent in past Sudanese elections, and its popularity has not grown. Turabi himself was defeated when he stood for parliament in 1986. Even if there were elections, the probability is that the results would be rigged, the Sudanese say, because the NIF would never put its rule in jeopardy.

My own sense is that popular dissatisfaction with the Islamic state runs deep, but that Turabi and his followers have effectively succeeded in entrenching themselves in power. Turabi's government is by far the strongest since independence. Though Sadiq al-Mahdi and other rivals routinely issue manifestos, the regime has managed to outmaneuver all of them, neutralizing any real threat to its survival. It has done very little to improve Sudanese life, but it has absorbed the war in the south into its daily operations and it exercises total control of the machinery of the state. I suspect that the upcoming generation of Sudanese, whatever its politics, may find that getting Turabi's government out of power is all but impossible.

· V ·

HASSAN AL-TURABI is a man of winning ways. Even those who fear and loathe him—and there are many—acknowledge that the personality he projects is enchanting. Though rather small and slim in build, he has handsome dark features and delicate hands, which move gracefully when he speaks. His voice is soft, and he smiles easily. He has poise. His presentation, without being pompous, is confident and self-assured.

Turabi likes to call himself an "Islamist." He rejects the term "fundamentalism" to define the movement currently radiating through the Muslim world. The term he prefers is the less descriptive "Islamism," the goal of which is "Islamic revival."

"History is a process of continual change," said Turabi. "For centuries Islam and Muslim civilization were on the rise, but the succeeding centuries brought decline and retrogression. Islam ceased generating new ideas. Muslim thinking, even its law, became fossilized. The *shari'a,* established as a means for people to grow closer to the Almighty by becoming more civilized, declined into little more than a relic. Intellectual life is now something in the past, to be revered rather than practiced.

"That is how we Muslims became subject to the depredations of others. Contemporary Islamism is a movement for historical change, and Islamic renaissance."

Students of Turabi say that, for foreign audiences, he adopts a tone of reason, different from his pronouncements at home. Sudanese joke that there is a Turabi for domestic consumption and "Turabi export." But the ideas he articulates, wherever he expresses them, are often daring and sometimes deep. If some of his assertions seem preposterous in relation to Sudanese reality, it is not because he is unaware of the contrast. Turabi commands skills that American slang associates with snake-oil salesmen. In his presence, it is hard not to find him compelling.

Asked about his own place in public life, Turabi answered with a true-to-form mix of pride, self-deprecation and cant.

"I would not characterize myself as a major power," he said. "I am not involved in actual policy-making. I have a role in society rather than in government. I am a Muslim thinker, and my writings and my thoughts are inspiration for Islamists who seek to realize Islam . . . in particular of course in Africa and the Middle East, where I belong.

"To see me as the power behind Sudan's government smacks of a certain naiveté, or a desperate stab at a conspiracy theory. I am a major figure in the world Islamic scene. That's all."[3]

Turabi credited the Gulf War of 1991 for arousing the Muslim masses to the defense of the faith. Though an Arab defeat, it was, he said, a "blessing in disguise" for the worldwide Islamic movement. It was not that the masses supported Iraq's invasion of Kuwait, he said, but that they were indignant at the presence of Western armies on the soil of Arabia, in proximity to Islam's holiest places.

Turabi said that in the months after the seizure of Kuwait he spoke throughout the Muslim world against waging a war on Iraq. He led mass meetings of Muslims—Africans and Asians as well as Arabs, even ex-Nasserites and Arab nationalists—as a popular protest. From the meetings an organization evolved, he said, with the delegates agreeing "to join a conference which is essentially Islamic and to assign the post of secretary general to someone like myself who is known to be Islamist."

It was in the headquarters of the organization, known as the Popular Arab and Islamic Conference, that I met Turabi. The building, on a boulevard in downtown Khartoum, is a low-lying quadrangle that embraces an ill-kept garden made up largely of dried bushes and wilted flowers. Having been met by a guard at the gate, I was led to a crowded waiting room, where busy-looking young men and women in Islamic dress scurried back and forth. On a wall was a sign, unusual in Arabic, reading: NO SMOKING.

After a few minutes of waiting, I was taken to Turabi. I found him in an office that was surprisingly small, though decorated cheerfully with Islamic calligraphy. Seated behind a desk, dressed in a white turban and a white cotton robe, he stood up and shook my hand warmly.

Having by then read widely from Turabi's writings and recorded interviews, I was prepared more for grand exposition than for precise answers. Turabi, I had learned, uses questions to establish a beachhead for the philosophical terrain that he wants to occupy. My own talk with him was no exception.

Turabi, I knew, uses concepts associated with modernism and Sufism to challenge Islamic orthodoxy. He condemns orthodoxy's rigidities, articulating in their place a personal, liberal and often humanistic faith. He also conveys the ideals of Mahdism and the Muslim Brotherhood to call for the Islamization of all of life, which he calls "unitarianism." Turabi holds that such Islamization can succeed only in an Islamic state.

Turabi's thought is distinguished from that of most other Islamic reformers by this eclectic combination. In our meeting, he opened with a historical rundown of how his philosophy emerged.

"I'll begin with the unitarian principle," he said. "To Muslims, it is not just that God is one but also existence is one; all life is just one program of worship, whether it's economics, politics, sex, private, public or whatever. And society is also one. So unitarianism is a fundamental principle that explains almost every aspect of doctrinal or practical Islam.

"But the Quran reveals that there is always a tendency to bifurcate. Power becomes the end, people are dedicated to personal power rather than using power in the service of God. You are familiar with the course of Christian history and how it brought secularism. There was a bifurcation, and then a confrontation between church and state, each vying for supremacy. Ultimately religion was defeated and relegated to private life.

"The same disease afflicted Muslims very early, during the Umayyad period, less than forty years after the Prophet.* The *ulama* noticed that government, based not on Islam but on dynasty or usurpation, was not legitimate, and so they claimed that *ijma*—that is, the consensus that stands higher than government in the lawmaking process—was to be organized by themselves. The *ulama* are not holy, and they have no religious monopoly. Yet they took away the powers of *ijma* from the people and made themselves the highest lawmaking body, breeding the seeds of secularism.

"The real secularization of public life in Islam came about with Western imperialism. For Christians, religion had already been reduced to a hobby. The Westerners disestablished Islam in the Muslim world and, in the place of the *shari'a,* they installed positive laws, French or English or whatever, and secular institutions, like the army, the civil service, the economic system.

"The current Islamic revival is the response. I remember those early days, the 1940s, when the most important thing about Islamic movements was the slogan *din wa dawla,* 'Islam is a state and a religion.' People suddenly became aware of what they had forgotten. *Din wa dawla* became our essential theme.

"I plead with everybody that our movement isn't just political. We are a religious movement for the education and spiritual development of the individual. Our achievements in the field of reforming society, in changing individuals and in moral education, are more substantial than our achievements in politics.

* See Chapter 5, pp. 141–43.

"Critics make fun of the current slogan 'Islam is the solution,' because it is not specific. But it is more important than specific programs, which develop gradually, over time. We Islamists first have to argue the principle to the people, persuade them of the validity of Islamic unitarianism, which they forgot under imperialism, and which is the first principle of Islam."

In advocating the resurrection of the unitarian idea, Turabi's positions are consistent with fundamentalist ideology. But he departs from fundamentalism in insisting that the Islamic state be small and forbearing. Turabi insists he does not share the fundamentalist conception of a government that is coercive in imposing orthodox religious practice.

In substituting a pluralist morality for Islamic rigidity, Turabi tips toward Sufism and modernism. Sufism authorizes Muslims to set their own terms of their relationship with God. Modernism holds that the state cannot impose its reading of the scripture on individual Muslims. Both reject the orthodox notion of a single standard of human righteousness.

"What would an Islamic government mean?" Turabi asks. "The model is clear: the scope of government is limited. Law is not the only agency of social control. Moral norms, individual conscience, all these are very important, and they are autonomous. Intellectual attitudes to Islam are not going to be regulated, nor codified at all. The presumption is that people are free.

"An Islamic government will guarantee the religious freedom not just of non-Muslims but even of Muslims who have different views. I personally have views that run against all the orthodox schools of law on the status of women, on the court testimony of non-Muslims, on the law of apostasy. Some people say that I have been influenced by the West and that I border on apostasy myself. But I don't accept the condemnation of Salman Rushdie.

"If a Muslim wakes up in the morning and says he doesn't believe anymore, that's his business. There has never been any question of inhibiting people's freedom to express any understanding of Islam. The function of government is not total.

"Islamic government is not total because it is Islam that is total. To reduce Islam to government is not Islamic. An omnipotent state is not Islamic. Government has no business interfering in one's worship or prayer or fasting—except, of course, someone's public challenge to fasting. The Prophet himself used strong words against those who didn't come to the prayers but he did nothing to them. In things like dress, for example, there are moral injunctions for women and men, but they are not part of the law. We don't confuse what is moral with what is legal.

"Ideally, the Muslims always look to minimum government. If you read the Quran, very little is said about government. The Quran entrusts authority to the people. Public officials are chosen through consultation, *shura*. Muslims developed their health and education systems, all their social systems, away from government, through trusts and volunteer action. Lawmaking is ultimately based on *shura* and *ijma*. That's why Muslims have always worked on consensus, on something that would unite them."

Turabi rejected the charge that his own movement, even in practice, is undemocratic and anti-Western. Unlike Egypt's Muslim Brotherhood, it is not patriarchal or tribal, he said. On the contrary, it is elective, consultative and accountable. His movement, Turabi insisted, was striving toward the ideal of democratic Islam.

"Islamists like me look to the West as a challenge to respond to and also as a model to emulate," he said. "There are many positive values of Islam that have been developed in the West: participatory and free consultative government, dignity for the individual, free enterprise."

Turabi scoffed at the American charge that Sudan gives support to international terrorism. Islamists do not initiate aggression, he contended, though neither do they turn the other cheek. "Those who initiate aggression," he said, "should expect retaliation in kind, word for word and blow for blow. That, in short, is the meaning of *jihad*." But he insisted that, as a principle, Islam favors friendly relations and rejects force.

Among Turabi's favorite causes is the liberation of women, which he maintains is intrinsic to the Islamic system of values.

"Segregating women is not in the text of Islam," he said. "Like other religions, Islam has been abused by men to dominate women. The suppression of women is sanctified not by the Quran but by convention, just as tribalism is, and we evoke religion against both. The convention of oppressing women can resist Western influence, but it cannot resist religion."

Though admitting that women had not yet achieved full parity in Sudan, he maintained that the principle of their equality was now a settled issue, and its realization only a matter of time.

Turabi also defended, in our talk, the official policy for settling the war with the non-Muslim south. He acknowledged that the *shari'a*'s provisions on criminal justice were the central issue in the dispute. The government rejects a dual legal system, with different rules for Muslims and non-Muslims, he said, since it would impose on the police the requirement to determine the religion of the accused. Such a requirement, he said, would make a mockery of the law.

Instead, the government chose regionalization, waiving for the south not only laws against drinking alcohol but also the *hudud,* particularly the provisions on amputation. Under this system, he said, non-Muslims were guaranteed their rights, while Muslims were assured of the full practice of their faith.

Turabi, I found, had an answer for everything, including the charges of state tyranny. I pointed out that the government's punitive practices against dissent hardly constituted the minimalism he extolled. I reminded him that Sudan's indifference to human rights has been internationally condemned. But he was set for the question, and replied with no loss of composure.

"In many respects," he said, "Sudan recognizes that it has not achieved the model it has set for itself. Sudan is going through a transition, and in times like these, with a war going on, we haven't the capacity to observe normal procedures.

"We are an Islamic state but we are still studying the following issues: the form of government, the electoral system, the constitution, *shura,* the improvement of the economy by Islamic means. The role of Islamic banks and insurance companies is being debated, as is the nature of Islamic justice, the ways in which music and the arts may be encouraged.

"The democracy with which the Sudanese people are familiar is based on the ideas of the Ansar and the Khatmiyya, which are nineteenth-century sects. With respect to human rights, I'm not claiming that we have reached an ideal situation, where the optimum equation between liberty and state and society is maintained.

"How can you expect a complex country like ours, which is economically in very bad shape and politically in a state of civil war to maintain a constitutional system without some limitations on liberty? We admit we've tipped too far to government control; we need more freedom. But we haven't forgotten the model, and we are working actively to attain it."

I had heard before—in Baghdad during the Iran-Iraq War, for example—how difficult it was to realize political ideals in wartime. As soon as normality is restored, I was assured, the Ba'athi government would return to its real nature and embark on political liberalization. It did not happen in Iraq. It seemed equally unlikely, I thought, to happen in Sudan.

But Turabi also argued that Islamization must precede liberalization. The social and historical experiences which other peoples have in common and which have transformed them into nations, he argued, are absent in Sudan. If it is to become a nation, he maintained, Sudan has no alternative but to build its nationalism on a popular attachment to Islam.

"We can't have a Sudan which has no identity," Turabi said, "which has no direction, a Sudan which doesn't know whether to go for a socialist economy or a capitalist economy, whether to adopt Islam or adopt post-Christian Western ideology.

"Sudan is deeply divided between an elite which is Westernized and is pulling out and away, and a traditional society that is divided tribally, in a sectarian manner, without consciousness of its commonality. You can't have a country which is so disparate. You have either to search and work for a minimum of consensus, a minimum of unity, or break up. We have to have common objectives, a common language so we can communicate, common axioms so that we can settle our disputes and our arguments.

"In other countries, nationalism might be the alternative to Islam. But the only nationalism that is available to us, if we want to assert indigenous values and originality, as well as independence of the West, is Islam. Islam is the only modernity. Only Islam can serve as the national doctrine of today."

Asked whether he thought the rest of the Islamic world would follow the lead set by Sudan, Turabi did not give the facile reply, the categorical affirmative, that I had expected. In fact, he answered with an engaging tentativeness.

"I am quite sure," he said, "that every single Muslim country is now moving, slowly perhaps, swiftly perhaps, in the direction of an Islamic revival. But I don't believe in historical determinism, and this is not final history, because movements can be reversed.

"I know most of the Muslim countries. I know most of the Islamic movements. I've been every place and spoken to most government figures, as well as to many observers, not only Islamists but nationalists and leftists. It may be what I distill from all this wisdom is wishful thinking since, after all, I am committed to Islam. But I see the same process happening everywhere, and I believe that Islam will ultimately prevail. Still, I confess that I might be thinking wishfully."

5

Making the Shari'a

HISTORY AND LAW for Muslims play a different role from what they play in the West. The distinction weighs heavily on the outlook adopted by the members of the Muslim community toward themselves and toward the world around them.

History, for Westerners, is a secular discipline, like literature or sociology. Studied as a guide to the living world, it is in another domain from faith. Law, in the West, has also been, at least since the Middle Ages, a secular concern. Westerners may debate God's place in the annals of human affairs, but man takes responsibility for making his own rules of conduct.

For most Westerners, both the history and the law of Islam are mysterious. To those with conventional Western backgrounds, Islam unfolds on unexplored terrain, amid unfamiliar events. The names of the players, ringing exotically in the ear, are hard to remember. It is small wonder that Westerners' understanding of Islamic culture tends to be shallow.

The intimate link between history and law in Islam is particularly elusive to Westerners. Like Islamic law, the West's law is a product of its history. But in Islamic society, which regards all of life as religious expression, history's chief function is as a religious record. For Muslims, history contains the laws laid down by God for human behavior.

Having originated very differently from Islamic law, both Jewish and Christian law have lost much of their social role. For Jews, historically stateless and peripatetic, law emerged in exile through the interpretations by scholars of the Torah's divine admonitions. For Christians, whose faith was founded under the dominion of Rome, religious law grew within the embrace of the Roman legal system. Islamic law was not subjected in its seminal era to foreign sovereignties, and to this day remains at the core of Islamic consciousness.

When Muslims, after the Prophet's death in 632, recognized that the Quran left too much unsaid to constitute a system of law, they were presented with a quandary. How were they to create a comprehensive body of law? It took Islamic scholars three centuries to agree on a legal system that would go beyond the strictures of the Quran but would nonetheless remain divine.

To resolve the dilemma, Islamic jurists took their cue from the Quran, which said that Muhammad possessed God's mandate to assert the laws of right conduct. Following this logic, they agreed that Muhammad, though not divine himself, expressed God's will in whatever he did. From the Quran's premise, they concluded that the words and deeds of the Prophet had to be God's law.

Islamic law resembled Jewish law in emerging out of the deliberations of wise men intent on discerning God's will. Islam, however, left its scholars much less breadth to apply their own judgment or reason. Islamic scholars agreed, beyond the Quran, to be guided by the *sunna* of the Prophet, the precedents set by Muhammad during his lifetime. Islamic law was thus the direct product of Islamic history.

In the thousand years that have passed since the *shari'a*'s adoption, Muslim behavior has been ruled by the Prophet's precedents. Christians acknowledge a moral imperative to model themselves after Jesus. For Muslims, modeling themselves on Muhammad is more than a moral imperative; it is required conduct. Muslims believe that how faithfully they observe the law determines whether they will spend their afterlife in heaven or in hell.

Though it took three centuries to produce, the *shari'a*—the laws governing a believer's relationship with God—has since become the dominant force within Islam. It is more important than spiritual piety, more important than noble intentions, more important than inner purity. Muslims are not commanded to contemplate the grandeur of God; they are told to obey the law.

It is fair to say that the imperative to observe the *shari'a* has shaped not just Muslims but Muslim civilization. Far more than Jewish and Christian law, Islamic law has oriented the faith to the moment of its origin, keying Muslim society to an idyllic past when the Prophet was in command. It imparts to the Muslim utopia a historic rather than a spiritual nature.

In Muhammad's era, says the *shari'a*, lies the ideal of holiness. The Prophet's life is thus a matter for religious, not secular, study. The chronicles of other eras might be of some intellectual interest but, in containing no religious lessons, they are of little importance. To Muslims, law is what God has expressed not just in the Quran but through the medium of the Prophet's life.

The intimate link between the life of Muhammad and the commandments of God freezes Islam in time, making the present suspect. This itself gives Islam a unique character among the monotheistic faiths.

About a thousand years ago the scholars of the *shari'a* pronounced their work complete. They had learned everything they needed to know about the Prophet's life, they said, and had drawn the proper lessons from it. Having devised God's law, they pronounced it divine. Being divine, they said, it was subject neither to criticism nor to change.

That the *shari'a* is immutable remains the orthodox Islamic position. The doctrine of immutability has deprived Islamic law of the organic quality that characterizes law in secular societies. Islam rejects the evolution of law, proclaiming that Muslim life must adjust to the *shari'a*, not the *shari'a* to Muslim life.

Yet existence for Muslims, as for all others, is not static. Willingly or not, Islamic society is part of a dynamic universe. No culture, however conservative, can stop change. Nor can any build a barrier high enough or thick enough to avoid the impact that experience and technology have on human values.

The *shari'a*, however, presumes to set rules that guide Muslims, for all time, to a life that emulates the Prophet's. This aspiration contains much that is noble. But it also condemns Muslim society to remain a pristine island of faithful observance, whatever the changes taking place in the sea around it.

Many societies entertain a vision of a golden age somewhere in their past, but acknowledge that it is gone forever. They may aspire to a new age that will be equally golden, but inevitably different in character. Muslim believers, however, retain a conviction that, if only man can be guided into right conduct, the one and only golden age, the Prophet's age, can be regained.

According to this belief, whatsoever has gone wrong in Islam derives from the Muslims' weakness of engaging in misguided conduct. Only conduct that follows the *shari'a*, says Islam, will return Muslims to a better age. Following the *shari'a*, moreover, means that the age will inevitably look like the Prophet's.

Islam thus denies to Muslims the right to participate in the changes that take place from one moment to the next in the real world. It rejects adaptation, places constraints on accommodation. As human history moves on, the doctrine of the *shari'a*'s immutability imposes a burden so heavy that Islamic society has been unable to keep pace.

A few Muslims have always disagreed with this doctrine. The *shari'a*, they have argued, is not like the Quran itself, the precise words of God. Not only was the Prophet mortal but his history was written by mortals, and mortals acquire new information, shift their judgments, correct their mistakes. Therefore, they say, the *shari'a* should always be open to review.

Throughout the Middle East, Muslims in our own day have made this contention the subject of vigorous debate.

Yet all the schools of Islamic thought accept the Prophet-centered principle on which the *shari'a* was crafted. This principle acknowledges the Quran as the first source of Islamic law but regards the Prophet's precedents as an equally legitimate basis for fixing the rules of Islamic behavior.

The term Muhammadanism is no longer used in the West as a synonym for Islam. Muslims, offended by it, point out that "Islam" means submission to God, not the Prophet. Yet it is no offense to say that Muhammadan, as an adjective, aptly describes Islamic civilization, even as it exists today.

Muhammad, as Islam has enshrined him, is more than the founding father. However important the memory of Moses and Jesus are to their faiths, neither has been as dominant as Muhammad in the shaping of a culture. Muhammad is not just the paragon of life on earth. He is the link between God's will and the laws of human behavior. And since God measures the conduct of believers against the standard of Muhammad's conduct, he became—however inadvertently—the gatekeeper to Islamic eternity.

The principle of Muhammad's preeminence is at the foundation of orthodoxy, but at the same time it determines the character of Islamic reform. It makes Islamic radicalism—as contemporary fundamentalists make clear—necessarily reactionary, while imparting even to modernism a nostalgia for a bygone era.

The differences that divide orthodox Muslims from modernists and fundamentalists is over the *shari'a*. Orthodoxy holds that it is perfect as it is. Modernists argue that, being the work of man, it must constantly be reinterpreted to adapt to the requirements of changing times. Fundamentalists maintain that, Islam being indifferent to changing times, it must be reexamined only for intrusions upon its original purity.

The stakes of this debate is the direction that Islamic civilization will take in dealing with the real world.

· II ·

SHARI'A, as the name for Islamic law, appears originally in the Quran. Speaking to Muhammad, God says: "We have set thee on a clear road [*shari'a*] of our commandment. Follow it, and follow not the whims of those who know not" (45:18).

Among the titles the Quran gives to God is *shari,* the lawgiver. Muhammad is referred to by the same term, with the definition stretched a bit by Islamic scholars into "preacher of law."

Shari'a is derived from a root which means "the road to the watering place" or simply "the way." The word offers a glimpse into the bedouin origins of Islamic law, and the tribally rooted sense of duty which many Muslims feel toward it to this day.[1]

The Quran provides plenty of evidence that Islam's legal system derives from the bedouins. The stringency of life in the desert encouraged obedience to established procedures, discouraging individualism and social experimentation. Survival was thought to depend on the solidarity of the bedouin community. The tribe was guided by the proven ways of its forebears. Tribal law, indistinguishable from tradition, was based on a common dedication to clearly understood precedents.

In the hothouse environment of Arabia, cut off from other cultures, Islam's character was forged. Judaism evolved under diverse gentile sovereigns; Christianity developed under the legions of Rome. But under Muhammad, Islam from the start had its own state and its own army. Though foreign influences pressed at its frontiers, they did not penetrate to its heart.

Muhammad softened the nature of bedouin society, but he did not tamper with its spirit, and he left most bedouin practices in place. The changes he imposed in shaping a more equitable society were far from revolutionary. Islam today preserves much of the character that Arab culture possessed before Muhammad was born.

The word *sunna*—meaning "tradition"—was used by the Arabian tribes as the equivalent of law. It is no coincidence that the Islamic scholars who made the *shari'a* later applied the word to Muhammad's sayings and deeds. As a word, *sunna* also evolved over time to refer to the mainstream of Islamic belief, distinguishing it from Shi'ism. Some nine tenths of Muslims today are Sunnis, which quite literally means "the followers of tradition."

The tribes of Arabia ultimately embraced the Prophet's rules of behavior more fully than his theology. Indeed, the Quran is hardly a theological document. God, the Quran says, determines each one's fate in the afterlife, based on the degree of obedience to His rules. Islam, being consistent, is less concerned with God's nature than with God's laws.

Muhammad, the evidence suggests, had no great interest in theology himself. Many verses of the Quran—as related in Chapter 3—address the concerns of a merchant and a social reformer. Muhammad's instructions from God were specific, earthbound. Not surprisingly, Islam became a religion of temporal law.

When scholars after the Prophet's death undertook to make the *shari'a,* such issues as conscience, love of God and inner piety were not among their concerns. Very quickly, many Muslims perceived a void in their conception of the faith, which became an invitation to Sufism, the rise of which would add a mystical dimension to Muslim life. Though many believers have found simultaneous fulfillment in the *shari'a* and Sufism, the two have remained basically contending poles within the religious structure. For Muslim orthodoxy, Sufism, though not quite a heresy, is a deviation from commitment to the *shari'a,* Islam's mainstream belief.

During the Prophet's lifetime the Islamic system of law, still undeveloped, consisted of an improvised mix of Quranic injunctions and bedouin tradition. When neither applied to a problem at hand, the Prophet personally declared what the law was. As lawgiver, his authority was unquestioned.

But, on Muhammad's death, the law was nothing but a hodgepodge of rules and admonitions. Many believers feared that unless Islam found something more compelling to offer, it would not survive. Creating a comprehensive system thus became a high priority. Significantly, the scholars who assumed the task took for granted that the law would be based on tribal tradition. No other source of law ever occurred to them.

The challenge lay in the absence of codification. Tradition, by definition, was not written down. Moreover, the scholars who set out to build a legal structure were urban dwellers, largely unfamiliar with tribal practice. Before they could inscribe the laws, they had to determine what the tradition was, a problem that was more difficult than first appeared.

Besides, there were other matters on the social agenda. Muhammad had given top priority to taming and reorganizing Arabia, and after his death the society was distracted by the struggle to succeed him. The next generation of leadership, the *rashidun,* conquered an empire and then had to absorb it. Few anticipated that the process of making the *shari'a* would take three hundred years.

The decades after Muhammad's death, though extolled as the golden age of the *rashidun,* were actually very tumultuous. The dispute over succession was followed by a civil war and then by a coup d'état, which brought the Umayyads, a dynasty of usurpers, to power. It is impossible to understand the development of Islamic culture without reference to the politics of this crucial, early age.

Muhammad had no male heir when he died in 632. His nearest male relative was his son-in-law and cousin, Ali. Though patrilineal descent was not a tribal tradition, Ali promptly claimed the caliphate, the office of the Prophet's successor. Ali argued that only by keeping the office in the family could the preservation of Islamic piety be assured. But the Prophet's companions, those who had long been at his side, had other ideas.

Following tribal practice, they met in *shura,* "consultation," and bestowed the caliphate on Abu Bakr, who was Muhammad's closest friend and the father of Aisha, his favorite wife. Ali and his supporters interpreted the process as a conspiracy of cronies, though the Quran specifically calls for *shura* as a part of decision making. At Abu Bakr's death two years later, the companions met in *shura* again and elected Omar, another of the Prophet's intimate circle.

The trouble began when Uthman succeeded to the office after Omar's assassination.* Uthman, though a Quraysh and a companion of the Prophet, was not a member of his clan, the Hashemites. On the contrary, he was an Umayyad, a member of the powerful clan that had led the opposition to the Prophet during his vexing years in Mecca. Muhammad's family, led by Ali, considered the choice unacceptable.

To many, Uthman represented the return to power of the old Meccan oligarchy, whom Muhammad had defeated. On what basis Uthman was selected is unclear; why he is considered a *rashidun,* a "rightly-guided" caliph, is even more so. History records Uthman as a weak ruler, given to nepotism and profligacy. His reign precipitated a civil war, and the Sunni-Shi'ite schism that lasts to this day.

The conflict began when Ali, sensing the Umayyads' dynastic ambitions, began recruiting troops to challenge Uthman. Most of the bedouin tribes, wooed by both, were undecided whose side to take. While rival contingents were lining up, Uthman was murdered by an

---

* See Farag Foda's account, Chapter 2, pp. 31–35.

insurgent soldier. Ali, whether or not complicit, was elected by the *shura* to succeed him. When the Umayyad clan rejected the election, the civil war broke out.[2]

Leading the Umayyads was Muawiyya, a nephew whom Uthman had appointed governor of Syria. Ali, at the head of a stronger army, won some early battles, and on a field in Syria in 657 he prepared for another encounter against an inferior Umayyad force. By a ruse, however, Muawiyya persuaded Ali to accept a truce, which dragged on and on. It ended when Ali was murdered, though the assassin was apparently one of his own followers and provided Muawiyya with an irresistible opportunity.

Muawiyya seized the opportunity and pronounced himself caliph, with no reference to the *shura*. It was Islam's first coup d'état. Muawiyya then severed the link with the Prophet's family and with the Arabian heartland by abandoning Muhammad's capital in Medina. Muawiyya located the Umayyad government in Damascus, which proceeded to become the new center of the Arab world.

In the view of many Muslims, the Umayyads were not just usurpers but secular kings. They did not, like their predecessors, claim to derive their authority from the Prophet. They declined to perform their religious obligations. Never secure on the throne, the Umayyads were soon under heavy pressure from segments of the faithful who called for a restoration of Islamic legitimacy.

Ali's old followers encouraged this dissidence. His son Hussein formed a party—*Shi'ate Ali,* from which comes the name Shi'ism—to resume the civil war. (*Shi'a,* conventionally translated as "party," more accurately means "group with a different opinion.") In its ranks were non-Arabs, among them many Persians newly converted to Islam and resentful of the disdain the Arabs showed them. As a dissident movement, Shi'ism attracted the surly and the poor, and to this day it is a movement of outsiders, resentful of the Sunni Arabs, the Islamic mainstream.

In 680 the Umayyads defeated a Shi'ite army at Karbala in Iraq, where a giant mosque now stands as a memorial to Hussein. The victory ended the prospect that Shi'ism would take over Islam. But the Shi'ite movement lived on, chiefly at the eastern reaches of the empire, in Persia and Iraq. To Sunnis, it has always been a heresy. But to its faithful, Shi'ism is the backbone of the faith, loyal to the Prophet's real family and to his belief.[3]

Under the Umayyads, the jurists began crafting a legal system that was unlike any other. Crucial to its emergence was the shadow of illegitimacy that hovered over the dynasty. This sense of illegitimacy persuaded the jurists shaping the *shari'a* to build a vehicle for asserting Islam's interest over that of the usurper. Their work initiated a system of law whose relationship to government differs sharply in conception from the one familiar to the West.

Westerners understand law as an instrument of the state; it is the government that makes and enforces rules of behavior. The *shari'a*, however, in claiming to be divine, denies to the state the authority to make law. This authority is asserted by the *ulama*, the body of senior jurists, as Islam interpreters. Since Muslims in the Umayyad era generally regarded the state as non-Islamic, the jurists working in their behalf created a *shari'a* meant to supersede state authority.

Since Umayyad times, regimes have conventionally proven stronger than the *ulama* and have bent them to the service of state interests. States, to be sure, have made law, in defiance of the *shari'a*. Nonetheless, the Islamic theory of the *shari'a* as a watchdog over an impious state remains intact to this day.[4]

Because of their confrontational posture, the scholars who labored on the *shari'a* took pains to preserve their independence of the Umayyad regime. These men have been depicted in history as pious amateurs, dedicated to the task of writing laws to govern the conduct both of believers and the state. The Umayyads, who surely knew what they were up to, apparently accepted a truce with them. As long as the scholars worked quietly, not roiling the realm, the regime did not interfere with them.

By Islam's second century, the makers of the *shari'a* had broken up into several schools. The most notable among them were in Kufa and Basra in Iraq, and Mecca and Medina in Arabia, far from the seat of imperial authority. The schools probably maintained a network of communications. It was out of prudence, no doubt, that there was no school in Damascus, the Umayyad capital.

By the nature of their work, the scholars were designated "traditionists." The term—distinguished from "traditionalist," with a quite different meaning—described a specialist in the search for legal codes within the body of tradition.

The traditionists were defiantly Islamic. In these early centuries Islam found itself infiltrated by ideas from Judaism and Christianity, even from Hellenism, Buddhism and Zoroastrianism. Indeed, from the Byzantines the office of judge, the *qadi*, found its way into the *shari'a*, along with the concept of the *dhimmi*, which provided for a tax on Christians and Jews in return for communal protection and autonomy. But the traditionists on the whole went their own way, holding that Islam already had all the wisdom it needed. The neighboring legal systems, they said, had nothing to teach them. Tradition-ism as a source of law served as a wall, protecting Islam from foreign intrusion.

The traditionists' duty was to establish "traditions," which in Arabic are called *hadith*. Their search began within the community as a whole but in time it narrowed to precedents set by Muhammad alone. The term *hadith* has therefore passed into the language meaning the "tra-ditions of the Prophet."

But in the early Umayyad years the traditionists took as their source of law the "living tradition," which led them in their inquiries to the established practices of all believers, but particularly the tribal nomads. A scholar of that era, for example, might learn that tribesmen routinely washed their hands before prayer. If the traditionists obtained and verified evidence that this was so, the practice became a "tradition," thus legally binding.

Traditionist principles, particularly during the Umayyad period, bear a resemblance to the English common law. The precedents that the scholars sought to establish were, in theory, the existing and an-cient practices of the community, as were English common law codes. In reality, in looking for law derived almost exclusively from the Ara-bian tribes, the traditionists were preserving the practices of Arab soci-ety's most closed and conservative segment.

In meeting to codify specific traditions, the traditionists debated according to strict rules. They were not permitted personal opinions or interpretations of what the law should be. Least of all were they permitted to propose innovations. They were allowed to use analogy but not pure reason to derive a conclusion. The traditionists were also required to resolve their disagreements by consensus, which was long-standing tribal practice.

Once the traditionists validated a precedent, it became an Islamic norm, and Muslims were expected to live by it. When, after extended debate, they reached consensus on a tradition, they proclaimed it by the formula, "We follow this."[5]

Contemporary observers might question the reliability of the tradi-tionists' methods. Historians tell us that working jurists more often selected their precedents by consulting scholars in other schools than by going out into the community themselves. Why they limited them-selves in this way is unclear but, being city people, they were probably ill at ease in the desert. This self-imposed limitation may also explain why the "living tradition" was, before long, judged inadequate and abandoned as a source of law.

Near the middle of the eighth century the traditionists shifted their method, adopting in place of the "living tradition" the precedents set by the companions of the Prophet, the *rashidun*. The idea apparently began at the Kufa school, then spread to the school in Mecca. The companions, the jurists concluded, were a more reliable guide to tradition than tribal practices.

The Umayyad caliphs, however, were unhappy with the change. The stigma of their usurpation refused to go away. They had hoped their tolerating the traditionists would stabilize the political order. But the traditionists, in shifting their attention to the *rashidun,* were exalting the very leaders from whom the Umayyads had snatched their power. Of the Prophet's companions, all except Uthman had been Hashemites, Umayyad enemies. Ali's supporters, the Shi'ites, continued to proclaim that they had been cheated of the throne, and constituted a major opposition force in the realm. The Umayyads had a point. What the traditionists described as a methodological refinement may actually have been a blow aimed at weakening the Damascus regime.

Indeed, in the search for sources of law, the authority of the *rashidun* proved even less trustworthy than the "living tradition." The traditionists argued that inquiries addressed to the companions' families would yield the needed data. But the last of the companions had died many decades before, and the traditionists surely understood that the information acquired about them would not be reliable.

In the end, the traditionists abandoned the companions too. Though we cannot know for sure, it is plausible that the Umayyads applied pressure on them. Whatever the case, the traditionists experimented only briefly with the *rashidun* before moving on to still another source.

The traditionists finally turned to Islam's ultimate earthly authority, the Prophet. There was logic in looking to Muhammad for the law, and the wonder is that it took so long to recognize. The "traditions of the Prophet" were the source which led to the *shari'a* that Muslims have since known. The change, however, did not achieve its full momentum until the next dynasty, after the Umayyads fell.[6]

· III ·

IN A.D. 750, THE NINETIETH YEAR of its reign, the Umayyad caliphate came to an end. Its state had been weakened by the resumption of ancient tribal warfare. The absence of a fixed rule of succession had repeatedly set brother against brother. The Shi'ites had never given up their struggle, nor had the Sunni pietists who were disturbed by the caliphate's secular ways. The issue of Islamic legitimacy had never been laid to rest.

The Umayyads' downfall was brought about by the Abbasids, a Hashemite family related to both Muhammad and Ali. Residents of Iraq, the Abbasids claimed a divine mission to restore the Prophet's kin to power. They persuaded not only the Shi'ites but many other dissidents to support them. Generations of Muslim historians, adopting the victors' perspective, have popularized—and exaggerated—the notion that, after fourteen Godless Umayyad caliphs, the Abbasids restored an Islamic state.

The Abbasid triumph was as much the product of social shifts as of military power. Iraq had become the empire's most heavily populated region, and non-Arabs outnumbered Arabs there. "Arab," a term that had referred to the conquerors from Arabia, had come to embrace whoever spoke Arabic, an index of the demographic reality. But if Arabic remained the empire's lingua franca, and Arabic practices the norm, Arab dominance was gravitating to Muslims of other cultures, particularly the Persians.

The Abbasids successfully exploited these shifts to put together a powerful coalition of Sunni believers, Shi'ites and new Muslims, most of them from the Persian province of Khurasan. Their defeat of the Umayyads signaled the eastward shift of the Arab heartland from Syria to Iraq, a transformation that was as much cultural as strategic.

The Persians, with their deeply rooted culture, were influential among the Abbasids, imparting a special cast to the dynasty. Life under the Umayyads, though hardly austere, had largely followed Arabian tribal ways. Under the Abbasids, the Arabs embraced a Persia-oriented worldliness. Baghdad, the capital on the Tigris, epitomized the new regime: on a foundation of bedouin values rose a society of unprecedented splendor.

The Abbasid caliphs, politically dependent on their reputation as believers, were outwardly more devout than the Umayyads. They recited prayers, built mosques and made pilgrimages to Mecca. But behind the veil of piety they venerated the newly rediscovered wisdom of the Greeks. They also practiced a cosmopolitan self-indulgence that was much in excess of Umayyad ways.

Under the Abbasids, the rough economic and social egalitarianism which insured the cohesion of desert society yielded to class hierarchy. At the bottom were the Muslim masses, who, events would show, retained a nostalgia for a simple life of shared austerity. Only later did the Abbasids perceive that the yearnings of these masses could not with impunity be ignored.

The Abbasids erected great palaces on the riverside, with spacious reception chambers lit by huge chandeliers. They built luxurious apartments for royal concubines and their eunuch servants. They kept slaves, wore the finest fabrics and furs, and bedecked themselves in jewels. They bathed their bodies with scent and dyed their hair. They raced horses and camels, and hired performers to amuse them with song. They dined on gold and silver plates, and ignored the Quran in getting drunk with wine.

At their apogee from the late eighth to the mid-ninth century, the Abbasids presided over the world's most powerful empire. No city was richer or more sophisticated than Baghdad, celebrated globally for its commerce, its scholarship and its arts. Whatever the external influences, the Arabs' transformation over the course of a century into an accomplished urban culture was a remarkable achievement. For the Abbasid elite, Islam was hardly more than a distraction. Yet the Arab core of the society remained profoundly religious, which the Abbasids did not recognize until painfully late.

The most eminent of the Abbasid caliphs was Harun al-Rashid (764–809), familiar to the West for the correspondence he conducted with the Frankish king Charlemagne. While Arab literature and science were reaching glorious heights, Europe was living in the Dark Ages. History records that Harun sent Charlemagne a gift of a brass water clock, surpassing in technology anything the West had ever seen, astounding the Frankish court.

Harun is also remembered for his appearances, as caliph and lover, in *The Thousand and One Nights*. The work is based on stories from the Persians, Indians, Greeks and perhaps even the Hebrews, though in the form that has reached modern times it is a fantasy that is profoundly Arab. The tales it contains testify to the cosmopolitanism of the Baghdad elite.

Sinbad, the sailor who is the central figure in the collection, is a model of the far-ranging Muslim merchant of the Abbasid era.[7] Sinbad's account of his last voyage, which follows, conveys some of the flavor of Harun's reign.

One day, one of my servants came and told me that an officer of the caliph's inquired for me. I rose from the table and went to him. "The caliph," said he, "has sent me to tell you that he must speak with you." I followed the officer to the palace where, being presented to the caliph, I saluted him by prostrating myself at his feet. "Sinbad," said he to me, "I stand in need of your service; you must carry my present to the King of Serendib." . . .

This command of the caliph was to me like a clap of thunder. "Commander of the Faithful," I replied, "I am ready to do whatever your majesty shall think fit to command." . . . He was very well pleased, and ordered me one thousand sequins for the expenses of the journey.

I prepared for my departure in a few days, and as soon as the caliph's letter and present were delivered to me, I went to Basra, where I embarked, and had a very happy voyage. . . . I was conducted to the palace, where I saluted the king [of Serendib] by prostration, according to custom. The king testified very great joy at seeing me. "Sinbad," said he, "you are welcome; I bless the day on which we see one another once more." I made my compliments to him and delivered the caliph's letter and gift, which he received with all imaginable satisfaction.

The caliph's present was a complete suit of cloth of gold, valued at 1,000 sequins; 50 robes of rich stuff, 100 of white cloth, the finest of Cairo, Suez and Alexandria; a vessel of agate broader than deep, an inch thick and a half-foot wide, the bottom of which represented in bas-relief a man with one knee on the ground, who held a bow and an arrow ready to discharge at a lion. He sent him also a rich tablet, which, according to tradition, belonged to the great Solomon.

The caliph's letter was as follows: "Greeting in the name of the sovereign guide of the right way, from the dependant on God, Harun al-Rashid, whom God hath made vice-regent to the Prophet. . . ."[8]

Harun's son al-Ma'mun, who succeeded to the caliphate in 813, is less known in the West but played a critical role in reviving the works of the ancient Greeks. A legend recounted by a tenth-century Arab chronicler—the tale reveals how non-Islamic the Abbasids had become—holds that al-Ma'mun, on seeing Aristotle in a dream, posed the question, "What is beauty?" Aristotle's reply was characteristically Hellenic: "That which is beautiful to our reason." Al-Ma'mun, the chronicler tells us, was thus won to Hellenic culture.

Intellectual as he was, however, al-Ma'mun is also remembered for his lavish tastes. At his wedding in 825, it is said, he sat with his bride, Buran, on a golden mat studded with sapphires, while minions showered thousands of pearls upon them. Arab literature has immortalized the occasion, one of the extravaganzas of the age.[9] It says much about the Abbasids' isolation that al-Ma'mun, shrewd as he was, never perceived his subjects' disapproval, either of his Hellenist passions or of his spending habits.

Yet even within court circles were many believers who disapproved of the era's intemperance. "The caliph and the courtiers," wrote a Baghdadi, "guzzle wine while imposing legal punishment on other drinkers." Abu Nuwas, a celebrated Abbasid poet who was Harun's favorite drinking partner and who often wrote in praise of wine and love, also suffered pangs of conscience. The following verse reveals the brooding Islamic melancholy that lay just beneath Abu Nuwas's veneer of joyful drunkenness.

> Stunned by my sin in its enormity,
> I took heart, Lord, and laid it side by side
> With that great mercy which is Thine alone,
> And measured both with yardstick up and down.
> My sin is great; but now I know, O Lord,
> That even greater is Thy clemency.[10]

What distinguished the Abbasids from the Umayyads more than their prodigality, however, was their willingness—a direct product of their attraction to the Greeks—to open the doors of the fortress of Islamic belief.

Baghdad was by then in a position to reap the return of more than two centuries of Arab conquests. Greek works of science and philosophy were in currency, and were acquired by deliberate orders of the caliph. Baghdad's new class of worldly intellectuals were assigned to pore over their meaning. Under al-Ma'mun, Islamic society experienced an intellectual explosion.

Many Greek manuscripts had been stored for centuries in Byzantium. Arab armies had often tried and failed to capture the great city, but when the two empires were not at war, Abbasids and Byzantines engaged in commerce. The manuscripts became a precious commodity at the Abbasid court.

The caliphs were first attracted to Greek medicine, which was far in advance of the healing arts among the Arabs. Later they acquired a fascination with astronomy, which had religious applications, like finding the direction of Mecca and determining the proper hours of prayer. Harun had sent to Byzantium for texts to compile astronomical charts. Al-Ma'mun, going a step further, dispatched a mission to bring back the works of Aristotle.

At first the Abbasids had to depend on Jews and Christians to translate. But Arabs gradually took over, and they quickly became avid students of the foreign learning that they held in their hands.

From the start, however, the society made a distinction between Islamic knowledge, which came from the Quran, and foreign knowledge—called *hikmah,* "wisdom"—which was derived from the

Greeks. In A.D. 830, al-Ma'mun built the Beit al-Hikmah, the House of Wisdom, in Baghdad. Its shelves contained no Islamic books. A combination library and academy, it offered only works of the Greeks, and for a time was the world's most celebrated educational institution.

Remarkably, Arab scholars absorbed within a few decades learning that had taken the Greeks centuries to produce. The historian Philip Hitti has written that, "While al-Rashid and al-Ma'mun were delving into Greek and Persian philosophy, their contemporaries in the West, Charlemagne and his lords, were reportedly dabbling in the art of writing their names."[11] Though condescending, the observation accurately conveys the superiority that Arabic culture, by any standard of measure, then enjoyed over the West.

The era of translation laid the basis for a surge of Arab creativity, in fields from mathematics, for which Arab thinkers showed a particular aptitude, to astronomy to medicine to geography. Arab architecture excelled. Arabic, a language hitherto limited to Quranic studies and popular poetry, suddenly became the vehicle of communication among the learned throughout the entire Mediterranean region.

Yet hidden somewhere in this brilliant culture was a flaw. The Arabs showed no real interest in the Greek humanists—Homer, Sophocles, Herodotus, Thucydides. They never narrowed the chasm between the quest for God and the quest for philosophical understanding. The civilization, including its intellectuals, continued to look inward on itself. The Arabs failed to integrate Islamic knowledge with *hikmah,* the wisdom of the West.

To be sure, faith and reason have never been comfortable companions anywhere. To this day, the West itself has not succeeded in fully reconciling them.

But in Islam the defenders of faith have historically been more sharply at war with the champions of reason. The Abbasid era was unique in exposing Islamic culture to an open, critical, humane body of thought. The era witnessed a dialogue, though often rancorous, between faith and reason. But the dialogue ran its course, having made few ripples on the Islamic pond, and since Abbasid times such dialogue has rarely taken place at all.

Under the Abbasid caliphs, the principal challenge to orthodoxy was undertaken by a movement of Islamic intellectuals known as the Mu'tazilites. Though their tactics were not always gentle, their message contained the promise of preserving, within the context of the faith, the creativity on which Islamic civilization had hopefully embarked. The Mu'tazilites were the product of the same invasion of new knowledge that produced great mathematicians and astronomers. They did not cause the surge of creativity among the Arabs during the Baghdad years, but, for a dazzling moment, they foreshadowed the revolution of the mind that the West experienced centuries later in the Renaissance.

The Mu'tazilites, who were Sunni Muslims, were both dedicated theologians and avid readers of the Greeks. Their name, derived from a word meaning "neutralists," suggests a state of suspension between belief and unbelief.[12] Their origins, in Basra, went back to Umayyad times, even before Greek texts became common. Partisans of an open Islamic vision, they were players in the political and religious disputes that began under the Umayyads and came to an end only under the Abbasids.

The Mu'tazilites introduced Sunni Islam to the principle of rational inquiry into the nature of God and the Quran. Such practices had hitherto been linked chiefly to Shi'ites. The Mu'tazilites also promoted a belief in free will, at odds with the orthodox doctrine of divine predestination.

The Umayyads had had no use for either rationalism or free will. Being enemies of the Shi'ites, they were suspicious of rationalism. Claiming legitimacy on the basis of predestination—they had no other basis for their claim—they possessed an equal distaste for the doctrine of free will.

The Umayyads persecuted the Mu'tazilites and executed at least one of their leaders on charges of subversion. The Abbasids, at the start of their dynastic uprising, recognized the Mu'tazilites as potential allies and extended them a welcome.

As strategy for coming to power, the Abbasids tried to bridge the gap between Sunnis and Shi'ites. They saw an advantage in balancing their own claim of orthodoxy with a patronage of Islamic dissidence. While they portrayed themselves as orthodox to unseat the usurpers, their victory over the Umayyads would not have been possible without Shi'ite help. It seems likely that the Abbasids also contemplated bringing the Shi'ites, after more than a century of schism, back into the Islamic fold.

Apart from political strategy, the Abbasids as a clan had long been receptive—as are the Hashemites today*—to making a place for reason in Islamic thought. It was not just expedient for them to seek allies in the Mu'tazilites and the Shi'ites. To overthrow the Umayyads, the Abbasids chose a strategy, which sent a signal of welcome to many

---

* See discussion in Chapter 10.

potential supporters but which they also found ideologically congenial.

In today's terms, the Mu'tazilites were far from freethinkers or even
agnostics. They were conventional Muslims in professing awe of God
and the Quran. But they deviated from orthodox thinking in rejecting
traditionism. In the view of the Mu'tazilites, orthodoxy was misguided
in taking tradition as the preeminent source of Islamic law. They called
for law based on divine justice, admittedly an abstraction, but one
which they believed could be readily defined by human reason, guided
by the Quran.

The Mu'tazilites did more than challenge traditionism as the root of
law, however. They denied the orthodox contention that law was the
highest expression of Islam. In the Mu'tazilite view, each believer had
personally to verify God's existence, a duty requiring an exercise of the
mind. Their doctrine, in short, proposed to transform Islam from an
externally to an internally directed set of convictions.

Orthodox thinkers had no interest in such a revolutionary shift. The
traditionists, who had by then become the dominant school of
thought within the Islamic establishment, saw Mu'tazilism as a dangerous enemy. They were consistent in arguing that human reason, at
best a faulty instrument, had no place in ascertaining God's will. If
God's word needed clarification or elaboration, they maintained, only
tradition could supply it. The traditionists, in self-defense, declared
Mu'tazilite belief to be heresy.

To traditionists, Mu'tazilism's exaltation of the human mind was an
assertion that human powers were at a level with God's. The traditionists dismissed the Mu'tazilite plea for a role for human reason. They
also rejected the doctrine of free will, considering it a presumptuous
attack on God's omnipotence.

It should be understood that the Mu'tazilites, though more speculative than was customary in Islam, were not partisans of the speculative philosophy of the Greeks. They did not pose such philosophical
questions as, "What is God?" Only much later would Arabs—most
notably Avicenna and Averroes—contribute significantly to speculative philosophy, and their impact would be far less on Islamic than on
Western thought.

Mu'tazilism's view of God had more in common with the mysticism
of the Sufis, as well as the controlled rationalism of the Shi'ites. In
adopting Greek premises, however, the Mu'tazilites proposed to lead
Islam in a wholly different direction from where traditionism was
taking it. Their aspirations would have made Islam unrecognizable not

just to the traditionists but, it might be conjectured, to Muhammad himself.

The caliph al-Ma'mun was the Mu'tazilites' greatest partisan. Not only had he an ideological commitment and a political interest, but there was more. His mother, it was said, was a Persian concubine, and perhaps a Shi'ite. His power base in the wars to secure and retain his power was the Persian province of Khurasan, a Shi'ite stronghold. Some historians think he may have become a Mu'tazilite himself, if not a secret Shi'ite.

Shortly after being named caliph in 813, al-Ma'mun took a gamble to strengthen the Abbasids' links with the Shi'ites. In an unprecedented action, he named Ali al-Rida, a Persian who was the Shi'ites' *imam*,* to succeed him. He also gave al-Rida his daughter in marriage, a political device that the Prophet had favored. Looking back, al-Ma'mun's effort was a clear move to repair the breach between Islam's two hostile branches. It turned out to be the last.

Al-Ma'mun overreached. The Sunni masses were mortified at the prospect of having a Shi'ite caliph. Far from being a unifier, the gesture jeopardized Abbasid rule and brought the empire to the brink of yet another civil war. Al-Ma'mun backed away rather than fight, and soon afterward al-Rida mysteriously died, along with several of his supporters. In a gesture of respect, the caliph had him buried next to Harun, his father, in a tomb that remains a Shi'ite shrine.

But al-Ma'mun's retreat did not resolve the domestic crisis. Orthodox Muslims were by now convinced that the caliph was hiding his conversion to Shi'ism, while the Shi'ites in Khurasan, dismayed by his weakness, effectively seceded from his increasingly fragile realm. Al-Ma'mun responded with yet another audacious move, declaring war on orthodoxy by pronouncing Mu'tazilism the official state dogma.

Al-Ma'mun's aim was to cripple the traditionists. But, ironically, he stripped Mu'tazilism of its theological credentials by reducing it to a political pawn in the empire's internal wars. Anti-Mu'tazilite sentiment soared, and dedicated Muslims protested against the caliph outside his House of Wisdom.

Al-Ma'mun then flexed his political muscles by ordering the clerics of his realm to swear allegiance to Mu'tazilism. Specifically, he commanded them to announce publicly their acceptance of the Mu'tazilite doctrine that the Quran had been "created."

The doctrine that the Quran was "uncreated"—examined in Chapter 3—has long been one of orthodoxy's curiosities. Orthodox schol-

---

* The title is used by Shi'ites to designate the leader of the faithful.

ars have historically held that the Quran had existed for all time and was revealed to Muhammad at a time of God's choosing. They intended by this to reaffirm that the Quran—and, by extension, Islamic doctrine—were eternally changeless.

The Mu'tazilites ridiculed both the logic and the political implications of their theory. They argued that God, having "created" the Quran, gave it to Muhammad to deal with specific earthly conditions. Their position implied that God might offer new revelations when new conditions demanded. They argued further that the text, having been "created" in response to one set of circumstances, should be reinterpreted in the light of other circumstances. On this issue, the line between the two Islamic schools was drawn.

Al-Ma'mun threatened serious punishment to whoever rejected the official line, and followed with a campaign of persecution, known to Islamic history as the *mihnah,* or "inquisition." For the Mu'tazilites, the hand had spun full circle. A century before, they had been persecuted by the Umayyads; now, under an Abbasid, they were effectively the persecutors.

The regime imprisoned, flogged, exiled and barred defiant clerics from their mosques. Al-Ma'mun personally abused some of them. Among Muslims today, the *mihnah* is far better remembered for the persecution of orthodoxy than are the Mu'tazilites for arguing in behalf of reason or a "created" Quran.

Most clerics yielded to al-Ma'mun's pressure, renouncing their beliefs to swear to the dogma of creation. But some refused, the most celebrated being Ahmad Ibn Hanbal, a jurist, whose courage made him a popular martyr. The sympathy that the masses showed him was evidence that the hearts of the Sunni believers, whatever the tastes of the Baghdad intellectuals, were still embedded in orthodoxy. The popularity of Ibn Hanbal's defiance signaled rising anti-Abbasid sentiment. In the end, al-Ma'mun assured Mu'tazilism's defeat by suffocating it in his political embrace.

Though the *mihnah* continued after al-Ma'mun's death in 833, its zealotry diminished and it soon died out. Meanwhile, the Mu'tazilites, like the caliphate itself, grew weaker. When al-Ma'mun's successors gave up official courtship of the Shi'ites to rally Sunni support, Mu'tazilism no longer served a political purpose. The caliph Mutawakkil (847–61), al-Ma'mun's nephew, revoked the state's allegiance to the doctrine of the "created" Quran and restored the traditionist dogma to favor. Without the caliphate's protection, the Mu'tazilites became the target of popular retribution. Ibn Hanbal's disciples, with impunity, were soon treating the Mu'tazilites as harshly as the Mu'tazilites had treated them.[13]

The theologian Abu al-Hasan al-Ash'ari, himself a Mu'tazilite, hammered the final nail into Mu'tazilism's coffin as the *mihnah* drew to a close. Al-Ash'ari is said to have lost his Mu'tazilite faith when he was forty, after recognizing that reason could not explain God's judgment on the Last Day.

The story is told that al-Ash'ari asked a Mu'tazilite sage how God would rule on the death of three brothers, one a believer, another a sinner, the third an innocent infant. The teacher replied that God would send the first to heaven, the second to hell and the third to limbo. Al-Ash'ari followed by asking why the infant should have died at all, and the Mu'tazilite answered that it was God's way of saving him from becoming a sinner.

"Then why," al-Ash'ari asked, "did God let the sinner live to adulthood?" To this, the sage had no answer. Al-Ashari then abandoned Mu'tazilism to follow Ibn Hanbal's school of law. In one of the dramatic moments of Islamic history, al-Ash'ari, on the day after Ramadan in the year 912, is said to have stood on the steps of the pulpit of the great mosque of Basra. Tearing off his robe, he cried aloud: "As I cast away this garment, so do I renounce what I formerly believed."[14]

Yet al-Ash'ari did not discredit all use of reason in Islam. Acknowledging reason's usefulness to metaphysics, he applied it himself to repudiate the Mu'tazilite position on the Quran's creation and mankind's free will. On matters of law, however, al-Ash'ari endorsed the orthodox principle that tradition alone served as a valid source of authority.

In preserving, while limiting, the application of reason, Al-Ash'ari widened the gap between legal and speculative thought in Islam. Orthodoxy tolerated reason's use in metaphysics, a subject in which it had little interest. At the same time al-Ash'ari, in stigmatizing reason's role in making law, strengthened orthodoxy in the province it cared about most.

Traditionists took satisfaction, in fact, in al-Ash'ari's dualism. Its orthodox conclusions, dressed in fresh arguments, only facilitated their work. In extirpating the influence of the Greeks from the law, Al-Ash'ari helped assure the triumph of a traditionist *shari'a*. The surviving remnant of Mu'tazilism proved no obstacle to the spread of the traditionist vision.

Mu'tazilism endured vestigially for another century or two, influential in philosophy but far from Islam's main current. As it faded, there rose in Europe the school called scholasticism, dedicated as the

Mu'tazilites had been to the reconciliation of faith and reason. It was inspired by the same Greek thinkers, translated now into Latin from Arabic, who had inspired the Mu'tazilites. Scholastics also owed a debt to the work of the Arab philosophers, Avicenna and Averroes, Mu'tazilism's heirs.

As a force behind scholasticism, Mu'tazilism, it might be argued, enjoyed a second wind in the West. It may also have been an influence when the Renaissance exploded in scholasticism's wake with the ideas that made the modern world. But in Islam, Mu'tazilism was by then no longer a force.

Though Mu'tazilism was itself far from secular, it was the closest that Islamic culture ever came to unleashing a secular movement of intellectual reform. It never completely disappeared from Islamic memory: Muhammad Abduh in Egypt, at the beginning of our own century, was consciously affected by it. But before the Abbasid era was over, the competition between reason and traditionism for the intellectual leadership of Islam had been settled for all time. In walking away from the Mu'tazilites, Muslims made a decision with which Islamic civilization has lived ever since.

· IV ·

THE TRADITIONIST Muhammad ibn Idris al-Shafi is known to history as the *shari'a*'s preeminent contributor. A Hashemite, distantly related to the Prophet, al-Shafi was born in the seaport town of Gaza in Palestine in 767. But, raised in the austerity of Mecca, he spent much time among the bedouins, imbibing their culture.

As a teacher in Yemen, he dabbled in Shi'ite politics and was taken prisoner by Abbasid forces in a skirmish with Shi'ite dissidents in 803. He arrived in Baghdad at a time when the talk of a Sunni-Shi'ite reconciliation was everywhere. Pardoned by Harun al-Rashid, he resumed his studies, and later became a teacher of classical traditionism. Al-Shafi died during al-Ma'mun's reign in Cairo, where his tomb remains an object of popular veneration.

Like other seminal traditionists, al-Shafi could not be called original, much less innovative. Such terms, in their Islamic context, would in any case be considered disparaging. Al-Shafi put his own formidable intellectual powers to confirming tradition as the principal component of Islamic law. His genius resided in imparting a new orientation to traditionist thought, laying the foundation of the system that has since endured.

Al-Shafi maintained that there were not just two—Quran and tradition—but four sources of Islamic law.

The Quran, a divine authority though limited in scope, was naturally the first. There was also the consensus of believers (*ijma*), which in theory referred to the entire Muslim community but in practice became a consultation among scholars. A third source was reasoning by analogy (*qiyas*), which al-Shafi regarded as useful for filling occasional gaps in the law, but lacking the divine quality which he believed the legal system required.

The most important source, he argued, was the Prophet himself. At a time when the companions were still part of the debate, al-Shafi's arguments in behalf of the Prophet were a groundbreaking contribution to the development of the law.

We might speculate that al-Shafi's youthful flirtation with Shi'ism, enemy of the first three caliphs, influenced his predisposition to the Prophet. Like al-Ma'mun, his caliph, al-Shafi probably aspired to repair the Sunni-Shi'ite breach. But as a traditionist, he took issue with al-Ma'mun on the importance of reason, and he especially disliked the Mu'tazilites.

Al-Shafi's thinking cannot be understood without reference to his opposition to Mu'tazilism. His teaching entered the public discourse at a time when the Mu'tazilites were politically ascendant. To al-Shafi, the Mu'tazilites' Greek inspiration was a stain on Islam, and to overcome it he had to promote an authority with even greater inherent appeal. Neither the "living tradition" nor the companions would do, but the Prophet was revered by Sunnis and Shi'ites alike. Al-Shafi's embrace of Muhammad's omnipotence appealed to the Shi'ites, and thereby proved to be an excellent anti-Mu'tazilite strategy.

Al-Shafi had problems with his fellow traditionists, however. Earlier scholars had rejected Muhammad as an authority on the grounds that one man's practices did not make a tradition. The Quran had told them, after all, that Muhammad was just a messenger, and a human like others. Al-Shafi argued that in the verse which commands "Obey God and the Prophet," the Quran established Muhammad as Islam's eternal guide. God, he contended, meant this command not just during Muhammad's lifetime but for all time.

Al-Shafi recognized Muhammad as second in authority only to God Himself—and, to the dismay of many believers, not second in all cases. Conventional jurists had held that the Prophet's *sunna*, if it had validity at all, was superseded by the word of God. Al-Shafi maintained that the sequence of God-first-Muhammad-second only confused the schools of law and puzzled believers, and so required major reconsideration.

So vast were the powers that God conveyed to the Prophet in the Quran, al-Shafi argued, and so great Muhammad's wisdom, that he clearly outranked other sources of law. Al-Shafi even had the audacity to hold that when the Prophet's *hadith* differed from the written rules of the Quran, Muhammad had the authority to overrule God. Al-Shafi argued that the Prophet, as God's delegate, had established traditions to cover all aspects of human conduct.

Al-Shafi's claim upset most traditionists no less than everyday believers. But he is said to have made his case so skillfully that the doubters were forced to submit. Al-Shafi failed to persuade the Shi'ites to accept a system of law free of the *rashidun* and return to the fold. But in resolving the long-standing dispute over the source of traditions, the principal obstacle to finishing the *shari'a,* his undertaking was a huge success.

By the time he died in 820, al-Shafi had won over his most prominent student, Ibn Hanbal, who had delivered the mortal blow to Mu'tazilism in resisting the *mihnah.* Other prominent converts followed and, within a few decades, al-Shafi's ideas had been absorbed by all of Muslim jurisprudence.[15]

Al-Shafi, having erected the scaffolding for the *shari'a,* left it to others to lay the bricks. Once his theory was adopted, the traditionist schools had no shortage of disciples willing to seek out *hadith,* the individual sayings and acts attributed to Muhammad. Their call touched off a frenetic search that would last for the remainder of the ninth century, producing a huge literature of Prophetic precedents. It also established a scholarly specialty in collecting, verifying and classifying the *hadith.*

The seekers of the *hadith* were not jurists but legal reporters, whose voyages of discovery took them to every corner of the Islamic world. Some researchers were very serious about this work; for others, it was sport. Given the competitive atmosphere that the process engendered, most researchers emphasized quantity; few made qualitative distinctions. Together, the researchers returned home with some 600,000 samples of Prophetic maxims.

Understandably, the process had its skeptics. Muhammad had died two centuries before the search began, and any saying attributed to him would have had to pass from one mouth to another at least a half dozen times, and usually many more. Believers were tempted by the prestige of giving testimony about the Prophet, and no doubt they embellished what they knew. As one contemporary observer said, "I have come to the conclusion that a true believer is never so ready to lie as in matters of the *hadith*."[16]

Indeed, traditionism, as far back as the "living tradition," had had its doubters. The Umayyads trumped up traditions to serve political ends, but they were only the first. Apart from the deliberate forgeries, there was the problem of witnesses' subjectivity and the outright failings of memory. The Mu'tazilites focused on the flaws to mock the entire process, but even conventional Muslims admitted to serious questions.

Islamic scholarship never developed a technique for confirming the authenticity of *hadith*. Obviously, none was available. The closest scholars came was to set rules for verifying the chain of transmission (*isnad*), from the Prophet's act or assertion to the researcher's transcription. These rules led to a classification system, the "science of the *hadith*," which established categories ranging from "sound" to "weak" to "mendacious." But it hardly inoculated the process from error.

Al-Shafi recognized there would be problems with *hadith* transcribed two hundred years after the Prophet's death, but he was undaunted. He never admitted that the quest for a perfect body of law might be disqualified by the imperfection of the sources. N. J. Coulson, a British specialist in Islamic law, also takes a tolerant view. He dismisses the later scholarship, most of it non-Muslim, which cast doubt on the reliability of *hadith*. He takes for granted that most of the statements attributed to the Prophet are apocryphal. But, he contends, the *hadith* as a body reflect the values of the era, and so might well represent what the Prophet would have said or done. In that sense, Coulson maintains, the *hadith* are authentic.

However one judges this question, by the end of the ninth century six great collections, containing tens of thousands of *hadith*, had been published. To this day, their reliability is debated, though they remain central to how Muslim believers conduct their lives. These *hadith* became the raw material of the *shari'a*. The traditionists had pronounced them sound and declared them juridically binding.[17]

Once the *hadith* were collected, the traditionists initiated the deliberations known to history as *ijtihad*—from *jihad*, in the sense of "personal judgment" or "struggle." *Ijtihad* refers to the analytical process undertaken by the scholars to transform the raw material into the comprehensive body of law at the heart of Islam.

The deliberations followed the well-established procedure which required that all differences be settled by consensus. Once consensus was reached and the pronouncement made that "we follow this," the dossier on any given matter could not be reopened. The Prophet himself, it was said, had given his stamp to this consensus, declaring in one of his best-known *hadith*, "My community shall never agree on an error."

The *ulama* interpreted these words to mean that whatever their deliberations produced was infallible. Once a law was established, it had no appeal. It was then recorded in manuals, accessible to all Muslims. On exhausting the available body of *hadith*, the scholars declared the *shari'a* finished. When they said "finished," furthermore, they meant finished for all time.

"The door of *ijtihad* was closed" is an expression known to all Arabs. It refers to the period from the end of the ninth century to the beginning of the tenth, when Islam's most distinguished scholars pronounced what they said to be the last word on the law. After that, nothing remained to be established.

At that point the exercise of *ijtihad* gave way to the duty called *taqlid*, "the acceptance of the truth," required of all believers. Henceforth Islamic jurists were required to apply without question the *sunna* of the Prophet, as presented in the *shari'a*. Believers had a similar obligation to obey.

Since the closing of the door of *ijtihad*, Islamic scholars have added little beyond ornamentation to the tenets written by al-Shafi's disciples. The *ulama* have settled disputes, conducted trials and served as watchdogs, all based on avoiding the risk of change. Many Islamic scholars have written learned disquisitions, elucidating one point or another of law, but few of them have tried to reopen the door. On each of the rare occasions of challenge, according to the Muslim scholar Fazlur Rahman, orthodoxy has shown a remarkable "shock-absorbing capacity" to bury without a trace any threats to the status quo.

The work that al-Shafi initiated is the vehicle through which Muslims express their faith. It has preserved through the generations an almost corporeal link between the Prophet and believers. Observance of the law provides Muslims with visible religious credentials, much like battle ribbons. The highest term of approval that the society conveys to a believer is *salafi*—"one who imitates the Prophet."[18]

The *shari'a* possesses immense authority, to which secular governments, however reluctantly, defer. Its rocklike certainties, as much as anything else, explain the capacity for survival that Islamic civilization has demonstrated over the difficult centuries since the Abbasid age. In imparting to Muslims a strong sense of God's will, the *shari'a* is surely the foundation of the society's remarkable stability.

But Muslims, it is fair to add, have paid heavily for the comfort the *shari'a* has brought. Islamic law, bound to a fleeting moment which purports to have witnessed mankind's apotheosis, has limited the culture's vision. The message of the law is that the highest human aspiration lies in re-creating the distant experience of the Prophet. In de-legitimizing the search for a society grounded in modern values, new methods and a sense of enlarged possibilities on earth, it shackles the Islamic mind.

The *shari'a*, as a guide to the conduct of life, has turned a civilization that once shone brilliantly away from the future. The Arabs proved their genius, beyond any doubt, in Abbasid times. Where have the originality and creativity of that era vanished? A strong case can be argued that they were locked away in a storehouse of ideas by the triumphant traditionists, whose rigid concept of the law still governs the Arab world.

· V ·

VIA THE *SUNNA* of the Prophet, the *shari'a* blankets Islamic life. The Prophet's precedents apply not only to life's grand concerns but to its trivialities, like social manners, forms of greeting and items of dress. Islamic scholars point out that true Muslim believers regard the *shari'a* less as a diverse set of laws than as "the whole duty of man."[19]

Joseph Schacht, a Columbia University expert in Islamic law, wrote a quarter century ago that the *shari'a* leaves little to individual judgment. It informs the pious Muslim not only "what his religious duties are [and] what makes him ritually clean or unclean, [but] what he may eat or drink, how to dress and how to treat his family, and generally what he may with good conscience regard in the widest sense as lawful acts and possessions."

The Hungarian scholar Ignaz Goldziher says that the *shari'a* provides instructions on how to respond to someone who sneezes; it determines the permissibility of wearing a gold ring. Ibn Hanbal—who himself collected and published 29,000 *hadith*—refused to eat watermelon, on the grounds that there was no precedent of the Prophet's eating such a food. Some Muslim clerics are said, for the same reasons, to be unreconciled even now to the use of the knife and fork.

Unlike legal systems that are the arm of the state, the *shari'a* is essentially self-enforcing. God, under the *shari'a*, is in most cases—

though not all—the enforcer, determining the fate of each in the afterlife according to the number and seriousness of the sins committed. This gives Muslims, even in states ruled by Islamic law, some flexibility over which provisions they choose to observe and which they do not. But believers recognize that whatever choice they make will be judged by God on the Last Day.

The *shari'a*, for example, contains no earthly penalty even for the Muslim who eats pork or fails to fast on Ramadan, very basic Islamic tenets. In Saudi Arabia and Iran, both Islamic states, the authorities have assumed the power to enforce many of these provisions. But the *shari'a*, nonetheless, reserves payment to the afterlife for a large proportion of human sins.

Some legal scholars, for this reason, argue that the *shari'a* is not law at all. A code linked only to a set of moral imperatives based on ideals of behavior does not, these scholars say, meet the definition of law. The description is a reminder that the *shari'a* is, before anything else, a Muslim's compact not with the state but with God.

But to regard it as only a moral code overstates its limits. Offenses classed by the Quran as affronts to God (*hudud*)—adultery and false allegations of adultery, wine drinking, theft and highway robbery— explicitly require penalties. The penalties specified in the Quran are death for adultery, lashing for drinking and amputation of the hand for theft. The community is expected to apply these penalties, and application is in theory the responsibility of all believers. In practice, however, the authority for enforcement usually devolves upon the state.

The Quran, curiously, does not specify the penalty for homicide. Its silence is no doubt a vestige of the principle of family retaliation inscribed in the *lex talionis,* the law that governed the Arabian tribes in Muhammad's time. The *shari'a* fills in the gap left by the Quran in many such matters, but the responsibilities of the state have nonetheless often been left unclear.

The *shari'a* is never far from pre-Islamic practice. It makes no provision for monetary fines, for instance, and it regards prison as a place not for punishment but for repentance. It treats accidental homicide as did the tribesmen of Arabia, as a private matter to be resolved by agreement between the victim's family and the perpetrator.

More complicated is apostasy, condemned repeatedly by the Quran but without citing an earthly penalty. The ambiguity was illustrated in Chapter 2, in the debate among Islamic jurists over the killing of Farag Foda. The orthodox Islamic position, however, accepts the *hadith* in which the Prophet says, "Whoever changes his religion, kill him."[20]

Exhaustive as the *shari'a* is on rules of personal conduct, on matters of politics it seems to make its point by what it leaves unsaid. Notwithstanding the fundamentalists' contention that Muslims can live religiously only in an Islamic state, nowhere does the *shari'a* enjoin the establishment of such a state.

On the contrary, the law, as stated earlier, assumes a natural antagonism between the *ulama* and the state. The makers of the *shari'a* were indifferent to the form that government took. The *shari'a* requires simply that the state be just and offer no obstacles to the practice of the faith. The traditionists never confused the *shari'a* with a political constitution.

That is not to say that the law has no impact on politics. Many states within Islam have seen fit throughout history to apply the *shari'a*, in part if not in whole. Some rulers have routinely acknowledged curbs on their power based on the *ulama*'s claim of moral authority to review the *shari'a*'s enforcement. Others have resisted such curbs, or rejected them outright.

Over the course of history the *shari'a*, in promoting religious over temporal supremacy, has probably weakened Muslim political systems. It has surely weakened the believer's sense of loyalty and responsibility to the state.

"If there is an action on the part of a caliph and a contrary tradition from the Prophet . . . ," al-Shafi wrote, "that action must be rejected in favor of the tradition from the Prophet." Imbued by its creators with divine perfection, the *shari'a* has denied what is generally regarded as sovereignty's fundamental attribute: the duty to make and enforce law. This loss, distancing the state from the realities of everyday life, has paralyzed normal political development.

It is true that no state, Muslim or otherwise, has been able to ignore everyday reality. Political institutions need some freedom to respond to change, whatever the *shari'a* says. Islam's way, however, has not been to legitimize lawmaking but to fictionalize it.

The process even acquired a name, *hiyal,* which is defined as "legal fictions." States regularly designate new laws, with the *ulama*'s consent, as "regulations to enforce the *shari'a.*" Islamic officials make fanciful legal interpretations to justify them. Banks evade the Quran's explicit ban on interest, for example, by resorting to financial tricks.[21] No Muslim is fooled by such actions, and fundamentalist reformers routinely denounce them. But they enable Muslim states to claim fidelity to the letter of the *shari'a*, even while wringing out the Islamic spirit.

Ironically, the case can be made that the *shari'a*, even while debilitating the state, has also laid the groundwork for despotism. This was

not the intention of the traditionists, who regarded the law's autonomy as a barrier to tyranny. In designing the *shari'a* as an essentially
moral force, however, they left a vacuum of power that states typically
rushed in to fill. In failing to provide for positive law enforcement, the
traditionists also failed to provide positive curbs on state tyranny.

It should be no surprise that, throughout history, governments
have promoted the *hadith* that best serve their power. In a legal system
ruled by hundreds of thousands of prophetic assertions, one might
expect that the strongest forces in the society would decide which ones
matter and which do not. In effect, many governments have crafted
their own *shari'a,* on the basis of the *hadith* that suit them.

Among the most frequently cited are the Prophet's counsels against
rebellion. One hears little from the Islamic governments of Saudi Arabia or Sudan, for example, of the *hadith* that authorize resistance to
political injustice.

"You must pray even behind a sinner," Muhammad said. Since the
ruler conventionally leads the Friday prayer, this *hadith* means that
Muhammad enjoins loyalty to the existing regime, whatever the
ruler's misconduct. Another hadith that governments have popularized is: "One day many, very many, evils will arise in my community,
but he who undertakes to split the common cause of the Muslims is to
be killed with the sword."[22]

When I inquired about popular dissatisfaction in Saudi Arabia during my visit there—described in Chapter 7—officials cited these *hadith*
to illustrate that good Muslims would never presume to challenge
their leaders.

In yet another *hadith*, the Prophet commands: "Do not insult those
who govern you. . . . If they act badly the sin rests with them and
you must be patient." These words sanction despotism, as long as the
despots are willing to take their chances on God's judgment on the
Last Day. As for the believers, they are told to accept their earthly fate,
while waiting for reward in the afterlife.

Patience in the face of injustice is, in fact, a theme that threads
insistently through the *shari'a*. The *hadith* that command passivity add
weight to the doctrine that God predestines humans to their fate—
examined in the discussion of the Quran in Chapter 2. The passivity
that pervades Islamic culture is persuasive evidence of the impact of
such *hadith*. It is no coincidence that the Arab masses have nearly
always been docile in confronting oppression, at least the oppression
of Muslim governments. In this sense, the *shari'a*, whatever its services
to justice, has also promoted injustice. Both belong to the heritage
that the traditionists have left to Islamic society.

· VI ·

UNTIL THE EIGHTEENTH CENTURY, Islamic society was so isolated from the outside world, and so static within, that the *shari'a*, using the various stratagems (*hiyal*) at its command, accommodated comfortably whatever changes in law were required.[23]

But in 1798, Napoleon—taking advantage of the Ottoman Empire's accelerating decline—occupied Ottoman Egypt, setting off shock waves. Since then, Islam's involvement with the West has been unrelieved, and calls for legal reform, notwithstanding the *shari'a*, have resonated across the Middle East.

The Turks were the first to experiment. Their early reforms, based on Western codes, concentrated on the areas of trade and finance, where Muslims often encountered the West. The Islamic establishment, trying desperately to hold the line, contested most of the reforms but was steadily beaten back.

The early reforms took place under the cover of revisions in administrative regulations. But Muslims recognized the changes as a foreign graft on their ancient trunk. What emerged was a dual system, consisting of Western codes plus a residue of the *shari'a*, a compromise which left the community generally confused.

The *ulama* succeeded almost everywhere in saving the *shari'a*'s hold over family law, particularly the provisions dealing with women and children.[24] They also managed to preserve the death penalty for apostasy, which they linked to safeguarding Islam. They were less successful in criminal law, which by the end of the nineteenth century had been modified throughout most of the Middle East to correspond with Western procedures.

Legal scholars agree, however, that, psychologically, most of the Western grafts have made very little impact. Coulson, the British specialist, says the era's reforms had an "opportunistic character," imparting a feeling of transience. "The fortress of traditional law," he wrote, "had been breached beyond repair, but the complex structure that had taken its place did not yet rest upon solid foundations."

Certainly none of the reforms were incorporated on the basis of *ijtihad*, a scholarly rethinking of the *shari'a*. Besieged, Muslim authorities were more willing to swallow foreign codes than to tamper with Islamic law. The *shari'a*, though bloodied by the reformers, largely survived the attacks, and continued to exercise its moral influence over the culture.[25]

Muhammad Abduh, Egypt's grand *mufti* as the nineteenth century ended, was among the Muslims who recognized that reforms were needed to reverse their society's decay. Much of the Arab world, Egypt included, was then occupied by Christian armies. Arab students, turning their backs on Islamic education, were flocking to European universities. Abduh understood that too little had changed in Islam since Napoleon's arrival. In fact, the gap with the West, by any measure, had grown wider. Abduh saw a danger that Islam itself would be a casualty of the Western presence.

Abduh proposed the first serious effort in a thousand years to reconsider the *shari'a*. He was no secularist, and he did not seek to Westernize *shari'a* law. He also recognized that Islam faced a dilemma in trying to take what it needed from the West while preserving its integrity. Abduh never gave up his commitment to the *shari'a*. But he believed that many of its layers could be peeled off without placing the faith in jeopardy.

In combining piety with an openness to inspiration from outside Islam, Abduh shared much with the Mu'tazilites. He was conscious himself of the parallel, and seems even to have been influenced by the doctrines. He declared openly that reason was central to advancing the human condition and that disdain for reason was at the root of Islamic decline. But he distanced himself from public identification with Mu'tazilism. Orthodox circles still regarded the Mu'tazilites as heretics, and sought to discredit Abduh's proposals by labeling them "neo-Mu'tazilite."[26]

Much of Abduh's personal credibility lay in his belonging to two groups whose outlook on the world had changed curiously little since Abbasid times: the *ulama* and the Muslim masses. He was born into a pious family in the Nile delta, long the cradle of Egyptian leadership. Educated in mosque schools, he rebelled against the rote memorization that characterized Islamic learning. He nonetheless went on to Al-Azhar, Islam's official university, where he studied logic and mystical theology.

In Cairo, Abduh became a disciple of Jamal ad-Din al-Afghani, a modernist reformer and nationalist agitator. This led to his forced exile from Egypt. In London and Beirut, Abduh absorbed European thought and refined his activist theology. On returning home, he was appointed a judge, and then Grand Mufti, the highest official of the *shari'a* courts.

As political thinker, Abduh speculated that the masses, while historically submissive to Muslim despots, could be roused to action against Christian rule. He put the *shari'a* to an unfamiliar kind of political service, citing *hadith* that favored the overthrow of an unjust ruler.

Abduh's pleading helped to bring religion into the struggle against colonial oppression.

In theology, Abduh challenged orthodoxy with no less vigor. The *ulama*, he maintained, must repudiate the notion that the door to *ijtihad* was closed. *Ijtihad*, the creative use of the mind, must rebuild the faith on the basis of Islam's seminal values, which had been distorted by traditionism. *Hadith* that have no bearing on the times should be discarded. Islam, he argued, offered lessons from within itself, if only Muslims practiced *ijtihad* to perceive what was applicable in the *shari'a* to modern times.

Abduh argued that the *ulama* had grossly distorted Islam over the centuries. Islam, he said, not only permitted but required innovation. Reason, he maintained, was not just an option but a Quranic imperative. Abduh sought to persuade Muslims that Islam was served, not threatened, by Western scientific thought.

Abduh also tried softening the rigidly Prophet-centered vision of the *shari'a*, echoing Mu'tazilism in urging a more humanistic orientation to the law. Muslims need not abandon the *shari'a*, Abduh argued. Islamic scholars, he wrote, had to weigh the Quran and the traditions of the Prophet "in the scales of human reason . . . so that God's wisdom may be fulfilled and the order of the human world preserved."

Islam, Abduh believed, was poised to build a prosperous and dynamic Islamic community. The obstacle, he said, was that too few believers were willing to reexamine the meaning that orthodoxy had placed on God's words a millennium ago.

Abduh may not have been a modern man in the Western sense, but he understood the problem of Islamic civilization. Reform of the *shari'a*, he said, would do more than make law compatible with the requirements of the times. He saw it also as a channel to something more important: preparing the Islamic mind to escape its medieval shackles.

The problem Abduh faced as a reformer was that Muslims were not, on the whole, prepared to escape medievalism. Most were satisfied to cling to Islam as it was. Abduh did not deny that it would be painful for Muslims to transform old habits of the intellect, but he miscalculated the number willing to endure the pain. Wherever he turned he encountered resistance to the transformation that he proposed. Most Muslims, he learned, were no readier for changes in Islamic orthodoxy than they had been in Mu'tazilite times. Abduh's modernist disciples find them no readier today.

6

Khomeini's Triumph

· I ·

I WAS SURE I KNEW what I would find when I arrived in Teheran for the first time in the spring of 1996. Its reputation had preceded me. After seventeen years, Ayatollah Khomeini's Islamic revolution was, I knew, still brimming with zealotry.

Iran is neither culturally nor ethnically Arab but, since Islam's early days, its ardor has influenced the faith. I wanted to visit there to learn about Shi'ism, the schism that began soon after the Prophet's death. Shi'ites, though a small minority of Muslims, have had a huge impact on Islam's course. It might even be argued that one can understand Sunnis only by contrasting them with Shi'ites. Since overthrowing a secular monarchy, Shi'ism has also been offering lessons to those Arabs who believe their own future lies in establishing a fundamentalist Islamic state.

So, primed for fanaticism, I was not surprised at the airport by a sign at passport control which said, DEATH TO AMERICA, a slogan directed at the erstwhile Shah's chief supporter. Seated in a cab on my way to town, I spied a banner hanging over the street that proclaimed: HEJAB IS DIGNITY, referring to one of the revolution's dress symbols. In my hotel, even as the bearded clerks warmly welcomed me, I was notified by a wall poster that WE WILL INFLICT ON AMERICA A SEVERE DEFEAT. The next morning a taxi took me down Khalid Islambouli Avenue, named for the Egyptian fundamentalist who led the assassins of Egypt's secular President, Anwar Sadat. That's Teheran, I told myself, gritting my teeth.

But from then on the unexpected took over.

Visually, Teheran looked to me more like an Eastern European than a Middle Eastern city. The boulevards were wide and clean, the traffic heavy but well regulated. I saw few limousines, fewer beggars, and scarcely any presence of the army.

The pedestrians bustled along, as if on their way to conduct important business. The men wore Western clothes; the women, though wrapped from head to toe in black, gave no ground on the sidewalks. Children, looking very healthy, romped in playgrounds and in deep green, well-kept parks.

Food was plentiful, both in outdoor markets and in popular restaurants, and the store windows were filled with consumer goods, including pretty dresses, cosmetics and lacy lingerie, all designated by the revolution as *haram* ("forbidden").

In the Arab world, the street scene normally conveys a certain lethargy, which suggests societies that are no more interested than Islam itself in serious change. But after a few days of rarely hearing a muezzin's call, Teheran's energy proclaimed to me that the city was hardly Islamic—in the social sense of the term—at all.

My first interview was with two political science professors at the Imam Sadeq University, situated on a campus that in the Shah's day was a branch of the Harvard Business School. Since the revolution it has been under the presidency of an ayatollah and offered a religiously oriented curriculum. The two men, in their late thirties and costumed in tweeds, were Western educated, but neither was apologetic at being back home.

The two professors agreed that the end of the Iran-Iraq War in 1988 had opened the door to a wide-ranging debate among intellectuals—unrestrained, though mostly underground—on the legitimacy of the Islamic regime. Even the clergy, backbone of the revolution, was examining the validity of the principles of absolute clerical power since Ayatollah Khomeini's death in 1989. In the classroom, they said, students scoffed at the notion that Islam had all the answers to contemporary problems. Increasingly, they maintained, the religious and secular elite talked of political pluralism as the basis of the state.

"Iran is now a fairly open society," said Hadi Semati, a 1993 Ph.D. from the University of Tennessee. "Public discussion of some subjects is still taboo—the dominance of the clergy, the Rushdie *fatwa*, the dress code for women. Though the government still tolerates no political organizing, some people think—though I am not convinced—that we will soon have political parties.

"Undoubtedly, however, secularism is rising and people are raising questions about Islam. Political magazines, if they are discreet, can discuss sensitive issues. Any time intellectuals get together over coffee, they compete in denouncing government policies. The atmosphere has changed since Khomeini's death."

Semati was mistaken in suggesting that Iran had opened up for good, however. A few months after my visit, reports coming out of the country revealed that a crackdown on dissent was under way. Steady liberalization seemed less likely than periodic ups and downs, depending on who was on top in political power struggles. I had the good fortune to make my visit during one of the ups.

Then, in May 1997, a cleric named Mohammed Khatami was elected President of Iran, having campaigned on a platform of political and cultural moderation. I never heard Khatami's name during my visit. Most Iranians assumed that President Ali Akbar Rafsanjani would be succeeded by Ali Akbar Nateq-Nouri, the extremely conservative Speaker of the Parliament. Khatami not only defeated Nateq-Nouri in a free election, however, but he owed his victory largely to the votes of women.

"The experience of governing has undermined absolutism," Semati had said in our talk; and Khatami's victory seemed to vindicate him. "So did the cease-fire with Iraq, which was a humiliating defeat. Having accepted huge sacrifices—a million casualties, including 400,000 dead—for what we were told was a holy *jihad,* the people suddenly discovered that God did not defeat Satan, who was Saddam Hussein. Out of this trauma emerged a different perception of the clergy and of the state."

Semati argued that Iran, even while idolizing Khomeini, had never reached a consensus on Islamic rule. Khomeini's vision of clerical government was based on Islamic theories that were disputed even by much of the clergy. Mehdi Bazargan, the revolution's first Prime Minister, had called for a democratic state with, at most, clerical guidance. Ali Shariati, an influential thinker of the prerevolutionary era, had advocated an Islamic state based not on clerical power but on social justice and egalitarian ideals.

The current favorite of reformers, Semati said, was Abdolkarim Soroosh, a Muslim thinker who questions Khomeini's authoritarian premises. He has been compared in Iran with Martin Luther, for challenging the clergy's political monopoly.

"Soroosh is reexamining the basic texts of Islam, where our politics has its roots," Semati said. "His background is in the philosophy of science, and he was an early supporter of the revolution. A very religious man himself, he now says Khomeini's absolutism is only one of many ways to interpret Islam.

"Most of my students like his being both religious and open-minded. The government recently banned Soroosh from television, but he still writes and teaches. His influence is growing."

Javad Tabatabai, a tall, slim man in his forties, is a specialist in Islamic law, working at the Encyclopedia Islamica, a government publication and research center. Tabatabai was also an irrepressible critic of the Islamic state, which in 1994 fired him as a professor at Teheran University. Iran, unlike Iraq, has a tradition of intellectual freedom, however, and for several weeks, he said, students and teachers demonstrated in protest. Though never hired back by the university, he said, he was offered compensating work at the Encyclopedia.

Tabatabai, like most Iranians, feels no nostalgia for the Shah, despite his cheerful prediction that the Islamic regime is doomed. Iran's language is religious, he said, but its spirit is political. The Shah's regime was totalitarian, he said, but unfortunately, the regime was too identified with America for the opposition to consider Western democracy as an alternative. Religion was the opposition's only available weapon, and now that it has become an instrument of oppression, the people are unwilling to put up with it. The Islamic state, he said, will not survive another decade.

"Khomeini seized upon the idea of theocracy," he said, "proposing to use the clergy as agents of the Prophet. Making Iran into an Islamic state meant transforming Islam into a political faith. This government will never legitimize a secular opposition, so it will never evolve. It will stay as it is, or fall.

"Khomeini, like the Shah, was a political, not a religious, man. Most religious leaders had reservations about his ideas but abandoned them under repression, and dissidence still runs into the wall of government power.

"But the regime has no real legitimacy, and the crisis is growing. Some cities are already in revolt. Khomeini's personality was strong enough to keep the system intact, but he did not succeed in showing that Islam could govern. If the state falls, Islam will pay the price."

In a society that bans opposition parties, Ebrahim Yazdi leads a nebulous organization called the Freedom Movement. Created in the 1960s, it survives on the reputation of its founder, Mehdi Bazargan, a respected Islamic reformer whom the Shah kept in prison for six years for opposition activities. Bazargan, named Prime Minister by Khomeini, resigned soon after the revolution to protest Khomeini's refusal to call off the popular occupation of the U.S. Embassy.

When Bazargan died in 1994, Soroosh spoke at his commemoration, but the state, fearful of his popularity, would permit no public ceremony. Yazdi, who had been Foreign Minister in Bazargan's short-lived government, succeeded him as the Freedom Movement's head.

"We left the government in 1979 when we saw the direction in which it was moving," said Yazdi in his spacious home in prosperous north Teheran. "Our movement had been instrumental in making the revolution, as a member of the coalition that brought Khomeini to power. We are loyal to it still. But we think that, since the revolution was pluralistic, the state should be too.

"We stood by the regime in the war with Iraq until our troops drove the Iraqis from our soil. Then we advocated a cease-fire because the nation was no longer in danger. But Khomeini went with the hard-liners, who have dominated ever since.

"We also dispute the view that Khomeini's constitution is the word of God. We disapprove of *velayat-e faqih,* his authoritarian philosophy, which he contended was above the law, and we think it must be changed. The Islamic Republic must find a way to absorb what is valuable not just inside but outside Islam.

"The Freedom Movement is democratic, and so it rejects an electoral system in which the government must approve every candidate. We protest the restrictions the government imposes on the people and the press. The clergy that makes up the government is not evil but it does not understand democracy, and will not put up with organized opposition. It does not understand how much turbulence lies beneath the surface of our society."

Yazdi repeated the dark assessments I often heard in Iran of the government's performance: widespread corruption, nepotism, cronyism; inflation ranging from 50 to as high as 100 percent; economic reform succumbing to inflated state budgets, bloated public industries and a currency that loses value daily. The mullahs, he said, have proven as proficient at graft as were the Shah's officials. Disturbances, directed at the government, erupt sporadically in Teheran as well as the provinces. Many Iranians, Yazdi said, feel that no one is in control.

I met with Abdolkarim Soroosh, the intellectual luminary, in the cluttered office of a small publishing firm in north Teheran, where he does his writing. A slight, balding, unprepossessing man, he speaks with a soft voice in a clear English that dates from his postdoctoral studies in the philosophy of science at the University of London.

Soroosh told me that, after six years abroad, he returned to Teheran as the revolution was picking up momentum. He was captivated by Khomeini, who, soon afterward, named him to a committee to set the terms for reforming and reopening the universities, which had been closed for two years for being insufficiently Islamic. But he soon tired of the task, he said, largely because religious radicals had come to dominate the campuses.

During the 1980s, while not writing and teaching, he spent his time giving lectures on religion in mosques and on television. When I arrived to see him, he was clearly falling from favor and was permitted far fewer public appearances.

"I still support Imam Khomeini and can't resist praising him," Soroosh said, "but he was a human being, and so a fallible man. What is worse, the clergy who made the revolution are intellectually stagnant, leaving Islam in an intellectual straitjacket. They are suspicious of educated people, particularly those who have studied in the West. They want you to be 100 percent with them. If not, you do not have their confidence.

"My quarrel is not with the clergy as such, any more than it is with the government. I am not a political man and I was not a fifth column in the cultural revolution. I am challenging Islamic orthodoxy, and trying to introduce new ideas, but the clergy who run the government see me as a political threat."

Soroosh, of course, was stretching in denying that he was a political man. Khomeini's authoritarianism, he argued, is a misstatement of Islam. Iran needs full democracy, he said, within a free and open society. The government is remiss, he contended, in failing to attend to education and the economy. Soroosh may not have been a candidate for office, but his concerns were very political.

Yet Soroosh described himself as a believer, even a mystic, and he argued the need for Islam to establish an ethical social order. Religion's real domain is the next life, he said, not this one. He challenged the orthodox tenet that the Quran and the scriptures contain all the knowledge that is required to solve the problems of modern society. They may set boundaries for human conduct, he maintained, but they cannot replace reason and the scientific method as tools for dealing with daily life.

"Islamic scriptures say your hand should be cut off for stealing," Soroosh said, "but they do not guide you to be happy and prosperous, to avoid stealing. I have studied Islam under the *ulama* and my credentials are not often questioned. I am a good Muslim, and I pray five times a day. I have learned Islam's strengths and limitations, and I do not think Islam is all-powerful. On the contrary, the danger of the Islamic revolution is that its failures will give Islam a perpetual bad name."

Soroosh lamented that the West is "homocentric," having lost its spiritual core. But he criticized those Muslims who turn their backs on the West or, what is worse, who are intimidated by it. He expressed disdain for the revolution's demonizing the West, particularly the United States. Muslims, he insisted, must be "daring in selection," eclectic about what the West offers. "Islamic values," he argued, "are strong enough to guide the process."

Stating his Islamic vision metaphorically, Soroosh has written: "We do not want religion to become an impediment of science. We want religion and science to be closely linked. Religion must act as the lights do in a car and not as the brakes do."[1]

It is characteristic of Soroosh's style to contrast lights with brakes. The language in which he talks and writes is simple, which no doubt accounts for his popularity on the platform. He likes to set off his images in vivid contraposition.

"The Quran is divine," he told me, "interpretation is human. . . . The text of the scripture is silent; it is up to us to make it speak. . . . The scripture is immutable; interpretation is changeable. . . . Khomeini has two aspects: personality and theories; I am fond of his personality and I disagree with his theories."

In the year after I left Iran, Soroosh became an increasing target of political intimidation. Bands of Islamic zealots called *basijees,* typically devout youths from poor families, repeatedly harassed him during lectures. He was mugged twice.

"As a professor, how can I tell my students," he wrote in an open letter, "to be brave and to think freely . . . when I see so many things that are a sin in our community?"

The government responded by closing the magazine that published the letter. Soon afterward, Soroosh left for self-imposed exile in Britain.[2]

· II ·

IRAN IS A SHI'ITE SOCIETY, which means that it professes a form of Islam that separates it from the Arab majority of the Sunni world. About 85 percent of Muslims are Sunnis; slightly more than 10 percent are Shi'ites. Being Muslim, Shi'ites share many beliefs with the Sunni mainstream, but dividing the two are differences in both religious and political doctrine.

Westerners who read newspapers and watched television during the Khomeini revolution of 1978 and 1979 no doubt came away, as I did, with an image of Shi'ite society as peculiarly violent. At times—in taking over the American Embassy, for example—it seemed to embrace the irrational. The most that observers can say about those days is that people are not likely to be on their best behavior in the tempest of revolution.

A corrective to this impression set in for me during my visit to Iran. Only then did I entertain the possibility that normality in Iran is much like it is elsewhere. I also began to see how different Iranian culture is from the culture of the Sunni Arab world.

As I noted in Chapter 5, the origins of the breach between Sunnis and Shi'ites date back to the struggle over the succession to the Prophet Muhammad. Shi'ites do not accept the Sunni contention that Muhammad made no provision for a successor. They maintain that he indicated a clear preference for a family member to govern the Islamic community by a kind of divine right.

The Shi'ite candidate was Ali, Muhammad's cousin and the husband of his daughter Fatima. He was the closest of the Prophet's male kin. But the companions of the Prophet met in a *shura* and selected instead Abu Bakr, one of their own, as caliph. In the Shi'ite view, this was squalid power politics.

After Abu Bakr's death the *shura* successively named two more companions, Omar and Uthman, to the caliphate. Ali was preparing a military challenge when Uthman was assassinated, and in 656 the *shura* finally made Ali caliph. The moment appeared propitious to repair the breach. Instead Uthman's family, the Umayyads, went after Ali on the battlefield. In 661, Ali was himself assassinated and the Umayyads seized the throne.

Sunnis conventionally regard all four caliphs as *rashidun,* the "rightly-guided" ones. Curiously, they regard these years, tumultuous as they were, as Islam's golden age. But Shi'ites regard the first three caliphs as usurpers, and their rule as illegitimate. They consider Ali the Prophet's only valid successor.

The real barrier to reconciliation, however, was the Umayyads, who had no viable claim whatever to legitimacy. On the tenth of the Arabic month of Moharram in 680, an Umayyad force attacked and slaughtered an army led by Hussein, Ali's son, near Karbala in Iraq. Afterward, most Sunnis, albeit reluctantly, accepted Umayyad rule. The Shi'ites, however, flatly rejected it.

For the Shi'ites, the Umayyads became the sworn enemy, and Hussein's martyrdom an eternal tragedy, commemorated each year on the battle's anniversary by mass mourning. The mourning, reminding Shi'ites how distinct they are from Sunnis, includes a ritual of self-flagellation. It also proclaims Shi'ism's abiding commitment to an Islamic legitimacy based on Ali's dynasty, descending in time through his son Hussein.

While Sunnis bowed before their caliphs, Shi'ites gave their allegiance to their "Imams,"* Ali and his descendants. The two institutions were not parallel: the caliphs were temporal, ruling presumably, according to Islamic law; the Imams were Islamic scholars, the supreme guardians of the faith. The dominant Shi'ite belief, called "Twelver" Shi'ism, holds that there were only twelve Imams. The last Imam, Shi'ites believe, disappeared mysteriously in 873 and has been unheard of since.

Because the last Imam's fate is uncertain, Shi'ites refer to it as an "occultation," a hiding. Twelvers hold that Islam still lives under the reign of the Hidden Imam, who at a time of his own choosing will reappear. When he does, he will be the Mahdi—a messianic figure probably taken from Judaic or Christian belief—to rule, as the Prophet intended, over all Islam.

Though Shi'ite doctrine has spread throughout the Islamic world, Shi'ite communities have historically been most heavily concentrated on Iran's western border. As noted in Chapter 5, Shi'ites played a major role in overthrowing the Umayyads, Hussein's killers, and installing the Abassids in Baghdad in their place. Historically, however, Shi'ites have been more cautious, generally keeping a low profile, avoiding involvement in Islam-wide struggles.

Some theorists, in fact, contend that the doctrine of "occultation" was actually devised to permit Shi'ites to hold on to their beliefs without appearing to threaten the Sunni majority. Shi'ism, perhaps unique among the faiths, even has a rule called *taqiya,* which condones the dissembling of belief in a hostile environment. Yet, while taking pains to avert conflict, the Shi'ites have kept alive the grudge that divides them from the Sunni world.

Scholars contend that the doctrinal differences between Sunnis and Shi'ites lead them in opposite directions. The belief in the Mahdi's reappearance orients Shi'ism toward the future; the Sunnis' fixation on the Prophet turns them reflexively toward the past. The Imam promises Shi'ites to reappear to make a new and better world; Sunnis are taught to strive to return to the proven ways of the Prophet. These dogmas may explain why Shi'ites seem more comfortable than Sunnis with the demands of modern times.

Shi'ism assigns to the *ulama,* as surrogates for the Hidden Imam,

* Literally, "exemplar or "model." For Shi'ites, the term is the highest accolade of the faith, and when Khomeini accepted it for himself some eyebrows were raised. For Sunnis, the term refers simply to the prayer leader of a mosque. It was, however, the title also used by Saudi rulers before they called themselves kings.

the imamate's principal religious duty: interpreting the law. The Shi'ite *ulama*, like its Sunni counterpart, has historically served to check the powers of the secular state. But, unlike the Sunnis, who have closed the doors to *ijtihad*, they also assert the Mahdi's power to derive new legal norms. Shi'ism's most qualified legal interpreters are called *mujtahid*, "those who practice *ijtihad*." Unlike Sunnis, Shi'ites recognize a clerical hierarchy, which is not rigid but which the *mujtahid* dominate. Its members, though generally known as clerics, exercise their authority not as agents of God but through their knowledge of Islamic law.

Though Shi'ism's twelve Imams were considered infallible, *mujtahid* are not. Indeed, their interpretations are often disputed vigorously, both among themselves and within the society. In acting in the Mahdi's behalf, however, they enjoy in Shi'ite society a status which is far above that of the clergy of the Sunnis.

Shi'ites had no direct role in producing the *shari'a* but they generally accept it both as valid and divine. This acceptance is vindication for al-Shafi, the great traditionist, who—as noted in Chapter 5—sought to reconcile Sunnis and Shi'ites. But Shi'ites also attribute a high value to the directives that have come down from their own Imams. In addition, they reject the Sunni belief that *ijtihad* is closed, as well as the Sunni suspicion of reason; the Shi'ites honor reason not just in law but in all human affairs.

Indeed, Shi'ite thought is infused with a spirit of rationalism that is absent from Sunni doctrines. This was true in Abbasid times, when Shi'ites allied with Mu'tazilism in endorsing the use of reason. It is also true today among Shi'ites, who exalt human reason and free will far more than do the Sunnis.

In accepting the ongoing validity of *ijtihad*, Shi'ism never succumbed to the intellectual lethargy that overcame Sunnism. It is true that Shi'ism, like Sunnism, was untouched by the shock of secularism that spread the practice of rationalism through Christian culture. Yet Shi'ism, in contrast to Sunnism, found within its own resources the means to keep its beliefs open to constant rational debate.

The two, in the early days, also adopted conflicting attitudes on the nature of the state. The Sunnis devised the caliphate and imparted to its actions a divine character. To Shi'ites, the caliphate had usurped the rightful claims of Ali and his heirs to rule. When the Twelfth Imam, the last of these heirs, vanished, the Shi'ites lost their last claimant to legitimacy. Since the "occultation," they have held that, until the Mahdi appears, authority can be neither legitimate nor divine, and all government is at best a temporary improvisation.

This outlook has meant that, while accepting the Islamic premise of inseparability of religion and state, Shi'ites have accommodated over the centuries to a dualism. Shi'ites have owed permanent allegiance to no government. In the absence of a clear doctrine of legitimacy, Shi'ites have been offered by their faith a range of political options.

Until the sixteenth century, Iran was not officially a Shi'ite state. Shi'ites in Iran coexisted not only with a Sunni majority but with non-Islamic faiths. This changed when the Safavids, a militant Sufi order, chose Shi'ism to promote the goal of supplanting the Ottomans, quintessentially Sunni, as the principal power in Iran. In making Shi'ism the state religion, they upset the long-standing harmony between Shi'ite and Sunni communities, but they succeeded in establishing a dynasty that ruled Iran for two hundred years.

The Safavids achieved their objective of winning over the Iranian masses to Shi'ism by enlisting the *mujtahid* in their campaign. But though they promoted conversion to Shi'ism, the *mujtahid* refused to endorse the Safavid claim to be the surrogates of the Hidden Imam. Instead, they preserved a balance between the monarchy and themselves, acknowledging the Safavids' temporal supremacy while reaffirming their own power as the *ulama,* the unique interpreters of Islamic law.

Since Safavid times, vigorous competition between the *mujtahid* and the secular state has been a constant of Iranian history. Ayatollah Khomeini's revolution in our own time was a major triumph for the *mujtahid.* Khomeini's constitution, in fact, presumed to transform the terms of the relationship by Islamizing the state. But Iran's long tradition of withholding legitimacy has not died. As long as the Mahdi remains hidden, an Iranian consensus is unlikely, and the state will continue to be insecure.

· III ·

RUHOLLAH KHOMEINI—his given name means "inspired of God"—was born in a village south of Teheran in 1902. A son and grandson of Shi'ite scholars, he gravitated naturally into religious schools, and then into a career as an Islamic jurist, in which the excellence of his own scholarship was in time recognized. He lived for eighty-seven years, spanning almost the entire twentieth century. He was surely the most charismatic Shi'ite cleric of the age, and among Shi'ism's most audacious thinkers. But Khomeini is best understood within the context of the deep feelings of nationalism, rather than of piety, that swept through Iran during his long lifetime.

Modern Iranian nationalism made its first appearance only a decade before Khomeini's birth. Iran was then an arena of competition between Russia, pressing southward toward the Persian Gulf, and Britain, determined to protect its maritime trade routes to India. Iran's problem—unlike, say, Egypt's and Algeria's—was not that it was under colonial rule. But its government, while Iranian, was so weak that it could not stand up to escalating British and Russian demands.

When the Shah, in 1891, sought to curry Britain's favor by granting a monopoly on tobacco to a British company, Iran's clergy organized a massive protest. In alliance with the merchant class, the clergy achieved an almost unanimous boycott of tobacco products, and the Shah was forced to cancel the grant. But the monarchy was not chastised. Self-indulgent and constantly in need of loans, it extended other concessions to foreign powers, surrendering its sovereignty bit by bit.

Khomeini was still a child when London and Moscow, in response to a growing threat from Germany, composed their differences and divided Iran into spheres of influence. All Iranians had difficulty bearing the humiliation of its government being forced to the margins of internal political control.

In 1905 the Iranian masses, led largely by the clergy, rose up in protest against their government. The rebellion won a constitution, a parliament (*majlis*) and a variety of political freedoms. The constitution was not secular; it affirmed the preeminence of Shi'ite Islam and the *ulama*'s right to review legislation. Still, not all clerics approved of it. Many had no use for democracy, which was championed largely by the secularists who had seized a share of the power.

Britain and Russia also opposed the constitution. When the Shah, seeking to evade the limitations it imposed on him, turned to them, they willingly backed him up. With the monarchy's complicity, the European powers succeeded in suppressing the revolutionary reforms and, by the eve of World War I, Britain and Russia both had troops in occupation in the country.

By the 1920s Iran, though still nominally independent, had effectively become a British protectorate. The constitution and the parliament survived until Khomeini swept them away. But they were little more than historical landmarks.

In this contentious atmosphere, Khomeini grew to manhood. In contrast to Egyptians or Algerians, he was exposed to a double imperialism, Britain's and Russia's, from which emerged a nationalism that was turned against both West and East. It was, in fact, a nationalism that was hostile to foreigners generally.

A former student of Khomeini at Qom, the principal seat of Shi'ite studies, noted: "The two issues he emphasized were the necessity for Islam and Iran to be independent of both Eastern and Western colonialism and the need to get clerics out of the mold of an academic straitjacket."[3] Later, Khomeini was considered a subversive by the monarchy for promoting a clerical activism against Iran's friends, the Americans, as well as against its foes, the Russians.

Khomeini had already started as a teacher at Qom when Reza Khan, an Iranian army commander, seized the government. Reza Khan had been Minister of War in 1921, promising to rebuild a society destabilized by World War I. Both the British and the *ulama*, admiring his decisive qualities, gave him their support. By 1925 he had mobilized the force needed to overthrow the reigning Qajar dynasty. In its place he installed a secular monarchy he called the Pahlavis, a name meant to recall the glories of ancient Persia. Reza Khan named himself as Shah.

To modernize Iran, Reza Shah emulated Turkey's Ataturk in embarking on a secularization program. He broke the clergy's monopoly over the schools and the legal system, promoted Western dress and relaxed restrictions on women. While professing a love of Islam, he struck at Shi'ite symbols, banning the public self-flagellation that took place on the anniversary of Hussein's martyrdom. He also ignored the 1905 constitution to run a brutal dictatorship.[4]

In those days Khomeini did not regard the monarchy as illegitimate. In fact, he showed no interest in politics at all. When the British deposed Reza Shah during World War II for consorting with the Germans, Khomeini expressed no anger at Britain's action. If he had bitter feelings, he expressed them only after the accession of Reza Shah's son, Mohammad Reza Shah, who became the last of the Pahlavi monarchs.[5]

The young Shah faced a new wave of nationalism when World War II ended. He helped trigger it himself in the late 1940s by bringing accusations of fraud and negligence against the Anglo-Iranian Oil Company, the British firm that held a monopoly in the oil fields. In 1950 a parliamentary election was won by a nationalist majority under Mohammed Mosaddeq, a veteran politician with a reputation for probity and courage. Mosaddeq, as Prime Minister, promptly nationalized Iranian oil.

The American government, responding more to a presumed Soviet than an Iranian threat, at that point snatched away the leadership in the dispute from Britain. The Americans had not supported Britain's bargaining position; on the contrary, they acknowledged the justice of the Iranian claim. But, convinced that Mosaddeq was planning to deliver Iran to the Soviet Union, they called for a boycott and block-ade of the country.

The confrontation, ironically, turned Iran's pro-Soviet Tudeh Party, never more than a minor player in Iranian politics, into a major influence. Mosaddeq was left with the choice of allying with the Tudeh or submitting to the Americans. He became an Iranian hero by refusing to submit to the foreigner's power.

The Shah, faced in 1952 with a Prime Minister who was growing both more radical and more popular, embraced the Americans and dismissed Mosaddeq from office. In response, huge crowds shouting anti-Western slogans took to Teheran's streets. The army, loyal to the Shah, suppressed the demonstrations, inflicting hundreds of casualties. The crowds, nonetheless, frightened the Shah into reappointing Mosaddeq, who emerged a more formidable leader than ever.

The following year Washington tried organizing a coup d'état against Mosaddeq and, when it failed, evacuated the Shah and his family to safety outside the country. In a second, more violent coup soon after, however, Washington succeeded in restoring the Shah to his throne. The Shah's return under American patronage opened a new era of royal tyranny.

"The Mosaddeq affair was the big turning point in modern Iranian history," said Ebrahim Yazdi, the head of the Freedom Movement. "It killed our experiment with popular government. It also blackened the image of America which, having never been involved in colonialism here, had been our ideal in freedom and democracy. I think there was a good chance for our democracy had Mosaddeq survived. Instead, the Shah came back and, in the eyes of all Iranians, he was an American agent. The Shah never overcame that, and neither did the Americans."

Khomeini stayed on the sidelines during the Mosaddeq affair, as he had during the earlier contest with Reza Shah. He apparently was among those who considered Mosaddeq—as he had once considered Reza Shah—too secular to support, even against foreign devils. Like most of the clergy, he shared Mosaddeq's nationalism but feared that Mosaddeq's modernization, like Reza Shah's, could be achieved only at clerical expense.

Khomeini's idol at the time was Ayatollah Mohammad Borujerdi, who was not a nationalist partisan but a dedicated quietist. Borujerdi, Iran's leading *mujtahid*, believed in deferring to power, which was the prevailing practice of Shi'ite clerics. Historians note that Khomeini's political activism, though rooted in the popular outrage provoked by

America's anti-Mosaddeq coup, dated only from Borujerdi's death a few years later.[6]

Soon after ending his political reticence, Khomeini became recognized as the Shah's principal clerical opponent. His first test came over a proposed law to grant women and non-Muslims the vote in local elections. Denouncing the law as non-Islamic, he taunted the Shah by linking him to Jews and Zionists. Iran was the only Muslim country, save Turkey, that had diplomatic relations with Israel. Khomeini's attacks persuaded the government to withdraw the voting proposal. His actions struck a popular chord among the masses and drew a major segment of the clergy into political activism.

After this victory Khomeini attacked the Shah's proposals for rural reform, which would have distributed land to the peasantry. He also kept up the drumbeat of opposition to the women's vote. Though he often spoke of Islam's concern for the oppressed, in practice Khomeini showed much less interest in rectifying social inequities than in preserving the clergy's exercise of power.

Khomeini's eloquence attracted a large and dedicated following among the divinity students at Qom. During a 1963 sermon, before a huge crowd, he once again linked the Shah to Israel and accused him of seeking to destroy Islam. The Shah's response was to order Khomeini's arrest but, after street protests that the security forces savagely suppressed, he consented to Khomeini's release.[7]

In July 1964 the Shah made a serious tactical mistake, proposing a law to permit criminal trials in American courts of Americans assigned to military missions in Iran. Many countries where Americans were based had enacted similar laws. But Khomeini, with his finger on the popular pulse, saw an opportunity. The bill recalled to Iranians the humiliating capitulatory rights that Western powers had once imposed in Iran, a tailor-made issue for an assault on the monarchy.

The bill, Khomeini said in a sermon in Qom, was "a document for the enslavement of Iran. . . . [It] has declared that Iran is a colony. . . . It has struck out all our Islamic and national glories. . . . The misfortunes of Islamic governments have come from the interference of foreigners in their destinies." Iran, having once been under England's control, was now "a prisoner of America." Khomeini's message was that only by turning the state over to men of religion could Iran be saved from subversion at the hands of America's lackey, the Shah.[8]

Within a few days of the sermon, Khomeini was arrested and banished to Turkey, where he remained for a year. He was then permitted to relocate in the Shi'ite shrine city of Najaf in Iraq, where he stayed for thirteen years more. Loath to make Khomeini a martyr, the Shah was convinced that he would be forgotten in exile.

But while he was in Najaf, Khomeini's army of followers still heeded his guidance. They listened to his words on cassette tapes that were readily available in bazaars. They came to visit him at the court he established. They recognized him, the banished *mujtahid*, as chief of the Islamic opposition. In Iraq, Khomeini stayed constantly in touch with home, planning his return while working out new doctrines for the government of an Islamic state.

· IV ·

BY MOST ACCOUNTS, Khomeini did not arrive in Najaf with a fixed political philosophy. He was not yet convinced that Iran's monarchy had to be overthrown and a theocracy established to replace it. He knew he wanted the state reformed. But he still accepted the traditional Shi'ite position that, until the return of the Twelfth Imam, any government subject to the guidance of the *ulama* was acceptable to Islam.

He apparently changed his mind as the Shah became increasingly dictatorial, brutal and subservient to Washington. He also saw the Shah gravitating toward a secularism that weakened clerical prerogatives. Khomeini was profoundly shaken, though Iran was not itself involved, by the humiliation to Islam inflicted by Israel's arms in the Six-Day War in 1967. He began to reexamine his earlier conviction that rededication to the faith was enough by itself to save Muslim society.

In a series of lectures in 1970, five years after his arrival in Najaf, Khomeini laid out his plan for Islamic rule. His theory of *velayat-e faqih*, conventionally translated as the "mandate of the jurist," had its roots in the Shi'ite Imamate. But in a bold innovation, Khomeini took the *mujtahid*'s responsibilities to interpret the law beyond what they had ever been. He who holds the *velayat-e faqih*, the mandate of the jurist, is the heir, Khomeini declared, to the Hidden Imam. His theory gave religious sanction to fusing the duality of authority in Shi'ite society—the *ulama* and the state—into a single source of power.

"The mandate of the jurist," Khomeini declared, "is to govern and administer the country and implement the provisions of the sacred law."[9] Only *mujtahid*, he argued, are able to assure the rule of law. "Since Islamic government is a government of law," he said, "those acquainted with the law or, more precisely, with religion must supervise its functioning. It is they who supervise all executive and administrative affairs."[10] Khomeini further said, adding divine endorsement to the jurist's responsibilities, "The jurist's regency will be the same as enjoyed by the Prophet in governing the Islamic community, and it is incumbent on all Muslims to obey him."[11]

Khomeini knew, of course, that his theories would stir controversy. His followers, with his encouragement, had already acclaimed him Imam. It was the first use of the title, a link with the Hidden Imam, in Iran's Shi'ite history. Though it carried no official power, it implied great deference. Its use seemed also to confirm that Khomeini had designed his theories to have himself recognized as *faqih*. His fellow *mujtahid* did not, on the whole, approve of his plans. Many, in fact, found them presumptuous.

Khomeini's aspirations, furthermore, ran into the obstacle of a chaotic clerical structure. Shi'ite clerics are not organized into a recognized hierarchy; their rank is a function of the personal following they attract. Even an ayatollah is not appointed; his peers call him the name in deference to scholarly eminence.[12] Not only were few clerics won over to Khomeini's plan; as a body, Iran's clerics had no process for adopting it.

"The political conception that Imam Khomeini developed in Najaf was not based on a consensus of Shi'ite religious ideas," said Hasan Taromi in an interview. "It was the product of his own thinking. The Imam's vision of the Islamic state was not the collective ideology of the *mujtahid*, though it became the ideology of the regime that he established after the revolution."

Taromi, a cleric of about forty, talked with me in a small office at the Islamic Encyclopedia. Like most mullahs, he wore a thick beard, a gray robe and a white turban. Taromi had studied religion at Qom and now worked at the Encyclopedia, preparing articles on Islamic theology and jurisprudence for publication.

"While Khomeini was in exile," Taromi said, "his ideas circulated in clerical circles in Iran, but there was no public debate on them. Supporters of his ideas did not speak out, because the Shah was putting Khomeini's people in prison. But the clerical opposition did not speak out either, for fear of disrupting the *ulama*'s solid front against the Shah. So the public really never knew much about what Khomeini had on his mind.

"Privately, however, the debate was intense. Being Shi'ites, we do not reject *ijtihad* the way the Sunnis do, and we are ready to explore new ideas. Until Khomeini, no *mujtahid* ever made the claim to rule over the entire Islamic community. Khomeini did not pretend to be relaying the word of God but, through *ijtihad*, he challenged long-standing practices and beliefs among the *mujtahid*. Khomeini's ideas were quite revolutionary."

The principal theological counterargument to Khomeini was that the authority imparted by Shi'ism to the *mujtahid* was not to govern but to interpret Islamic law for those who did. Even while the twelve Imams were alive, they had left the actual conduct of government in others' hands. The second major rebuttal was that the inheritance of authority from the Hidden Imam was collective, and that no single *mujtahid*, not even Khomeini as *faqih*, had the right to assert it for himself.

"Eventually, Khomeini's ideas triumphed," Taromi said, "but not because the *ulama* were persuaded. Many *mujtahid* still have serious doubts about *velayat-e faqih*, in terms of both theory and implementation. Since Khomeini's death, the government has allowed more open debate on *velayat-e faqih*, and it has led only to more serious criticism, in forums and in the press.

"To understand why *velayat-e faqih* was adopted, when it was not at all popular, you have to think back to conditions in 1979. Iranians saw Khomeini then not as a thinker but as head of the revolution. In winning, he got to choose the state that he wanted. In returning to Iran in victory, he was not about to be challenged by the few *mujtahid*, either politically or philosophically."

When Iranians began to riot against the Shah in 1978, the *mujtahid* turned to Khomeini for guidance. Their strength lay in their disarray. Khomeini himself was out of their reach, and his lieutenants had no chain of command that could be disrupted by arrests. The Shah had no idea how to deal with the disintegration around him and, in desperation, beseeched America for help. In doing so, he only confirmed Khomeini's charge that he was a lackey of the United States.

With the state crumbling, Khomeini became the organizing focus not just for clerics but for the left and center. The left, Communist-oriented and anticlerical, assumed it would be able to manipulate him once the Shah was overthrown. Bazargan, leader of the centrists, was committed to restoring Iranian democracy, but urged Khomeini to soften his attacks on America, the democratic bastion. Khomeini, however, was not interested in advice from Bazargan or anyone else. Far from soliciting Washington's favor, he stepped up his condemnation. Though he remained silent on his theory of *velayat-e faqih*, he made clear that his aim was establishing an Islamic republic, whose constitution would be the law of Islam.[13]

· V ·

ENOUGH HAS ALREADY been written of Khomeini's relocation to Paris in October 1978, the Shah's flight from Iran in January 1979 and Khomeini's return to Teheran in triumph two weeks later. The revolution had already been won when he arrived.

With his authority unchallenged, Khomeini moved first to vest power in a Revolutionary Council, dominated by clerics. The moderate Bazargan, whom he named Prime Minister, provided a facade of legality, while *Komiteh,* armed vigilante groups operating in his name, roamed the country enforcing his authority. Hastily organized revolutionary tribunals routinely spilled the blood of ex-supporters of the Shah after summary trials.

Many Khomeini supporters, however, saw no need of legality. So intoxicating were the times that his claque referred to him as the forerunner of the Mahdi, if not the Mahdi himself. The conclusion they drew was that Khomeini, as God's agent and the savior, could act as he chose.

Khomeini, while not discouraging such worship, was aware of how the clergy had been shoved aside after the 1905 revolution by Reza Shah's secular state. With a strong sense of the politics of the moment, he recognized that his own revolution, unless legitimized and institutionalized, might not survive. Khomeini instructed Bazargan to conduct a national referendum, and in March, 98.2 percent of Iranians approved the establishment of an Islamic state.[14]

Bazargan then set out faithfully to provide for the transition. In a draft constitution, he and his cabinet proposed a Western-style presidential regime, with a parliament whose orthodoxy would be assured by the supervision of an Islamic council. *Velayat-e faqih* was not mentioned. Khomeini—perceiving, some say, that his support was still rising and that delay was on his side—sent the draft for review to an elected Assembly of Experts, which was yet to be chosen.

The revolutionary fervor that prevailed during the campaign for the Assembly's election, made the outcome foreordained. Of the Council's seventy-three seats, fifty-five were won by clerics, and several more by lay sympathizers of an Islamic state. The secular opposition won only a handful. By the time the Assembly met, Khomeini had made clear that he considered Bazargan's proposed constitution too timid, and he called for a document crafted in his own image.

The delegates then went seriously about the work of replacing Bazargan's draft. Records of the debates show no signs that dissent was suppressed. Some cool heads did indeed question Khomeini's constitutional designs, but they failed to slow the rush to Islamic radicalism.

The Assembly of Experts created a theocratic state, based on the *velayat-e faqih* doctrine. The constitution it produced says, "During the Occultation, the mandate to rule . . . devolves on a just and pious *faqih*, who is acquainted with the circumstances of his age; who is courageous, resourceful, and possessed of administrative ability, and accepted as leader by the majority of the people." Few Iranians had any doubt whom the Council was describing. The constitution gave the *faqih* the power to name all major officials and approve all candidates for President, but imposed no other specific responsibilities on him. Khomeini was to be *faqih* for life, serving *de jure* in behalf of the Hidden Imam. No Iranian ruler had ever been given such powers.[15]

"All civil, penal, financial, economic, administrative, cultural, military, political or other laws and regulations," said the constitution, "must be based on Islamic criteria."

The constitution provided, beneath the level of the *faqih*, for the election of a President and a single-chamber parliament to perform the day-to-day duties of governing. It created a clerically dominated Council of Guardians to pass on the Islamic credentials of candidates for office. It set up Islamic courts, ruled by clerics, to enforce the law and limited personal freedom to clerically approved Islamic norms. It also contained an appendix, which cited the Quranic verses and Shi'ite *hadith* as its legal sources.

Bazargan deeply disapproved of the constitution, and a segment of the clerical establishment agreed with him. Khomeini answered them with claims that were significantly more sweeping than those he had made while in exile.

"The *velayat-e faqih*," he said, "is not something created by the Assembly of Experts. It is something that God has ordained."[16]

Khomeini ordered a referendum on the draft of the constitution, which he proceeded to describe as a contest between God and Satan. The polarization that his words implied assured its ratification. Still, he took no chances. America's anger at the revolution, still smoldering months after his triumph, offered him an opportunity to radicalize Iran even further.

Washington had not only refused to extradite the Shah to Iran for trial, as Khomeini demanded, but had offered to grant him permanent refuge in the United States. Khomeini was furious. On October 22 "students faithful to the line of the Imam" occupied the American Embassy, sharpening the contest between God and Satan. Calling the embassy a "nest of spies," they took fifty-two staff members as hostages.

Khomeini, though he may not have instigated the occupation, took note of its huge popularity and understood its usefulness. Not only did the Islamic masses applaud but the pro-Communist left, cheered by the introduction of anti-Americanism into the revolution's doctrines, quit the opposition. Bazargan, the Prime Minister, pleaded with Khomeini to call off the occupation, then resigned when he refused, casting doubt on the loyalty of the pro-democracy forces. The chief foes of *velayat-e faqih* had been neutralized. In the December 1979 constitutional referendum, the electorate endorsed the Islamic state by a huge margin.[17] Khomeini had played his nationalist cards brilliantly.

· VI ·

OVER THE REMAINING decade of his life, Khomeini gave his energies to consolidating his work. Whatever the power the constitution had conferred on him, it was not a simple task. After the euphoria over the embassy's occupation passed, the left turned on him, determined to salvage the revolution it believed he had stolen. Willing to spill blood, pro-Communist elements launched a small but vicious civil war, which claimed victims from as high as the top ranks of the clerical hierarchy. Khomeini, however, proved he could be equally violent, as violent as the Shah had ever been. Tens of thousands of Iranians died before the resistance was stanched.

Meanwhile, Khomeini moved to widen popular acceptance of his rule and of the revolution's controversial doctrines. He stacked the state bureaucracy at all levels with the faithful. He organized a corps of prayer leaders to travel the country to preach revolutionary fidelity in the mosques. He encouraged the founding of Islamic associations to rally support to his cause in factories and bazaars. He ordered *velayat-e faqih* taught as absolute truth in the schools. He personally delivered sermons in mosques and on television on the importance of loyalty to the new Islamic state.

Recognizing the revolution's dependency on the clergy, he took particular steps to keep it in line. He placed reliable *mujtahid* into the major positions of command, maneuvering dissenters to the margins. He gave lesser clerics a vested interest in the revolution by nominating them to posts in government agencies and in the state's many new schools, mosques and religious societies. Some 10,000 clerics were soon on the public payroll, their professional fate tied to the republic's survival.

Khomeini also reshaped the armed forces and the security services, which had remained faithful to the Shah to the end. He had hundreds of security agents executed, and thousands purged from the ranks. In rebuilding the security organizations, he imparted to them a character as ruthless as that of the Shah's agencies. The armed forces were only a bit more difficult.

It is probable that Khomeini meant to destroy the military services outright, and he first set up a parallel force called the Revolutionary Guards, which was conceived as replacement. But then the war against Iraq began, requiring all the available military help. All three military arms fought valiantly against Iraq, and so were not disbanded. But to this day, they have not overcome the suspicions engendered by their longstanding loyalty to the Pahlavi regime.[18]

The war against Iraq started Khomeini on the path of "exporting the revolution," a term he himself used. It had been on his mind since his days in exile.[19] "Islam is not peculiar to a country," he had said, ". . . Islam has come for humanity." Khomeini frequently referred to Iran as "the starting point" for worldwide Islamic revolution. In the constitution, the Iranian republic's goal was described as "the happiness of all human beings in all human societies."[20]

Khomeini carried a particular grudge against Iraq's Saddam Hussein, dating to his exile in Najaf. Though Iraq initiated the war in the fall of 1980, even Iranian historians agree that Khomeini had done much to provoke it. He then prolonged it, with the goal of overthrowing Saddam, long after Iraqi forces were driven from Iran's soil.

The eight bloody years of the war sorely tested the republic. After Iraq's early victories, Iran went on the offensive but had to trade horrible losses of life for small territorial gains. Mixing Shi'ism with nationalism, Khomeini exhorted his troops to capture Karbala, site of great Shi'ite shrines, as well as to fight for the "beloved homeland." But after nearly a million casualties, public opinion had turned against the war and even he lost the knack for keeping the country's fighting spirit at the pitch that victory demanded.

Far from winning the Arabs to the side of the revolution, Khomeini found they believed Saddam's claim that Iraq was fighting to save the Arab world from Persian imperialism. Nor did he lay to rest Saddam's boast that Iraq was defending Sunni Islam against the Shi'ite heresy. On the contrary, Khomeini's heated rhetoric only confirmed to the Arabs that their community was in danger. To Khomeini's dismay, Iraq's Shi'ites, the bulk of Saddam's forces, rejected his revolution, while Arabs elsewhere grew increasingly hostile as the war dragged on.

In 1988 the fighting reached a climax. Ironically, it was not Iraq but the United States, Khomeini's nemesis, that again stood at the hub of events. Concerned about its oil supplies, Washington had been escorting tankers through the waters of the Gulf, edging closer to the conflict. In April 1988 an Iranian mine struck a tanker, and the U.S. Navy in retaliation shelled Iranian offshore oil platforms, then sank two Iranian ships. In July, Americans shot down an Iranian civilian airliner with a loss of 290 lives. Iran charged premeditation; Washington called it an accident. Whatever it was, the airliner tragedy became the pretext for Khomeini's acceptance of a United Nations cease-fire proposal, effectively acknowledging his defeat. America's intervention had saved Khomeini from having to concede victory to Saddam Hussein, whom he considered a Muslim apostate. He was also able to exploit this intervention by the Great Satan to sustain Iran's revolutionary ardor.

Nonetheless, Khomeini described the cease-fire as "worse than taking poison." It was not easy to explain to his followers the defeat of a cause for which he claimed God's endorsement. The cease-fire halted the revolution's military momentum. If Khomeini wanted to continue the policy of "exportation," he would have to find other means.

In my own visit to Iran some years later, America still cast a huge shadow. Iranians had not forgiven America's patronage of the Shah, or its unwillingness to accept his overthrow. But among Western-oriented Iranians, I heard nostalgia for friendlier times, and I discerned rather little anti-American animosity. Many Iranians, uncomfortable with isolation, seemed anxious to rejoin the world community.

Few Iranians, even among believers, talked to me of the blessings of Islamic rule. Fifteen years after the revolution, Iranians were unforgiving of the Shah, and rejoiced at Iran's independence of American domination. But I heard little praise for the Islamic state, which led me to question the depth of the religious impulse behind the revolution in the first place.

On my trip to Qom, I visited with retired Ayatollah Ahmad Azari-Qomi, who had been the chief prosecutor of Khomeini's revolutionary tribunals after the Shah's overthrow. When I asked him to list the major achievements of the revolution, I expected a lecture on the virtues of the Islamic state. Instead, he talked about the United States.

"Our best achievement," he said, "is that we are independent now vis-à-vis America. Our policies are our own. We are perhaps the only really independent country in the world. That is the best thing that Imam Khomeini did for us."

One day I was invited to join a seminar at Teheran University to discuss U.S.-Iranian relations with some graduate students. A dozen men and three women—unlike the lower schools, the universities are coed—were in the classroom. They were older than their American counterparts, the result of the suspension of instruction in the 1980s during the "Islamization" of the curriculum. They were also well informed and articulate.

Asked what the revolution meant to them, their answers, without being strident, resounded with a pride in a country that now lived in a manner of its own choosing.

"Before the revolution," said a man in a shabby jacket, "our intellectuals looked to the West as the model to be copied. That's changed, and now they are looking for an Iranian way."

"Iranian identity had always been dependent, marginal," said a woman in a *chador*. "Under the influence of Islam, Iran has changed to its true identity. We are now standing against the United States and, for the first time, America takes us seriously."

"Before, we barely knew Iran," said a well-combed man in a sweater and jeans. "Now we're looking to rediscover everything about it. The Shah tried to invoke patriotism out of Iran's past but failed. Since he fell, we've internalized Iran and Islam.

"The government is still clamping down on opposition, but the fear has vanished. There's a greater sense of tranquillity. We may oppose the regime, but we still identify with it."

In a mansion in a walled, wooded tract in north Teheran, I heard a harsher view in a talk on U.S.-Iranian relations with Mohammed Shariati. An Islamic cleric, Shariati had been a classmate and close friend of Ahmad Khomeini, the Imam's son. Shariati, in his late forties, had graduated from a seminary in Qom, then joined the ayatollah in exile. Since the revolution, he said, he had served successively in the cabinet, the diplomatic corps and the parliament.

When we met, Shariati was the director of *Ourouj,* an institute housed in the mansion. Its mission, he told me, is to preserve every last word that Khomeini pronounced, and every last scrap of film that shows Khomeini's face. Shariati told me that he himself articulates what he called "the Imam's line," which he reveres. He began by challenging the premise of my first question, that the United States and Iran had once been friends.

"There was never a friendship between the American and Iranian peoples," he said, "though before the revolution there was a friendship between the U.S. Government and the Shah. We have always been aware of America's contempt for Third World countries—Vietnam, Cuba, Latin America, the Arab world. We applauded your help in saving us from Soviet Communism after World War II, but your reason was not generous: it was to dominate Iran.

"Sometimes what you did was understandable; sometimes it was intolerable, like overthrowing Mosaddeq. All American relations with the Third World have been based on domination.

"You personally are welcome here"—he smiled to reassure me—"but we are the generation of the revolution, and I cannot imagine that relations between our countries will ever be good."

I pointed out to Shariati that we Americans also have grievances, the most memorable of which is probably the occupation of the embassy, where the fifty-two Americans were held hostage for more than a year. In terms of U.S.-Iranian relations, I volunteered, seizing the embassy was surely shortsighted. He disagreed.

"I respect your viewpoint," he said politely; our entire talk was polite, "but let me tell you mine. The United States was the biggest supporter of the Shah. It aggravated all of Iran's problems. The American Embassy was the headquarters of the plot against Iran. What the Americans did was not normal diplomatic work. Their embassy was a nest of spies.

"America did not accept our revolution and tried to crush it, as it once crushed Mosaddeq. The taking of the embassy was not a mistake. It was a confrontation with our oppressor, and we have no regrets."

I asked Shariati if he thought there was any hope of improved relations between our countries. He did not hesitate.

"Some events are unpredictable—like the fall of the U.S.S.R. or the Iranian revolution itself. So better relations may also happen, without predictability.

"But we cannot forget the past, and we can't start over without putting relations on an equal basis, which you don't want. We remain loyal to the values of our revolution, and they will not change. Our view is that the United States wants to be the only decision-maker in the world. We in Iran will not be oppressed, however, and will continue to resist your domination."

When we had finished talking and were drinking tea and nibbling cookies, I asked Shariati whether his hard-line answers represented a consensus of Iranians. It was the only question on which he paused to reflect. I was surprised by the modesty of his answer.

"What I expressed," he said at last, "is what some people in Iran think. Basically, the opinions I express are those of the people who made the revolution."

Khomeini was surely seeking to rally "the people who made the revolution" in 1989, in issuing the now famous *fatwa* ordering the death of the Anglo-Indian writer Salman Rushdie. In the months after Iran's defeat by Iraq, revolutionary morale was in sharp decline. Many voices were calling for normalization of Iran's foreign relations, even with Washington. For Khomeini, the revolution's future appeared in danger and, with his uncanny political instinct, he seized the moment to reignite the flames of anti-Western hostility.

Khomeini's reach was very wide. Rushdie had no ties whatever to Iran. He was not even a Shi'ite. But his book had already provoked riots among Muslims in England and in Pakistan. Khomeini maintained that it was his clear duty to impose Islamic punishment on Rushdie for apostasy.

Khomeini's *fatwa* represented the ultimate exportation of the revolution, though neither by armies nor by the international terrorism of which the regime had frequently been accused. Khomeini's claim of jurisdiction over all Muslims was pure Islamic imperialism. Such a claim, unequaled since the Prophet and the companions seemed particularly presumptuous in being asserted by a Shi'ite. Though upsetting to many *mujtahid,* it thrilled the militant followers of the Imam's line.

On February 14, 1989, Radio Teheran read Khomeini's text.

"I would like to inform all the intrepid Muslims *in the world,*" Khomeini declared, "that the author of the book entitled *The Satanic Verses,* which has been written, printed and published in opposition to Islam, the Prophet and the Quran, as well as those publishers who were aware of its contents, have been sentenced to death.

"I call on all zealous Muslims to execute them quickly, wherever they find them, so that no one will dare to insult the Islamic sanctions. Anyone killed in doing this duty will be regarded as a martyr."[21]

Khomeini followed by saying that he had found Rushdie "an agent of corruption," who had "made war on God." In the message, Khomeini called *The Satanic Verses* an anti-Islamic plot, masterminded by the United States, Britain and the Zionists.[22]

Clear-sighted as he was, Khomeini understood that he had provoked a major cultural collision. The *fatwa,* for the West, was a challenge to free expression, the right to trial, the right to choose one's own religious beliefs, the sovereignty of nations. To Islam, it was a defense of the inviolability of God, the right of the faith to limit speech and suppress apostasy, the jurisdiction of the *shari'a* over all believers. Khomeini knew very well that he was drawing a line which partisans on neither side could cross.

Since the *fatwa,* Islam and the West have been unable to find common ground to resolve the dispute. All the proposals in public discourse have been judged unduly compromising to one side or the other. For Khomeini, the *fatwa* was a way to stiffen the backbone of Muslims. Compromise was not on his agenda.

Khomeini died three months after issuing the *fatwa*, and the Iranian government took the position that his death changed nothing. Some supporters even argued that, since he alone had control over the *fatwa*, it would remain valid for eternity. A $2 million bounty, privately offered but officially condoned, was placed on Rushdie's head. As late as 1995, an Iranian diplomat made the mistake of telling a foreign government that the *fatwa*, while technically valid, had in reality expired; he was promptly fired.

Of wider significance, Khomeini achieved the objective of raising a barrier to Iran's reconciliation with the West. It was not the only issue between them, of course. But the *fatwa* has helped keep Iran as isolated as it has ever been from the world community, a decade after Khomeini's death.

Many Iranians still defend Khomeini's decision on the *fatwa*, maintaining that it was an unavoidable Islamic duty. "He was a mystic," said a theology professor at Teheran University, "and he had intuitive feelings toward the Prophet Muhammad, whom Rushdie blasphemed. Rushdie's words left the Imam with no choice.

"The Satanic Verses was an indisputable heresy. Khomeini saw the willingness of the Western countries to publish it as an attack on the revolution. Politically, he had to respond.

"Still, his motives were not essentially political. Rushdie was a *murtad*, a Muslim who abandoned Islam. Islamic law provides for the death of a *murtad*. Khomeini was a believer, and in the final analysis he issued the *fatwa* as an act of Islamic piety."

A Teheran University professor, looking at the world through a more secular lens, took a quite different position.

"Criticizing the Rushdie *fatwa* remains one of our taboos," he said. "We all believe the *fatwa* was a terrible mistake, but no one can say it publicly. That's because Khomeini is so identified with it. He is worshiped by Iran's masses and, though we can talk more about Khomeini's mistakes than we once did, these feelings on the part of the people are not subsiding.

"To the masses, the *fatwa* still represents the courage and Islamic integrity of the revolution. It symbolizes defiance of the West and imperialism. It is almost the revolution itself.

"If the government tried to reverse it, there would be demagogues mobilizing crowds in the streets. Like it or not, we have to live with it."

· VII ·

THOUGH OTHERS DID, Ayatollah Khomeini never described the revolution that he made as fundamentalist. He probably never thought of it in those terms. Iran, of course, has its fundamentalists, some of them in high ranks of the clergy. Some even hold influential positions in the government. Yet Khomeini, while indulging them, was also disdainful of their views.

Khomeini is often quoted by Iranians as saying that Islam is for all time, not for fourteen centuries ago on the Arabian peninsula. He specifically took on the fundamentalists in two *fatwas*, one concurring in the presentation of women on television and radio, the other approving the playing of chess and the commercial sale of musical instruments. Hardly radical, these *fatwas* nonetheless elicited protests from fundamentalist clerics. Khomeini rejected their protests with contempt.

"I feel it necessary," he wrote to them, "to express my despair about your understanding of the divine injunctions and that of the Shi'ite traditions. . . . The way you interpret the traditions, the new civilization should be destroyed and the people should live in shackles or live forever in the desert."[23]

Iranians like to point to these modernist *fatwas*, along with Khomeini's defense of them, as evidence of the forward-looking character of the revolution. That was not the message, of course, of Khomeini's *fatwa* on Rushdie, but a *mujtahid* in Qom insisted to me that it should not be understood as a serious theological statement, much less as a barrier to creative thought. He urged me to see it exclusively as a political weapon selected by Khomeini to preserve the revolution. In another time and place, the Imam's response would have been to ignore Rushdie, the *mujtahid* said, as he ignored most other sinners.

The isolation that Khomeini cultivated to keep revolutionary zealotry at a high pitch, however, has imposed severe costs. Iran's soaring birth rate has created long-term economic problems, which can be treated only with an infusion of investment and technology. Poverty is already provoking social instability. Whatever the benefits Khomeini believed the Rushdie *fatwa* would have on morale, it surely aggravated the prospects for the return desired by many Iranians to economic developement and international normality.

Many Shi'ite thinkers today are sensitive to Iran's practical problems. Rejecting fundamentalism, they talk of forging a culture that encourages scientifically based patterns of behavior, the basis of a modern state. Abdolkarim Soroosh is only the most eloquent member of this school. I heard his echo in *mujtahid* wearing turbans and beards in Teheran and in Qom.

In Iran, such thinkers are not considered infidels, as they might be in orthodox circles in the Arab world. Shi'ism's openness to *ijtihad*, even to "innovation," helps to create an atmosphere that is generally tolerant of their work. The government, conventionally authoritarian, is more likely to attack advocates of reform for political deviation—as Soroosh has been—than for religious heresy.

Meanwhile, the signs grow that revolutionary zealotry is on the decline.

"Under the Shah," quipped an Iranian during my visit, "we engaged in public drinking and private prayer. Under the republic, we practice private drinking and public prayer." But many Iranians rarely see the inside of a mosque, and more than a few boast of the wine, homemade or bootlegged, that they serve at parties with family or friends.

Western television, though against the rules, is also common. During my visit the government cracked down on satellite dishes, arguing that Western TV placed the population in "cultural jeopardy." The population howled audibly in protest, and the government admitted that the move was only likely to increase the traffic in contraband video tapes.

The newspapers while I was in Teheran also carried the curious notice that a hundred Central Asian women had been arrested in the bazaar for violating Islamic dress codes. Knowing Iranians explained to me that this was a euphemism for their real offense, which was to serve the city's thriving prostitution industry.

Khatami's election as President in 1997 with a 70 percent majority seemed to confirm that zealotry is waning. But it is by no means dead. Revolutionary vigilantes, called *basijee*s, still roam the streets. Unemployable youths recruited in villages and poor neighborhoods around the country, they are heir to the revolutionary-era *komiteh*, enforcing revolutionary morality. They serve the Islamic state in return for a small income and the promise of free education, as well as for the gratification of bullying others.[24]

The *basijee*s, no doubt under orders from a high place, roughed up Abdolkarim Soroosh in 1996, persuading him to leave the country. More commonly, they monitor women, generally from the richer classes, who take liberties with the dress code—exposing a little ankle, throat or hair. (Censors, incidentally, black out barelegged women from Western magazines, which circulate widely, while men in bikinis strut through the pages.) Among the favored targets of the *basijee*s are the teenage children of more prosperous, Westernized families, giving their efforts an egalitarian, class flavor.

Yet even the Iranians who test the bonds of traditionalism in their dress or their drinking do not seem to be signaling a desire to abandon the revolution. Rebelling against the strictures of Islam does not translate into sympathy for the Shah.

Indeed, though Iranians may divide along class lines, I saw no nostalgia in any class for the Shah's era. Many Iranians have had enough of revolutionary ardor, in contrast to others who remain committed to promoting Islamic causes. Many complain of the government's incompetence in dealing with the country's dire economic conditions, and some take to the streets to protest. But the revolution itself, whatever its disappointments, is not in dispute. It is surely a fait accompli.

What does Islamic revolution in Iran say about the prospect for Islamic revolutions elsewhere? The fact of its survival is probably its most compelling message. The Russian Revolution conveyed the same lesson to several generations of Communists. The establishment of an Islamic state in Iran proved that it can be done. If in Iran, then why not anywhere that there are believing Muslims?

Sunni radicals in, say, Egypt or Algeria have taken heart from the Iranian experience, but they have not taken much else. What Iran has shared with them is not money or arms—the money Arab militants receive, ironically, has come mostly from the West's allies in the Gulf— but a revolutionary example. Islamic zealots throughout the Muslim world were thrilled when Khomeini overthrew the Shah. Khomeini's image helps to keep the Islamic movement's hopes alive.

Yet Iran's example has its limits. Sunni fundamentalists need a model of revolutionary government, but Khomeini's doctrine of *velayat-e faqih* is probably too tangled in Shi'ite history to serve them. Shi'ism's esteem for the application of reason and for *ijtihad*, without which the revolution may well have been impossible, are probably even more difficult for Iran to teach others. Such uniquely Iranian concepts make barely a dent where Sunni fundamentalism dominates.

Perhaps most important, there probably will not be another Khomeini. While he lived, he transformed political dynamics throughout the Islamic world. He was one of those rare men who, for good or evil, changed history. A successful revolution may require a powerful personality like his, but it is unlikely that one like him will come along very soon.

7

The Saudi Dilemma

BURAYDA is a quiet oasis city, three hours by car from Riyadh, in the heart of the Arabian desert. Once a crossroads of caravans, it may well have been visited by the Prophet Muhammad during his voyages across the peninsula as a merchant. Burayda is still noted for its thriving camel and goat markets.

It is also known for the rigorous devotion of its 100,000 inhabitants to the austere form of Sunni Islam—Wahhabism, most call it—that is Saudi Arabia's state religion. In recognition of the city's piety, King Fahd bin Abdulaziz, out of his personal resources, built a magnificent mosque a few years ago near the central square. But after the Gulf War of 1991, dissident politics shattered the city's tranquillity, raising questions about the character of Burayda's piety.

Saudi Arabia is rightly regarded as the most Islamic of the Arab countries. The birthplace of the faith and of the traditions that make up the *shari'a,* it takes pride in the authenticity of its Islamic practice. The Saudi king considers himself not only an Islamic ruler but the guardian of the Islamic holy places in Mecca and Medina. For many years the Saudi regime thought it was immune, because it was already so Islamic, from the criticism of the fundamentalists who were disrupting other Arab countries. What the disorders at Burayda announced was that, while some Saudis were aggrieved that their state was too Islamic, others were angry that it was not Islamic enough.

The disorders began in the fall of 1993 when the Burayda police issued a warrant for the arrest of Sheikh Salman al-Audah. Audah, a brilliant cleric in his late thirties, had captured the attention of law enforcement authorities for harshly criticizing the royal family from the *minbar* of his mosque. The Sauds, Audah declared, had committed both political errors and religious sins. Forewarned by the arrest in Mecca a few days before of Dr. Safar al-Hawali, another clerical critic of the royal family, Audah was already in hiding when the police arrived at his home.

But Audah decided abruptly against becoming a fugitive and returned home to meet the police at the head of a twenty-car motorcade of supporters. After a brief negotiation with police officials, he agreed to surrender on the condition that he be permitted to address the thousand or more of his followers who had assembled to greet him. A contingent of riot troops was by then on hand. In front of a microphone set up in his courtyard, Audah delivered a fiery anti-Saud diatribe. He then rejoined the motorcade, which had grown by many more cars, and to the accompaniment of blaring horns drove to the governor's mansion, where he gave himself up.

News of these unusual events, though blacked out by Saudi press and television, was spread by word of mouth during the ensuing weeks throughout the country. The action was also recorded on videotape and bootlegged to viewers outside Saudi Arabia. I acquired one of the clandestine tapes.

Audah's was only the most spectacular arrest of that week. His supporters claimed that as many as a thousand dissidents were arrested in country-wide sweeps. Characteristically, the government announced that leaks of the arrests published in the international press were all "lies and misleading information."

But a few days after the Burayda events, the Interior Ministry, which commands the police, admitted holding 157 men on charges of sowing dissent in the kingdom. The ministry said that most were released after confessing error, and it warned of dire consequences for any who repeated their crimes. The ministry further vowed to take "deterrent measures" against any others who committed "actions that undermine the faith or the [internal] security of the country, be it in writing or otherwise."

Twenty-seven of the detainees seized that week, however, were not released. The ministry had singled them out for playing the "principal harmful roles" in defying the government. Hawali, a cleric and teacher at Mecca's Islamic university, was, along with Audah, the most prominent of them. Since September 1993 the two have remained political prisoners—an accurate term, albeit resented by the government. Both have declined to make public repentance of their acts, the condition of their release.

Saudi Arabia was not accustomed to such a crisis. It is basically a stable and law-abiding society, obedient to the Islamic injunction against popular disorder. But since the Gulf War's end, discontent had been discernibly rising. The Burayda roundups looked like the climax, though in fact there was still more trouble on the way.

No Saudis had endorsed the occupation of Kuwait by Saddam Hussein's Iraq in August 1990. Nonetheless, the war to liberate Kuwait aroused no patriotic fervor. Even less was it perceived as a defense of Islam. Saudis were disturbed by the arrival on their holy soil of foreign soldiers—many of them Christian, Jewish or, perhaps most shocking of all, female—to prosecute the war. At best, most saw the war as a necessary evil.

Shedding their normal docility, many Saudis criticized the government for deferring to the United States in not trying hard enough to avoid the war. Since not a single Iraqi soldier had crossed into Saudi Arabia, most were unconvinced their own country was ever in danger.

Unhappy themselves at the presence of this foreign army, many Saudis were embarrassed at the contempt heaped on them by Muslims worldwide for inviting the infidels in. If they were so threatened, Saudis asked, why would their own army, or a coalition of Muslim armies, not have been enough to keep the aggression at bay? Ominously, they questioned what had happened to the billions of the national fortune spent to assure the country's defense.

At first the royal family seemed not to have discerned the resentment, or else to have been convinced it was only a dark cloud that would pass. The Burayda episode alerted them. But then the government failed again, in not anticipating the violent antigovernment turbulence that followed the Burayda arrests.

On November 13, 1995, a car bomb exploded at a military training center in Riyadh, killing seven persons, including five American advisers. The government proclaimed initially that Iran, Iraq or Sudan was to blame. But six months later the police arrested four Saudi citizens, who in public confessions said the government's pro-Western policies, which they regarded as apostasy, had persuaded them of the need for a *jihad*. Convicted of murder, all four were beheaded.

Three of the convicted were "Afghans." That is, they were among the estimated 15,000 Saudis who had fought in Afghanistan in the 1980s against the Soviet invaders. They returned from Afghanistan with military skills and very radical Islamic views.

The government, ironically, had provided much of the financial support for the Islamic resistance in Afghanistan. It had, in fact, given money to groups promoting fundamentalist views in many Islamic countries. Its generosity toward the international fundamentalist movement had often made trouble for other Arab governments. Now the trouble was home, haunting Saudi Arabia itself.

To acknowledge the culprits as Saudis was distressing to a government which routinely maintains that all is well in the kingdom. Its position is that Wahhabism is beyond the reproach of any believers. The royal family was outraged by the presumptuousness of the Afghans in challenging their Islam.

The government's anguish was summed up by Prince Nayef, Minister of Interior and brother of the King, who is one of the country's most powerful men. "It is painful to us all," he said of the bombers, "that they belong to this beloved homeland, which is known for its . . . adherence to its religion and its cohesion."

In June 1996, barely a month after the four were beheaded, another car bomb exploded, this one on the rim of an American army compound in Dhahran. It destroyed a military barracks, killing nineteen U.S. airmen and wounding about two hundred.

By now the government recognized that American servicemen were being targeted as a way of destroying the intimate military relationship established between Saudi Arabia and the United States in the wake of the war. Some 35,000 Americans, tied to the management of the Saudi oil fields, had lived peacefully in the country for decades. Under a postwar agreement, they were joined by an estimated 5,000 American military personnel, some deployed as combatants and others as trainers. Many Saudis thought the American military presence was a bad idea. Islamic extremists considered it a heresy.

The Saudi government tried to hold non-Saudis responsible for the explosion in Dhahran, as it had for the car bomb in Riyadh. Within a few weeks it claimed to have proof that the attack was committed by native Shi'ites in the pay of Iran. Shi'ites, about 15 percent of the otherwise Sunni population, have long been victims of Saudi discrimination. Even the government acknowledges as much. The police were said to have arrested about forty Shi'ites in connection with the bombing. Despite American skepticism about their involvement, Saudi officials were said to have pressed Washington to bomb Iran in retaliation.

Upset by the religious flavor of these postwar disorders, the Saud family also vowed to regain the Islamic initiative.

The Sauds went first to Sheikh Abdulaziz bin Baz, the *mufti*, who is the highest official of the country's *shari'a* system. A blind cleric, bin Baz in 1966 made a celebrated claim that, according to the Quran and the Prophet, the sun rotates around the earth. The government has since tried to overlook the assertion, and accords bin Baz great deference for his Islamic learning. Addressing the bombings, bin Baz issued a ruling which declared that to jeopardize the life of foreigners living under the protection of an Islamic state is a violation of Islamic law.

A few days later the Saudi *ulama,* a historic ally of the Saud family, met in council in Taif and, in a widely publicized statement, recalled a *hadith* in which the Prophet Muhammad said that "a person who kills an ally will not smell the fragrance of Paradise." Referring to the bombing, the *ulama* added: "Anyone who carries out such an act will never go to heaven. Real Muslims, and the Islamic faith, have nothing to do with this criminal act."

· II ·

TO MANY SAUDIS, basing infidels on the holy soil was not just a religious but a political lapse, defaulting on the compact by which the Saud family rules.

This compact is rooted in a desert tradition by which smaller, weaker tribes paid a "brotherhood tax," a *khuwa,* to a larger, powerful tribe, in return for physical protection. The Sauds, before becoming the ruling family, were a strong and noble tribe. The *khuwa* they levied emerged as the heart of their present political legitimacy, as well as of the deference that Saudi citizens almost without exception bestow on them.[1]

As sovereigns, the Sauds have proven for the past two and a half centuries extremely deft at holding the tribal system together. Through muscle, money and marriages, they have brought—save for two brief periods out of power—consistent stability to the peninsula. The question raised in the minds of many Saudis by the Gulf War was whether the family had lost its touch. Had the terms of the *khuwa,* Saudis asked, been violated? Notwithstanding the ultimate victory, the price that Saudis paid for the war drew a cloud over the House of Saud's right to rule.

"The Gulf War taught us," a Saudi businessman said to me, "that the security we thought we had could be snatched away overnight by Saddam Hussein or Uncle Sam or even our own rulers." Like most Saudis, the man was willing to talk on the condition that I not identify him. "The status quo for us was like the desert: we took it for granted. For as long as we could remember, tranquillity had characterized our national life. We trusted our rulers. Now we sense that each of us is responsible for ourselves. We see that nothing is permanent—not even the Saud family."

In the privacy of his home, where he knew he would not be overheard, a university professor said to me:

"Saudis are not used to being in danger. Riyadh took only a few Iraqi Scuds during the fighting, but we didn't like it. I mean, we know it wasn't like living in France or Poland in World War II, but the danger to us was real enough. Of course, these matters were not discussed publicly. The newspapers, as always, were obediently silent. But we all knew that soldiers from other countries were defending us because we were unable to defend ourselves. We were very humiliated, and very angry.

"Even now, we see ourselves surrounded by neighbors that don't like us—Iran, Iraq, Sudan, Yemen, even Egypt and Jordan—and we wonder what's next. The West seems to think that the impact of the war was cultural, that we were upset by women in T-shirts driving jeeps. There's some truth to that, but we've become used to foreigners. The more fundamental truth is that we felt the royal family had let us down."

To organize for political ends in Saudi Arabia is in itself illegal. The ban is harshly interpreted. The American-born wife of a Saudi told me the authorities had stopped her from organizing a PTA in her child's school. The clergy sometimes circumvent the law by working through mosque associations. Unlike other Saudis, clerics can also express political criticism, by veiling it in sermons that deplore deviation from the true course of Islam.

In May 1991, barely two months after war ended, some 400 Islamic clerics, supported by some nonclerical intellectuals, submitted a letter to King Fahd calling for a series of reforms. The arrest in 1993 of Audah and Hawali, who were among the organizers, has its roots in this document. The criticisms expressed, albeit phrased in religious terms, were by worldwide standards mostly of a political nature.

The letter contained such familiar Islamic demands as the abrogation of measures in conflict with the *shari'a* and more generous financing for religious institutions.

But it went further to propose the establishment of a *shura* to give advice to the King; the personal accountability "without exception" of all officials, with punishment for the corrupt; the guarantee of civil rights in the context of the *shari'a;* the fair distribution of public wealth; and the organizing of a strong army and an indigenous arms industry for national defense.

Notwithstanding its Islamic language, the aim of the letter was clearly to curb the political absolutism of the House of Saud. The royal family was shocked. The letter, however respectful in tone, was daring in its challenge to royal authority. The Sauds considered it the most insolent act committed since the violent occupation of the Great

Mosque in Mecca in 1979, which occurred in the wake of an earlier Gulf trauma.

The attack on the Mecca mosque took place a few months after Khomeini's seizure of power in Iran. Khomeini's talk of "exporting the revolution" had made the royal family, as well as other Saudis, very nervous. The attackers, however, were Sunnis, not Shi'ites and not Khomeini's supporters, though they were clearly inspired by his overthrow of Iran's monarchy.

In a well-planned operation, some 250 armed radicals surprised security guards to seize the holiest shrine in Islam. Accusing the Sauds of corrupting the faith, they denied the family's legitimacy and demanded its abdication.

Buoyed by Shi'ite rioting in the Eastern Province, the rebels were initially confident of overthrowing the state. But after two weeks of siege, during which dozens were killed, government forces, with some help from abroad, reestablished control. The rebels had failed to repeat Khomeini's success. After summary trials, the heads of sixty-three of the attackers fell.

Though the Sauds emerged as victors, the pressure from Iran continued. In the name of "exporting the revolution," Iran began a campaign of harassment, organizing political demonstrations in Mecca, at the *hajj,* the holy pilgrimage, every year. A demonstration in 1987 ended in the death of 275 Iranian pilgrims and 85 Saudi policemen. Though these episodes failed in their revolutionary purpose, together they did considerable damage to the reputation of the Sauds, and seriously undermined the kingdom's sense of security.

The Sauds, reacting to the 1991 clerics' letter, tried to link the signers to the Sunni zealots at the Mecca mosque. There were similarities, to be sure. Both, grounding their grievances in Islamic values, called for an end to the Sauds' corruption, ostentation and imitation of the West. Though cloaked in piety, the two sets of demands were essentially political.

But between the two groups lay a difference which made the 1991 challenge much more significant. While the 1979 rebels were Muslims at the social margins, without much popular support, the signers of the 1991 letter were in the Islamic—or, at least, the Wahhabi—mainstream. Being nonviolent, they did not provoke the same fears as the besiegers of the Mecca mosque, but the public gave them more serious attention.

The Saudi government, in the months after receiving the letter, fumbled about in confusion. The *ulama,* while issuing admonitions, were equally uncertain what strategy to adopt. Audah and Hawali were, after all, distinguished clerics, presumably destined in the next generation to occupy the top places in the religious hierarchy. Not just intelligent but devout, these men could not be readily dismissed or casually punished.

Sensing the indecision, the dissidents issued more statements, which attracted further signers. In September 1992 they addressed a thirty-eight-page manifesto, more radical than the 1991 letter, to Sheikh bin Baz himself. Most of the signatories were young, which suggested a generational split in the society, and particularly within the religious establishment.

The manifesto boldly attacked the clerical elders for uncritically endorsing royal policies, including the war. It also proposed a series of drastic reforms to insure greater supervision by the *ulama* over the government.[2]

Meanwhile, a wholly other protest was being organized outside the bounds of the clerical establishment. To describe it as secular would be inaccurate; Western-style protests are of little interest to Saudi Arabians. Saudis, a professor reminded me, respond not to Rousseau or Jefferson but to the Prophet and his companions. Any serious reformer, Saudis agree, understands that his cause must be carried aboard an Islamic vehicle.

Many of those who joined the new protest had collaborated with Audah and Hawali in the 1991 petition. Since women in Saudi Arabia are totally excluded from public life, all were men. But those identified with it were not so much clerics as professors, judges, professionals and businessmen.

The new protest's organizer was Muhammad al-Massa'ri, a practicing Muslim, about fifty, with a doctorate in theoretical physics from an American university. His father had been a distinguished member of the *ulama*. The son, a professor at King Saud University in Riyadh, was long known as a sporadic critic of the state. The Gulf War turned him into a full-time dissident.

In May 1993, Massa'ri publicly announced the formation of the Committee for the Defense of Legitimate Rights in Saudi Arabia (CDLR). "Legitimate" was a code word which Saudis understood to mean *"shari'a*-based." Massa'ri described the CDLR not as a political party but as an association devoted to human rights and political reform within the context of Islamic law.

Massa'ri's announcement shattered the government's lethargy, and several days later he was arrested in a raid on his home in Riyadh. Over the following months, dozens of CDLR sympathizers—many of them

Massa'ri's kin—followed him to prison. Massa'ri himself was held for six months before being tried and convicted of blasphemy. Released in early 1994, he slipped illegally across the border into Yemen, and in April showed up in London, where he set up a CDLR office.

Since then, Massa'ri and a handful of associates have provoked the Sauds by feeding out information and criticism via telephone, fax and bootlegged cassettes. Much of it condemns the corruption of Saudi princes, whom it depicts as home-grown mafiosi. Both the international press and the country's intellectual grapevine have hungrily consumed their communications.

Shortly after Massa'ri announced CDLR's formation, the Saudi government—surely no coincidence—began reaching out to the country's Shi'ite minority. Not only had the state discriminated against the Shi'ites; the *ulama* officially regarded them as heretics. Many Saudi Shi'ites had fled abroad, where they maintained opposition organizations and published opposition journals.

But in July 1993 the government and the London-based Shi'ites negotiated a reconciliation. The government released forty Shi'ite political prisoners and promised to reform its anti-Shi'ite practices. The Shi'ites abroad, in return, agreed to stop publishing hostile journals.

The government also did some damage to the CDLR in its counter-offensive. Though it did not accuse the group of involvement in the Riyadh car bombing, it persuaded one of the convicted killers to declare in a televised confession that he had been swayed by Massa'ri's faxes from London. The assertion, while proving no culpability, suggested to believers that Massa'ri was abetting disorder. Massa'ri countered with a move to undermine the government's truce with the Saudi Shi'ites.

The rapprochement between the Sauds and the Shi'ites was already foundering when Massa'ri reached London in mid-1994. A year of quiet had been overtaken by a resumption of mutual recriminations. The truce remained officially in force, however, until November 1996. That is when the government publicly accused the Shi'ites of the bombing at Dhahran.

Massa'ri responded to the opening by announcing a plan to establish a Sunni-Shi'ite coalition against the royal family. He no doubt recognized that, in promoting a coalition with the Shi'ites, he was going against the grain of Saudi culture. The Sunni-Shi'ite conflict in Arabia goes back to Ali's time, more than thirteen hundred years before. In proposing a reconciliation, Massa'ri was propounding a doctrine of tolerance that was foreign to Saudi Sunnis. His fellow dissidents, also shaped by Arabia's history, were themselves uncomfortable at the prospect of cooperating with Shi'ites.

Asked by journalists to lay out the political changes he envisaged in setting up a Sunni-Shi'ite front, Massa'ri answered by advocating a very non-Islamic separation of religion and the state. Wahhabis had to be bewildered by his meaning.

"The state," Massa'ri said, "will be responsible for the defense of the country based on Islam, for the economic system based on Islam, for keeping public order and public morals as agreed upon by all Muslims . . . [but] the state will get out of sectarian affairs [and] not interfere in matters of worship and private cults or in questions of creed."

Proposing such religious freedom as Saudi Arabia had never known, he said the government "will not be involved in deciding if this or that school of thought is more suitable. That is for everyone to decide on his own."[3]

Massa'ri's plans were far too radical—too liberal, to be precise, too revolutionary—to sit comfortably, not just with Saudis generally but with his own organization. Massa'ri's strategic views were similarly evolving, to the point of his proposing CDLR's political cooperation not only with Shi'ites but with any others, not necessarily Saudis, who might be useful to his campaign. Strains within resistance movements in exile are not unusual, of course. But Massa'ri's strategy, predictably, split CDLR. The schism produced wings that were not so much hostile to each other as committed to different courses.

The split in London only intensified doubts among Saudis about whether the ideas of the opposition in exile were compatible with those of the dissidents at home. The two movements held some negative ideas in common. Neither argued for popular democracy, free expression or women's equality, all foreign values. Neither concealed a suspicion of the West, and an aversion to Zionism. Both made their case to Saudi Arabians within the framework of traditional Islamic reforms.

Some Saudi sympathizers feared, however, that geography had tilted the exiles toward Western-style liberalism, while repression had tilted the locals toward Khomeini-style absolutism. The gravitation of both away from the center strengthened the royal family, leaving it in a position to claim that alone, unreformed, it represented national authenticity and religious purity.

When I visited Saudi Arabia in 1995, most of the known dissidents were still confined either in prison or house arrest. But sympathizers were surprisingly easy to find and, with appropriate caution, ready to talk. All admitted to uncertainty about where the two dissident groups stood.

These sympathizers acknowledged that dissent had not reached the stage of a popular movement. Their explanation was that Saudi culture was averse to political risk, attributable in part to an Islamic habit of accepting authority and in part to a recognition of economic dependency on the Sauds. Massa'ri's calls for sit-ins in the mosques, for example, had evoked no response. Yet I was told repeatedly that the dissidents represented an "attitude," which was steadily spreading.

Royal-family loyalists dismissed the dissidence as unimportant. Some contended that it was simply the rebellion of one generation against its elders. The Sauds will survive it, they maintained, as the Sauds have survived earlier challenges.

It is true that most of the dissidents were in their thirties and forties, while the elite who dominated the Saud family and ran the country were in their seventies and eighties. In a society as tediously conformist as Saudi Arabia, the reformers' youth was in itself attractive. The loyalists were mistaken, however, in arguing that the appeal of the dissidents was limited to the young. Even family partisans admitted to a widespread popular feeling that the ruling elite was geriatric, and that the time had come to pass the torch.

In the final analysis, what stunned the royal family was the audacity of the dissidents' Islamic claims. The Sauds have always taken pride in their piety. They never describe their foes as fundamentalists, because they reserve the term to describe themselves. In their counterattacks, they denounce the dissidents as fanatics who are degrading Islam to promote impious ends. But they could not conceal their pain, since what the dissidents were doing was challenging them at their own Islamic game.

· III ·

IN THE CENTURIES after the Prophet Muhammad received the Quranic revelations, Arabia drifted away from the rigorous monotheism that Islam had introduced and retreated to the primitive religious practices of *jahiliyya,* the era that preceded Muhammad's revelations. Both townspeople and bedouins resumed praying to saints, making pilgrimages to tombs, venerating trees and stones, offering sacrifices to lesser gods.

After Muhammad's death in 632, the centers of Islamic teaching had moved away, to Baghdad and Damascus, and to cities beyond the

Arab world. Mecca, though still the object of the annual *hajj*, became an intellectual backwater. So did Medina. The state that the Prophet created had disintegrated, ceding political preeminence to a patchwork of tribal sovereignties. Arabia's inhabitants were still Muslims, their relations vaguely governed by the *shari'a*. But they had largely resumed the life of their ancestors in *jahiliyya*, the time of ignorance.

Like the Prophet Muhammad eleven hundred years before him, Muhammad ibn Abd al-Wahhab, an itinerant preacher, was deeply troubled by the condition of his homeland. Born in a southern oasis in 1703, he had studied in Medina, then in Iraq and Iran, and returned home committed to leading an Islamic renaissance.

The Ottoman Empire was the major power in Arabia at this time. Though the Ottomans had troops based in many of the towns, the inaccessibility, harsh climate and nomadic social structure of Arabia saved it from total conquest. Wahhab loathed the Ottomans' toleration of paganism in the peninsula. His aim was to drive them out and establish a strong Arabian political authority that would restore authentic religious practices.

Wahhab proceeded to lead a fundamentalist crusade that contained the germ of what would one day be called nationalism. It aspired to ending foreign influence in Arabia. But in its puritanism and xenophobia it was also an introduction to the fundamentalism that, two centuries later, aroused the enthusiasm of believers throughout the Islamic world.

Wahhab's intellectual guide was Taki al-Din Ibn Taimiyya, a fourteenth-century jurist of the rigid school of law founded by Ahmad Ibn Hanbal, the pillar of orthodoxy who—as noted in Chapter 5—had defied the *mihnah* during the reign of the Abbasid caliph al-Ma'mun. As a teacher in Damascus and Cairo, Ibn Taimiyya had won a following during an era that was similarly upsetting to Islam, when rationalist philosophy influenced by the Greeks and by Sufi mysticism appeared to be on the rise.

A literal interpreter of the scriptures, Ibn Taimiyya castigated both Greek philosophy and Sufism as *bid'a*, innovation. He did not claim to be an original thinker; in fact, he was consistent in denouncing all original thinking as heresy. His vision of himself was as a restorer of the era of the *rashidun*. Ibn Taimiyya also argued that the local *ulama* served Islam more faithfully than the caliphs in distant Baghdad. Four centuries later his work became the text for Wahhab's Arabian crusade.[4]

Wahhab's goal was to bring all Muslims back to Prophetic Islam, in which believers followed a charismatic and devout leader. "Unity is a sign of divine clemency," Ibn Taimiyya had written. "Discord is a punishment of God."[5] To Muhammad ibn Abd al-Wahhab, Ibn Taimiyya brought the vision of a rigorous orthodoxy, not only in religious practice but in social behavior.

The Islam that Wahhab preached was starkly puritan—no singing, no dancing, no smoking. Its model was the life he presumed Muslims led under the Prophet. Not only did he classify much of existing ritual as pagan; he left little margin for human foibles. Though the world attaches Wahhab's name to the beliefs he preached, his followers prefer to call themselves "unitarians." The term reflects the claim that theirs is not a variation of Islam but the Prophet's doctrine itself, the one true faith.

Wahhabism became the backbone of Saudi political development. But, by a historical quirk, its success grew out of early failure. Muhammad ibn Abd al-Wahhab's preaching—like the Prophet Muhammad's—made very few converts to his version of the faith. So Wahhab shifted strategy. He set out in search of a tribal leader who had the armed might and the will to enforce the puritan dogma he espoused. Wahhab found such a leader in 1744 in Muhammad ibn Saud, an ambitious chief living in the village of Diriyah, now a suburb of Riyadh. The two forged an alliance that has endured.

As nearly as historians can tell, the Saud clan, town dwellers rather than bedouins, had arrived in central Arabia, the region called Nejd, from the desert of the northeast only a few decades before. The clan was well organized, and when Saud heard Wahhab out, he was persuaded that Wahhab's ideology could serve his tribal ambitions.

The two men not only exchanged oaths of fidelity; Saud also married his daughter to Wahhab, sealing the family bond. When Wahhab urged a declaration of holy war against heresy, Saud was glad to comply. Together they envisaged establishing an Islamic state based on pure Prophetic principles, under the rule of the House of Saud.

With the Wahhabs providing religious guidance, the Sauds over the ensuing decades sent emissaries throughout the peninsula to teach the tenets of their reformist faith. But, like the Prophet, they were more successful in making converts on the battlefield, winning a series of major military victories that subjugated towns and tribes. Gradually, the Ottomans withdrew, leaving the Saud leaders in charge of a widening area, on which they imposed the *zakat*, the Quranic tax, as symbol of Islam's and their own authority.

The Sauds, it should be noted, applied their authority not just on Sunni tribes, who accepted it more or less willingly, but on the Shi'ite tribes spread throughout the region, who did not. In 1802 a Saudi army spilled out of Arabia and sacked the Shi'ite town of Karbala in Iraq, laying waste the shrine of Imam Hussein. The incident fixed the terms of the Sauds' relations with Shi'ism into a permanent mutual animosity.

But tribal shrines in Arabia fared no better than Karbala. By the beginning of the nineteenth century the House of Saud had unified the peninsula. In doing so, it had reduced all pagan monuments—as the Prophet himself had once done—to piles of ruins.

Wahhabism, in alliance with the Sauds, remains the backbone of the state to this day. The Wahhabs impart Islamic legitimacy; the Sauds are the enforcers of religious orthodoxy. In the nineteenth century the Saudi empire was brought down once by the Ottomans and once by a rival tribe, the Rashids; meanwhile, the British navy in the Gulf nibbled off bits of the periphery—Kuwait, Oman, Bahrain, the Emirates. Yet throughout the years the Saud-Wahhab alliance has retained Arabia's loyalty. After each fall, popular support helped the Sauds to pick themselves up and restore their sovereign rule.

The Saudi state, in preserving its sovereignty, has had over the years to modify its ruling institutions very little. It retains today the same parallel hierarchies, royal and clerical, that first governed 250 years ago.

In theory, the Saudi monarchy is the executive, the Wahhabi *ulama* the moral guide. In practice, the relationship is more complex. The two institutions, while allies, are often rivals, each tugging constantly at the other.

The clerics prefer to call the head of the House of Saud "Imam," to convey the holy source of his power; the Saudi monarch, having adopted the title Custodian of the Two [Mecca and Medina] Holy Mosques to assert his piety, likes being called "King," though in Arabic the title has a foreign ring that clerics scorn.

Yet, while each hierarchy tries for a leg up on the other, they acknowledge their mutual dependence. Whatever the Saudi dissidents' current demands for reform, history suggests that the regime has survived this long precisely because it has never, in its basic structure, given serious thought to reform at all.

· IV ·

ABDULLAH bin Muhammad al-Alshaikh is an example of how the system works. A direct descendant of Sheikh Muhammad ibn Abd al-Wahhab—the family has since adopted Alshaikh as its surname—he gravitated through his kinship ties into the clerical establishment. Educated at Riyadh's Imam Muhammad bin Saud University—usually called Imam University, where most of the country's high clerics are trained—he received a doctorate in Islamic law, then became a professor and a dean. Married, with four children, he was in his late forties when we met.

Alshaikh, heavily bearded, talks softly but his manner conveys great certainty. He is currently the Minister of Justice, which means that he supervises Saudi Arabia's Islamic system of law, the *shari'a*. It is the only law the country has.

"Islamic law requires the presence of a state," he told me in a meeting at his ministry. What he proceeded to articulate were the governing principles of the state, and the peculiarly Saudi view of the link between government and law.

"My ancestor, Muhammad ibn Abd al-Wahhab, could have gone to the mosque to seize political and religious power through the people, but he understood his limitations. He imparted to Muhammad ibn Saud the wisdom he needed to become caliph, a successor to the Prophet Muhammad. Such is the path of succession of whoever rules by Islamic law. Abd al-Wahhab's mandate was to be the ruler's guide, but the state is the final authority, even in religious matters."

When I asked Alshaikh how Islam responds to the corruption of which I had heard so much in Saudi Arabia, he did not dismiss the question. On the contrary, he had a ready answer.

"It is forbidden in Islam to raise a hand against the ruler. If he makes a mistake—even a big one like corruption, and that includes adultery or stealing or drinking—it is prohibited to overthrow him. If he forces others to violate Islam, you may refuse to follow him but you can go no further. You can advise him to change his ways, but you cannot publicize his faults.

"The one exception is heresy; if the ruler does not believe in God or the Prophet, then action is required.

"Otherwise, to overthrow a ruler is not permitted. When a people is without a ruler, what results is *fitna*—public disorder—and that is worse than corrupt rule. Obedience to rulers is part of Muslim practice."

Obedience, enforced under the *shari'a,* is the linchpin of the jointly exercised rule of the Sauds and the Wahhabs. The notion that obedience is a duty comes from the Hanbali school of law, whose interpretation of the *shari'a* rules in Saudi Arabia. The admonition to obey, while backed by *hadith,* also relies heavily on interpretation of the

Quranic verse that, according to the translation by Helms, says: *"Fitna is a greater sin than killing"* (2:217).*

Ahmad Ibn Hanbal, founder of the Hanbali school, provoked *fitna* himself—as we saw in Chapter 5—during the Abbasid caliphate of al-Ma'mun. Alshaikh would no doubt exculpate Hanbal, however, on the grounds that al-Ma'mun, having embraced the Mu'tazilite heresy, fell under the exception clause to the *fitna* rule,

Quranic scholars variously define *fitna* along a continuum from civil disturbance to doctrinal challenges to Islam.[6] In Saudi eyes, the Ottomans who overthrew the Sauds in the nineteenth century committed *fitna;* so did Saddam Hussein in invading Kuwait and Khomeini in promoting protests in Mecca during the *hajj*. But *fitna* might also describe *bid'a*, innovations of any kind, including rebuttals of orthodoxy or the introduction of new practices. Obviously the doctrine, selectively employed, is a useful instrument for preserving both the social order and the political status quo.

Alshaikh's remarks make clear that not only Massa'ri and his fellow exiles but Audah, Hawali and the other clerical critics of the Sauds can be accused, under the official definition, of promoting *fitna*. Unlike Hanbal, moreover, none of them is likely to qualify—as long as the Wahhabi *ulama* does the interpreting—under the exception that authorizes *fitna* against heresy.

The present generation of dissidents are by no means the first Wahhabis, dissatisfied with the state's level of piety, to engage deliberately in *fitna*. Such deviance from the norm is not astonishing. Any state whose legitimacy is based on an extreme religious doctrine (Wahhabism) that is constantly fanned by professionals (*ulama*) risks being theologically outflanked. As we are about to see, the Sauds were outflanked by zealots earlier in the century and barely survived. In pretending to be surprised by the current wave of Islamic dissidents, the Sauds are being either disingenuous or remiss in not having learned that lesson.

When the century began, the Sauds still depended for their military power on contingents of volunteers, which they recruited on an ad hoc basis. At first they relied on townspeople, their chief political base. Later they shifted to bedouins, many of whose tribes had recently been converted to Wahhabism. The most ferocious were the Wahhabi zeal-

* Pickthall renders the verse as "Persecution is worse than killing"; Dawood as "Idolatry is worse than carnage"; and Cragg as "Subversion is more heinous than slaughter." The variety illustrates the difficulties with Quranic translations. The Helms translation is the closest to the Hanbali view.

ots who called themselves Ikhwan ("brothers"). Though they sometimes resisted Saudi discipline, the Ikhwan became the Sauds' chief military agents.

A century ago, during a period when the the Sauds were out of power, many of the Ikhwan decided to abandon desert life to regroup—in emulation, they claimed, of Muhammad's *hijra* to Medina—in agricultural settlements. Within their communities, walled and generally clustered around a simple mud brick mosque, they practiced a cultlike Islam, requiring members to attend the mosque five times daily and segregate themselves rigidly by gender. More than any known fundamentalist society, the Ikhwan planned literally to recreate the Islamic golden age, to the point of shunning all technology that was unknown to the Prophet.

The Sauds endorsed and even helped finance the movement, which by 1915 numbered some two hundred settlements. The Ikhwan, in return, contributed soldiers to defeat the Sauds' enemies, first the Rashid tribe, from whom they wrested back the north of the peninsula in 1921, and then the Hashemites, from whom they conquered Hejaz, the western region that included Mecca and Medina, in 1924. With the Ikhwan's arms, the Sauds also imposed their rule for the first time on the bedouins living in the desert of central Arabia.

By the late 1920s the Ikhwan had become addicted to a fighting *jihad*, which in their eyes justified the massacre even of the women and children whom they regarded as insufficiently pious. They also waged war on Shi'ites, foreigners and Sunnis of non-Wahhabi faith. The royal family, while continuing to use Ikhwan volunteers, also understood the need to restrain their excesses.

The Ikhwan overreached in raiding the territory of Iraq and Transjordan, which the British after World War I had awarded to the Hashemites, long-standing rivals of the Sauds. The Ikhwan invaded the Hashemites' domains, even converting some of the local tribes to Wahhabism. Then Britain struck back with armor and aircraft, causing heavy casualties in Saudi towns and villages, and the Sauds, over the objections of the Ikhwan, decided to adopt a less aggressive strategy.

Meanwhile, the Saudi monarch had declared himself "Custodian of the Two Holy Mosques," Mecca and Medina, in recognition of his new responsibilities. These responsibilities included managing the *hajj,* the Muslim pilgrimage. No longer could the Sauds be simply Wahhabis, presiding over their own, isolated realm. In administering the pilgrimage, they had to accommodate to Muslims from outside Arabia, most of whom practiced a far less severe form of Islam.

The Ikhwan disapproved of the concessions the royal family extended to the more than 130,000 Muslims who, as early as 1927, made the *hajj*.[7] The Sauds supplied the pilgrims with cars and buses, electricity and places to sleep. They accredited foreign consuls, some of them Christian. With the approval of the *ulama*, they even offered visitors the luxury of radio.

The Ikhwan, denouncing the Sauds for impiety while continuing to provoke the British, had now become a real menace to regional stability. Some of its members called openly for the Sauds' downfall. "They thought they were right," said Abdulaziz, the Saudi monarch, "because of their love of religion. They became fanatics, and their affairs were against the instruction of the *shari'a*."[8] Though good Muslims, he said, they were guilty of *fitna*.

The Sauds responded to the danger by turning to their old constituency, the Arabian towns, to organize a rival army. With help from the British, they equipped this new army with modern vehicles and supported it with British-piloted planes. In a battle in March 1929, the loyalist forces beat the Ikhwan badly. It took more fighting and further assistance from Britain, but within a year the power of the Ikhwan had been broken for good.

The rebellion and defeat of the Ikhwan taught the monarchy many lessons. One was that reliance on a single army to defend the state placed the monarchy itself in danger. Since then the country has always had two armies, neither very strong, positioned to compete with the other.

The victory also taught the Sauds to be vigilant in the defense of their Wahhabi credentials. In administering Mecca and Medina and in humbling the Ikhwan, they had shown a capacity to be practical as well as pious. But practicality, to many believers, was by its nature the enemy of piety. Consorting with infidels, whether to suppress *fitna* or build a telegraph system, deeply offended some Wahhabis. The war against the Ikhwan showed the Sauds that their perpetual need to renew their Islamic credentials would always narrow the limits on their political options.

The war against the Ikhwan in 1929, in a sense, foreshadowed Saudi Arabia's current political crisis. That the Sauds were serving Muslims during the *hajj* was not enough; they were also bringing innovation to the kingdom. Nor was it enough during the Gulf War that the Sauds were defending Arabia; they were also consorting with infidels. Then as now, these were sins that many Wahhabis were not prepared to forgive.

But the Sauds, in our own era, helped to bring the problem on themselves in rejecting any shift, even a gradual one, to popular participation in the affairs of state. In refusing to share political responsibility, in times of both tranquillity and danger, they have failed to build a constituency of support for their political system.

Committed as they are to a monopoly of power, they have inevitably courted conflict between the temporal and religious demands of the unusual society that they govern. They faced a real dilemma in 1991 in being unable to keep both the Iraqi army at bay and Western forces from sullying the holy soil. The dilemma, even in retrospect, offers no ready solution. As long as the Sauds exercise total authority in the kingdom, they will be unable to unload any share of the blame for mistakes. They are also likely to find, as long as they depend on the favor of clerics sworn to Wahhabi purity, that, whatever the dangers the country may face, their responses will never be quite pious enough.

· V ·

ON A BARREN PATCH of desert at the edge of Riyadh, a huge, beautifully landscaped, white marble building stands beside a busy highway. The building is identified only by a small plaque inscribed K.F.C.C. The initials stand for King Fahd Cultural Center, a concert hall that seats 3,000 and boasts laser lighting, a hydraulically operated stage, air conditioning and plush salon chairs. It has never been used.

In an article in the *Washington Post,*[9] John Lancaster reports that the hall was completed at a cost of some $140 million on the eve of the Gulf War. The *ulama,* witnessing the arrival of hundreds of thousands of foreign troops, mostly American, pressured the government to keep the doors of the auditorium closed. They feared, Lancaster writes, a deluge of immodestly dressed performers, Western music and dancing, and mixed-sex audiences. After the war the *ulama* persisted in its objections, and the curtain at the K.F.C.C. has still not been raised.

Since the defeat of the Ikhwan in 1930, the Sauds have aspired to coax the *ulama* into accepting the modern world. But as a matter of tactics, they have eschewed confrontation. When Sheikh bin Baz said the sun rotated around the earth, the Sauds did not contradict him, and bin Baz has since become one of the family's most faithful retainers. Whenever they have met resistance from the *ulama,* the Sauds have preferred to retreat rather than fight.

When the first radio stations were installed, for example, the Sauds, in return for clerical approval, saw to it that broadcasts of the Quran would flood the airwaves. To win consent for public education, they conceded the predominance of Islamic studies in the curriculum. To bring girls into the educational system, they granted the *ulama* the administration of all girls' schools. Even now, the clergy are the most important force in the Saudi Arabian school system.

After Khomeini's triumph in Iran in 1979, followed by the seizure of the Mecca mosque, the government made heavy concessions to the clerics to shore up their Islamic support. They closed the movie houses and barred music and drama from television. Soon after, they revoked the right of women to travel or study abroad in the absence of male relatives.

As a further response to Khomeini, the Sauds increased the power of the *mutaween,* street-level enforcers of Wahhabi belief. Once the *mutaween,* mosque employees, had been empowered simply to summon men to the mosque to pray. In the 1980s they were incorporated into the civil service and authorized to close shops during prayer time. They also took over the supervision of women's dress, assuring the modesty even of foreign women.

The *mutaween* ended the tolerance of private worship by non-Muslims, largely Christians. Millions of foreigners, invited by the government to do the work that Saudis will not do, now live in the country. The *mutaween* keep them from meeting to pray, and have even raided the religious services of diplomats.

During the Gulf War, when Western servicewomen were appearing publicly in uniform on city streets, forty-seven Saudi women organized a demonstration to win the right to drive. Notwithstanding international publicity, the King seized their passports, fired all of them from their jobs and made the driving ban on women even more stringent than before. A *fatwa* justified the action as observance of the Islamic injunction to preserve women's dignity.

"The King, deep down, is less rigid than the clergy," an editor of an Islamic paper said to me. "By Saudi standards, he is probably very enlightened. But the people are Wahhabi, and I'm not sure how much social change the people want.

"We have an enlightened, Western-oriented middle class, which favors reform. Its members behave differently when they go to London or Cairo, and even behind the doors of their own homes. They're tired of the gap between ideology and practice, and they'd like to end the hypocrisy. But the national consensus remains Wahhabi, and no one successfully challenges it.

"The women who demonstrated for the right to drive did not get public support, and the King was applauded for punishing them. The clergy may be an obstacle to modernization but they are not alone. Fahd can't be more liberal than the people."

A Western-educated intellectual had a slightly different reading of the clergy's power.

"In recent years," he said, "this country has exploded with new experiences in technology and in such areas as banking and management. These changes have been absorbed with no conflict.

"But the old social issues remain untouched. Islamic society has not resolved three questions: where women fit in, what the goal of education is, and how much freedom of dissent to grant the people and the media. Everyone is concerned about these questions. But no one talks of them in public, not in the universities or the chambers of commerce, and certainly not in the press. We can't even buy books unless they are approved by the Ministry of Information, and then we know they say nothing."

This man argued that the Saudi *ulama*, even though not a formal clergy, is more powerful than the Catholic hierarchy. Its Vatican is Imam University, which funnels a great number of Islamic Ph.D.s into the government system. Young as they are, he said, these clerics get jobs with substantial authority. Some go abroad, to other Muslim countries, to proselytize for Wahhabism. Many go into education, he said, where they enforce the *ulama*'s directives and brainwash the students.

"A few decades ago," he said, "our country was almost illiterate. Now thousands of young people graduate from our schools every year. They used to go to universities abroad, and many came back with modern ideas. Now we have seven universities of our own, and our students stay home and become ingrown. Many graduate as teachers—especially the women, since no other work is available to them— and go on to reinforce religious thinking in the schools.

"It is ironic that when the schools were established they were regarded as liberalizing instruments. But under the rule of the clergy, they are making the society even more conservative.

"The situation has developed this way because the royal family's policy has been to respond to every crisis by granting a few more concessions to the clerics. It thinks it is co-opting them, but they keep demanding more. As they grow stronger, they bring us not higher spiritual values but more ritual, which translates into greater social and doctrinal conformity."

The man pointed out that, as a sign of religiosity, Saudi men increasingly wear beards, while more and more women wear the full veil and the black *abaya*. The *mutaween* patrol the streets and the markets with greater dedication, making sure that women's arms are covered. Men want to be seen reciting prayers. Yet, he said, Saudis are not better Muslims. On the contrary, the more they ritualize religion, the more they marginalize belief.

"I'm not sure whether Audah and Hawali, rebellious as they are, depart from this pattern. They come from the trend that says women shouldn't drive and Shi'ites are not Muslims. They demand political accountability, but they seem to be urging even greater restrictions on popular freedoms.

"As for Massa'ri and the CDLR, they are new to us, and they apparently are still developing their ideas. I think they represent progressive Islam, more so than Audah and Hawali. But it's like the opening frames of a movie: we still don't know the plot.

"King Fahd will be succeeded by one of his brothers, who is more or less his contemporary, and I don't think anything will change. We hope the younger generation of the royal family will be different. The sons still go abroad to school and are said to understand that the country is in a straitjacket. But that's a surmise. Everything about the royal family is secretive.

"Besides, if all we do is wait, it will be a long time before the old men who now rule us give way to the next generation."

· VI ·

THE SAUDI ROYAL FAMILY is convinced it presides over a country that is peculiarly blessed. It feels that it has created an ideal fusion—not just for an Islamic society, for any society—of political and religious power. In talking to family members, they say they are puzzled about why their system is not emulated by other states, and at least by other Muslim states.

The Saud family looks at its neighbors Egypt and Iraq, and it vows that it will not have an army, like theirs, that can overthrow a monarchy and take over the state. It considers the disorderly parliaments of Kuwait and Jordan to be convincing evidence of the disadvantages of democracy. And it takes satisfaction that when Saddam's army stood at the gates, the Saudi people rallied around, and the family came through intact.

But many Saudi citizens are disenchanted at their rulers' failure to have learned useful lessons from the war.

Everyone knows the war was costly; no one knows how costly. The government releases whatever financial data it chooses, and no outsider can pretend to have a clear picture of the state's finances. A reasonable guess holds that the war cost Saudi Arabia about $60 billion. This is beyond the $30 billion the government contributed in the 1980s to defray the expenses of Iraq's war against Iran. The government may have spent another $50 billion after the Gulf War to refit its own forces. To pay these huge bills, the government has had to draw down its reserves, but it still has no foreign debt, and since the war its reserves may be rising again.

The royal family, though currently pinched, has shown no disposition to change its spendthrift practices. The state still levies no income or profits taxes, though to demonstrate its fiscal responsibility it has reduced by about a fourth its subsidies to the public on the consumption of water and electricity, on medical services and on agriculture. Few Saudis that I met complained of having to endure this austerity. On the other hand, I heard many complaints about the royal family's refusal to share in it.

King Fahd, unlike his predecessors, is said by Saudis to impose no spending limits on family members. According to estimates, 5,000 princes, and an equal number of princesses, now receive large monthly stipends for no reason except kinship. Family members still build lavish palaces and, unlike other citizens, pay nothing for utilities, airplane tickets and other state services. They pocket huge commissions on foreign contracts and, recently the King is said to have dropped his guard against the princes' muscling in, Mafia-like, on private businessmen. These practices, hitherto strictly barred, are reported to be straining the patience of the bourgeoisie, a class that has always been loyal to the status quo.

Just as the war produced no cutbacks in the financial liberties taken by the Sauds, it produced no restructuring of the national security policies which left the country totally dependent on foreigners for its protection. Though the country is now investing heavily in air defense, it is doing little to upgrade its ground forces. Clearly, the unhappy memory of the war against the Ikhwan remains vivid; no steps have been taken to unify the ground forces.

Pentagon sources told me that Saudi defense strategy is to build only enough power to slow an aggressor, while preparing for the infrastructural needs of a friendly—meaning American—expeditionary force that will, in time, arrive to save the country. This strategy is acknowledged to be a carbon copy of the Desert Storm operation of 1990–91.

In interviewing Saudi officials, I found the most embarrassing question I could ask was why the country, with substantially greater population and wealth, could not build an army like Israel's to defend itself.

The reply generally consisted of thin sociology. When pressed, officials reluctantly admitted that the royal family had no appetite for a strong standing army.

"Moving from a state of scarcity a few decades ago, our priority was a good life, not a defense force," said Prince Saud al-Faisal, the Foreign Minister and nephew of the King. "Building an army takes time as well as money. We have to develop our human resources, to learn how to use modern weapons. It cannot be our top priority. The comparison with Israel, where the people came from Europe, isn't fair.

"In the Gulf War, hundreds of thousands of foreign troops were based on our soil, and our society retained its cohesion. That was our achievement. We do not dismiss its importance.

"No one wants someone else's sons to come here to die, and in theory every country should be able to defend itself. But collective security is an honorable strategy. Remember that the West, in dealing with the Soviet Union, relied on it for decades. In dealing with Iraq, both we and our allies found it a useful strategy, and we are prepared to rely on it again."

The principal political change after the Gulf War has been the King's establishment of a *Majlis al-Shura,* a national consultative council, as well as thirteen provincial councils responsible to local governors. *Shura*—conventionally interpreted as consultation between the ruler and the ruled—is enjoined in the Quran. As we noted before, it is one of Islam's few political commandments and was applied for the election of the first four caliphs. *Shura* was among the demands contained in the clerics' letter to the King in May 1991. Though some Islamic thinkers take it as a call for a democratic state, the House of Saud interprets it more modestly.

Shura, emerging out of bedouin practices, became part of the Saudi state machinery under King Abdulaziz, who founded the present kingdom at the turn of the century. It fell into disuse in the 1950s, when the Sauds, bowing to pressures to modernize government, adopted a cabinet system around the King.

King Fahd, on assuming the throne in 1982, promised to restore *shura* to the political system, and in 1985 actually built a sumptuous palace in which the *Majlis*—the word means "discussion group"—was to sit. But no *shura* was established and, in the void, Saudis became skeptical that one would ever be. The King finally issued a *shura* decree in 1992, a year after the Gulf War, and in 1993 the body met for the first time. The provincial bodies began meeting a year later.

The *Majlis al-Shura* has sixty-one members, including its chairman, Muhammad bin Jubair, who is an old tribal leader and a former Justice

Minister. The entire membership was appointed by the King, who, to the surprise of most Saudis, named no princes to seats. Rather, he tipped the body toward academics, then added some engineers, businessmen, doctors and lawyers, religious scholars and retired civil servants.

The selections, to be sure, contained no hint of representativity, whether geographical, class or tribal. Predictably, the King named no dissidents; the *shura* has no formal opposition within it. But the appointments were not frivolous. They were weighted heavily toward nonclerics with practical experience and intellectual attainment. More than half the members named were Ph.D.s, and two thirds had studied in the West.

"When King Abdulaziz established the *shura,* there were very few educated people in the kingdom," said Sheikh Jubair, its elderly chairman. Jubair, circled by aides, received me in a richly carpeted, vanilla and gold sitting room of the *Majlis* building. "The educated people were all clergy. The luminaries were tribal chieftains. Nonetheless, the King relied on it for advice on legal, financial and management problems. By the 1950s, however, the King had more qualified people available, and the world was more complicated, and so the *shura* lost its role.

"But it never really disappeared. It is required in Islam. God in the Quran instructs the ruler to ask advice of the *people who know* before reaching a decision.* The laws of Islam were written fourteen hundred years ago in the Quran and the *sunna,* and they do not require a legislature. To make the *shura* into a representative body would not be Islamic.

"Of course, times change. Not everything is in the *shari'a.* The King cannot change the laws against drinking, for example, but when we need traffic regulations, he issues a decree and everyone is required by the Quran to obey it. But the *shura* is not a step toward democracy. It is our own system, coming from our religion and habits and tradition.

"Furthermore, if we had an election, we wouldn't get such educated men to serve. The voters would not choose members qualified to offer the King advice. They would elect tribal chiefs, unable to read or write. Our *shura,* composed of experts, fulfills its Islamic mandate of advising the King, who has the responsibility to rule."

Under the royal decree, the *shura*'s mandate is to consider drafts of laws and international agreements which are submitted to it. Consid-

* In fact, the Quran's requirement of a *shura* does not specify "people who know," though the Prophet is quoted on such a principle in the *sunna.*

eration of the national budget, which the royal family treats as a private matter, is not included among its responsibilities.

Organized much like a parliament, the *Majlis al-Shura* has committees which hear testimony and, after discussion, propose action to the plenary body. The *shura* can summon officials and request state documents, but it has no watchdog functions. The *shura* debates and votes, then sends its recommendations to the King. All of its proceedings are recorded. What most distinguishes it from parliaments is that its actions have no binding force.

Abdulaziz al-Fayez, a respected political scientist on leave from Riyadh University, told me he had no indication in advance that he was a candidate, and was stunned by his nomination to the *shura*. All members agree to serve full time for four years, for which they are paid a small stipend. They are very conscientious about their work, he said, and debate the issues thoughtfully and respectfully. All accept the limitations on their power.

"We have no illusions," Fayez said. "We're Saudis, and we're used to paternalism. Our job is to give our honest judgments on public issues, and we do. We are a source of information and analysis that is outside the ministerial circle. In short, we are a body of advisers to the King, and nothing more."

Fayez said the King has shown respect for the *shura* and seems to take its recommendations seriously. The rules of procedure, however, not only make its deliberations secret but bar its members from discussing any items on its agenda with the press.

Since citizens have little idea what the *Majlis al-Shura* does, and even less what the provincial *shura*s do, the entire process becomes an easy target of mockery, which Fayez says it does not deserve. Critics regard the *Majlis al-Shura* as a political lapdog, designed to give the King cover against charges of despotism. In fact, the *shura* process is shrouded in so much secrecy that most Saudis, having been introduced to it as a step toward accountability, have now all but forgotten that it exists.

Dr. Abdullah al-Naseef, who is deputy chairman to Sheikh Jubair, told me he regrets that the *shura* does not play a more prominent role in Saudi affairs.

Naseef studied in the 1960s at Berkeley, where he said he learned to cherish American democracy, though he was appalled at its absence of spiritual content. By profession a geologist, he has also served as executive director of the World Muslim League, where he said he has worked to promote an Islam that is gentler than what the world generally perceives.

"We Arabs are now emerging from the Dark Ages," Naseef said. "We turned away from Greek thought under the Abbasids; we suffered from intellectual aggression during colonialism; we gave up *ijtihad* during the Ottoman years. We largely lost our ability to think and criticize. Now we are frustrated and have a deep inferiority complex. Coming out is very hard."

Naseef said he saw the *shura* as the beginning of a social transformation. He wants its sessions covered by the press, even televised, but the government refuses. The Saud family fails to understand, he said, that the people now want to participate in the life of the country. The *shura* has been conducting itself responsibly. Opening it up, he said, would give Saudis a greater sense of themselves, and even enhance social stability.

Naseef contended that Saudis are ready to build on the experience they already have had with elections in universities, chambers of commerce and professional associations. Nothing in Islam bars elections, he argued, or even women's suffrage. Sheikh Jubair is mistaken, he declared, in asserting that elections will bring in unsuitable people. Vigorous debate may not be part of the Quran, he said, but it is part of bedouin tradition, and Saudis are ready for it.

"Sheikh Jubair is right, however, in saying there are limits to speech in Islam," Naseef continued. "Indeed, I was shocked by the speech and the disorder I found in Berkeley in 1964. They were not good for America. Those young people, in their absence of values, were failed by their families. Such an experience would not be good for us. Totally free speech can lead to free sex, illegitimate children, wild behavior. Fortunately, Islam provides signposts. Our moral precepts, based on our faith, are our strength.

"Nonetheless, we have to have dialogue in Islam. One man can't issue *fatwa*s, not even Sheikh bin Baz, on what the Quran or the *sunna* says. Egypt is having so much trouble with its young people because they have never been introduced to the gentle side of Islam. A Godless society has made heroes of the radicals, who want to kill for Islam. When the young are not taught that Islam is tolerant and loving, how can they grow up to be reasonable?

"We Muslims are the greatest enemies of Islam. We blame Western conspiracies for our problems rather than look into ourselves. We applaud Khomeini's foolish *fatwa* against Rushdie. We are still fighting Mu'tazilites and *ijtihad,* when we should be reaching out for fresh ideas within our own culture.

"That's why the *shura* is important. Islamic doctrine does not limit it in any way. The government says that opening up the debate will confuse the people. I think it is just the opposite. I believe television will be covering our meetings before very long. I'm among the Saudis who think this is the beginning of something very good."

· VII ·

PRINCE Salman bin Abdulaziz, the youngest full brother of King Fahd, has since 1962 been the governor of the province of Riyadh. He has been a good governor, most say.

Born in 1936, he is on the record as King Abdulaziz's thirty-second son. Though the Saudi system empowers the King to designate his successor, in practice the decision is subject to the advice—the *shura*—of the closest family members. Many believe that Salman one day will become King, but the royal succession has always contained uncertainties.

Currently, Salman is not even the crown prince. The present heir to the throne is Prince Abdullah, a half brother who was born in 1923, two years after the King. In a society that reveres blood relationships, it has been a puzzle to Saudis why Abdullah, son of King Abdulaziz by a different mother, was selected. He is said to be more austere, less worldly, than his half brothers. It has also been common knowledge that he is not close to King Fahd.

Still, in early 1996, it was Abdullah who served as acting King while Fahd was recovering from a serious illness. Reports leaked from the palace indicated that he did not get along with his half brothers, and few were surprised when they managed to cut his tenure short. Nonetheless Abdullah, as commander of the tribally based National Guard, controls one of the kingdom's two armies, and his influence cannot be lightly dismissed.

Prince Salman, on the other hand, is one of King Fahd's close advisers. In a meeting with me, he denied the frequently heard claim that the royal family is aloof from the people. We met in his office at the governorate in downtown Riyadh, where he conceded the importance of the intelligence services in keeping the royal family informed of what the people are thinking. But he contended that all of the princes meet with Saudi citizens personally, and so get direct exposure to what is on their minds.

He himself conducts a *majlis*—a consultation with the people—twice daily, he said, in which his doors are open to all Saudis who wish to bring him their problems.

At Prince Salman's invitation, I witnessed his own *majlis,* held after the noon prayer in a huge and opulent receiving room in the palace.

Dozens of robed men, most with the sun-dried faces of bedouins, sat waiting in chairs around the periphery, then rose deferentially when Salman entered. Forming a line, each in turn approached the throne, shook the prince's hand, presented him a petition, and for a few seconds delivered a personal plea. The issues were private, I was told, like getting an elderly mother admitted to a hospital or releasing a miscreant son from jail. The prince, after listening to the petitioner, handed the petition to an aide, to whom he whispered instructions.

The *majlis* struck me as a fascinating adaptation of ancient customs to the present day, if not to present values. It was a scene of desert governance, a display of comradeship between the ruler and the ruled. What I witnessed, however, was not a hearing on public policy but a system for dealing with intimate personal needs. Certainly, none of the petitioners proffered a comment that the prince did not want to hear. I left the *majlis* dubious about whether these encounters conveyed to the prince anything at all of the people's attitude toward his family, current political problems or the nature of the Saudi state.

"Yes, the royal family is aware that there is discontent in the kingdom," Prince Salman told me. "It does not disturb me that the people are looking for the best for their country. We are looking for the same thing.

"But, as Sauds, we have a special responsibility not to undermine our cultural strengths. Unlike some countries, we do not want to adopt practices that do not suit us. Our most important goal is to preserve our country's unity. The King loves all Saudis like his sons. Arabia used to be a collection of regions and tribes; now we are becoming a single family.

"Such troublemakers as Audah and Hawali don't represent anything in our culture. Intentionally or not, they are promoting *fitna,* anarchy. We are not deluded into thinking we have attained perfection—there is no ideal system on earth. But we do believe in development that is faithful to our traditions. That is the direction in which our family is moving."

Pretending to some humility, the royal family—as Prince Salman's words confirm—does not take the line that it is faultless. Echoing Minister of Justice Alshaikh, Wahhab's descendant, one leading prince conceded to me that princes from time to time lapse from Islamic morality. He even admitted the substance of the repeated charge that family members engage in corruption. It seemed to me he had adopted, as strategy, the position that confession is good for the state. By adopting the "we're only human" argument, Prince Salman appeared to suggest that family members deserved absolution for their sins.

Indeed, the family line seems to be: Though not saints, we have not in the final analysis done so badly by our country. The proposition I often heard, phrased in one way or another, went as follows: "Look at other countries that have been blessed with oil riches. We could have slipped into social chaos, like Algeria or Venezuela or Nigeria. But we did not. Just take a look around at the nation we have become." One need not be an apologist for the Sauds to see much truth in these boasts.

Whatever its flaws, Saudi Arabia has risen from the desert in a few generations to have prospering cities, efficient communication and transportation systems, state-of-the-art factories and seaports, well-run universities and hospitals. Its oil industry, where Saudis are increasingly replacing foreign managers, is competently run and dominates world markets.

Moreover, Saudi Arabia has spread its oil wealth widely, if not equitably. Though more than half its citizens are under twenty-one—the birth rate, about 3.8 percent, is among the world's highest—it has, without a pervasive police presence, maintained a remarkable level of public order. Indisputably, the culture is stifling to individual expression; but it is also undeniably infused with a pride of collective achievement.

The House of Saud is troubled, however, that so many of its citizens do not regard these accomplishments as enough. Massa'ri and his group on the one hand and Audah, Hawali and their followers on the other may well be—to use a local metaphor—the camel's nose poking under the tent. The Sauds do not know how many more there are like them. The problem is that they regard all their critics as ingrates, misguided at best, and probably outright sinful.

Prince Nayef, born in 1933, is another of the King's full brothers. He is indignant at challenges to the character, as well as to the integrity, of the Saud family's governance.

As Minister of Interior, Nayef is the kingdom's chief law enforcement officer. Cleanly shaven, with a small mustache and a paunch, he wore a simple white gown to our meeting, with tan slippers on his feet and a white *kufiyyah* on his head. His translator was dressed more elegantly. Nayef's office, though large, was decorated only with photographs of Saudi kings. His desk was without a computer but, for reasons I did not understand, had on it a battery of thirteen separate telephones.

Nayef is said to be the hard-liner of the King's entourage, though any real distinction between the brothers' opinions was not readily apparent in talks with me. The most affable of the princes that I met, Nayef spent ten minutes on ceremonial amenities before getting down to business.

We talked first of the Shi'ites in the Eastern Province, with whom he said the Sauds were on good terms. Our meeting took place during the government's truce with the Shi'ites, some months before the bombing in Dhahran. Nayef insisted that Iran was still trying to stir up the Shi'ites, but was no longer achieving the success it had enjoyed during Khomeini's early years.

"The Shi'ites of Saudi Arabia," he said, "have too much national pride to pay attention to Iran. Those who went into exile are now returning to the kingdom. They will be welcomed by us, as long as they remain good citizens."

Nayef also spoke of the ban on driving by women, which he said— to my surprise—was not an Islamic issue at all.

"The applicable rule," he said, "is that anything which does not contradict Islam is permissible. But any rule must be acceptable to society, which decides whether it is good or bad. Driving by women is obviously not forbidden by the *shari'a,* but a social consensus holds that it will lead to bad deeds.

"In a case like this, the King makes the decision, but he considers the consensus that the *ulama* express, and none of them favors women driving. *Ijtihad* is important here. On Islamic principles, the doors to *ijtihad* are closed. But on matters not covered by the *shari'a,* the scholars apply *ijtihad,* as they have throughout history. The scholars now think that driving by women is dangerous, and the King agrees. But that can change."

For the most part, Nayef answered my questions softly and with patience. His thought process was sometimes hard to follow, being arabesque in design. But only once did he show the temper for which he is known, when I asked about the reformers' demands. His exasperation was visible on his face and in his words.

"Muslims say that a petition provides guidance to an Islamic leader," he told me, "so we found it normal to receive the petitions organized by Audah and Hawali after the Gulf War. The King has an open heart and an open door for any citizen concerned with the well-being of the country. We will examine any proposal that doesn't contradict Islamic law.

"But the reforms they called for are not legitimate. They presented them as demands, and exposed them to the world. They knew they were embarrassing to us, and that was unacceptable. Proclaiming their positions in sermons in the mosque was also wrong. It contradicts Islamic principles. The public is as disturbed by their mistakes as I am. Ours is an Islamic state, and our family does not need such people to tell us about Islam."

Nayef contended that many of the family's critics have been influenced by external forces. Among the forces he cited were Egypt's Muslim Brothers and the "so-called liberal reformers" elsewhere. He denounced the British government, without mentioning its name, for providing hospitality to Massa'ri, who he said was acting in behalf of people who were seeking to destabilize the kingdom. The Sauds, he said, will never be affected by foreign thinking.

"The citizens who have been causing so much trouble are seriously misguided," he continued. "Though their beliefs have an Islamic face, behind them are their own personal or political interests. The majority that signed the petition apologized and were released. The others will either be convinced of their wrongdoing and repent—the King usually accepts a sincere apology—or they will be subjected to the punishment of Islamic courts."

At this point, Prince Nayef digressed, unasked, into a long defense of Saudi justice, denying charges made by Amnesty International and other human rights organizations of torture, kangaroo trials and indiscriminate executions by public beheadings. Then, after a few minutes, he returned to the Saudi dissidents.

"These misinformed men are damaging themselves more than they are damaging our country," he said. "They are like mischievous sons in the family and they must receive paternal discipline. After listening to them, we see no reason to change our course and we will not— neither I nor our family."

No Saudi that I encountered—and I asked the question repeatedly— expressed a belief that the dissidents whom Prince Nayef reviled had any immediate prospect of triumphing. The Sauds' roots in the culture are too deep, skewing the odds against their challengers. But many Saudis pointed out that the contest was only beginning, and that without concessions from the royal family it was sure to intensify.

My own sense is that the Sauds have sheltered themselves from any real grasp of the breadth of the popular discontent. But only at their peril can they ignore it much longer.

Admittedly, in a society as closed as Saudi Arabia's, it is hard to gauge the depth and intensity of discontent. Similarly, in a government as secretive as Saudi Arabia's, it is impossible to measure official receptivity to the popular grumbling. Since the end of the Gulf War, however, there is enough evidence to conclude that the discontent will not go away of its own accord. Nor are invocations to Islamic duty by princes and clerics likely to extinguish the fire that lies underneath it.

Justifiably or not, the Gulf War provoked a sharp turn in the public mind. Whether Saudis prefer lives with more Wahhabism or less, it seems very apparent that most want greater accountability from their government. It will not suffice much longer for the family to hide its rejection of reform behind Islam. Saudis are beginning to see through this device. As long as the House of Saud refuses to acknowledge the yearning for a more accountable state, I believe, the feeling of dissatisfaction in the culture will continue to grow.

8

The Anguish of Algeria

THE BADR MOSQUE—named for the Prophet's decisive military victory in Arabia in 623—stands on a steep, winding street in a middle-class quarter of Algiers. I visited it at midday one Friday, just as the civil war that has since consumed Algeria was getting under way. Though Algeria was never considered very religious, the mosque was overflowing when I arrived, an hour before prayer time. The presence of so many believers at devotions was clearly a political as well as a religious statement.

While a loudspeaker blared a religious message from inside, several hundred men, most of them in working clothes, milled about on the street. Women approached in twos and threes on foot, glancing neither right nor left as they passed through the gamut of the men. They entered by their own door, which led directly to a women's gallery upstairs. Nearly all were dressed, as the Algerians say, *à l'iranienne,* that is, not in the decorous veil (*haik*) that is customary in Algeria but in the long robes made fashionable by the Khomeini revolution.

At about one-thirty the loudspeaker sent a signal that the prayers were to begin, and automobile traffic was halted. It was, I knew, illegal to pray on the street. Some weeks before, the police had banned street prayers in response to the antigovernment protests incited by the harangues of *imams* over their loudspeakers. Nonetheless, the men unrolled the prayer rugs that each carried and formed a series of tight ranks, shoulder to shoulder, across the pavement.

The protests, some of them violent, had begun after the government revoked the parliamentary election won by the Islamic Salvation Front, the fundamentalist party that everyone called the FIS (for *Front Islamique du Salut*). The government, the biggest loser, then outlawed the FIS and arrested most of its leadership. Though it replaced pro-FIS *imam*s in most mosques with its own clerics, it had failed to stop the protests. They subsided only with the onset of Ramadan, a month-long fast of penitence, but recently there had been signs that they would resume.

Not a policeman was in sight at the Badr Mosque on the day of my visit, a week after Ramadan. But the taxi driver who had brought me, and who stayed to recite his own prayers, told me the worshipers took for granted that dozens of plain-clothes agents had already infiltrated their ranks. He also predicted that, without police provocation, there would be no trouble.

He was right. Though the tension in the air was palpable, the prayer hour went peacefully. The sermon the men heard over the loudspeaker was a Quranic lesson on kindness. When it was over they rolled up their prayer rugs, broke ranks quietly and headed home for lunch. The worshipers inside followed them.

But my experience at the Badr Mosque was the beginning rather than the end of the story. That evening the police twice stopped the car in which I was riding with friends to inspect the trunk for weapons. The next morning the papers announced the killing of several soldiers in a town south of Algiers. Over the following months, killings became commonplace; within a few years the number of dead approached 60,000. Algeria's strife had by then become the most bloodthirsty religious war of our age.

The Algerian civil war, from one perspective, was the tragic culmination of the rise of religious zealotry in the Islamic world. Though the war in Afghanistan, while producing many more casualties, had a sharp Islamic flavor, it began as a struggle to liberate the country from the Soviets and evolved into a contest among local sects. Algeria had won its war of liberation from France many years before. It was now in a war in which its secular regime fought religious forces over the establishment of an Islamic state.

The war had reverberations throughout the Islamic world, and particularly in the Arab countries, which had experimented so unsuccessfully over the decades with secular rule. Some observers saw it as a sign that stability within the Arab community was precipitously disintegrating. A few went further to contend that the Arabs would be following Khomeini's Iran into an era of Islamic rule. Was Algeria-style bloodletting, many asked, the fate that awaited Egypt and Tunisia, where the contest between mosque and state was already violent? Could it also be the future of Syria, which was presently calm, but where a deep Islamic rancor toward the government lay beneath the surface?

Algeria's tragedy was compounded by the hopefulness with which it had embarked on its independence. Unlike the Arab states that had been handed their freedom, Algerians had, with their own resources, defeated the French in 1962 in ferocious combat. The victory imbued Algerian society with a deep sense of achievement.

Algeria emerged from the war with an educated elite, at ease in the West, speaking French, a Western language, in addition to Arabic, its native tongue. It boasted substantial wealth from its fertile fields, as well as from the hydrocarbons beneath its soil. It had inherited a useful physical infrastructure; its geography placed it close to its natural markets. Surely, few ex-colonies had begun their independence with as much promise.

Fervent believers argued that Western-style secularism was the flaw that neutralized all of these advantages. The argument, if plausible at all, failed to take key factors into account. The post-independence government was not just secular; it was also corrupt, repressive and incompetent. It rigorously excluded all popular participation in its deliberations. It was not up to coping with one of the world's highest birth rates. When bad times came—and they came rather quickly—the government found that, while it had an army to enforce its will, it had little popular support.

No wonder the rest of the Arab world watched Algeria's disintegration with anxiety. Algeria's problems applied, in some form and to some degree, to every Arab society. Obviously, many Arabs were intoxicated by the prospect of an Islamic regime; "Islam," their slogan says, "is the solution." But, to others, Islamic government was no solution at all; on the contrary, it would inevitably make the problems worse.

In Algeria, however, the Islamic movement was the only organized opposition to the regime, and so Islam—by default, some said—became the vehicle of protest. To be sure, Islamic societies were not alone in being corrupt, repressive and incompetent. These characteristics can be found anywhere. But are piety and prayer their substitute? Is the *shari'a* the answer? Religions normally promise only better odds on salvation; Islam, in Algeria, was also promising better government. The Islamic experience in Sudan and Iran belies the prospect. The evidence they offer suggests that Islamic revolution, at best, may solve one problem—the overthrow of a corrupt secular state—only by creating many others. Was Algeria going to be an exception, setting a glittering precedent for the Arab world?

Given the organization of Arab societies, it is understandable that Algerians were not alone in the temptation to turn to Islam to replace a secular government that is unfit to rule. The Arabs have not succeeded at democracy; even in Moscow's heyday, they never mobilized more than minorities in behalf of Communism. Islam, to many, seemed to be the only available recourse.

Is not Algeria's crisis, whatever its peculiar variation, all too typical of the Arab world's? Indeed, there is reason to fear that in time the entire Arab world will, in one form or another, recapitulate the Algerian experience.

It was no coincidence that the Badr Mosque, when I visited in the spring of 1992, looked only half finished. It had been in use, I learned later, for a half dozen years, during which its exterior cement walls, which its designers surely intended to have surfaced, remained deliberately untouched. I could imagine those walls covered with painted ceramic tiles, Moorish style, a décor that imparted a lively color to buildings throughout Algiers, a city which I found otherwise grim, even depressed.

The explanation for the unfinished look, I learned, lay in an Algerian law which gave the state the power to appoint a mosque's *imam,* but only on completion of construction. Unfinished, thousands of Algerian mosques, like the Badr Mosque, remained under the control of the mosque associations that had built them. Most of these associations were dominated by antigovernment fundamentalists.

The systematic takeover of Algeria's mosques was not of recent origin. The process had started soon after the country freed itself from French rule in 1962.

The FLN (*Front de la Libération Nationale*), a coalition of secular and religious forces, had launched Algeria's war of independence eight years earlier. Throughout the 130 years of colonial rule, the *ulama* and its Islamic allies had been at the forefront of resistance to the French. Its representatives became the FLN's Islamic wing, known familiarly as the "bearded FLN."· In setting out to free Algeria of Christian occupation, it regarded the war as a *jihad.* The proclamation that launched the hostilities against France in 1954 promised the creation of a state "within the framework of the principles of Islam."

Muslim nationalists of that era—fundamentalism, as the term is understood today, did not yet exist—called for not just a political but a psychological liberation. Algeria, believers argued, could be truly freed from colonialism only by establishing—"reestablishing," a few maintained, citing a mythical precolonial era—an Islamic state. These revolutionaries talked of a contract, to be executed after liberation, between Islam and the FLN.

But the FLN at the end of the war was not what it had been at the start. As in other liberated Arab countries, the army, with indifference to the rest of the society, seized control of the state. It hammered the FLN, as a political party, into a docile instrument to run the government in its behalf. The institutions of the "FLN-state" were modeled not on the Prophet Muhammad's Medina, furthermore, but on the secular socialism of Gamal Abdel Nasser's Egypt. For aggrieved Muslims, Algeria's mosques held the greatest promise for redressing the state's character.

When a million French colonists fled the country in the wake of the peace agreement, the state turned the churches and synagogues they had left behind into mosques. But, with a soaring birth rate and rapid migration from the countryside to the cities, these were not enough. So a huge building program was undertaken, in part financed by the Gulf states. Mosques rose at the rate of a thousand a year in the seventies and eighties, not even counting the simple prayer rooms set up in schools and factories, and in the clusters of tacky high-rises, soon to become urban slums, where the exploding population was lodged.[1]

The many new pulpits created vacancies for *imam*s whose beliefs covered the spectrum of Islamic interpretation. It was occasionally noted in these years that older and working-class Muslims attended the formally established mosques, whose *imam*s, paid by the state, faithfully followed the government line. Undereducated and unemployed youths, an increasing number, gravitated to the improvised, back-room chapels, where preachers of more radical doctrines were likely to preside.

Far from trying to contain the Islamic wave, the Algerian government abetted it. High officials told themselves that the replacement of French influence by Islam was a reminder to Algerians of the FLN's victory in the war and its services to the people. The government saw the mosques as a symbol of its well-earned political legitimacy.

The government, moreover, was persuaded that Islam would immunize the society against Communists, whom it saw as a real danger, notwithstanding its own socialist policies. One scholar points out that Sadat in Egypt, the Shah in Iran, Nimieri in Sudan, King Hussein in Jordan and Zia ul-Haq in Pakistan, as well as the United States in Afghanistan, pursued a similar pro-mosque strategy to counter Communism. "Such opportunism," he notes, "has now come back to haunt nearly all the regimes" that adopted it.[2]

For the same reasons, the Algerian government promoted the society's Arabization, discouraging the use of French—the language, iron-ically, in which the FLN had successfully conducted the war. Promoting Arabic inevitably meant promoting the Quran, providing a terrain favorable to Islamization. Teachers of Arabic often doubled up as *imam*s. Funds from the Gulf nourished them. To staff its newly Arabized schools, the government also invited teachers from abroad, mostly from Egypt. Many were Islamic activists.

One of them was the Egyptian sheikh, Muhammad al-Ghazali, whose key role in the events surrounding the murder of Farag Foda was examined in Chapter 2. The government took pride in recruiting such an erudite scholar, whom it named as president of a major Islamic university. Via television and the press, al-Ghazali helped spread the credibility of a strict Islam, soon to emerge as fundamentalism, throughout Algerian society.[3]

From the start, the government had banned all popular organizations, fearing their potential for political troublemaking. But, seeing no inconsistency, it made an exception for associations whose purpose was to build and run mosques. Algeria was not alone; Saudi Arabia and the Shah's Iran did the same. They were among the Islamic despotisms which failed to recognize that, in permitting freedoms to Islamic associations that were denied to others, they were inexorably channeling political opposition into the mosques.

While organizing their members, Algeria's mosques, on the whole, kept a low political profile. Algerians were careful not to provoke the security police, which were assumed to be omnipresent. In 1966, al-Qiyam ("the values"), a fundamentalist society, tested official resolve by leading protests against Nasser's execution of the extremist thinker, Sayyid Qutb. The government, which regarded Nasser as its friend, promptly dissolved al-Qiyam. Occasionally a declared dissident received a prison term. More commonly, an *imam* was summoned by the police, or jailed briefly, for saying too much in a sermon. Overall, however, the government gave the mosques a rather long leash to build political structures, which they exploited quietly but systematically.

By the 1980s the generation that was Islamized in the mosques was growing more audacious. In 1982 a Communist student was killed by Islamic zealots, and the government did not respond. It also failed to stop the recurring harassment of women on the streets for their un-Islamic dress or their uncovered hair. Its indifference would soon prove costly. When, by the end of the decade the FLN was showing signs of collapse, the mosque associations were ready to enlist in the struggle to deliver the fatal blow.

· II ·

THE FLN STATE'S long-looming collision with fundamentalism took place in October 1988, on the streets of Algiers. Since independence, Algeria's population had nearly tripled to 24 million, 60 percent of whom were under twenty-five. Through careless management, the government had acquired a huge foreign debt. In the mid-1980s, when the oil and gas market collapsed, the income on which the FLN relied to provide its social services dropped sharply. In the face of economic crisis, the government had no disposable income. Massive riots were the people's response.

The riots' origins are obscure. They appear to have begun as purely economic protests, without ideological content, but in their rapid spread from Algiers to the provinces many saw signs of a well-ordered plot. Though no evidence supports the theory, it is true that Islamic leaders quickly seized command of the streets, providing direction to the thousands of young men who were stoning and burning to express their rage.

After few days of rioting, a popular *imam* named Ali Benhadj issued a list of demands in the name of the Islamic movement. On the list was an end to corruption, a guaranteed minimum income and a reform of the system of justice. More grandly, the list also included the "cleansing" of Algerian law of all principles contrary to Islam.[4] A year later Ali Benhadj would be known to all Algerians as the chief luminary of the FIS.

The riots evolved swiftly into confrontations between crowds of adolescents and army tanks. The government declared martial law, and when it failed to stop the fighting, its soldiers fired into the crowds, killing hundreds. Young fundamentalists made up a large proportion of the victims. To many observers, the army's excesses were the last straw, persuading a majority of Algerians that the one-party socialist state had to go.

Chadli Bendjedid, an ex-officer whom the army had made President in 1979, apparently acquired doubts himself about the FLN state. His response was a promise of prompt democratization. In retrospect, the promise appears ill considered, even to democrats. Though the French had introduced Algeria to democracy, they invariably cooked elections in favor of their own candidates, giving the process a bad name. The country, moreover, lacked the experience and the institutions—political parties, a free press, trade unions, human rights guarantees—considered essential to the operation of a democratic society.

On paper, Bendjedid wiped out these deficiencies in a constitution hastily drawn up in February 1989. Benhadj, who saw democracy simply as a secular state in another form, led a boycott of the referendum to ratify it. Ironically, his failure to block the constitution enabled his followers to promote their goal of an Islamic state by organizing their efforts legally.

Bendjedid's constitution revoked the FLN's monopoly of power. It authorized free speech and a free press, as well as free political parties. It also contained an escape clause, permitting the banning of religious parties, but Bendjedid chose not to invoke it. He was apparently persuaded by the polls which showed that the FLN would regain via elections the power it no longer possessed by right. But the Islamic movement, once in the political arena, had no intention of forfeiting the match.

The founding of the FIS as a political party was publicly announced in March 1989, after an agreement was reached among Algeria's chief *imam*s. They said they were guided by the Quranic verse, "Ye were on an abyss of fire, and He did save you from it" (3:103). In choosing the Islamic Salvation Front as their name, they delivered a message that the party was not just political but spiritual.

The founders of the FIS had had no trouble rallying to the clichés of Islamic politics; they rejected secularism, the class struggle and socialism. Unanimously, they supported the idea of an Islamic state. Yet the agreement did not come easily. Their negotiations revealed serious differences in Islamic ideology, as well as regional and generational rivalries.

Whatever debate they conducted focused on strategy, since they could not agree on a social program. They were silent on fundamentalist theological positions, as well as on the institutions of an Islamic state. Moderates attacked Ali Benhadj, the most active among the organizers, for his provocative leadership of the October riots. But in the end the founders papered over their differences in the interest of common political objectives. Their published platform was bland, conveying a decision to defer the hard ideological issues until the Islamic state actually came into being.[5]

Named as head of the FIS was Dr. Abassi Madani, who was both a sophisticated psychology professor with a British doctorate and a practicing *imam*. Born in 1931, the son of an *imam*, he had fought in the war of independence as a member of the Islamic wing of the FLN and, after the war, held office before his imprisonment for involvement in an Islamic student strike. Madani's presence aligned the FIS with Algerian nationalism and enriched it with his experience in politics. Pragmatic about strategy, Madani also served as a restraint on the more impetuous Benhadj.

Sheikh Benhadj, still in his thirties, was named the second in command and became the FIS's most recognizable voice. From the pulpit of his working-class mosque in an industrial quarter of Algiers, he called not only for an Islamic state but for an armed *jihad* to attain it. Having often been jailed for his sermons, he was the hero of the "October generation," the street-wise youths whom he led in the riots of 1988. Austere and mystical, Benhadj was a brilliant and arousing speaker. Convinced by Iran's experience that victory was near, he identified the FIS with more extreme positions than a leadership consensus was prepared to take.

Within a few months some sixty political parties, including the FLN and the FIS, were legally registered and preparing for elections. Most consisted of a single ambitious leader and his entourage, without much ideology. A few had a regional base, which limited their scope. The weakness of these secular parties left the FLN, its wealth and organization intact, in a formidable position. The FIS, having united the country's religious forces, was its only serious rival.

Under the constitution, the government promised first municipal, then parliamentary elections. The pitting of the FLN against the FIS presented, in retrospect, a clear choice between secular and religious rule. But Algeria's voters, in the giddiness of unfamiliar freedom, saw the FIS essentially as a challenger to the status quo. That it was taking on the detested FLN was clearly considered more significant than its Islamic program. Popular disillusion with the FLN, more than religion, had made the FIS into the channel of Algeria's discontent.

In the elections for municipal offices on June 12, 1990, some eight million Algerians cast ballots. It was the first free, honest, multiparty election in the nation's—perhaps the Arab world's—history.

The results were stunning. The FIS won control of 853 of Algeria's 1,541 municipalities, including the major cities of Algiers, Oran and Constantine. The FIS received 4.5 million votes, or about 54 percent of the total, including a huge majority from the voters under thirty. The FLN came in second, with 34 percent. The remainder of the vote was split among the smaller parties, none of them figuring significantly in the outcome.

The losers tried to make something of the 40 percent of the eligible voters who had chosen to stay home. They argued that in the rigged balloting conducted by the French, Algerians had acquired the habit of abstaining as a protest. The victors' mandate, they argued, was more limited than it seemed. But though their claim, if valid, would have reduced the FIS percentage to a third of the electorate, it was still a huge plurality.

The FIS's country-wide victory gave it an unmistakable popular base but relatively little direct power. The funds put at its disposal were barely sufficient to administer municipalities, much less reform them. The mosque associations showed ingenuity in collecting money to help FIS officials. But interested not in running parks and playgrounds but in founding an Islamic state, the FIS expended little effort on making a distinguished record in Algeria's city halls.

Nonetheless, the FIS made its presence felt. On the facades of its buildings, it replaced the motto of the republic, "For the people and by the people," with "Islamic Municipality." In many localities it outlawed the mixing of genders at school and work. It banned the sale and consumption of alcohol and the wearing of revealing clothing. In taking possession of local voting rolls, it also obtained a weapon of more than symbolic importance—determining who would be enfranchised in the parliamentary election, promised for 1991.

The FIS's triumph, however, failed to put an end to urban disorders. When Iraq's Saddam Hussein invaded Kuwait in August 1990 and the United States, heading a coalition of Western and Arab states, began landing troops in Saudi Arabia, Algeria's government supported the coalition. Madani backed the government and denounced Iraq, but Ali Benhadj persuaded him to change his mind. Donning a military uniform in place of his usual *imam*'s robe, Benhadj took to the streets to demand that volunteers be recruited to fight for Iraq. Western forces, he proclaimed, must not be permitted on sacred Islamic soil.

In the turmoil that ensued, Bendjedid found an excuse for indefinitely postponing the parliamentary elections, scheduled for early 1991. He then had a new law enacted that scandalously gerrymandered electoral districts to favor FLN candidates. The FIS, supported by the other opposition parties, called a general strike, which once again brought demonstrators into the streets. Madani, under heavy pressure, threatened to proclaim an armed *jihad* and Benhadj issued a plea to soldiers to rebel against their officers. For the second time in three years, the government declared martial law and the army fired into the crowds, killing several hundred protesters.

A few days later the government, claiming to have discovered large stores of arms belonging to the FIS, arrested Madani and Benhadj, along with some seven hundred FIS militants, charging them with armed insurrection. But Bendjedid again defused the powder keg. He withdrew the gerrymandering proposal and set the legislative election for December 26, with a runoff three weeks later. He did not, however, release Madani and Benhadj.

With its leaders and much of its rank and file in prison, the FIS faced the dilemma of whether to participate in the election. From his cell, Madani took the initiative, issuing instructions for the FIS to resume the legal, public competition for political power. Benhadj's followers did not submit easily but, at a conference in July, Madani's backers turned back their challenge. Only then did the FIS formally announce that, at its leaders' instructions, it would join in the election campaign.

The campaign in the fall of 1991 proved to be unexpectedly calm. The candidates held rallies, distributed literature and debated their programs before orderly crowds. They painted graffiti, in both Arabic and French, and when I visited several months later, walls throughout the country were still covered with such slogans as *Votez FIS Contre Blisse* ("devil," in Arabic) and *Le FLN Battent les Fissistes; Vive les Démocrates.* At FIS meetings, replicas of prison bars were put on display, a reminder that Madani and Benhadj were in jail. But FIS candidates, ordered to follow the rules, conducted themselves decorously.

On election eve the pollsters were still predicting an even split, and Bendjedid declared that he was prepared to live with the outcome. He even hinted that he might invite the FIS to take a few seats in the cabinet.

But when the results were in, the FIS had no need of Bendjedid's charity: it stood ready to swallow up the whole government. Of the assembly's 430 seats, the FIS won 188 outright and led in 140 of the 199 outstanding contests. Not only was it on its way to a majority; it appeared likely to win two thirds of the seats, enough to fulfill its campaign promise of replacing Bendjedid's constitution with the *shari'a.*

The FLN took only fifteen seats. Of the forty-six other parties on the ballot, all but one were shut out.

If there was a flaw in the FIS's sweep, it lay in its receiving a million fewer votes than it had won in the municipal elections the year before. Its percentage of the vote declined from 54 to 48 percent, while abstentions rose to over 40 percent. Both sides made charges of irregularities, and there were indications that FIS municipalities had disenfranchised some nonbelievers. Yet there was no doubt about the overall magnitude of the FIS landslide, and the right that it imparted, under the rules of democracy, to make profound changes in Algerian society.

Algeria's secular leadership went into shock over the election. Its initial reaction focused on averting disaster in the runoff, which was scheduled for January 16. On December 29, three days after the balloting, the government publicly pleaded with Algerians who had abstained in the first round to save the constitutional state by going to the polls in the second. On January 2 a coalition of opposition parties, women's groups and the country's largest labor union assembled an estimated 300,000 marchers in Algiers to protest the prospect of Islamization. It was the biggest popular demonstration since the war of independence. But confidence that the situation could be salvaged was quickly eroding.

A handful of party leaders called on Bendjedid, in the interests of democracy, to finish the election process, insisting that the government's constitutional powers were sufficient to block the FIS's more radical designs. Most secular leaders and a major segment of the independent press, however, took the opposite tack, imploring the government to cancel the second round, on the grounds that the impending FIS victory would destroy the new democracy.

Bendjedid, during these crucial days, entertained talk of giving the FIS a free hand to enact its social program in return for his retaining control of defense and interior, the security ministries. Such a deal, however, did not sit well with the army. Its position was more than the product of a secular disposition. The repression it had conducted on Algeria's streets since 1988 had made it the FIS's implacable enemy. The generals were apprehensive that, in power, the FIS would exact bloody retribution.

The ruling elite deliberated in secrecy throughout the first ten days of January 1992. Then, on the eleventh, Bendjedid announced his resignation, saying that his continued presence was "gravely harming national cohesion."

His departure left no equivocation about who was in charge. For thirty years the army had let the FLN govern on the condition that it maintain order. Algerians had endorsed the fiction that the FLN was in charge. But, since 1988, the FLN's failures had gone from bad to worse. In the new constitution, Bendjedid turned the FLN loose to sink or swim like other parties, and it was sinking. Now, with the FIS poised to take over, the FLN's usefulness was at an end, and the army faced the problem of devising another structure to cover its rule.

Three days after Bendjedid's departure a five-member High State Council was named by the army to assume presidential functions. It was dominated by an army general. To preserve a democratic facade, the Council had a moderate Islamist and a human rights activist among its members. But, for a country that had enjoyed a giddy moment of democracy, this was thin constitutional cover. Algerians were not fooled: the army was in charge. The Council's first decree was to cancel the runoff round, revoking the election. The action has since passed into the national lexicon as the "January coup d'état."

· III ·

DURING MY VISIT to Algeria just after the coup, I met with the Council's human rights appointee, Ali Haroun, a highly regarded lawyer, a veteran of the war of independence and a longtime critic of the excesses of the FLN state. On taking his post, Haroun described the coup to a French television network—whose programs were beamed to Algeria—as "an exceptional situation in a nation's life," essential to preserve human rights.

"The FIS," Haroun told the TV, "has had the honesty to declare that it is not democratic, that it is against democracy . . . that when it takes power there will be no more elections; there will be the *shura,* the religious men who meet together and decide in your behalf. The FIS says it would use elections to gain power; afterwards, there would be no more elections. . . ."

The statements that Haroun paraphrased were accurate, and he was justified in his apprehension. But whether they represented FIS *policy* was another matter. Some of Madani's followers may have been genuine democrats; most of Benhadj's surely were not. Given their differences, it is unlikely there was a formal decision by the FIS on the principle of elections, or that there was any FIS policy on democracy at all.

"Am I going to allow a situation," Haroun continued, "where, in a month or two, people will no longer have any rights? I cannot do that. . . . We are going to take the time to set up real institutions to lead this country toward real democracy—not some pretext of using a democratic process to kill democracy."

A few weeks later I met with Haroun in the presidential palace, built after the war of independence. It is a series of modern, low-lying buildings, hidden behind a stone wall. Its white color evoked Mediterranean cities, its pointed arches, gardens and hand-woven rugs recalled Middle Eastern folk tales. Escorted by a security guard, I followed a path bordered by trees, then walked through a carpeted corridor decorated with nineteenth-century martial paintings. Haroun waited for me in his office behind a sculptured table. An elegant man, he seemed very French.

"On December 26," he said, "we were struck by a tidal wave of fundamentalism. If we had followed democracy to the letter, we'd have let it go on, and we'd have been washed away. It would all have been very democratic. Don't forget that the Nazis took power democratically in 1933, and nobody stopped them for fear it would appear antidemocratic. Like the Germans, we could also have done nothing and witnessed the death of democracy. If the FIS has the right to use democracy to destroy democracy, then don't count me any longer among the democrats.

"For any democrat, what happened in January was traumatic. But I could not stand by while we became like Iran or Sudan or Afghanistan. Many Algerians—trade unionists, professionals, women, students, supporters of human rights—shared our worries, and if we had followed the election process to the end, we would necessarily have wound up in civil war.

"For now, the government has avoided disaster, and we have remained more or less within the framework of legitimacy. In determining our course, the army was the dominating element, but if the people had all denounced the putsch, the army would have had to back down. Now the army's role is over and the responsibility belongs to the political classes. Honestly, we are not fully clear where we go from here."

As eloquently as Haroun made his case, I could not accept his claim that, if the people had spoken, the army would have obeyed. The army had deposed Algeria's provisional leadership after the war of independence, killing thousands. It had chosen presidents, suppressed insurrections and made coups d'état. It even controlled its own history. I remember thinking how strange it was that I was unable to find a single account in Algiers bookstores on the army's role in the events since independence; later I was told that such books, plentiful in France, were banned in Algeria.

Notwithstanding the blackout of information, all Algerians—including Haroun—knew that the army, when faced with calls for democracy, had never backed down.

"I think all Algerians," Haroun continued, "now accept the principle that relations between the governors and the governed will be conducted democratically, that is, by means of multiparty elections, but we're not yet sure how to achieve it. What we did was to put off the choice of a government until later. We have not abolished the choice.

"I am not anti-Muslim. On the contrary, I regard myself as a strong Muslim, and I will not allow myself to be excluded from Islam by Ali Benhadj, who wears a beard, because I shave and wear a suit and tie. The fundamentalists can pray as they like, and we can still have a

united and free society. They have laid down the choices. Shall Algeria
be republic or caliphate, nation or *umma,* democracy or *shura*cracy?

"Nothing guarantees, of course, that we will not face the same
outcome in another election. But we can create institutions to respond
to current conditions, and if we do our work well, Algerians will reject
theocracy and choose real democracy as the foundation of the state."

Algiers in the wake of the January coup was tense but calm. The
threat of violence lifted perceptibly when the FIS promised—at least
until the government clarified its intentions—"to remain within the
legal framework without renouncing its plan for an Islamic state." A
few days later the FIS went further, conveying a more defiant nuance
to its intentions: "We will go down the path of your constitution, not
because we believe in it but because disregarding it would give you a
pretext to crack down."

By then, the armored cars patrolling the streets and the tanks watching over the ministries had been withdrawn and were replaced by
lightly armed foot soldiers.

But the army, far from mollified, had made up its mind to destroy
the FIS. On January 14 security forces conducted a new wave of
arrests of FIS leaders, while sweeping through the streets of Algiers to
detain anyone wearing the loose-fitting white tunics which identified
FIS members. It also moved to regain control of the mosques, replacing fundamentalist *imam*s by the dozens, cutting off loudspeakers,
banning street gatherings.

By the end of January, with nearly all of its leaders jailed and its
press heavily curbed, the FIS was effectively decapitated. On February
8 the Interior Ministry filed court papers to outlaw it. Over the next
weeks the government closed FIS offices and removed the municipal
officials who had been elected to their posts in the FIS landslide of
1990.

By then, FIS supporters had begun the campaign of Friday demonstrations around the city's mosques. The army reacted with restraint
until protesters, in a fundamentalist district of Algiers, turned over
trucks to form barricades, filling the air with the smell of civil strife.
On February 7 the army killed 40 protesters outside a mosque. A few
days later the FIS declared that the next Friday it would hold a march
to bring down the state. The army, ominously, brought in contingents
from the provinces and positioned them along the parade route. Facing massacre, the FIS backed down, from what was probably the high-
water mark of its power.

By the end of February, masses of young militants, the shock troops
of the FIS, had been rounded up and sent to camps in the Algerian

Sahara. The government admitted to 5,000 detainees; the FIS put the number at 30,000. Whatever the figure, the detentions stopped the protests and, for the moment, put an end to the prospect of a popular uprising. In March the government declared the FIS, after twenty-nine months of legality, officially dissolved.

A few months later I was in Algeria again, and took a car to Setif, a middle-sized city on a rich plain about two hundred miles east of Algiers. Long a nationalist stronghold, Setif was the site of a portentous uprising against the French in 1945, in which a few *colons* were killed; the French army replied by massacring thousands of Algerians. After Setif, Algeria was never the same. When Algeria won its independence, the *colons* all left, but the French style of the town square remained untouched, a reminder to visitors not only of the colonial era but of the influence that its long relationship with France continued to exercise on Algerian society.

In Setif, I met Hocine Mekias, a small man of thirty-four with a fuzzy beard, who a year before had returned from the United States with a Ph.D. in mathematics. A political activist since his student days, he ran in the parliamentary election on the FIS ticket and won, defeating a veteran politician who, though he had quit the FLN, could not shake his long association with it. On March 11, Mekias was arrested and sent to a detention camp in the Sahara, where he was held for three months. Mekias told me he was informed neither why he was arrested nor why he was released. During his stay he was not even interrogated. Life at the camp, he said, was tolerable, and detainees were free to pray and to discuss politics. He said he also read books, brought to him by his family.

Apologizing for not inviting me to his home, he explained that the police had recently questioned him about a visitor from an international human rights organization, and he did not want them to summon him again. Since it was raining, we talked in his automobile, parked near the town square.

Mekias described himself as a moderate within the FIS, and a fierce opponent of political violence. The first priority of a FIS state, he said, would be the elimination of corruption and the restoration of justice. Such goals, he admitted, were not exclusive to Islam, but he insisted that, in a country of Islamic culture, secular parties were unlikely to attain them.

A FIS state would be democratic, Mekias said, and it would not outlaw secular parties. But, he said, he was confident that people would lose interest in secularism, and it would wither away. While criticizing a violent streak among FIS hard-liners, Mekias acknowledged sharing with them—"I'm proud to say that"—a commitment to the *shari'a* that included a man's right to rule his family and take up to four wives, the banning of alcohol, capital punishment and the amputation of the hand as a penalty for theft.

By the time Mekias and I met, FIS supporters were routinely engaged in violent activities, though the FIS did not take responsibility for them. Occasional dispatches from the underground leadership took the line that the FIS, though faithful to its promise to negotiate an end to the crisis, nonetheless understood how popular indignation might lead to violence. The FIS claimed to be in no position, because of its spontaneity, to stop the violence.

Soon after the coup, coordinated attacks on government forces became common. Within a few months, local and state police were being assassinated at the rate of one or two every few days. Most attacks were in and around Algiers, but even small provincial towns and villages were not exempt. By spring, about fifty security men had been killed, most in carefully planned and executed actions, with the assassins seizing the weapons of their victims.

Most Algerians were convinced that the FIS, from the underground, was commanding the attacks. Later it appeared likely that the FIS had little control over the bands of killers operating in its name. But in its declarations of policy the FIS was equivocal—or, more likely, divided. It proclaimed the theory that its electoral victory had given it the right not just to rule Algeria but to enforce this right with arms. For the time being, the FIS said, it was willing to negotiate with the government a return to democratic legality—but it reserved to itself the choice of when to exercise its military option.

· IV ·

TO UNDERSTAND something about the development of Algeria, let us start at the seventh century, when Muhammad's armies extended their conquests from Arabia across North Africa, which was nominally under Byzantium and largely Christian. Algeria's natives, apart from a scattering of Jews, were tough tribesmen known as Berbers, who tended their flocks and tilled the land. Though they shared Semitic roots with the Arabs, they were culturally much closer to the Romans, who had left behind a strong civilization when Rome fell. The Berbers had produced outstanding Christian thinkers, most notably the conservative St. Augustine. They were also known for spawning heretical religious movements.

For a time the Berbers put up a vigorous resistance to the Arabs.

Then suddenly they embraced Islam and joined the Arabs in crossing into Spain, exercising a dominant influence in the shaping of Muslim civilization there. But the occupation of Spain also produced a prolonged cross-fertilization, exposing the region to European values. This exposure gave North Africa a distinctive character within the Arab world.

The first wave of Arab conquerers, having founded no colonies, made little impact on Algeria. Real Arabization began only in the eleventh century, when the caliphate in Cairo sent tribes of nomads westward from Arabia. A contemporary historian described them as a "swarm of locusts," who destroyed towns and turned farmland into grazing pastures. In the cities, however, they established what became Algeria's dominant culture. Meanwhile, the Berbers, for the most part, maintained their separateness in the countryside. There they spoke their own language, followed their customary laws and practiced schismatic forms of Islam, their adopted religion.

France's 132-year occupation, which began in 1830, helped preserve the Arab-Berber split. French influence fell most heavily on the Berbers, more open than the Arabs to foreign culture. Though Berbers participated as fiercely as Arabs in the war of independence from 1954 to 1962, they have since shown much less hostility to France's ongoing cultural influence.

It is noteworthy that Algiers is closer, psychologically as well as geographically, to Paris than to Mecca. "We have thirty flights a day to Europe," an official said to me, in explaining the contrast between Algeria and the Middle East. "How many does Syria have?" At least 2 million Algerians also live in Europe, most of them in France. This constant contact across the Mediterranean lightens the weight of traditional Islam, especially for the Berber community, on Algeria's cultural life.

Berbers, after fourteen centuries of sharing Algeria with Arabs, retain a strong identity today. A fourth to a third of Algerians call themselves Berber. A common allegiance to Islam has kept the two peoples from perpetual conflict, but a tension remains. Some Algerians date the sequence of events that brought down the Bendjedid government not from 1988, when protesters first took to the streets, but from 1980, when Berber university students went on strike against the FLN to demand recognition of their historic language. Though Berbers speak Arabic, they look upon Arabic culture as Middle Eastern, quite different from their own.

It is my observation that Algeria is in general warier toward Islam than are the Arab societies to the east. Algerians have a stronger sense of individuality than Syrians or Egyptians or Saudis. It manifests itself in greater willingness—in books, conversation and even in the press—to question religious and social orthodoxies. I was astonished at how much critical debate took place in Algeria, particularly among Berbers, on Islam's role in the society and in their lives. The explanation, I suspect, lies in the slightly rebellious attitude that the Berber heritage contributes to Algeria's civilization.

One afternoon, in a bookstore near Algiers University, I picked up a slim volume by Redha Malek, whom I had known as ambassador to Washington. Malek, in addition to his career in diplomacy, had long been active in liberal Islamic organizations. After the January coup he served briefly as an anti-FIS Prime Minister, though his hard line was without notable achievement.

"If we in Algeria want to hasten our arrival as a modern state, and a member of the international community," he wrote, "one of our first postulates must be, without mincing words, freedom of individual conscience in questions of religious belief. . . . Religious tolerance is a basic virtue, and we must put an end to the prohibitions applied by theologians a thousand years ago to muzzle free thought. . . . 'Islam, the friend of reason,' that must be the central theme of our philosophical discourse today."[6]

I have rarely seen such sentiments in books on counters in the Middle East. Later I read a series of columns in an Algiers newspaper which examined Islam with unusual detachment. The author, Zahir Ihaddaden, was a university professor and a former member of the "bearded FLN," as well as a cofounder of an independent Islamic party called *El Umma*.

"In our society, we have a tendency to let myths determine how we live and act," he wrote. "Once these myths . . . may have been useful, but in our time they have been reduced to empty slogans. Let me cite two: the myth of political union and the myth that bars *bid'a*, religious innovation.

"Since the Muslim world slipped into decadence, reform movements have spouted appeals to union. When the Arab states were striving for sovereignty, such appeals were useful, but now they . . . paralyze our societies by distorting the difference between the dream and the real, between utopia and reality. . . ."

I read this paragraph as criticism both of Nasser-style Arab nationalism and of the fundamentalist dogma which holds that an Islamic state must ignore the present boundaries of Muslim countries to embrace the entire *umma*. It was meant as an appeal to Islamists to deal with

Algeria first. This doctrine was one of many that divided the factions within the FIS.

"As for the second myth," Ihaddaden went on, "in our system of beliefs, all religious innovation is taboo. Our theologians fear the modern world, and promote this taboo to avoid discussing ideas that might ease our adaptation to it. They would have us forget that modifying worn-out ideas is a source of life. This taboo keeps Muslims in a state of perpetual stagnation. . . ."

Impressed with Ihaddaden's writing, I managed to arrange a meeting, which took place one evening at his home in Kouba, a working-class quarter known as a FIS bastion. A soft-spoken man in his fifties, Ihaddaden received me in the company of his wife, which I found unusual for a Muslim. The coffee table was stacked high with little cakes that she had baked to celebrate the end of Ramadan, and after we talked she insisted I take some of them back to the hotel with me in a paper bag. I did.

"The countries of North Africa were always ruled by local people," said Ihaddaden, when I asked why Algeria's culture was different from the Middle East's. "Even the Umayyad and the Abassid caliphs, coming from Arabia, were foreign to their Middle East subjects. Here, though sovereignty may have been claimed by the Arabs or the Ottomans, we kept Algerians in charge. Until the French came along, we always governed ourselves. Having accepted Islam, we were not ruled in its name by conquerors.

"The religious ideas developed here, through dialogue, had a great deal of variety. But the French occupation ruptured our normal evolution, leaving the people with a feeling of emptiness. The French treated us with total condescension. In their schools, we lost our history and our culture. They confiscated our mosques and used our clergy to do their bidding. Degraded by a Western, Christian power, we were filled with shame of our civilization. Our religious development stopped cold.

"Today, the FIS is picking up the pieces of our national tragedy. It has no program; it makes a mockery of democracy; it humiliates women. But it promises to fill a void in our history, which is important in a state that has failed to build strong institutions. Our culture has recently awakened, and we have reopened the traditional dialogue on our political and religious values. The people are listening. But as a social force, the FIS has an edge on the secular intellectuals: it is deeply Algerian, and it speaks a simple, direct language that is compelling to frustrated Algerians."

Algerians trace the modern reawakening of Islamic consciousness to

Abdelhamid Ben Badis, a Berber, called by his admirers "the *imam* of the century." Ben Badis, after a classical Islamic education, consecrated himself in the 1920s to the cause of Algerian freedom and Islamic reform. Freedom, in that era, meant anticolonialism. Reform meant the rescue of Islam from the folk cults that had grown up, particularly in rural areas, around marabout mystics and Sufi brothers. Because the French manipulated the folk cults to promote their interests, political nationalism and religious reform went hand in hand.

In organizing the Association of *Ulama* in 1931, Ben Badis took his inspiration from Egypt's modernist thinker, Muhammad Abduh. He called for *salafiya*, the word Abduh used to signify the need to return to the Islam of the Prophet. To Ben Badis, however, this did not mean fundamentalism, though he opposed drinking and dancing. Mostly, it meant a purging of Algeria's popular Islam of idolatry and superstition. Being a modernist of Abduh's school, he proposed not to replicate the society of Muhammad and the *rashidun* but to draw from its spirituality the lessons applicable to contemporary life.[7]

Ben Badis called for more Islamic education, but he argued for keeping the society open to Western ideas. As a patriot, he gave priority to a restoration of Algeria's cultural identity, from which he believed an independence of the spirit would emerge. The motto he imparted to the Association was: "Algeria is my country, Arabic my language, Islam my religion." In the spirit of Abduh, he promoted a tolerant reform based on Algerian—not Arab—nationalism.

In helping to suffuse Algerian nationalism with Islam, Ben Badis won converts to the cause of liberation. Much of the *ulama*, convinced he was subordinating Islam to secular nationalism, opposed his ideas. Islam and nationalism, Ben Badis answered, were equally important to Algerians. He died in 1940, but his vision was absorbed through the "bearded FLN" into the ideology of the war of liberation.

In the postwar era the FLN exploited Ben Badis's vision in attempting to place Islam at the service of the state. It did not succeed, and indeed, by the late 1960s, the mosques, rejecting Ben Badis, were passing inexorably into opposition. To counter the FLN's Nasserist ideology, young Algerians, chose to be guided by Egypt's experience. They echoed the fundamentalist line of Nasser's Islamic foes in the Muslim Brotherhood and entertained the violent ideas not only of Hassan al-Banna but of Sayyid Qutb. Algerian Islam grew increasingly harsh, leaving the moderation of Ben Badis in eclipse.

By the 1970s, the fundamentalist wing, calling itself *salafi*, had taken over a large proportion of Algeria's mosques. Its members were teachers, professionals, state functionaries—and unemployed youths. In 1979 the Iranian revolution aroused them to demand an Islamic state governed by the *shari'a.*

When the FIS was founded a decade later, they were deeply committed to the replacement of the FLN state.[8]

Yet Ben Badis's moderation had not altogether vanished. Inside the FIS were Abduh-style Muslims, Ben Badis's ideological descendants. They were known as *jaz'ara,* the Arabic word for "Algeria," in recognition of their link with Ben Badis's humane nationalism. They were university-based and, like Ben Badis, a bit elitist. Between the *jaz'ara* and the dominant *salafi* faction, there grew what has become in contemporary Islam a classical tension between modernism and fundamentalism.

A third wing involved in organizing the FIS was designated *mujahideen* ("makers of *jihad*"), a term used for Islamic fighters. The *mujahideen,* compared to the *jaz'ara* and *salafi* wings, cared less for ideology than action. Heirs to the brutality of the war against the French, they were particularly drawn to Qutb's bloody advocacy. They believed the Islamic state could be achieved only through "armed struggle," and they justified whatever violence it required. While the *mujahideen* prepared for violence, both the *jaz'ara* and *salafi* wings debated whether they should be in the Islamic movement at all.

The division among the wings was not always clean. Many within the FIS were eclectic, selecting doctrine from different factions. As the civil war intensified, the entire movement fragmented, with expediency beckoning members across factional lines. When the FIS went underground, its factions became even harder to track. Relations between them were sometimes supportive, sometimes deadly, based on a logic that was often obscure.

This maneuvering further blurred the character of the Islamic movement. Beyond a vague commitment to an Islamic state, Algerians had little idea what the movement stood for. Would its guide be the moderation of Ben Badis or the radicalism of Qutb, al-Banna and Benhadj? To preserve the organization from ideological disarray, the founders of the FIS had barely considered such questions, much less resolved them. Soon after the January coup the FIS's leaders vanished into prison or hiding or exile, or into guerrilla bands scattered about the countryside. The Islamic movement's great decisions were never made. They now appear unlikely ever to be.

· V ·

IN SEARCH of a further understanding of the FIS culture for this book, I went to Anwar Haddam, whom I met in Paris in 1992, a few months after the January coup. Stocky and bearded, not yet forty, he had been a member of the Islamic movement since his days as a student at the University of Algiers. Later a professor of nuclear physics at the university, he became a founder of the FIS, and ran in the legislative elections of 1991 from his hometown of Tlemcen in western Algeria. Winner of a majority in the first round, Haddam never made it to the parliament.

On the day in January 1992 that the army revoked the election, a sociologist from a Paris research institute happened to be in Tlemcen. She told an interviewer that "people had forgotten about the army, about the possibility of intervention." The city had been in exultation, she said; then everything stopped.

"The next day," she said, "I went out to see what the people were saying, how people experienced the end of the electoral process. I found consternation. . . . There was incredible restraint on the part of the Islamists, which was more important than what happened afterward: the coup d'état, the military takeover, the punishing of the FIS. There had been the feeling that a breath of liberty was coming and then—it collapsed."[9]

Haddam told me the FIS had anticipated the possibility of a coup and had made some plans to deal with it. He went into hiding when the government began arresting activists, then managed his escape from the country. When I made contact with him, he was the FIS representative in France. We talked in a dingy office in a shabby North African quarter in Paris.

Understandably, Haddam was outraged at events. "A crime against humanity" was his characterization of the January coup. "Though we are sure to take power," he said, "it is up to the junta to decide whether it happens by violence or the political process. Either way, this dictatorship will come to an end."

Optimistic then, Haddam predicted that Algeria's soldiers would disobey military orders to suppress the FIS. "The soldiers voted for the FIS," he said. "They are waiting for us to act. When the time comes, it will not take a civil war to overthrow the government, because they will come willingly over to our side." Events later proved the inaccuracy of his prediction.

When I saw Haddam again after four years of civil war, during which the army had remained loyal to the state, he was much less buoyant. Because of the French government's hostility to FIS activists, he had left France and wound up in the United States, where he had done graduate work in physics a decade before. I met with him in the small house in a Washington suburb where he lived with his family.

Haddam described himself as the FIS spokesman in Washington, and his business card carried the title "President, Parliamentary Delegation." The American government, though more hospitable to him than the French had been, was no friendlier to the FIS. Haddam was frustrated at failing to soften the American position. Even more frustrating, squabbles inside the FIS created some uncertainty about whom he represented, if anyone at all.

Haddam, in a series of interviews in 1996, described to me his background in Tlemcen. His family was, he said, Islamic in belief, Francophile in culture and nationalist in politics. It seemed to me to typify the character of the *jaz'ara* wing of the FIS.

Haddam told me his parents were religious, yet spoke fluent French and opened him to Western ideas. His father, a disciple of Ben Badis, had belonged to the Islamic wing of the FLN. After studying in France for a doctorate in mathematics, he returned to Tlemcen, where he taught in the local high school. He also founded and presided over a student mosque there. His parents, Haddam said, taught him that Islamic practice and Western-style intellectual attainment were complementary.

At eighteen, Haddam said, he went to Algiers to study at the university, where his older siblings were already enrolled. They all lived in the same apartment and belonged to the growing Islamic student movement. It troubled them, he said, that Marxism and secularism were then the dominant creeds and that there was no place for students to pray. After much badgering, the university finally agreed to the establishment of a mosque, Haddam said, which became the hub from which he and his friends organized Islamic outreach programs.

At the university, Haddam said, he came under the influence of Malek Bennabi, the modernist thinker, who taught that Islamic civilization's decline was the product less of Western colonialism than of its own inadaptability to changing circumstances. Bennabi, a cultural nationalist, introduced Haddam to the notion of *colonizabilité*, a weakness which Algeria would have to overcome before it could attain an authentic national life.[10]

I went back to look at Bennabi's work and found this:

"When the Muslim is denied the effective means of developing his personality and making use of his gifts, that's colonialism. But when the Muslim does not even dream of putting to good use the means that are already available to him, of making an extra effort to better his life, of building on his good luck, of using his time to a positive end, when on the contrary he resigns himself to the rules of the colonizer, assuring the success of the colonizer's techniques, that is *colonizabilité.*"[11]

As his Islamic guide, Bennabi took the Quranic verse: "God does not change the condition of a people until they have first changed what is in their hearts" (13:11).[12] Bennabi contended that Islam's decline began with the fall of the Mu'tazilites a thousand years before, and he argued for an embrace of reason and respect for innovation in interpreting Islam's essential doctrines.

"Europe in the nineteenth century," Bennabi wrote, "entrusted its destiny to three concepts: science, progress, civilization." These concepts have become the basis both of the West's global dominance and of a world civilization. But alone, he said, they leave Western society empty of spiritual content. Islam must absorb the West's three imperatives, while retaining its own spirituality, "to resume its rank among the great history-making ideas."[13]

Bennabi worked for much of his adult life in France as an electrical engineer, while writing on the theme of the decadence and renewal of Islamic culture. Disenchanted with Algeria's government after the war of independence, he studied and rejected the reformist vision of Saudi Arabia's Wahhabis and Egypt's Muslim Brotherhood before gravitating toward the views of Ben Badis. Bennabi concluded finally that Algeria's Islamic regeneration had to take place not within the context of the *umma*, the worldwide Islamic community, but within the boundaries of Algeria alone.

In 1967, Bennabi began inviting students, most of them with scientific training, to attend seminars in his apartment, conducted in French, focusing on Islamic themes. Haddam was among the invited.

"I came from a small, conservative town," Haddam told me. "Bennabi introduced me to a larger world. He talked of the need for an Islamic renaissance and of our personal transformation to achieve it. He taught us to be planners, and to be aware that our enemies were also planners."

The seminars, which probably touched several hundred students in all, ended with Bennabi's death in 1973.

They gave birth in the 1970s, Haddam told me, to a secret association. Its members, all worshipers at the university mosque, called it simply *jama'a* ("group"). Its fundamentalist rivals, scornful of Bennabi's call to Islamize Algeria without reference to the *umma*, contemptuously dubbed the group *jaz'ara*. Haddam told me he disliked the name, on the grounds that it was divisive, but *jaz'ara* was the name that stuck.

Jaz'ara students, Haddam said, circulated among university and secondary school mosques, largely in Algiers, seeking converts to their Islamic vision. Among their basic principles, he said, was the rejection of political violence. "We had just come out of a violent revolution," Haddam told me, "and we did not believe an Islamic state that came to power through violence could be just."

Though elitist in character, largely nonclerical and heavily francophone, the *jaz'ara* brought Ben Badis's lessons of tolerance into the FIS. Though it was never more than a minority, it was for a time remarkably influential.

The majority who came together to organize the FIS were *imams* and their disciples, most of *salafi* tendencies. They viewed Islam within the context of fundamentalist imperatives. They were more nationalist in being anti-French and anti-Western than pro-Algerian. Overwhelmingly arabophone, they came not out of the universities but out of Algeria's network of Quranic schools. The *salafi* power base was the masses, barely schooled, highly responsive to Islamic populism. Most members, when the FIS was born, were too young to have experienced Algeria's war of independence. But, ironically, they were old enough to feel they had been betrayed by it.

Abassi Madani, FIS's president, though known for promoting compromises, at heart was a *salafi*. He resented the *jaz'ara,* not just for its modernist views, which he regarded as non-Islamic, but for its worldliness and elitism, and for the social privilege that the bulk of its members enjoyed.

In June 1991, just before his arrest and six months before the military coup, Madani was asked to define his democratic principles. His answer only compounded the fear that fundamentalism, once voted into power, would not allow itself to be voted out.

"Islam is a religion which seeks the truth . . ." he said. "The truth is the truth, whether it comes from the minority or the majority. . . . The truth is that the need for Islam is greater today than at any time in human history. . . . Islam requires the government to follow the truth even if it is coming from a minority party of the society. . . . We go beyond what is called democracy to what is higher and more complete."

Ali Benhadj, FIS's second in command, was even more forthright in denigrating democracy. To Benhadj, democracy was not Islamic, and non-Islamic governing institutions were apostate. His goal was a state,

Sunni to be sure, but run much like Iran's, by a *shura* of *imam*s. Unlike Madani, he was not a compromiser, and fought vigorously against the concessions—such as the public disclaimers of violence—that the *jaz'ara* succeeded at first in imposing on the FIS.

Benhadj was still in prison, incommunicado, when I first visited Algiers and has remained there in the years since. While I was doing the research for this book, he was believed to be locked up in the Sahara but his followers, having had no contact with him, were unsure whether he was even alive. No one in Algeria identified with the FIS was free to talk to me, and so I had to go searching elsewhere for an Algerian qualified to discuss *salafi* ideals.

In France, too, hundreds of Algerian activists had been placed in detention, most of them without charges. Abandoning any pretense of neutrality in the Algerian conflict, France had openly gone over to the side of Algeria's government. In large measure it was responding to bombs set off in Paris and to the kidnapping and killing of its nationals in Algeria, all presumably by Islamic militants. More or less indiscriminately, France had rounded up Islamic activists—the police admitted to two hundred, the FIS put the figure at sixteen hundred. Those who had somehow eluded the police net were too frightened to talk.

So I tried London, where the police were more indulgent. The FIS network in France had directed me to Abdullah Messai, a red-bearded *salafi* in his fifties, a Benhadj disciple who said he was willing to interpret his mentor, though he did not claim to represent him. We met in the commercial district of a suburb at the end of an underground line, where half the pedestrians were in saris or turbans or *hejab*s. On the second story of a Burger King, drinking coffee while rock'n'roll blared in my ears, I listened as Messai discussed the fine points of *salafi* Islam.

"God talks to Muslims through the Quran, His book," said Messai. "When I want to know something, I refer to it. The answers are clear. We Muslims are told not to add or subtract, much less invent, in our doctrine. No innovation, no *bid'a,* is allowed. God has given us everything we need. Islam's problems began when believers began to complicate this simple principle. After the Prophet's death, humans started to embellish God's word.

"Ali Benhadj understands that the problems we face in Algeria are the result of *bid'a*. We who follow him are for revival, for getting rid of *bid'a*. To you Westerners, innovation sounds nice, but our goal is to free the Muslim mind from man-made beliefs, so that we can return to the God-given truth. These truths are not affected by time. God and the book are our references for all times.

"Being humans, we may fall short because of human whims or by following false gods. Categories like *jaz'ara* and *salafi* do harm, suggesting God can be interpreted as man chooses, which provokes mutual accusations. But most of the texts are clear, and need no interpretation. In the few verses that do, interpretation must be kept to a minimum. In the sense of having the truth of God's word at hand, we Muslims are all fundamentalists."

Messai acknowledged, however, that the scriptures do not provide guidance on the institutions of an Islamic state. Though the state's chief responsibility is to apply Islamic law correctly, the scriptures say only that it must be headed by a believer. Even without divine instruction, Benhadj is confident, he said, that sincere Muslims can design an Islamic state that pleases God and enforces the laws.

Not surprisingly, Messai did not express a high opinion of Bennabi, whom he described as an "Islamic scholar, one of the best of his time, with nice theories." But Bennabi's modernism, he said, addressed the problems of Muslims living under French oppression, without his fully grasping the *sunna*'s eternal truths. Too much of Bennabi's theories, he said, were his own and not God's.

"Benhadj has a deeper understanding, and generally tries to be objective toward the texts," Messai said, "but even he sometimes gives his own point of view, which carries him to the edge of the dangerous realm of *bid'a*."

Messai's example of Benhadj's *bid'a* lay in his tolerating the violence of the *mujahideen*, knowing it departs from Islam. "Even *jihad* has rules," he said, "and the *mujahideen* violate them." Comparing the *mujahideen* to Afghanistan's Taliban, he said, "These people give the faith a bad name." Benhadj embraces the *mujahideen*, Messai said, though their zealotry plays into the hands of Islam's enemies, the governments of Algeria and the West.

Benhadj's own writings on the *mujahideen* generally confirm Messai's observation. Benhadj, known as an orator, had written little about his beliefs in the years before his arrest. But in a letter from prison in 1993 he said that if the government did not respect its political commitments, the FIS would no longer be bound by its vow of peaceful struggle. A year later he went further by associating the *mujahideen*'s violence with the *salafi*, the majority wing of the FIS.

"What you call terrorism is in reality *jihad* in behalf of God on High and the exaltation of His word," Benhadj wrote in 1994 to Algeria's President. "Muslims have recourse to arms when they are severed from peaceful, legal means of change and the exercise of their political rights. Terrorism and violence are the product of a tyrannical and despotic junta.

"I support my brother *mujahideen* and I urge them to fight with all legitimate means. I advise them to observe the right of resistance against your junta, its auxiliaries and its riffraff, and not to lay down their arms until there is a legal and equitable solution which restores our rights."

Made public, Benhadj's letter did serious harm to the FIS. Nor was his defense of Islamic violence universally shared by the FIS leadership. Most FIS activists retained reservations about committing the organization to a civil war. They did not accept the *mujahideen,* a dissident faction at best, as equals in the campaign for an Islamic state.

The *mujahideen* had always been a stepchild within the FIS. Ali Benhadj was one of their few consistent sympathizers. Madani was afraid of them, and many of the FIS's most esteemed *imam*s had no use for their conduct in the struggle. The *mujahideen*'s history within the Islamic movement was, in fact, rather far removed from that of the *jaz'ara* and *salafi* wings.

The *mujahideen*'s roots went back to 1982, when Moustafa Bouyali, an ex-guerrilla fighter in the war of independence, launched a small insurrection against the "impious state" of the FLN. Influenced by Qutb, disillusioned by the refusal of Algeria's clergy to take up arms at his side, he resolved on a *jihad* of his own. Having recruited followers and stocked up on weapons, he directed a series of attacks on small-town wine shops, for which he was arrested and released. But after a brother's death in a police skirmish, he moved his band into the Atlas Mountains south of Algiers and initiated guerrilla warfare, to which Ali Benhadj gave his blessing.

For five years Bouyali frustrated the government with raids, assassination attempts and kidnappings. In magnitude and in casualties, his insurrection was not a threat to the government. But with a few dozen companions he captured the hearts of antistate Muslims, who saw him as an Islamic Robin Hood.

Part of the government wanted to negotiate with Bouyali, but the security services refused. In February 1987 the army ambushed and killed Bouyali on the outskirts of Algiers, and in the ensuing months rounded up much of his band. A few were executed and some were imprisoned. Within extremist circles, Bouyali became a martyr. He left behind a legacy of Islamic armed struggle, which believers who shared his outlook were avid to emulate.[14]

The survivors in Bouyali's band never disarmed, and after the January coup re-formed their groups. They were reinforced by comrades released from prison and picked up further recruits among local Afghans, who were experienced in guerrilla violence. The Afghans, renowned for being bloodthirsty, are thought to have shaped the strategy, as well as the character, of the entire *mujahideen* movement.

From its earliest days, the FIS leadership did what it could to bring the *mujahideen* under its command. But most of the *mujahideen* held the FIS in contempt for working within the government's rules, for consenting to elections, for rejecting *jihad*. Indeed, the FIS—both *salafi* and *jaz'ara*—had never prepared for armed struggle. Having come together in 1989 to participate in elections, both factions had thought little about taking the battlefield. The FIS indulged itself after the January coup with some vague threats, hoping to intimidate the government. But in failing, it also lost control of the *mujahideen* faction.

Bouyali's heirs probably never took orders from the FIS. For a while the FIS could count on the allegiance of the paramilitary units organized as the AIS (*Armée Islamique du Salut*), but they never amounted to much. From the start of the civil war, the major perpetrators of violence were the loosely affiliated bands known as the GIA, the *Groupes Islamiques Armés*. The deliberate use of the plural in their name proclaims the absence of authority, even among themselves. As violence became more commonplace, the GIA superseded the FIS in the public mind. As the FIS grew increasingly ineffectual, the GIA— thanks to the attention that the press and television gave to its depredations—co-opted the image of the Islamic movement.

As for ideology, many *mujahideen* appeared to share the worldview of Afghanistan's Taliban. They were antiwomen, anti-intellectual and antiforeigner, as well as being foes of the government. But some of the *mujahideen* were not ideological at all. They were common criminals, using Islam as a cover for banditry, kidnapping and rape. The government tried to persuade the outside world that such criminals were the majority. The claim was overblown, but it no doubt contained a substantial element of truth.

Algeria's security forces have successfully used mass arrests and torture to penetrate *mujahideen* units, diminishing their effectiveness. But the tactics of mass arrest have also been counterproductive, leading to a huge exodus from civilian society of young fundamentalists, for whom the *mujahideen* are a waiting source of shelter.

Life among the *mujahideen* is unquestionably hard. Suspicion is rampant. Power struggles among the groups are common. They have won the sympathy of few Algerians. It is not surprising that in this poisonous atmosphere they kill with insouciance, not just their adversaries and defenseless innocents but even one another.

The government's tactics have helped as well as hurt the GIA. In imprisoning the legitimate leadership of the FIS, and in refusing its offers to negotiate, the government, by default, has promoted the GIA into a position of dominance. Within the FIS, the *jaz'ara* and the *salafi* have clearly failed to achieve results. The FIS argues that discrediting the FIS is the government's real goal. In the GIA, the government can make the claim that its adversary is barbaric, and ignore all pleas to negotiate a fair conclusion to the civil war.

In 1994, Muhammad Said, an *imam* identified with the *jaz'ara* and serving as the FIS's provisional head, announced a merger with the GIA. The announcement, bewildering to outsiders, seemed to suggest an unlikely alliance between the two factions. Soon afterward Said was assassinated. The best explanation seemed to be that he had sought to impose restraints upon the GIA's violence and was killed by the *mujahideen* for his trouble.

Anwar Haddam, in Washington, loyally announced his support for Said's action, though he told me he had advised strongly against it. Said's course, suggesting abandonment of the political track, cast a shadow over the FIS both inside and outside Algeria. It was particularly painful for Haddam, who suddenly found himself listed in the terrorist camp, which seriously damaged his status in Washington. In December 1996, Haddam was arrested by American immigration authorities and placed in detention pending the execution of a deportation order.

And so the war has gone on, assuming an eerie resemblance in its brutality to Algeria's conflict against the French, when many citizens, asking only to be left alone, were punished by both sides for their indifference. In the summer and fall of 1997 the killing became particularly grotesque as masked bands practiced slipping into villages, some on the edge of Algiers itself, to spend the night hours slashing the throats of women, children and old men. As many as three or four hundred were killed in each of these strikes, while security units stationed nearby failed to respond to desperate calls for help.

For six years observers had assumed that the civil war's intermittent massacres were the work of the GIA, and in most cases they surely were. But the latest killings raised questions about the complicity of the security forces. With journalists intimidated by both state brutality and Islamic assassins, on-the-scene reporting of the war has always been spotty. But the evidence that has recently emerged suggests, at the least, that renegade military units and local militias armed by the government—perhaps accountable to no one—were deeply involved in the massacre. Clearly, the regime, if not an instigator of this violence, was powerless to stop it. At the latest count, the war is believed to have cost 60,000 lives, though some estimates are far higher.

· VI ·

SIX YEARS of civil war in Algeria have shown that neither side has the military strength needed to destroy the other.

The FIS, though organizationally in shambles, may survive in the hearts of its supporters, whatever their number may be. But its dream—to undermine the moral foundations of the state, causing it to fall of its own weight, as the monarchy did in Iran—has proven an illusion.

On the other hand, the government forces have been unable to bring the killing to an end. The *mujahideen,* who will not relent in their bloody *jihad,* have a counterpart in the *éradicateurs,* the segment of the military leadership that refuses any political compromise. It insists—apparently with significant civilian support—on maintaining its efforts to crush the rebellion totally.

Since 1994, Liamine Zeroual, an army general who came up through the ranks, has been Algeria's President. When chosen by the army to replace the High State Council, Zeroual, then fifty-two years old, was regarded as a cut above the rest of the officer corps in honesty and competence.

Whether or not he counts himself among the *éradicateurs* is unclear, but he has done little to promote a negotiated settlement of the war. Meanwhile, Madani and Benhadj, the recognized FIS leaders, have done no better in getting the GIA to end their killing and participate in any kind of talks.

Throughout 1994 the two sides felt each other out, seemingly offering the promise of an agreement.

Zeroual spoke of initiating a dialogue "that excludes nobody" and Benhadj, from prison, wrote letters which suggested that he, at last, might lay aside *jihad.* In August 1994, Madani notified Zeroual of the possibility of an armed truce. A month later both he and Benhadj were transferred from prison to house arrest, which observers took as a sign that substantive meetings were imminent.

But no dialogue ever took place. Negotiations to prepare for the talks—if they really were negotiations—collapsed over preconditions: the FIS wanted Madani and Benhadj released outright; the government wanted a condemnation from them of GIA violence. The collapse seemed to mean that both sides were subject to the veto of their own hard-liners.

By the time the preliminaries broke down in early 1995, the army and the GIA, the one more savage than the other, had raised the bloodshed to a new level. Since then there has been no prospect of the two sides meeting for negotiations.

But, as the two geared up for more fighting, another negotiation, quite different in character, was opening in Rome. In November the Sant' Egidio Community, a peace group affiliated with the Vatican, invited the FIS, along with the FLN and Algeria's other opposition parties, to meet under its auspices to draft a proposal to end the war. The government was also invited but declined to attend. The delegates who assembled at Sant' Egidio represented parties that had received more than 80 percent of the vote cast in the 1991 parliamentary election.

For the FIS, the meeting had the approval, conveyed from an Algerian prison, of Madani and Benhadj. Abdullah Messai, Benhadj's man in London, assured me that the meeting in no way represented a deviation from the goal of an Islamic state. "Islam authorizes an agreement with people who are not really on your side," he said, "to isolate the real enemy. Even the Prophet did that." One journalist quoted Benhadj as saying that if Sant' Egidio led to a dialogue with the government he would "go himself into the mountains to get the *mujahideen*" to accept the terms. For the first time, the FIS agreed to sit down with Algeria's secular parties. Never before had it seemed so enthusiastic.[15]

Anwar Haddam was the FIS delegate to Sant' Egidio. His presence was a source of some controversy among factions within the FIS. But he told me the arrangements for the meeting, as well as the initial draft of the platform, were prepared under the instructions of Madani and Benhadj. Haddam said he was the only member of the senior FIS leadership who was free to attend.

Sant' Egidio was a "big achievement" for the FIS, Haddam told me, in having the secular parties join in reaffirming the "enlightened Islamic principles" that had been set forth in 1954 in the declaration that launched Algeria's war of liberation. But the FIS, he conceded, also made significant concessions.

These concessions were foreshadowed in January 1995, when the FIS announced, in the name of Madani and Benhadj, its condemnation of "all [violent] acts directed at innocents, whatever their politics or religion, by whoever may commit them." Only a few months before, when it was sparring with the government over possible negotiations, the FIS had been unwilling to make such a statement, but it had clearly changed its mind. A few days after the statement was released, the Sant' Egidio platform was signed by the participants and made public.[16]

It was a significant retreat by the FIS to sign a document that made no mention of reinstating the results of the 1991 election, a long-standing demand. The platform also omitted the FIS claim, based on the 1991 election, to be Algeria's legitimate government. The document did not repeat the FIS line that it was the unique victim of the January coup. The platform also committed the FIS to *alternance,* which meant it was willing to go into peaceful opposition like other parties if voted out of office.

In terms of the fighting, the platform reaffirmed the statement by Madani and Benhadj in explicitly condemning attacks on civilians and foreigners. The document was also conspicuous in its silence on the right of the FIS to armed struggle.

The negotiations that the document proposed were to be conducted under the provisions of Algeria's constitution of 1989. The parties would be "the de facto authority and the representative political forces." Their mission would be to "decide the structures, modalities and duration of a transitional period, to be as short as possible, leading to free and pluralist elections that permit the people the full exercise of their sovereignty."

The Sant' Egidio platform was offered, moreover, not as an ultimatum but as an agenda for further bargaining. It was clearly conciliatory, and many Algerians placed great hope in it. Yet Zeroual flatly turned it down. He never announced his reasons, though, sardonically, he expressed shock that good Algerians would hold such a meeting abroad, rather than in the homeland. In Algeria, of course, the participants would surely have been arrested.

The search for an explanation of Zeroual's hostility falls most logically on a clause in the platform calling for the "nonintervention of the army in political affairs." To outsiders, it would seem only reasonable. But its acceptance would have nullified the Algerian military's long-standing supremacy in the political system. Whatever his other objections, Zeroual, as the army's surrogate, could clearly not tolerate such a radical change in the political system.

Two weeks after the Sant' Egidio signing, Zeroual returned Madani and Benhadj to prison. Benhadj has not been heard from since. The reimprisonment was Zeroual's signal that he would in his own way legitimize the political system established by the January coup. His subsequent acts have confirmed this was his intention.

In June 1995, Zeroual announced that elections for the presidency—"transparent, free, democratic and sovereign"—would be held in the first week of November. Soon after, he declared his own candidacy. The FIS, which was still banned, offered no candidate of its own. But neither did the other parties represented at Sant' Egidio, though they were presumably legal. All of them also boycotted the balloting.

Besides Zeroual, the electoral list contained the names of a moderate *imam,* a secular Berber and a businessman. None were friendly to the FIS. The campaign was conducted without incident and the balloting took place essentially as Zeroual had promised. Not only did the government run what most observers agreed was a fair election, but the *mujahideen* failed to disrupt it.

The results were even more favorable to Zeroual than had been anticipated; he won 61 percent of the votes. Equally significant, 75 percent of the electorate ignored the boycott and went to the polls, making the abstention rate lower than in 1991, the year of the big FIS victory.

The figures suggested that Algerians had repudiated the overwhelming endorsement given to the FIS four years earlier. Their vote for Zeroual could be taken as a renunciation of their revolutionary aspirations. But an equally persuasive interpretation of the outcome is that the electorate, exhausted by the civil war, was now asking only for an end to the violence, which Zeroual seemed in the best position to provide.

In a letter sent after the victory, a faction of the FIS linked to Madani tried reaching out to Zeroual, signaling a readiness to talk. Zeroual dismissed the offer. He responded by inviting the country's political forces—conspicuously omitting the FIS—to a conference to discuss Algeria's future. All but one of the parties that cosigned the Sant' Egidio platform stood together in declining his invitation.

It was the FLN that broke ranks. In an internal coup, the party leaders who had negotiated and signed the Sant' Egidio platform lost their posts to candidates willing to endorse Zeroual. The results suggest that the FLN's rank and file had tired of being excluded from power. Having spent four years in the cold, the party of Algeria's liberation had returned to the political game.

In mid-1996, Zeroual proposed a set of constitutional amendments to reshape the legislative assembly. While not explicitly banning Islamic parties, they barred the exploitation of religion—an ill-defined prohibition—for political purposes. They also empowered the President to appoint members to a new upper chamber of parliament, and to rule by decree during parliamentary recesses. Effectively, the amendments authorized the President to ignore the assembly. Their obvious intent was to deny to any Islamic party the power the FIS had come near to acquiring in 1991.

Algerians voted on the amendments on November 28 and, according to the government, more than 85 percent gave their approval. The official tally claimed 12.7 million ballots were cast, more than in the presidential elections the year before. It also said that only 20 percent of the voters had abstained, a new low.

Neither diplomats nor journalists had been permitted to monitor the voting, however, and more than one Algerian noted that the polling stations, characterized by long lines in 1995, were virtually empty in 1996. Many Algerians expressed skepticism at the government's figures.

Nonetheless, the amendments were ratified, and the question left was whether the FIS would ever be able to rise again. The FIS's leadership, some of it functioning underground and some of it abroad, had no effective means of appealing to the people. Moreover, the GIA, having become identified as *the* Islamic opposition, had largely pre-empted the FIS in the public mind. Its violence, which helped clear the field for Zeroual, had undoubtedly alienated the majority of Algerians and undermined the loyalty that the Islamic movement once enjoyed.

In retrospect, it appears the FIS took its last shot at staying a player in the political arena by going to Sant' Egidio. The effort failed. Since then, Zeroual has, by any measure, outmaneuvered it. He has offered the people a facade of democracy, while rewriting the constitution to preclude not only the FIS but any other party from winning political control. His amendments reaffirmed that the President, backed by the army, would retain the last word in running the state.

Where had the sentiment gone that produced a vote for an Islamic state in 1990 and again in 1991? Was the vote an illusion, in not being Islamic at all? Had Algerians, as the secularists among them claimed, been more interested in voting the FLN out than in voting the FIS in? Had they, in reality, never been interested in an Islamic state at all?

Certainly the Islamic movement, which includes the remnants of the FIS, perseveres in believing that Algeria is not prepared to abandon its cause. On the contrary, it continues to assert that the injustice of January 1992 will not prevail, and that the Algerians will, in the end, affirm Islam's right to rule.

On the day after Zeroual's constitutional amendments were ratified, a secular journalist whose newspaper had lost four staff members to Islamic assassins told the *New York Times:* "When I heard the results of the referendum, I felt complete despair for the first time. . . . What we have in place now is a time bomb. Nobody knows exactly when it will explode, but we all know that one day it will." He was saying that the civil war, far from over, had barely begun.

Yet for the moment there is no doubt that the President, acting in behalf of the army, is securely in charge. In 1997 he authorized two more elections. One was to fill the seats in Algeria's largely impotent parliament, the other to fill the municipal posts vacated by order of the regime after the coup. The GIA responded by intensifying its carnage, killing hundreds, many of them to no apparent purpose in isolated towns and villages. They did not, however, stop the elections, which foreign observers deemed to be, on the whole, honest. To no one's surprise, the President's party and its allies won substantial victories.

The 1997 elections completed the reassembly of the constituent parts—President, constitution, parliament, municipalities—of the Algerian government. The damage done in the January coup had ostensibly been repaired. Zeroual could now make a reasonable claim of legitimacy, which most foreign governments, as well as many Algerians, deemed they had no choice but to accept.

The putative reestablishment of legitimacy, however, did not resolve Algeria's basic problems. Not only had the killing grown worse, but the years of fighting had put a stop to any serious effort—if the regime ever intended a serious effort—to rebuild Algerian institutions.

The country's economy remained fragile while its population continued to soar. The level of political integrity had, presumably, not improved. A sense of social inequity still ate at popular morale. In short, the characteristics that were intrinsic to the FLN state were, nearly a decade after Bendjedid's great democratic reforms, still intact.

Many Algerians say that, though the FIS may now be dead, the Islamic movement is only in hibernation, waiting for the springtime. When the movement awakens, they say, its political organization may have a new name but it will profess the same commitment to a state based on Islam and the *shari'a*. None of the changes that Zeroual has made, they insist, have addressed the problems that lay at the heart of the FIS's electoral victories—and its subsequent downfall.

Yet it is also clear that the army will not again take the chances with democracy that it took before the January coup. Nor will it grant to the Islamic movement the opportunities for growth—through mosque associations or access to government posts—that it enjoyed in the decades after independence. Amply warned, it will not make the same mistakes a second time.

On both sides, the feeling is widespread that, though the civil war may have occasional moments of remission in the coming years, the struggle for Algeria's soul is far from over.

9

The Beleaguered Muslims
of France

· I ·

EVERY COUNTRY of Western Europe has, over the past few decades, come to live with the presence of a substantial community of immigrant Muslims. They have arrived from different places and for different reasons, and they have received many varieties of welcome. But their experience everywhere is shaped by an absence of precedent. Their migration is the first ever of Islamic communities attempting to integrate in the Christian world.

France's community is by far the largest. By rough calculation, France now has between 4 and 5 million Muslims, nearly a tenth of its population. Though still preponderantly Catholic, France now has more Muslims than either Protestants or Jews, its historical minorities. Islam is France's second largest religion.

The presence of these communities is the product of the soaring population and stagnant economies of the Arab world. The Arabs are not alone in dealing with these twin problems, of course. The continuing explosion of population in all of the developing world imposes huge pressures that redound indirectly on the West. These pressures, moreover, are likely to keep rising if—as seems quite likely—life in the Third World becomes more impoverished and governments less stable. But, for now, Muslim society is leading the charge.

France, by force of circumstances, has taken the leadership in absorbing Muslim emigration. Like communal migration throughout history, the process has not always gone smoothly. France's difficulties raise serious questions about whether—or, perhaps more accurately, for how long—Western society can deal with populations spilling over from the developing world without seriously undermining its own equilibrium. But France's experience also suggests that Muslims may create special problems of their own for the West.

A large majority of France's Muslim community comes from the former North African empire of Algeria, Morocco and Tunisia. A half million more originate in the Middle East, most from the ex-colonies of Syria and Lebanon. Several hundred thousand Muslims in France are blacks, from the former colonies of West Africa. Turks make up about 150,000, and about 35,000 are French who have converted to Islam. The rest originate from the hundred or so countries that the Ministry of Interior describes as "diverse."

Approximately half of the Muslims living in France have French nationality. As many as a fourth may be in residence illegally, though generally with the toleration of the police. The French have learned that trying to expel them can produce more headaches than it cures.

The French government, it should be added, acknowledges that the figures on Muslims are imprecise. The French state, being legally secular, is forbidden to make religious inquiries, whether of citizens or noncitizens. France takes no religious census.

But, as the diversity of origins indicates, France's Muslims make up a far from unified community. Though all regard themselves as members of the *umma,* their cultural differences, their ideological disputes and their old-country rivalries divide them much more than their shared commitment to Islam unites them. This disarray is frustrating to the French government. The French state, albeit secular, maintains official relationships with religious communities through representative bodies of their choice. The Muslims lack such a body.

The French classify these bodies as "associations," enabling the government to deal routinely with religious communities on matters of common concern. An official explained to me that the procedure is not regarded as a violation of secularism. The same legal principle, the official said, permits the government to deal with, say, football clubs or literary societies.

The Ministry of Interior, through its Religious Affairs Bureau, has responsibility for dealing with the religions. It is no coincidence that this is also the ministry that runs the police. In 1905, when France severed official relations with the Catholic Church, it took the position that religious groups, particularly militant Catholics, were a potential source of disorder. To deal with them under the same roof as the police seemed logical.

On local matters, the ministry commonly delegates its power to the municipalities. The mayors of towns and villages deal with the religious associations on matters relating, for example, to holiday celebrations or building permits or youth programs.

But on grander issues the ministry consults with the Catholic Conference of Bishops, the Jewish Consistory and the Protestant Federation. It even meets with an association that represents a half million Armenians in France.

The ministry solicits their opinions, for example, on choosing prison chaplains. It assigns them time for religious programming on the radio and the television networks. Informally, it may even examine social or law-enforcement practices that bear on the community.

The government acknowledges that security issues, not holidays or TV time, are its chief interest in a relationship with the Muslims. Not surprisingly, French authorities find the Muslims, being the newest and the least integrated of France's immigrant communities, the most troublesome.

Until 1981, French law prevented consultations with Muslims, by denying to them—and to all foreigners—the right to form "associations." Most Frenchmen became conscious of this distinction only in the 1970s, and it was debated in the election campaign of 1981. After François Mitterrand became President, the parliament voted to lift the ban, opening the way for Muslims to organize in the same way as Christians and Jews.

Since then Muslims at the local level have formed hundreds of associations, some to build and run mosques, others to promote sports, political interests or education. Many of these associations have been linked into regional or nationwide federations. But the community as a whole, to the government's annoyance, has remained too fragmented to choose a body to represent it in treating the big problems with the umbrella organization, the Interior Ministry in Paris.

Muslims, in their defense, argue that the ministry should give them more time to settle their differences. Though present in France since World War I, Muslims arrived in large numbers only in the 1960s, long after the other religious minorities had established themselves. The government is not insensitive to this response but points out that the Muslims are no closer to agreement now than they were three decades ago.

The major Muslim influx came when Algeria's war of independence ended in 1962. First came a wave of "Harkis," hundreds of thousands of Algerians who were granted asylum, with their families, for having fought against other Algerians in the French army. Soon afterward, a million more Algerians arrived, mostly young men, responding to France's invitation to meet the need for labor of a suddenly burgeoning economy. Predictably, they were anti-Harki. The Algerians established two communities. If that were not division enough, since 1992 Algeria's civil war has fragmented its community in France even more.

The high tide of Muslim immigration—Algerian, Moroccan, Tunisian—lasted only a few years. By the late 1960s the economic boom had ebbed, reducing the demand for immigrant labor. But by then Muslims were already living in nearly all of France's cities and towns. Only slowly did the French perceive that, with few of the immigrants choosing to return home, a society of Muslims of substantial numbers had settled in the country to stay.

In the 1970s, France enacted a "zero immigration" policy, to halt the influx, but new laws did not stop the population increase. The newcomers had a higher birth rate than the French. Many Muslims also entered illegally, or through an exception in the laws which authorized the reunion of immigrant families.

This exception, based on genuinely humane concerns, has set the tone for French policy. Germany and Britain, each with a Muslim community of about 2 million, have followed different paths. Germany never accepted the immigrants' permanent presence and still promotes their repatriation. Britain, without a clear policy, practices a kind of laissez-faire toward its immigrant communities. Only France, faithful to a tradition of hospitality to foreigners, formally recognizes its Muslims and vows to integrate them into the larger society.

France, it is fair to say, never abandoned the egalitarianism in its revolutionary heritage. It has for two centuries absorbed outsiders more readily than any country in Europe. It retains a generous interpretation of the right of asylum. Despite a "zero immigration" policy, it has not dropped the practice of offering to immigrants the opportunity to become French.

This policy, in recent years, has fallen on hard times. Unemployment in France throughout the 1990s has been intractable. More important, Algeria's civil war, in which France has supported the military regime against the Islamic rebels, has brought bloodshed to French streets, curbing the disposition of the French to distinguish innocent immigrants from hostile terrorists.

Public opinion polls show that two thirds of the French now confuse Islam with fundamentalism and link them both with fanaticism. This attitude has fed the fortunes of Jean-Marie Le Pen's National Front, a far-right party that calls for expelling the Arabs entirely. It has not been easy, in this atmosphere, for France's government to persevere in its integration efforts.

France, in explaining its policy, maintains that it will integrate those Muslims who are already in residence, while building a wall against admitting any more. But integration has not proved easy and population pressures from North Africa continue to grow. France's execution of its Muslim policy is falling seriously behind the theory. France, as a result, is not inspiring its European neighbors to emulate the hospitality it has shown.

· II ·

THE PROCLAIMED OBJECTIVE of France's Muslim community is to become French in nationality, while remaining Islamic in religion. It has no guidelines, however, for adapting Muslim culture—that is, the everyday life of the community—to the context of a liberal, democratic, Western civilization.

Worship itself poses no problem. Within the framework of the religious freedom that the West conventionally offers, the Islamic community's rituals live comfortably side by side with the rituals of other faiths. There may be limits to what the West will tolerate. The self-flagellation of the Shi'ites, for example, would surely offend French sensibilities. France has already pronounced the genital mutilation of girls, common in Egypt and Sudan, illegal. But the Islam of most Muslims in France does not contain such indigestible practices.

Indeed, the Islamic rites performed in France are scarcely different in character from Christian or Jewish devotions. The Muslim community in France has never complained that it is denied the right to pray as freely as the members of other faiths.

Independent studies, in fact, suggest that Muslims resemble the French remarkably in their religious habits. Only 10 or 15 percent of both practice their religion on a regular basis. Like the French, most Muslims identify with their faith culturally rather than ritually—that is, by celebrating major holidays either in the mosque or in the context of family and friends.

But Islam is also a system of law, regarded by its believers as divine. As a practical matter, this law has been reduced throughout most of the Arab world to family affairs. But just as two solid objects cannot simultaneously occupy the same space, it is clear the *shari'a*, even as family law, cannot coexist within the legal system administered by a Western secular state.

The incompatibility goes further, however. Much more than contemporary Christians and Jews, Muslims—even those who do not practice—identify themselves as members of a religious community.

Muslims do not accept the state as a secular authority, as Westerners do. The duty of the state, in Islam, is to provide the community with conditions congenial to the practice of the faith. Far more than for a modern Christian or Jew, for a Muslim to be both a believer and French requires fidelity to communities in conflict, one secular, the other religious. This presents a serious dilemma.

Recently the Rushdie episode illustrated the pull of the divine felt by so many Muslims in the West. Muslims, like others, take pleasure in exercising secular freedoms. But Muslims in Britain protested the publication of Salman Rushdie's *The Satanic Verses,* on the grounds that it offended the Prophet. Then they protested when Britain offered to protect Rushdie from the death penalty pronounced in Khomeini's *fatwa.* Though no one in Britain died from the *fatwa,* it would be hard to imagine a more vivid conflict between Islam's values and the West's.

In France, polygamous marriages have long been illegal, but the government for decades tolerated immigrant families that arrived in a condition of polygamy. In recent years, however, polygamy, practiced mostly among West African Muslims, has led to serious social problems: multiple pregnancies, severe poverty, domestic disorders. Seeing the situation spin out of control, the government reversed itself and now treats all marriages after the first as effectively annulled.

Rather than deal in Islamic abstractions, France follows the premise that Islam's compatibility with French society will not be prejudged by the scriptural texts. Muslims are welcome to believe whatever they like, but they are expected to obey the same French laws as everyone else. They are judged not on the basis of what the Quran says but on what they, as individuals and within the context of French legal codes, actually do.

Whether France and its Muslims can reach an accommodation on such issues as women's rights of inheritance, on which the *shari'a* is very explicit, is still not clear. What cannot be accommodated in theory may be resolved in practice. The two parties, in matters of law, are still feeling out each other's limits.

Muslims admit that the French government has shown considerable generosity of spirit in confronting their peculiar needs. They acknowledge France's positive contributions—though falling short of Islamic ideals—to the integration process. France, they concede, has respected Islam's religious distinctiveness.

The state, for example, provides Muslim chaplains and Muslim dietary rations to believers in the military and in prisons. Business and industry offer time and facilities for prayer to Muslim employees.

Some 30,000 members of the Muslim community, with official blessing, go on pilgrimage to Mecca each year.

More visible are France's mosques. France has eight "cathedral-mosques," each accommodating a thousand or more worshipers. Around the country there are also more than a hundred smaller mosques, in which several hundred believers can assemble. Muslims say they need more mosques, and that bureaucratic obstacles at the local level prevent their building them. There is truth to this charge. Yet Muslims, free to improvise, have transformed stores, houses and apartments into prayer rooms. Though less satisfactory than mosques, more than a thousand exist, in every French province.

If the French government had its way, the Grand Mosque of Paris would be the Muslim papacy. At the edge of the Latin Quarter, it was dedicated in 1926 to the Muslim soldiers, largely North African, who fought for France in World War I. Classically Islamic in design, with high walls and a crenellated minaret that dominates the *quartier,* it has a courtyard paved in black and white tiles. At its hub is an octagonal fountain, where men in many costumes perform ablutions. Thousands of Muslims pray there every Friday.

France's most illustrious Islamic monument, the Grand Mosque, as an "association," receives subsidies for maintenance from the Paris municipality and the Ministry of Interior.[1] It also receives official greetings each year, as do the other major faiths, from the President of the Republic.

At first linked to Morocco, the Grand Mosque has been supported by Algeria, under an agreement with the French government, since Algeria's independence in 1962. Algeria also names the mosque's *imam.* This arrangement does not satisfy all of France's Muslims, a majority of whom are not Algerian. On the contrary, it says to them that the mosque, lacking the universality that the papacy represents to Catholics, is an arm of the Algerian state.

The newest "cathedral-mosque" opened in Lyon, France's second city, in September 1994. Built largely with Saudi money, but on municipal land, the mosque is snow white in color, fusing modern with historic Islamic architecture. Its construction was preceded by a decade of wrangling, during which Lyon's Muslims, to avoid offending the Lyonnais, agreed to shorten the minaret and muffle the call of the *muezzin.* At its dedication, its *imam* described it as standing "midway between two cultures—the marvels of the Quran and the wisdom of Descartes."

The dedication was a major event in French Muslim life. Charles Pasqua, a man who boasts of his own immigrant roots, represented the state. Pasqua, then the Minister of Interior, was in charge of relations with religious associations. But as the state's highest police official, he also brought a reminder to the Muslim community that the government, however tolerant, still looked upon Islam in the context of internal security.

France, Pasqua declared in his speech, would not compromise its secular traditions to accommodate any faith, and expected Muslims in France to accept French law over the *shari'a*. He issued a further challenge: "It is not enough simply to have Islam in France," he said. "There must now be a French Islam."

The idea behind a "French Islam" is identical to what France expects of its Christians and Jews. But to Muslims it is an odd idea, alien to traditional Islamic dogma, and it did not sit well with most of them. France, Pasqua's words warned, would tolerate Islamic practices, whether religious or cultural, but only so long as they did not challenge the integrity of French society.

Pasqua's speech was an admission that all was not harmonious between France and its Muslim community. He reflected a widely felt anxiety about Islam's impact on France's national life. He also articulated a concern over whether Muslims were different from the immigrants who preceded them, the Poles or the Portuguese or the Jews. Pasqua's speech contained a recognition that France was uncertain whether Muslims could be integrated at all.

· III ·

CROSSTOWN from the Paris Mosque, in the grim 19th arrondissement abutting the heavily Muslim, industrial suburbs on the northern rim of the city, stands another of France's "grand" mosques—although, in the English sense of the word, it is not grand at all. Its Arabic name is Adda'wa, which means "the call," but it is more familiarly known as the Stalingrad Mosque, for a nearby Métro stop. It is the largest mosque in France, but its flat, unmarked facade makes it difficult to identify. I found it on a cold December day by following a crowd of men hurrying from both directions for their Friday prayers.

The mosque is a converted warehouse, purchased by an association of Muslims in the early 1980s with Saudi funds. The few partitions that have been installed have scarcely changed the interior's rough, unfinished look. On the second story are offices, an auditorium, a modest library and a few classrooms. On the ground floor is the mosque itself, an unheated cavernous ex-garage some 100 by 200 feet, interrupted at regular intervals by thick pillars. Missing panels leave dark, rectangular gaps in the low ceiling.

The men filing in to pray, many of them teenagers, seemed about equally divided between Arabs and Africans. Some wore colorful West African costumes or Middle Eastern *galibiyas,* but many more were wrapped in the shabby coats or ski jackets of manual laborers, and on their heads wore knitted hats. A few, in coats and ties, looked French. Some men left their shoes at the door, but most carried them in plastic bags or tucked them under arm. Standing at intervals around the hall were dozens of well-groomed men in their twenties wearing badges that said *Sécurité.*

The congregants began filling the hall about noon, lining up in tight, straight rows facing the *mihrab,* the niche on the eastern wall that points the way to Mecca. The entire space was without women, though about 500, I was later told, had assembled in the upstairs auditorium to follow the prayers on closed-circuit TV. By the time the *imam* entered at one o'clock, more than 2,000 men stood silently in the December chill, waiting for his words.

The *imam* was Dr. Larbi Kéchat, born in Algeria in 1952. Slight and with a trimmed beard, Kéchat is a product of French higher education; though still an Algerian national, he has been a resident of France for twenty-five years. Politically, he is considered hostile to Algeria's military regime and sympathetic to the Islamic rebels of the FIS. But he is, nonetheless, consistent in expressing his opposition to revolutionary violence.

Kéchat, among the most prominent of France's *imam*s, preaches an open-minded Islam and frequently participates in Muslim-Christian dialogues. The message of his sermon that day—delivered intermittently in French and Arabic—was that Muslims must not claim God's mercy just for themselves, but should recognize that it is bestowed equally on believers of every faith.

I chose Adda'wa for a visit because Kéchat had been the central figure in the controversial arrest in August 1994 of twenty-six Algerians suspected of sympathy toward Islamic terrorists. The roundup took place shortly after killers from Algeria's *Groupes Islamiques Armés* murdered five Frenchmen in Algiers.

Kéchat, seized by the police outside his mosque, was taken with the others to an abandoned military camp north of Paris. Twenty were promptly expelled to the African republic of Burkina Faso. In explanation, Pasqua's Interior Ministry described them all as "susceptible of presenting a danger to the security of our compatriots." "Susceptible," as many pointed out, was not the same as criminal. None of the men was charged with a crime.

Kéchat was among the six who, though kept in detention, were not deported. The influential newspaper *Le Monde* campaigned for his release, and so did a band of Catholic priests known for their support of reconciliation with Islam. One of them proclaimed that Kéchat had been "taken as a hostage to terrorize organized Muslims—whether sympathetic or not to the extremists—who are hostile to the Algiers military regime."

Even the Paris Mosque came to his support, but its overture was neutralized by intra-Muslim politics. When Dalil Boubakeur, the mosque's rector, came to visit, Kéchat shocked France by joining the other prisoners in refusing to receive him. He was an agent, they said, of the military junta in Algiers, which they blamed for creating the circumstances of their arrest.

After several weeks in detention, Kéchat was sentenced, without trial, to a version of house arrest. Under police surveillance, he was confined to the 19th arrondissement, the site of his mosque. The terms permitted him to continue as *imam* but barred him, as he joked, from crossing into the next arrondissement to visit his barber. The punishment was lifted only a few weeks before I paid him the visit.

In a shabby office above the mosque, Kéchat told me the mass arrest was meant as a warning to the Muslims of France not to provide any help to the Islamic rebels in Algeria's civil war. Though a "humiliation for our entire community," he said, Muslims would not be bullied by it. Referring to the Algerian elections won by the FIS and revoked by the government in 1992, he insisted that France must accept Algerian democracy, whether or not it liked the outcome of the balloting. The arrests showed, he said, how vitally important it was for France and its Muslims to intensify their "brotherly collaboration."

I asked Kéchat what he thought of Pasqua's call at Lyon for a "French Islam."

"What is being asked of us," he answered, "is not integration but assimilation, which requires us to leave our identity behind. Individuals can be assimilated; a community cannot. A workable integration is one in which each party accepts the other as it is, with its own special culture.

"Our community, which started thirty years ago with soldiers and workers, is now mostly native-born and knows no other home. The idea of returning to somewhere else is not part of our thinking. We have become part of the French family, and accept our responsibilities to it. But we cannot be alone in making accommodations.

"As Muslims, our ideal is a totally Islamic society, but that is only an ideal. Of course, we would like the life of our community to be guided by our own laws, but we know that in France the circumstances do not permit it."

Kéchat argued that Islam does not bar believers from adaptation to other cultures. Islam in France, he said, is different from the Islam practiced in, say, Egypt or Algeria. He called it a "diluted Islam," in which Muslims in France have learned to live with the separation of church and state, painful as the idea may be. Muslims in France accept these limitations, he said, because Islam decries *fitna,* commanding believers to safeguard the stability of the society in which they live.

"But France must also make accommodations to us," he added. "The arrival in France of Protestants and Jews required changes in French society. Now it is the time of the Muslims. As a start, we need more mosques, to replace the dingy basement rooms in which so many Muslims now pray. We propose that a committee of wise men of both cultures sit down to work out solutions to our differences. These changes need not be abrupt, but we have got to assemble around a table together and agree on them."

Clearly, Kéchat was staking out a position that was quite different from Pasqua's "French Islam." While acknowledging that Islam in France could not be rigid, he seemed to be saying that he expected the French to meet it halfway. Most of the French have so far shown little willingness to make such a journey.

· IV ·

THE *HEJAB*, the scarf that Muslim women traditionally wear to cover their hair, has become an issue that resists accommodation. Both sides have adopted it as a symbol to test the will of the other. So far, neither has shown much sign of yielding.

In 1989 three teenage Muslim girls—declaring themselves "believers but not fundamentalists"—were expelled from a high school in Creil, a town north of Paris, for wearing a *hejab,* which the school administration called a religious symbol. Until then, Muslim adolescents in the schools willingly followed the dress codes—jeans, sweaters, miniskirts—of their non-Muslim counterparts. French sociologists surmised that the *hejab* was selected by the first generation of Muslims born in France, by then reaching adolescence, in a search for personal identity.

But many Frenchmen did not view the issue so innocently. In explaining the deep feelings the *hejab* dispute aroused in France, one astute writer compared it to America's Watergate, in touching sensibilities that are so subtle that outsiders find them incomprehensible. The *hejab* affair can be understood only within the context of the struggle that France has waged since Voltaire's time to limit the power of the Catholic Church in French society.

In 1905, France more or less settled that struggle in adopting the principle of *laïcité*, a form of secularism that resembles but is not identical to America's. France replaced the state's special relationship with the Church by vowing equal treatment to all faiths. The French government, unlike America's, can now offer funds to religious "associations" for secular purposes, such as the preservation of religious monuments, even though it would never put "In God We Trust" on the currency. But both France and the United States—in a practice that Muslims find hard to understand—strictly prohibit state support of religious schools and the payment of salaries to the clergy.

Laïcité has never satisfied all French Catholics, some of whom still talk of reversing the practice. To most of France, however, it ended the long church-state struggle, with only a few scars remaining. To many of the French, Muslim demands for authorization to wear the *hejab* threaten to reopen the old wounds.

The standard Muslim defense of the *hejab* holds that it is not a religious symbol but a cultural artifact, linked to Muslim history. Larbi Kéchat told me—disingenuously, I thought—that it reflects the differences between the West's physical sense of beauty, acquired from the Greeks, and the more abstract notions of the East, where the highest art form is calligraphy.

A mantra of the pro-*hejab* forces asks why, if one teenager can attend classes in a miniskirt or torn jeans, another can't attend in a *hejab*? There was no easy answer. Playing on a perceived weak spot in egalitarian ideology, the *hejab*'s defenders proclaim that to deny to Muslim women a freedom of dress that is guaranteed to everyone else in France is pure racism.

The standard French counterargument, its roots embedded in the revolution of 1789, is that the schools have a mission to neutralize religious differences and imbue students with a common dedication to French culture. One prominent scholar wrote that French education "is incompatible with the preservation of immigrant cultures. We preach the universality of mankind." French intellectuals link the *hejab* to tribalism, seeing it as a barrier to the very integration that Muslims claim to desire.

The support given to the Muslim position by the organized clergy—Catholic, Protestant and Jewish—did not help to calm the waters.

Some Frenchmen saw it as evidence of a clerical conspiracy to amend the 1905 law, crushing *laïcité.*

Muslim leaders made heroines of the students at Creil, and negotiations between French authorities and their legal representatives proceeded for three years without an agreement. Finally the government banned the *hejab,* but enforcement was lax, and the Muslim community kept the issue in the courts. Meanwhile, the number of Muslim girls who wore the *hejab* to school soared exponentially.

The government understood that the *hejab* had become a symbol of protest but disagreed within its own circles on the significance. The Interior Ministry saw the issue in terms of national security and claimed that, of some 300,000 Muslim girls in French high schools, 15,000 were wearing the *hejab.* It meant, the ministry said, an alarming rise in fundamentalism, as well as support for the Islamic uprising in Algeria. The Education Ministry was less upset, putting the figure at only 2,000 girls. It described the protest in terms of harmless adolescent whimsy.

Some Muslim leaders maintain that, whatever the correct figure, the numbers do not adequately reflect the problem. Many girls, they say, are too embarrassed to be seen bareheaded in public and avoid school altogether. Anti-*hejab* teachers, on the other hand, contend that the issue has nothing to do with religious belief. They have testified that militants recruit Muslim girls to put on the *hejab* as a political statement, imposing peer pressure on fellow students to follow.

The *hejab* evoked passionate debate among French men and women of all classes throughout the early 1990s. One result, according to polls, was a sharp rise in concern among the French about the prospect of living with Islam.

In 1994 the government adopted a new rule relating to the *hejab,* which recognized a student's right to display religious symbols, unless they were "outrageous, ostentatious or meant to proselytize." The rule seemed to provide room for a cross or a kippa, while barring the *hejab,* but it left interpretation to the directors of each school. Predictably, the rule satisfied neither Muslims nor secularists, and so the dispute rages on.

Among the outspoken partisans of the *hejab* is the Union of French Islamic Organizations (UOIF), an umbrella for some 200 local associations active in promoting Islamic orthodoxy. UOIF, which is heavily Tunisian, is also said to control some 150 mosques.

Conventional wisdom holds that the UOIF is the French branch of the Muslim Brotherhood. Its leaders, when asked, answer ambiguously. But from its headquarters on a narrow street in the grimy Parisian suburb of La Courneuve, the UOIF produces books, videos and audiocassettes meant to advance the Islamic cause, and organizes courses and camps to train Islamic activists.

Included in the UOIF program is an Islamic fair held each December on the grounds of the old airport of Le Bourget, where Lindbergh landed in 1927. In 1994 the UOIF's differences with the Paris Mosque were so sharp that Dalil Boubakeur, the mosque's *imam,* declined to attend the fair. I was invited to attend the following year. Driving into the airport, I saw parked near the cavernous hangars dozens of chartered buses, with license plates from all over France. Thousands of people—30,000 attended in all, according to the French press—milled about.

In exploring the site, the first hangar I passed was set up as a temporary theater. I stopped for a few moments to listen to an *imam* lecturing in Arabic on Islamic doctrine. A notice displayed on the wall said that later in the evening an Arab chorus, accompanied by an Arab-style band, would entertain.

The next hangar had been turned into a primitive dormitory. Through the open door, where security guards stood checking credentials, I could see mattresses covered with blankets lined up neatly on the floor. One of the guards told me that believers who cannot afford the nearby motels slept there for a modest fee.

The third hangar was the center of activity. I presented my invitation at the turnstile, and when I entered I was stunned to find myself in a *souk,* a traditional Arab market.

Through thick cigarette smoke, thousands of men with beards and women in *hejabs*—some, in fact, in full veils—wandered among the aisles. They greeted friends, snacked on kebabs, fingered merchandise and clearly took pleasure in the dissonant Arab music that boomed from loudspeakers.

In booths identified by such banners as *Union Islamique des Etudiants de France* and *Association Islamique du Calvados,* young men, presumably volunteers, hawked prayer rugs, religious posters, embroidered Islamic gowns and trips to Mecca. They also sold CDs on which the sermons of some of Islam's famous preachers were recorded. In other booths, young people solicited donations to build mosques in France, or to help needy Muslims in Palestine, Bosnia and Chechniya. In a stall marked *Union des Femmes Musulmanes de France,* a large pennant announced: "France is my country; the *hejab* is my modesty."

The sign over a large table stacked with multicolored brochures identified its tenant as *l'Institut Européen des Sciences Humaines.* Just beneath this title was written a name in Arabic, which in translation read: "European Institute of Islamic Studies." Curious about the shift in meaning from one language to the other, I learned later that the institute had deliberately modified its French name to appease the French public, presumed to be more favorably disposed to the human sciences than to Islamic studies.

The institute, in fact, is an Islamic divinity school, founded in 1991 and located, incongruously, in Château-Chinon, a quaint village in Burgundy. François Mitterrand, the late French President, was mayor of Château-Chinon from 1959 to 1981. In poetry and song, the region around it is identified as *la France profonde*.

The institute, which I visited, is perched high on a Burgundy hill. Once a vacation site provided by a French manufacturer for his employees, it was bought in 1990 by some Muslim intellectuals affiliated with the UOIF. Saudi Arabia provided the money. Twice the anti-immigrant National Front brought in busloads of demonstrators to picket against its intended use, but the residents of the nearby towns and villages, I was told, refused to join them. The institute tries to be a good neighbor, its directors assured me, by consulting with the local residents and inviting them frequently to round-table talks and receptions.

At the center of the property are two handsome old villas, used for administration, classrooms and a library. Spread over the spacious grounds are a half dozen lesser buildings, serving as cafeteria and dormitories.

The institute claimed seventy-five resident students, half of whom were women, in addition to about two hundred students who matriculated in correspondence courses. Most residents, I was told, were enrolled in a four-year program to obtain master's degrees in Islamic theology, designed to prepare them for leadership positions in the Muslim community. Ten residents were taking a two-year program to become *imam*s in French mosques.

The genders mix academically but not socially, and I was assured that the students were not looking for spouses. When I visited the tiny library I found men and women at study, on different sides of the room. The men were in sweaters and jeans. The women, of course, wore long robes and the *hejab*.

Later, I met with the directors, who described the institute as Europe's first Islamic university, and said they aspired within a few years to enroll freshman classes of 300 students annually. Because expenses are high, the budget is dependent on subsidies from patrons, most of them in the Gulf. The institute's long-term dream, the directors said, was to have Château-Chinon rival Al-Azhar, Cairo's great seat of Islamic learning.

"Islam was losing this generation," said Ahmed Jaballah, the director of studies, born in 1956 in Tunisia. "French is the native language of most of our students. They arrive knowing little Arabic and less religion."

Jaballah, who has a Ph.D. in Islamic studies from the Sorbonne, spoke with me in his office, amid filing cabinets and computers. He said confidently that the institute was training the next generation of leaders of France's Muslim community.

"We start here by teaching them Arabic," Jaballah continued. "Then we teach them the Quran, the *hadith* and Islamic jurisprudence, like any other Islamic university. But there is a difference. Though our faculty was shaped in Arab institutions, most have advanced degrees from France. Knowing France, we understand that we must teach Islam within the context of Western reality. The religious training we provide has a Western orientation."

Several years ago Jaballah won a moment of fame by arguing in an open letter to France's Prime Minister, Michel Rocard, that the *hejab* was an obligation imposed by the Quran on all Muslim women. He is said also to have been instrumental in blocking concessions that promised to settle the dispute with the students at Creil. But, in talking with me, he maintained that the institute teaches an Islam that can adapt—a word he said he prefers to "compromise"—to life in the Western world.

The institute is far from fundamentalist, as some Frenchmen have charged, he said. Rather, it is influenced by the Egyptian reformer Muhammad Abduh. Muslims in France, he said, agree with Abduh in recognizing that the West has valid lessons to teach Islam.

Living in the West, said Jaballah, had opened him to a reexamination of formal Islamic doctrines. He no longer accepted, for example, the orthodox tenet that *ijtihad*—the interpretation of sacred texts—is closed. The institute, he said, considers this doctrine too rigid, and thus harmful to Islam.

"We see some advantage to living in the West, but we also see the obstacles," Jaballah said. "Muslims here fear Western hegemony. But the French fear our undermining their civilization. French pressure on us to assimilate is great.

"Some French say their civilization is available on a take-it-or-leave-it basis, without the slightest concession to our culture or our origins. We don't want to change French civilization, and we think we can be good Frenchmen. We accept the principle of *laïcité*, provided it is fair and neutral. But it must mean that we have the freedom to express our differences and be able to practice our religion as it is."

In reexamining Jaballah's words, he seemed to be expressing an ambiguity toward Islam's integration into French society. His thoughts largely echoed Larbi Kéchat's and corresponded with the line I heard from other leaders of France's Muslim community.

These men talked of the need for *ijtihad,* for the reexamination of Islamic doctrine. They acknowledged that the West had lessons to convey to them and that French *laïcité* left them plenty of room to practice their faith. Yet, as Muslims, they acknowledged some discomfort in living in a state that claimed neutrality between religious and nonreligious forces, and even permitted antireligious forces to participate in the culture.

In principle, these men favor Muslim involvement in France's cultural life, but in practice it frightens and bewilders them. Participation contains an insistent reminder that integration requires the revision of many of Islam's doctrines. They have not yet resolved the dilemma of how to be at once Muslim and French.

These men are no doubt sincere in denying that they are fundamentalists. They pay lip service to the need for change—accepting, in effect, *bid'a,* innovation—in Islamic belief. As good Muslims, this surely cannot come easily to them. But their words make clear that they feel obliged to keep this change to a minimum, requiring France to make as much of the adjustment as they can. As genuine believers, they can contemplate having an Islamic community living in France, but resist having France set the terms.

In provoking the dispute over the *hejab,* Muslim leaders have sent their battalions against *laïcité,* one of the ramparts of French culture. Though they have battered the wall, they have not breached it. Their strategy now commands their opening another front. Clearly, they regard the struggle as far from over.

· V ·

YET RELIGION, it is fair to say, is only one obstacle to integrating the Muslim community into French society. Earthly matters also loom large.

France welcomed the early waves of Muslims in an era that was short of manpower; it treats their offspring, in an era of labor surplus, as black sheep. The generation of the fathers contributed significantly to French society; the sons, economically superfluous, are more than the society can handle.

Young Muslim men, marooned in ghettos known colloquially as "hot zones," too often drop out of school, join gangs, take drugs, engage in violent crime. Young Muslim women, whatever the reason, seem to be more conscientious, and do better in careers. The government, failing to ameliorate the condition of the young men, has turned the problem over to the police. Not surprisingly, Islamic extremists have plowed the field of youthful discontent, which only compounds the police's burden.

In July 1995, Sheikh Abdelbaki Sahrawi, a well-known *imam* of a Paris mosque, was assassinated after condemning Islamic extremism in Algeria. A series of violent acts, related or not to the murder, followed in quick succession. The most celebrated was the bombing on July 25 in the Paris Métro, for which Algeria's *Groupes Islamiques Armés* took credit, describing it as retaliation for French support of the Algerian government. Over a few weeks, nine were killed and hundreds injured in Paris in terrorist attacks.

The terror reduced France to a state of panic and placed the police under great pressure to find perpetrators. On September 29, 1995, an antiterror squad killed a twenty-five-year-old Algerian in a shootout in an industrial suburb of Lyon. The government maintained that the killing had solved the crimes. But bombings and attempted bombings continued into 1996, and more arrests were made. On December 3, a few days after the presidential election in Algeria, a bomb killed two and injured dozens more in a Paris Métro station. The GIA claimed credit for this act too.

The victim of the 1995 shootout in Lyon was Khaled Kelkal, who was born in Algeria and raised in a dingy public housing block near where he died. His story was all too familiar.

Kelkal was one of ten children of a father who had migrated to France decades before in search of work. Having established a good employment record, the father lost his job in 1990, when the economy was scraping bottom. Shortly afterward Khaled, who had been a good student, was arrested and imprisoned for burglary. When he was released two years later, he joined his mother on a visit to Algeria, where the French police say he was recruited by Islamic extremists. After that, the police reported, he was without steady work and drifted down the road to terrorism.

On August 26, 1995, the police found Kelkal's fingerprints on a bomb attached to a railroad track, targeting an approaching train. Copies of his photograph were distributed around the country. Several weeks later, security forces, accompanied by a French television team, located him in an apartment hideout. TV audiences, watching the ensuing shootout, saw Kelkal in his final moments, lying on the ground, apparently trying to raise the pistol in his hand to fire. Notwithstanding the subsequent bombings, the police blamed the terrorist attacks that began with the Sahrawi assassination in July on the "Kelkal gang."

By chance, a German scholar studying France's ethnic conflicts had conducted a long interview in 1992 with Khaled Kelkal, providing a glimpse into his life. The text, published after his death,[2] depicted a thoughtful youth, raised by caring parents, drawn both to studies and to crime, angry at getting a lesser chance in life than his French schoolmates, attracted in prison to drugs and prayer, finally choosing fundamentalist Islam.

"All that guys like me want," he told the interviewer in his slangy, street French, "is work. Why can't they give us work so we can get ourselves together? . . . When a French kid gets his diploma, his father buys him a car. I see them all with their beautiful cars, and I don't even have a driver's license. . . . When I go for a job, I get the cold shoulder. I only have to say that I live in Vaulx-en-Velin [a poor Arab suburb]. I don't even have to tell them my name."

Kelkal said in the interview that in prison, guided by a member of the Muslim Brotherhood, he swore off drugs, went back to religion and learned Arabic. After that he recited his prayers every day and even listened to the lessons delivered by Muslim "savants" on cassettes. The goal he chose for himself, he said, was to make enough money to return permanently to Algeria, where he would set up a small business and be independent.

"I'm neither Arab nor French," he told the interviewer. "I'm Muslim. . . . When I walk into a mosque, I'm at ease. They shake your hand, they treat you like an old friend. No suspicion, no prejudices. . . . When I see another Muslim in the street, he smiles, and we stop and talk. We recognize each other as brothers, even if we never met before."

No sooner were Kelkal's dying moments shown on the television than young Muslim sympathizers vented their frustration by rioting in the suburbs of Paris and Lyon. They burned cars, smashed windows, looted stores and attacked police.

"The killing of Kelkal was the last straw," said Areski Dahmani, founder and president of France Plus, a secular organization of North Africans. "Kelkal was seen as a martyr by the *beurs*"—the term is widely accepted slang for North African youth—"a kind of Robin Hood who defied the state."

Dahmani described France Plus to me as the only organization in the Muslim community with a social, rather than a religious, agenda. It was founded in the 1980s as a rival to the Islamic associations that were then getting started. Its motto is: "All the rights and all the duties of the citizen." As its name implies, it urges young *beurs* to become more French—to vote, join the police, finish school, enlist in the army.

France Plus does not believe that Muslims need religious concessions. Muslims are at the bottom of the social heap, Dahmani said, because France has no policy to end racial discrimination and massive unemployment. He compared France Plus to American civil rights organizations and said that, unlike the religious associations, it gets its money not from foreigners but at home. France Plus endorses the policy of Muslim integration, he said, but questions how serious France is about implementing it.

"Kelkal is the product of the twenty-year failure to integrate the races," Dahmani said. "France never really accepted its North African immigrants. Now the authorities see that they have a potential fifth column of angry, state-hating young people, and they think that handing out a few peanuts will calm the situation.

"But French society is not working. More and more people are excluded from participation. Things have gone too far. Unless there is dramatic change, we could fall into the abyss of civil war within a few years."

France Plus defied the conventional Muslim position on the *hejab* by urging parliament to vote an outright ban, arguing that the state's neutrality on religious questions is the Muslim community's best long-term guarantee of the right to practice its faith. It claims that it has 11,000 militants in fifty regional organizations promoting its secular views. These views have earned Dahmani the opprobrium of the mainstream religious leadership, which routinely proclaims that, though France Plus may be North African, it is not Muslim at all.

"The demagogues in our community, in pushing for the *hejab* and the *shari'a,* are trying to achieve an ideological split," said Dahmani, a fashionably dressed and articulate man. Born in France in 1950, he calls himself a nonpracticing Muslim and is often said to have political ambitions for himself. "They see the perpetual combat between religious and secular forces in France as a model for polarizing Muslims. They emphasize the differences between Eastern and Western concepts of civilization.

"We advocate political means for solving the problems of our community. Our goal is power sharing at every level. As Muslims, we have long been powerless, and France Plus is trying to overcome our weakness in political experience.

"But we don't want to repeat the mistake of American blacks by supporting only the liberal parties. The left has taken our votes and given us little in return. The governments of France have created a modern state in terms of organization and technology, but on a human level—with left and right collaborating—they have made a disaster. We believe at France Plus that the more we spread our strength, the more the system will respond.

"Fortunately, in France we don't kill each other over our disagreements. Unlike Algeria or Egypt, we debate our differences openly. The extremists who try to silence debate, wherever they are, are Islam's worst enemy. We see France as a laboratory for an experiment with political values that can serve all Islam."

The high point of France Plus's efforts came in France's municipal elections of 1989, when candidates it supported competed for 2,000 seats and won a quarter of them. Sixty percent of the victors represented the left-wing parties, and 40 percent the right wing. Since that time, with the economy in decline, the trajectory of political power has been downward. Meanwhile, Muslim support for fundamentalism, particulary among the *beurs* in the industrial suburbs, has by every measure steadily risen.

In 1995, France Plus suffered a serious defeat when the National Front—calling for the expulsion of immigrants to reduce French unemployment—won 15 percent of the votes for President. In a more direct threat to Muslim communities throughout France, far-right candidates also won 1,000 seats in local assemblies and elected the mayors of three major cities.

Since then, with unemployment rising, the popularity of the National Front has shown continued growth. In increasingly strident terms, Jean-Marie Le Pen, the party's head, has called for sending 3 million Arabs back to their homelands. "Lepenization" also became a trendy new term in political life, referring to rising support for police crackdowns and expulsion proposals. Most French analysts think that the National Front has yet to reach its peak.

· VI ·

THE FRENCH seem unable to understand why their Muslims cannot agree on forming an "association" to speak for the community. Imbued with Catholic values, France regards religious hierarchy as a natural organizational principle. French Protestants, though doctrinally apart, nonetheless share the experience of hierarchy. French Jews, though their synagogues are autonomous, have been remarkably organized since the Middle Ages. Comfortable with centralized authority, the French are puzzled at the Muslim clergy's slack ties, and annoyed that the community is too riven to choose responsible political chiefs.

To the government, the solution is simple enough. It holds that the Paris Mosque has the necessary credentials for representation. The mosque's semiofficial character, shaped after World War I, goes further back than the Muslim community itself.

Given the violent spillover of the Algerian civil war, the government sees the mosque as even more than that. The leadership of the mosque promotes a peaceful Islam, an antidote to the militant fundamentalism that France sees behind local terrorism. The mosque also retains its links with the Algerian regime, which parallels France's own Algerian policy.

Somehow French officials ignore the widely held perception that the mosque is both a French government pawn and an Algerian government agent, which is what disqualifies it in the eyes of a majority of the Muslim community. That is not to say that the Muslim community supports the Algerian rebels. The Interior Ministry concedes that only a small minority of Muslims in France are sympathetic to them, and that only a few actively assist them. Many of France's Algerians, however, support Islamic political goals and even more dislike Algeria's military regime.

Yet there does seem to be a consensus: the Muslims in France do not want to suffer the penalties of mixing Algerian politics into their community life. That is understandable among the half of the Muslims who have no connection with Algeria. But it probably applies to most of those with roots in Algeria as well.

In 1995 the Interior Ministry tried giving the Paris Mosque a leg up over its rivals by awarding it the lucrative contract to supervise the slaughtering of meat under Muslim dietary laws. The fees involved, according to government sources, amounted to some $100 million a year, more than enough to assure the mosque's fidelity to the French government and free it from Algeria's embrace. The Muslim community, however, loudly protested the idea of giving the mosque a monopoly. Its opposition forced the ministry to drop the plan, leaving the government to lament that it still had no responsible Muslim authority to talk to.

Dalil Boubakeur has been the government's choice for the Muslim leadership since he was named the mosque's *imam* in 1992.

Boubakeur's father held the *imam*'s post during Algeria's war of independence, when he showed himself sympathetic to France. Some of the criticism of his positions rubbed off on the son, who was serving as his father's deputy. Boubakeur is now critical of the Algerian rebels but denies any loyalty to Algeria's military regime.

Born in Algeria in 1940, Dalil Boubakeur is a French citizen. Trained as both a medical doctor and an Islamic scholar, he has a mind that impresses French intellectuals, and a style that is not so French that it offends most Muslims. It is his political proximity to the French government that troubles a majority.

When I visited Boubakeur at the mosque, I found his office door guarded by an Algerian secretary without a *hejab* and, as a safeguard against potential assassins, a half dozen French cops.

"No one can categorically define Islam," said Boubakeur, a pudgy man with thinning hair, who wore a suit and tie but had an *imam*'s robe hanging on a hook nearby. "No one can precisely describe it as a culture or civilization or even as a religion. It comes in too many variations. The problem is that each Muslim thinks his own definition is the only real one.

"Here at the Paris Mosque, where Muslims from all over the world worship, we start with the premise that rationalism and modernity are components of religion. This view is guided by the uniqueness of the Muslim condition in France. We live as citizens under the laws of a non-Islamic country, and we must face issues in Islam that have never before been raised."

In his writings, Boubakeur acknowledges that his own rather liberal views of Islam were shaped during the years when his father was the mosque's *imam*. They are born of feelings of responsibility toward the small Muslim community that, forty years ago, was seeking to live harmoniously in France.

Boubakeur rejects, for example, the orthodox doctrine that fuses religion with the state. To support his position, he cites the Prophet's return to Medina to rule after conquering Mecca in A.D. 630. Preserving Medina as his capital, Boubakeur says, shows that Muhammad distinguished a holy city from a political city, and religion from the state.

Correspondingly, the Quran's Meccan suras are spiritual, he says, while the Medina suras emphasize rules for political organizing. From Umayyad times, Boubakeur argued in his talk with me, Islam has recognized a distinct temporal sovereignty. Mecca will always be holy to Islam, he said, but a political city can be anywhere—Damascus,

Istanbul, even Paris. Accepting the secular rule of France, he insisted, has a place in the Islamic past.

Echoing orthodox dogma, Boubakeur argues that *fitna*—rebellion against authority—is inadmissible. He also contends that the duty to make *jihad*, a holy war to spread the faith, has never been part of Islam. The term, he says, may be used to describe the Prophet's struggle against the Meccans, as well as Islamic wars of self-defense. But Islam understands *jihad* today as meaning an effort of will, he says, aimed at suppressing one's own evil instincts in the combat for the triumph of good.[3]

"The French recognize that we are willing to live under their laws," Boubakeur continued. "I sometimes think that French secularism is too static, too absolutist, in failing to take account of the spiritual needs of human society. But we do not want to deconstruct the patterns of French life."

However liberal his positions, Boubakeur argues in favor of the Muslim position in the *hejab* controversy, citing the Quranic injunction to women "to draw their cloaks close around them." But he suggests that, instead of prolonging the fight, believers might simply send their daughters to Islamic schools.

As for Islamic injunctions on family law, he acknowledges that they are at the heart of the *shari'a*, but he is ambiguous about their relationship to the French legal system. Boubakeur tries to please both sides in proclaiming that, while jurisdiction in family matters belongs to the mosques, all rulings must by necessity conform to French codes.[4]

"I don't like the term 'French Islam,' which Monsieur Pasqua and others have prescribed for us," Boubakeur said to me. "The issue for us is more complex than that. Many Muslims remain attached to a stagnant version of Islamic thought, and that is a trap we have made for ourselves. Islam certainly evolves. Here at the mosque, we are willing to practice Islam within the context of French values. We are ready to live our lives as good Frenchmen and French women. Still, I know Islam is at a crossroads."

In December 1994, Boubakeur set out from the crossroads. His direction, without his admitting it, was a French Islam.

After fifteen years of contentious deliberation, a committee of Muslim leaders organized by the Paris Mosque published a "Charter of the Muslim Faith in France." Three principal working groups—theological, social and legal—contributed recommendations, Boubakeur said, with the aim of making the charter consistent with both French law and Islamic scripture. The committee finished its work under pressure from the Interior Ministry. The charter was meant as a framework for the much-delayed organization of the Muslim community.

Boubakeur said his own contributions were based on the long experience of the Paris Mosque as the hub of a Muslim community living abroad. His studies of the Quran, Boubakeur wrote, left him no doubt that the mandate of the committee was to produce a charter laying out an Islam based on the Golden Mean.

The provisions of the charter express a clear goal of reassuring French society that it has nothing to fear from the Muslim community. The charter condemns theological fundamentalism and political extremism. It extols French values. It shows a side of Islam which Westerners cannot find objectionable.

According to Article 9: "Measure, moderation, kindness, patience, charity, love and forgiveness are the basis of Muslim piety. As a result, the solutions to community problems must be sought through dialogue and working together."

Article 11: "Islam preaches tolerance and fights racism, xenophobia and discrimination of every kind."

Article 15: "Respectful of the law of the French Republic, this charter commits the Muslim community to the preservation of the nonpolitical character of mosques."

Article 30: "The Muslims of France, faithful to their most authentic tradition, reject all extremism and bear witness to their attachment to the state which, by law, assures liberty of conscience to all, guarantees the free exercise of religion and treats all faiths equitably."

Article 33: "The Muslims of France intend to work for the emergence of an Islam of France, open to the Muslim world while being anchored in the reality of French society."

Asserting that Muslims "share with Jews and Christians the spiritual values of Abrahamic monotheism," the charter asked from the state only what it said the other faiths receive: help in building places of worship; in creating chaplaincies in schools, hospitals, prisons and the army; in reserving Muslim sections in cemeteries; in opening religious schools.

Still, the charter was much less a solicitation of favors from France than a pledge of allegiance.

Getting to the business of the organization of Muslims, the chief concern of the Ministry of Interior, the charter in Article 26 provided for the establishment of a "Representative Council of the Muslims of France" to assume responsibility to speak for the community at the national level.

Not surprisingly, Boubakeur had himself named president of the

Council. Though it was unclear who bestowed the title, he used it in signing the charter. Predictably, Charles Pasqua at the Interior Ministry promptly recognized the Council and Boubakeur's presidency. To many in the Muslim community, Pasqua's enthusiasm was proof enough of a coup d'état conducted jointly by the mosque and the French government.

As soon as the Muslim community read the charter, dissatisfaction with it spread quickly. The UOIF denounced Boubakeur's "hegemony." To the government's chagrin, much of the Muslim leadership declined to endorse it, not so much for what it contained as for who was regarded as behind the text.

Boubakeur, however valiant the try, failed to rally the community to support the Council. His defeat left the goverment with one more document on the growing stack of fruitless efforts to organize the Muslims of France. Boubakeur knew his star had faded when, for the new year of 1997, he did not receive the mosque's annual greeting from the President of the Republic.

· VII ·

CHARLES PASQUA, hoping to become Prime Minister, endorsed Edouard Balladur for President of France in 1995. When Jacques Chirac was elected, Pasqua naturally lost his post as Minister of Interior. He remained a popular figure, however, and the power he continued to wield as a provincial official helped to preserve some of his influence. More important, the team he had assembled at the Interior Ministry stayed intact, and Pasqua's policies toward France's Muslims were passed along to become Chirac's.

Pasqua received me in a handsome suite at the Conseil Général of the Département of Hauts-de-Seine, the provincial assembly of the wealthy Paris suburb that was regarded as his fief. His jovial style and thick accent, which the French call "Mediterranean," make him likable even to those who dispute his positions. Son of Corsicans who originated in Greece, Pasqua was quick to point out to me, as he apparently did to everyone, that as a boy he experienced anti-immigrant discrimination himself.

A rotund seventy-year-old when we met, Pasqua boasted of being fifty pounds lighter and in better shape than he was at sixty. Obviously, he was telling me that he was still fit for high office. Indeed, his policy pronouncements seemed to confirm my impression that he saw his absence from real political power as only temporary.

"The great majority of Muslims in France are loyal Frenchmen,"

Pasqua said. "But we have 50,000 or 100,000 who are influenced by fundamentalist doctrines, practice a hard-core Islam and are guided in their conduct by the Quran, not by the laws of the republic. Among them are maybe a thousand who are ready to turn to violence. We cannot allow such people to win in Algeria, and we can't allow them to affect our lives here."

But Pasqua made clear that he is no less frustrated than the Muslims themselves with France's failure to integrate them into the larger society. Nor is he indifferent, he said, to the sense of alienation that most Muslims feel.

"One of our major problems," he said, "is the lack of *imam*s who are French. Anyone can proclaim himself an *imam*, without speaking a word of our language. France does not want to intrude into religion. But we have to help promote a French Islam.

"The institute at Château-Chinon is too fundamentalist to be a solution to the problem. The Paris Mosque remains our best hope, but I see now that it has got to cut its ties to Algeria. The Moroccans resent the loss of the mosque. The King of Morocco, who has the title Commander of the Faithful, told me himself that the Moroccans in France, though they'll never come home, would not go to a mosque ruled by the Algerian government. The Paris Mosque has got to establish its independence.

"Boubakeur is intelligent and totally French. I'd like him to establish something like Cairo's Al-Azhar here, based on dogmas compatible with French life. We should help him. If we don't find a way to train French *imam*s, the extremists will take over, as they did in Algeria. We can't let the matter slide much longer."

Listening to Pasqua left no doubt that his concept of integration was different from that of most of the Muslim leadership. France is not like the United States, where ethnic groups retain their communal identity. French society is not a federation of communities. France, he said, has a tradition of assimilating individuals. Though one out of four citizens has a foreign grandparent, he said, all are considered fully French. France, he said, is accustomed to believers, whatever their faith, who have a personal relationship with God, as well as with the state.

One could deduce from Pasqua's words that, when he talked of a "French Islam," his emphasis was on the "French." That, in itself, distinguished him sharply from the Muslim leadership, which was much more concerned with the "Islam."

France will not accept polygamy, Pasqua said, any more than it will tolerate the *hejab*. The children of immigrants are welcome to become citizens, he said, but without reservations. The condition of their being French is to drop identification with competing religious or ethnic groups and become solely French.

Pasqua left no doubt that he was troubled by the lack of unity in the Muslim community. It opened the door to extremism, he said, which was the most immediate danger that France faced in dealing with its Muslims.

"The lack of structure is dangerous," he said. "The key to good relations is recognition by the entire community of the primacy of French law. This is a commitment that must be made, and the community itself must make. We are not going to commit the mistake of picking their leaders and trying to impose a commitment on them. But at stake is French security, which the government has the duty to safeguard."

As Pasqua's words suggested, the French increasingly see the Muslim community through the refractions of Algeria's violent civil war. The French think the Muslim community is not organized to cope with terrorism. The Muslims, on the other hand, resent French suspicions, and the excesses committed by the French police—like locking up Kéchat, and detaining hundreds of young Algerians without charges—in security's name.

The Algerian war, however, is only a passing problem, a temporary obstacle to integration. France's real fear is that its end, whenever it comes, will improve nothing. The conclusion to which much of France, Muslims and non-Muslims alike, seems to be gravitating— some with regret, others with satisfaction—is that Islam will not, or cannot, be integrated at all.

Virtually all Muslim leaders, it is true, claim to accept the principle that Islam must make accommodations. But Boubakeur, the most experienced of them, is also one of the few who has tried to think the process through to logical ends. Not many Muslims, however, are comfortable with his conclusion that the Muslims in France cannot remain a community apart. Most acknowledge the generosity of France's offer of a share in French civilization. But many are wary of accepting it, on the ground that their Islamic beliefs are not truly compatible with France's civilization.

Given the size of France's Muslim community, its alienation is not a minor matter. As an underclass, France's Muslims have shown little aptitude for economic mobility, and it seems unlikely they will soon improve their status. But in their lands of origin life is even worse, and they surely will not go home; on the contrary, the influx, notwithstanding legal resistance, will continue. Time is more likely to aggravate than to solve the community's alienation.

French society, out of self-interest, cannot ignore the danger of a permanent underclass. Inevitably, such an underclass spreads its discontent, whether in the form of labor disorders or crime or a level of lassitude that even public funds cannot overcome.

In Paris in August 1996, some three hundred illegal immigrants—all of whom were Muslim—barricaded themselves in a church to avoid deportation. A third of them were children. Fifty embarked on a hunger strike. In a climax that embarrassed France but may one day require repetition, French riot police dislodged them using tear gas. They were then dealt with harshly under French law.

The episode made clear to many of the French that their society dismisses the woes of the disaffected at its own ultimate peril. To perceive the Muslim community as a French problem alone, moreover, is naive. All the Western democracies face rising pressures of immigration from the developing world. Some are already feeling the pain; more will soon.

Most Muslims acknowledge that their civilization is in trouble. Without improved economic performance, the Muslim world will call on the prosperous societies, expecting help. The French experience suggests that Western societies are not likely to curtail their own good life in behalf of those who failed to make a good life for themselves. Few, in fact, are likely to be as generous as France.

An eminent American scholar, in a widely read work, has predicted confrontation in the next century at the frontiers where unfriendly civilizations meet.[5] One of the conflicts he foresees is between Islam and the West. The diagnosis, however, overlooks a more likely danger, foreshadowed by what is happening in France. The world is already engaged in conflicts between civilizations, not where their frontiers meet but within the frontiers of the Western states. How the developments play out in France will provide a clue to how they are resolved elsewhere.

10

The Hashemite Option

KING HUSSEIN of Jordan is the forty-second of the Hashemite line in direct descent from the Prophet.

He presides over a country of barely four million inhabitants, about equally divided between bedouins, most of whom have been urbanized over the last few generations, and Palestinians, refugees from the successive Arab-Israeli wars. His realm is mostly desert, poor in natural resources, with no oil at all and limited agricultural capacity. A buffer between hostile states—Israel to the west, Iraq to the east, Syria to the north, Saudi Arabia to the south—his country lacks the military power needed to assure its own security in the region.

On its face, Hussein's kingdom might well be a puppet state or an economic basket case. Or it might, like Lebanon, be paralyzed by communal fragmentation. Indeed, Jordan has had serious military, economic and communal crises during Hussein's five-decade reign. Yet it has also become a successful experiment—not perfect, but still striving—for what the Arab world might be: democratic, forward-looking, efficiently governed, tolerant.

Amman, the hilly capital where a third of Jordanians live, is clean, well designed and carefully maintained. It mixes a bustling old Arab city of small apartments and *souk*s with dazzling modern neighborhoods of stone villas and supermarkets. Its soaring boulevards are lined with high-rises, home to international businesses and banks. Amman also offers such bourgeois amenities as fine shops, luxury hotels, movie theaters, night clubs and pleasant coffee houses and restaurants.

Life outside the capital is more traditional. But nearly every Jordanian has access to electricity and piped water, and one sees no signs of hunger. More than 95 percent of school-age children are enrolled in elementary and high schools. Jordan has also established eighteen universities and fifty-two community colleges, nearly half of whose students are women. Literacy approaches 90 percent and newspaper readership has grown to a quarter million daily. The press, though more restrained than the West's, is easily the freest in the Arab world.

Aal al-Beit University, one of King Hussein's personal projects, offers an Islamic curriculum—but otherwise it has little resemblance to Al-Azhar. Inaugurated in 1994, its name means "People of the [Prophet's] House," a term which also refers to the Hashemite family. Aal al-Beit is located in an abandoned army base in the desert, near the Iraqi border. Uninviting as its setting is, it has a coeducational body of 3,000 students, Arab and non-Arab, from twenty-six countries. The students are Shi'ites as well as Sunnis, which is rare in Islamic institutions.

"We demand intellectual discipline but we do not expect loyalty to any specific school of Islamic thought," said Mohammad Adnan Al-Bakhit, a Jordanian who taught at American and European universities before becoming president of Aal al-Beit. "We train students to think rationally within the parameters of Islamic ethics. Islamic universities have not made much contribution to the world; we Arabs have been on the receiving end of knowledge. At Aal al-Beit we're trying to change that, by offering Islamic studies designed to deal with the world's real problems.

"We think there are many ways to practice Islam. The idea that *ijtihad* is closed led to the decline of the Muslim nation. Muslims got into trouble by persuading themselves that Islam had all the answers. Here at Aal al-Beit we don't accept a second opinion on some Islamic beliefs, like the oneness of God and the last judgment. But we think everything else is open to reassessment and review.

"We think we are backed by the Quran's many references to the intellect. We believe reason is an instrument for understanding God, and we are trying to rejuvenate the use of reason in Islam. In every mosque in the Sunni world, *imam*s shower the believer every Friday with slogans against *bid'a*, innovation. They think any idea coming from the outside, particularly from the West, is a sin. But here we tolerate all ideas, which is unique among Islamic universities.

"Some Muslims accuse us of teaching Shi'ite doctrine. The Saudis say this university was founded to graduate Hashemite disciples, undermining Wahhabi power. We're even the subject of suspicion that we're promoting a larger Hashemite scheme to take over the Arab world. In fact, all we're trying to do is to promote a tolerance of looking at Islam in many different ways."

One cool evening during my visit to Jordan, I drove out to Jerash, an ancient Roman town about an hour north of Amman. At its annual summer festival, started by King Hussein's American-born wife, Queen Noor, Jerash puts on display a wide assortment of both Arab and Western artists. A popular Iraqi crooner was creating much excitement, I was told, and so I made my way through the crowds to Jerash's stunning, 2,000-year-old amphitheater to hear him.

Under a sliver of moon I found nearly 10,000 young men and women waiting animatedly in the steeply tiered rows of seats. *Hejab*s and long robes were jammed next to tight T-shirts and jeans. Couples held the hands of their little children. I noted only a handful of foreigners, including a few Saudis in headdress. I also saw several brave youths who had shinnied up the ancient Roman columns at the edges of the stage for a better look at the singer.

A shy, slim man in his twenties, the singer was neatly dressed and combed, reminding me of a young Frank Sinatra. Accompanied by a string band, he triggered delirium with Arabic love ballads rendered in a deep, dreamy voice. With every note, the audience hooted, whistled, screamed, swooned and clapped. Entire rows linked arms to sway back and forth in unison. Dancers gyrated in the aisles. The crowd waved lighted candles and released balloons. Accustomed to the decorum, even the solemnity, of Islamic culture, I found the phenomenon unfamiliar. I had never seen Arabs having so much fun.

I wondered as I drove back from Jerash why Jordan seemed to be moving in a different direction from the rest of the Arab world. In Saudi Arabia the royal family submitted to the demands of the *ulama* to close all movies; in Egypt the government banned belly dancing, a traditional folk art, after the Islamic movement denounced it. Their concessions seemed to be an admission that, if life was not puritan, then it was not Islamic. Jordan's Islamic movement—it has an Islamic movement, after all—had tried to put an end to the Jerash festival, but the King would not hear of it.

Later, in talking with King Hussein, I asked whether, considering the atmosphere of liberality that one felt in Jordan, he regarded himself as an Islamic or a secular monarch.

"I'm an Islamic monarch, sir," he answered, with the exquisite politeness that characterizes his speech, "in believing that Islam embraces all, that it gives people their freedom, that it does not differentiate in the way it treats people. Maybe this is a different concept from what others in this part of the world hold. But I believe I'm a Muslim in advocating tolerance, in believing strongly that Jordanians, though they may vary, are one people with equal rights."

I had heard the King express such ideas before. The generally liberal principles according to which he exercised his powers confirmed that he meant them. But I wondered whether these were ideas that he had come upon independently, or whether they were somehow acquired as part of his heritage. Did they represent a valid school of Islam? Was there a Hashemite option in interpretation of the faith? It occurred to me that an answer to these questions might be uncovered in the history of the King's ancestors, the Prophet's progeny, the Hashemite family.

· II ·

KING HUSSEIN'S FAMILY, the Hashemites, takes its name from Hashem, the Prophet's great-grandfather. The family belonged to the Quraysh tribe, which became the rulers of Mecca several generations before the Prophet was born. The Hashemite lineage passed from the Prophet through his daughter Fatima and her husband Ali, who was also the Prophet's first cousin. Ali, Islam's fourth caliph, was the last of the *rashidun,* the "rightly-guided" caliphs.

It was the issue of Ali's succession, readers will recall, that provoked the breakaway of the Shi'ites from the mainstream of Islam. After the Prophet died, Ali's partisans argued for the preservation of Islamic piety by keeping the caliphate within the Prophet's family. They were overruled by the Prophet's Companions, who decided the succession by *shura,* consultation among themselves. After the reign of three caliphs, they agreed to bestow the office on Ali, but it was stolen away by a clan of usurpers, the Umayyads. The schism was never repaired, as Shi'ism has continued to challenge mainstream Sunnism over the doctrine that Islam must be governed by Ali's descendants.

When I asked King Hussein why he, as a direct descendant of Ali, was not accepted as the *imam* of the Shi'ites, he did not duck the question. The Hashemites throughout history, he said, respected the Shi'ites and regretted the schism. They reject the position of the Wahhabis, their longtime rivals, that Shi'ism is apostasy. In Jordan, he said, the Hashemites have sought to remove the wedge that Arab nationalism was driving between the Arabs and Iran, the largest Shi'ite society. Hashemites still favor Sunni-Shi'ite reconciliation, the King said. It is history and politics that keep the two branches of Islam irreparably apart.

The King brought to my attention that in 1980 he established by decree the Royal Academy for Islamic Civilization Research, also called the Aal al-Beit Foundation (not to be confused with Aal al-Beit University). He gave it a mandate to bring the Islamic sects closer together. Since then, three large meetings have taken place in Amman, and one in London, among Sunni and Shi'ite scholars. Their objective is to explore and, if possible, to narrow differences in dogma between the two branches.

Nassir El-Din El-Assad, a distinguished scholar who serves as the foundation's director, told me no one dreams that it is possible to bring Shi'ism and Sunnism together. In fact, at this stage of history, the idea of unification seems so far-fetched that it is never officially mentioned. But the Hashemites believe, he said, that Sunnis and Shi'ites can legitimately interpret Islam in their own way. It is the foundation's mission to promote the vision that no single orthodoxy defines Islam.

Assad said the vision dates back to Mecca, the Hashemites' home city. When the center of Islam left Mecca to move to Damascus and then Baghdad, the Hashemites stayed behind to assume responsibility for the holy shrines. In time, their domain encompassed all of Hejaz, the region of western Arabia that includes both Mecca and Medina.

Over the course of history, Hejazis, as caravan traders and seafarers, were more exposed than other Arabs to the outside world. They were also hosts to the annual pilgrimage to Mecca, which brought all kinds of Muslims, both Sunni and Shi'ite, together. Arabs agree that from these experiences the Hejazis, including the Hashemites, acquired an open-mindedness that was not characteristic of Arabs generally. They retain it to this day.

There are other Hashemite families who figure in Arab history. In the eighth century the Abbasids, Hashemites of a rival line, had become the dominant family in Islam; by the sixteenth century, however, they were extinct. Hashemite branches, over time, founded less powerful dynasties in Morocco and Yemen. But only the Hashemites of Mecca were recognized throughout history as the *Aal al-Beit*, the House of the Prophet. Their authority was legitimized by their service in safeguarding the holy cities, and in watching out for the pilgrims who visited each year.

Yet Mecca's Hashemites never became a military power. Over the centuries, in fact, they came under the suzerainty of a succession of more powerful Muslim states, which exploited a nominal control of the Prophet's birthplace to support claims to the caliphate. The Hashemites never made such a claim. While deferring formally to Baghdad, Cairo or Istanbul, they seemed content to serve the faith in

Hejaz. As guardians of the shrines, the Hashemites built up a reputation for honesty and fairness that served them with Muslims of all variations.

Late in the eighteenth century, however, a dark cloud moved in over the realm. The alliance that the Wahhabis formed with the Sauds in central Arabia had clearly targeted Hejaz. Aggressive and powerful, the alliance was also intolerant of deviations from the puritanical Islam that the Wahhabis preached. The alliance saw Hejaz as an objective fit not just for expansion but for conversion.

In raids in 1803 and again in 1806, the Sauds captured and sacked Mecca, reducing the Hashemite emir to vassalage. The Ottomans, nominally sovereign over Hejaz, recruited an army in Egypt, which drove the Wahhabi intruders back into the interior. But after the liberation Istanbul chose to administer the region directly, depriving the Hashemites of much of their traditional authority. With the Ottomans exercising tight controls and the Sauds thirsting for revenge, the pre-eminence that the *Aal al-Beit* had enjoyed for nearly a thousand years in Islam's holy places was for the first time in serious jeopardy.

With the coming of the twentieth century, the winds of Arab nationalism began to blow across the terrain. To many nationalists, the Hashemite family of Mecca was its logical leader. Arabs by now had an extended history of antagonism toward the West, which ruled over much of their patrimony. The nationalism they espoused was also directed against the Turks, who ruled over the rest. Some Arabs, adding an Islamic touch, even talked of wresting the caliphate away from the Turks to restore it to its rightful place within the Prophet's House.

When World War I began, the majority of Arabs responded to their Muslim instincts, lining up faithfully behind the Ottoman caliph against Britain and France. But Sharif* Hussein, the ruler of Mecca—great-grandfather of King Hussein—did not. Having his own grudges against Istanbul, he opened secret negotiations with the British, who pledged, in return for his help, to make the Middle East into an Arab nation at the war's end. Convinced he was to be the head of a great Arab state, the sharif in 1916 proclaimed an uprising against the Turks. It has come to be known as the Arab Revolt, the defining event of contemporary Arab political life.

The story of the Arab Revolt has often been told, as has the story of the secret Sykes-Picot agreement with France, under which Britain betrayed its vows to the Arabs. When the war ended, France occupied Syria and Lebanon, while Britain, still in Egypt, added Palestine and

---

* "Sharif" is a title designating a descendant of the Prophet.

Iraq to its empire. Britain's principal concession was not to the Arabs but to the Jews, who were promised a homeland in its Palestine mandate. Not only did Sharif Hussein receive nothing; in Arabia, the British now cultivated the Sauds, who, while the Hashemites were fighting for the Allies, had emerged as the peninsula's dominant power.

Ignoring Sharif Hussein's proclamation of himself as the Arab king, the British found it more congenial to deal with his sons. They gave Faisal, the third son, the crown in Iraq after the French dethroned him in Damascus. And they gave Abdullah, his older brother and grandfather of King Hussein, the emirate of Transjordan, the amorphous eastern segment of the Palestine mandate, after he threatened to march on Syria with an Arab army.

Sharif Hussein was not satisfied to have two sons as kings, however, and in 1924, when Turkey abolished the caliphate, he promptly claimed it for himself. The Sauds cited the claim as a pretext to complete their conquest of Arabia, ending the millennium of Hashemite dominion in the holy cities. The luckless sharif, exiled first to Cyprus, died in 1931 in Abdullah's capital of Amman and was buried in the Al-Aqsa Mosque in Jerusalem.

Though Abdullah inherited his father's ambition to lead a great Arab nation, he took consolation in Transjordan, where he set about establishing a responsible government. He became personally popular: the bedouins, many with roots in Hejaz, regarded him as one of their own; the town dwellers, many of them Christian, liked his flexible ways. An Arab historian has written that, "While taking religious tradition seriously, and observing accepted rules of social behavior, Abdullah was basically a tolerant and unfanatical person who kept an open mind."[1] By the force of his own magnetism, Abdullah, against heavy odds, shaped Transjordan into a real country.

His realm, however, remained by treaty heavily influenced by Britain. As emir, Abdullah was in charge, but a British adviser was in residence at the court and a British officer commanded his armed forces. With Britain's encouragement, Abdullah adopted a constitution in 1928, putting Jordan on a course toward democracy and limited monarchy. But as Arab nationalism in subsequent years grew fiercer, Abdullah's relationship with Britain became a shadow over Jordan's nationhood.

Meanwhile, Abdullah, his son mentally ill and often in treatment abroad, groomed his grandson, Hussein, for succession to his throne. Taking charge of the boy's education, he arranged private lessons in religion from Sheikh Hamzeh Arabi, a judge in the *shari'a* court, then sent the boy to Amman's Islamic Scientific College.

In his early autobiography, *Uneasy Lies the Head,* Hussein says that his grandfather supervised his religious lessons carefully. He also says Abdullah imparted to him a love of the desert and an appreciation of Jerusalem's spirituality. His grandfather, Hussein wrote, was "the greatest single influence on my life," adding that, "He loved me very much. . . . He was more than a grandfather, and to him I think I was a son."[2] Many Arabs would say later that they recognized much of Abdullah in his protégé, King Hussein.

Abdullah's realm acquired formal independence with the breakup of the British Empire after World War II. Its name was changed from the Emirate of Transjordan to the Hashemite Kingdom of Jordan, and his own title was upgraded from emir to king. A few years later, a new democratic constitution was adopted. But, in failing to sever all ties with Britain, Abdullah bequeathed a problem that would pursue the young nation for another decade.

Abdullah also had to confront the looming problem of the Jewish state that was taking shape across the Jordan River in Palestine. Still ambitious, he turned his attention to exploiting the conflict with the Jews to extend his realm. In Palestine, British rule was giving way to a plan for partition into Arab and Jewish states. Alone among Arab leaders, Abdullah raised no objection to the partition and schemed to annex the Arab sector.

In 1948, Abdullah joined other Arab states in waging an unsuccessful war against the Jews, but he was alone in taking profit from the defeat. By holding the West Bank against Israeli attacks, his army enabled him to realize the annexation that he planned. The defeat, however, brought Jordan a wave of refugees, who would create instability in the kingdom and whose numbers would be augmented with each succeeding Arab-Israeli war. Moreover, many Palestinians were never reconciled to Abdullah's seizure of their land and accused him openly of having colluded with the enemy.

In 1951, Abdullah, in the company of his grandson Hussein, was shot dead by an irate Palestinian during a visit to Jerusalem's Al-Aqsa Mosque. Hussein writes in his memoirs that he was saved from a bullet fired by the assassin only by a medal that his grandfather had only recently pinned to his breast.[3]

· III ·

HUSSEIN, born in 1935, was a student at a British college in Egypt when his grandfather died. His father, Talal, notwithstanding illness, was crowned King and officially designated Hussein the crown prince. During Talal's reign Hussein worked at Harrow in England on his secondary education. But after a year Talal's illness got the best of him and he abdicated. Hussein succeeded him in August 1952, three months short of his seventeenth birthday. Too young under the constitution to rule, Hussein turned his powers over to a regency council and enrolled as a cadet in the British military academy at Sandhurst. Six months later he returned to Amman and on May 2, 1953, he assumed the authority that he has exercised ever since.

These were scarcely easy times for a teenage King with little formal education or experience, who seemed more attracted to fast cars than to politics. The Arab defeat in 1948, at the root of his grandfather's assassination, had also led to the overthrow of the parliamentary regime in Syria and the monarchy in Egypt. Nasser, the charismatic colonel who became Egypt's President, had designs on *all* of the Arab world. The Sauds, grown wealthy from oil, also remained a Hashemite enemy. Throughout his early years, crowds aroused by Communism or Ba'athism, but mostly by Nasserism, routinely demonstrated in Amman's streets. Still dependent on the British, the young King was denounced as a stooge of imperialism. Few held out much prospect for his survival on the throne.

But Hussein proved to be a fast learner, demonstrating a shrewd political sense. He quickly identified and learned to rely on allies where he found them. In the army, while some officers responded to Nasser's shrill calls by organizing coups, others who were loyal to the bond established with Abdullah consistently thwarted them. The personal courage the King showed in these situations further enhanced his standing, both in the army and in the country.

Hussein, meanwhile, cultivated Jordan's Muslim Brotherhood, which emulated the anti-Nasserism of its Egyptian counterpart. Unlike the Sauds, he never curried favor with the Islamists by Islamizing the country. Instead, he accorded them a wide-ranging freedom to argue their beliefs, for which they reciprocated with their loyalty. When the Nasserists demonstrated, the Muslim Brothers mounted counterdemonstrations. Many informed Jordanians hold that, without the Brotherhood, the King would never have made it through the tumultuous early years of his reign.

But the turmoil took its victims, one of which was Jordanian democracy. After the 1956 election, Nasserists and Ba'athis dominated the parliament and cast doubt on the monarchy's legitimacy. Their radicalism was enflamed by the Suez attack made against Egypt that year by Israeli, British and French forces. The King, who had already deferred to the national mood by replacing the army's British commanders with Jordanians, was forced to agree to the full termination of the Anglo-Jordanian relationship. Still, his enemies were not satisfied.

In 1957, Ali Abu Nuwar, who had replaced a British officer as commander of the army, led a coup d'état, which forces loyal to the King quickly put down. But the momentum of Nasserism appeared unstoppable. Refusing to be intimidated, the King declared martial law, imposed censorship, suspended elections and dissolved the political parties. These antidemocratic acts remained in effect for nearly three decades.

But it is noteworthy that King Hussein permitted Abu Nuwar to flee into exile after the attempted coup. In a region where leaders order their executioners into action at any sign of disloyalty, he is unique in never having executed a plotter. There have been many. Characteristically, he has exiled or imprisoned them, then after a few years ordered their rehabilitation. Tough security services have buttressed his regime. But in sparing the lives of his enemies, the King has also spared Jordan the reign of fear that distinguishes politics in the neighboring Arab states.

In the early 1960s Jordan enjoyed a period of calm, but it ended abruptly in the June War of 1967, a greater military disaster than 1948. Jordan lost the West Bank, home of a third of its population, as well as Jerusalem's Islamic shrines. The defeat, in revealing the impotence of the Arab states, enhanced the appeal of the newly created Palestine Liberation Organization, which saw Jordan as a military base for the reconquest of the homeland. Jordanians did not take kindly to the PLO's designs and, in 1970 the inevitable collision touched off a brief but bloody war, known to history as "Black September," won decisively by Jordan's army.

Despite the victory, the ensuing years made clear that Hashemite suzerainty in Palestine was coming to an end. Palestinian nationalism was soaring, and the PLO, with the support of most Arab governments, demanded control of Palestinian affairs. In 1988 the King formally undid his grandfather's action, bowing to the PLO in renouncing all ties to the West Bank. His focus now shifted to building nationhood in a Jordan within the boundaries that Abdullah found when he arrived from Hejaz in 1920.

No longer was the survival of the Hashemite throne in doubt. But Jordanians, having left the old mix of discredited revolutionary doctrines behind them, now signaled a desire to return to democracy. In 1989, King Hussein lifted censorship and ordered parliamentary elections. He did not yet legalize the parties, but for the first time women were enfranchised. A spirited campaign followed, culminating in what all agreed was fair balloting.

The candidates, though running as independents, nonetheless identified their allegiances. The voters, ignoring the radicals of the 1950s—Communism and Nasserism were dead, Ba'athism had been discredited by the Syrian and Iraqi despotisms—gave a strong plurality to the Islamic bloc, an arm of the Muslim Brotherhood, the only political organization that had survived the authoritarian decades.

Some Jordanians feared the vote signaled a drift toward Islamic domination, perhaps even Jordan's "Algerianization." But the bloc's Islamizing efforts—pushing for gender segregation in the schools, for example—proved very unpopular. So did the limitations it sought to impose on women. In refusing to yield to the Islamists, the King had public opinion with him. In 1993 the Islamic coalition—now called the Islamic Action Front—faced tougher electoral rules and suffered a sizable defeat. Since then, most Jordanians have concluded that the Islamic movement, having reached its peak, is embarked on a decline. Its numbers diminished, it has since been in loyal opposition.

"We believe in the democratic system and peaceful reform," said Sheikh Abdulmajid Duneibat, the current president of the Muslim Brotherhood, still the umbrella organization of the Islamic Action Front. In his sixties, Duneibat is a practicing lawyer, who wears Western dress. "The King does not share our goal of applying the *shari'a* as the law of Jordan, but he is a Muslim like us and over the years we have been in continuous contact with him. We are legal in this country, and we are allowed to advocate what we believe. That is an important safety valve. We benefit from democracy and are not an extremist movement. In Jordan, no violence has been used, either by us or against us."

Before agreeing to the full resumption of democracy—that is, before restoring the legality of parties that had once challenged the legitimacy of the Hashemites—King Hussein called for the drafting of a "national charter." In his mind was not a new constitution—Jordan is ruled under a constitution promulgated by King Talal in 1952—but something different: a pact between all the members of Jordan's political community. A sixty-member drafting commission was named, representing professional and trade organizations, the bedouin tribes, labor unions, youth groups, women's associations and the Islamic movement. Some participants had once been the King's mortal enemies—Nasserites, Ba'athis, Communists, Socialists, even members of the PLO. When the commission finished its work, the charter was ratified by a conference of two hundred Jordanians and, in June 1991, it was promulgated by the King.

The charter is essentially a contract between King Hussein on the one hand and all of the groups in society with a political stake on the other. In return for his endorsing a democratic pluralism in which they would legally share, they gave their allegiance to the Hashemite throne. Some read the charter as a long-term promise, though it was not explicitly stated, of constitutional monarchy. But at the least, his opponents pledged to denounce the King no more as a Western puppet, while he renounced his power to disband the parliament or stifle the press.

The charter was more than political, however. It was also meant as a guide to Jordan's social character. While duly acknowledging that "Islam is the religion of the state, and Islamic law is the principal source of legislation," it is rich in imperatives that are alien to the conventions of Islamic orthodoxy.

The charter repeatedly asserts the equality of women with men in all domains. It extols human rights. It calls for an educational system that honors academic freedom and promotes "independent and creative thinking." Specifically citing religion, it insists on "Respect for the mind, belief in dialogue, recognition of the right of others to disagree . . . tolerance and rejection of political and social violence." In short, it is a commitment to a liberal humanism that surely has no equivalent elsewhere in the Arab world.

Soon after the charter was adopted, the issue of peace with Israel—long a priority but never close to realization—leaped to the top of the King's agenda. The region's most relentless promoter of peace, Hussein had inherited a respect for Israel from Abdullah, who had concluded in the 1940s that making peace with the Jews was better than waging a permanent war. Under the aegis of the United States, Jordan joined Syria, Egypt and the PLO to meet with Israel in Madrid in 1991 and embark on a negotiating process.

Palestine, by consensus of the Arabs, was the problem of the highest order. Starting at Madrid, King Hussein concentrated on promoting Israel's negotiations with the PLO, an acknowledgment that Jordan could not really be at peace as long as the Palestinians remained under occupation. On September 13, 1993, Israel and the PLO signed the Oslo Accord, which prescribed a series of partial withdrawals from the occupied territories, climaxing in a final-status agreement. The following day King Hussein signed a declaration that ended forty-six years of hostilities with Israel; it was followed in July 1994 by a formal treaty of peace.

The negotiations between Israel and the Palestinians soon disintegrated, however, leaving no doubt that the end to strife on the West Bank was still distant. The King persisted as an intermediary in Israeli-PLO talks but, more important to Jordanians, he continued to promote Jordanian-Israeli reconciliation. The King's message was that Jordan's development along the lines envisaged by the national charter could be pursued only within a framework of regional peace.

Though few Jordanians objected to peace, many disagreed with the King's policy of establishing normal relations with Israel as long as the Palestinian issue remained unresolved. The dispute has exposed even his emotions to scrutiny. Some scolded Hussein for weeping at the funeral of Israeli Prime Minister Yitzhak Rabin, with whom he had negotiated the peace. Some criticized his celebrated trip to Israel in the spring of 1997 to offer his personal condolences to the parents of seven Israeli schoolgirls who had been killed during a visit to Jordan by a deranged Jordanian soldier. In tenaciously pursuing not just peace but normalization, the King has provoked serious strains within Jordan's political system.

"What we have now is not peace; it is deferred peace," said Ahmad Obeidat, an independent centrist, a former Prime Minister and a prominent member of the opposition coalition. "We've left too many problems unsolved—Jerusalem, water, refugees. Some of us think that the peace treaty was an Israeli trick to create animosity between Jordan and the Palestinians. Whether we like it or not, Jordan has a special responsibility to Palestine.

"But as members of the opposition, we find it hard dealing with someone who's been ruling the country for forty-five years. We have learned to distinguish between the King and his policies, but we would like to see him more neutral. Instead of becoming more constitutionalized, our system has become more personalized. Though the charter is not legally binding, it is a moral obligation, and we think the King has not done his part in democratization. We don't expect the kingdom to be like Britain overnight. But there has not been enough progress. In that sense, the peace treaty with Israel has become the foe of democracy."

The dispute has, for the most part, been cordially conducted: the political parties continue to proclaim their loyalty to the King; the King remains faithful to the vow of democratic pluralism. The forms of democratic government remain essentially intact.

But the King had Jordan's electoral law amended, not unfairly but nonetheless to the detriment of the Islamic coalition, the most anti-Israeli of the political factions and the beneficiary of heavy support from Palestinian voters. He has also gone his own way in direct dealings with Israel, without real parliamentary consultation. In addition, he imposed a rein on the press after it became strongly critical of the normalization process.

The Islamic Action Front, backed by eight small left-wing parties, retaliated by boycotting the parliamentary election on November 4, 1997. Procedurally, their grievance was the amended electoral and press laws; substantively, it was normalization. The boycott enhanced the King's parliamentary support, but it confirmed that the peace treaty had undermined Jordanian democracy, as well as the cordial spirit of the national charter.

Yet Jordanians seem more exasperated than alarmed by these events. Many regretfully acknowledge the strains on democratic institutions, but only a few claim that Jordan's democracy is itself in danger.

· IV ·

ON AUGUST 6, 1997, I interviewed King Hussein in the royal palace in Amman. The slim, dark-haired youth who was crowned forty-five years ago had emerged into a solidly built man, wearing a patriarchal, snow-white beard. The King underwent surgery for cancer five years before but has since been pronounced cured. At our meeting he looked extremely fit. We spoke at the end of a long working day, and he was dressed in jeans and a short-sleeved plaid shirt. Having stopped smoking, the King sucked on hard candies as he talked.

The following are excerpts from the interview:

MILTON VIORST: What was the role of your forebears, the Hashemites of Mecca, during the centuries since the death of the Prophet?

KING HUSSEIN: My forebears were always the keepers of the holy flame in Mecca and Medina. But their great role in Arab history was to connect with the yearnings of the Arab people to lead the Arab Revolt, a reaction against the Turks who were trying to destroy Arab identity. Their objectives were unity and freedom, and a chance for the Arabs to take a place alongside other nations.

MV: Do you, as a Hashemite, retain a role in Mecca and Medina?

KH: No, sir, I have no role to play except that of a Muslim in a Muslim world. My family gave up a lot, losing their place in the holy cities, in the struggle for the Arab people. What happened after the Arab Revolt was a big price for them to pay. But now I'm a Jordanian, and I'm trying my very best to make this country a positive example in the Arab world.

MV: Sharif Hussein's goal was also to form a united Arab state. Is that vision lost forever?

KH: I believe that the Arab world is never going to be a united nation, as had been hoped in the Arab Revolt, but something in a more modern context, similar to Europe. It is the only way. We have developed within each part of the Arab world our own identities, and unity in the future must be a unity of sovereign equals.

MV: Have you shifted your family's sense of proprietary responsibility to Jerusalem?

KH: My family was involved in Jerusalem from the time that the Arab Revolt and the Sykes-Picot agreement and all the other surprises tragically took place, leading to Sharif Hussein's being exiled in Cyprus and eventually coming over here and passing away.

MV: Do the Hashemites have a responsibility there now?

KH: Yes, the responsibility to ensure that anything that can be done will be done to bring an end to the unfortunate struggle that has been the history of the children of Abraham. I think that Jerusalem should become the symbol of peace between the followers of the three basic monotheistic religions. It should be above the sovereignty of any country or the control of any side. Jerusalem, east and west, could become the capital of both Palestinians and Israelis. It could be two capitals. It could be whatever they choose in the future. But we will always have ties with Jerusalem. My great-grandfather was buried there. My grandfather fell there. Jerusalem is as important to us as any of the holiest sites in the Muslim world. Solving the problem of Jerusalem will symbolize the coming together of the children of Abraham, and until this happens we will do our duty, to help and push in that direction.

MV: Does that mean you consider yourself, as a Hashemite, a link between Jews and Arabs, the children of Abraham?

KH: To look back on my family heritage is one thing, but to think of the realities of the day is more important. Of course, I'm drawn to a very large extent to this heritage and I'm proud of it, but the difference between success and failure in the world of today is clear thinking and ideas, and ideals that people can gravitate around. So rather than talk of statues to the past, all of us, including myself, should put all our efforts into the future of the generations to come. This is my philosophy.

MV: Do you, do the Hashemites, have responsibility for leadership of Arabs beyond the borders of Jordan?

KH: I've stood for what I believe is for the best interests of Jordan, and also for the whole region. But I don't know about leadership. The Hashemites have a duty to supranational service but not in the sense of acquiring control. Nor do I seek it. I think that those who have sought that kind of control have brought enough damage to the Arab world. I believe that the Arab people themselves can decide what they want.

MV: What is the condition of the Arab community in our times?

KH: It is fragmented, no doubt about that. It is fragmented by religious belief and along nationalistic lines. But we are all Arabs, and we have the same language, so there is much that unites us. We must concentrate more on repairing relations between peoples than relations between leaders and governments.

MV: Can Arabs be twenty nations and one people?

KH: I suppose we can and we should be. But I don't think that we can be described as one people at this stage, when we have no central control.

MV: But, after the Prophet's era, there never was central control.

KH: That's true. But it was a far more coherent society then.

MV: Can't you do anything to make it more coherent now?

KH: I think of myself as someone who has tried to identify with the aspirations of the Arab people and to guide them to a collective life that makes sense. Most of us are Muslims and, as a devout Muslim, I am troubled by much in the Arab world that is portrayed as Islam or Islamic. In fact, I get very irritated when I see so many distortions of Islam carried out in the name of Islam. It is a problem I'm trying to do something about.

MV: What traditional Arab values do you consider vital to preserve?

KH: We still have many sound tribal values—chivalry, hospitality, courage, shame—but they are changing, in some cases sadly, as we open up to the rest of the world.

MV: What values might it be useful to shed?

KH: When *ijtihad*—the possibility of reconciling faith and present-day life—stopped a long time ago, that was the beginning of a very sad deterioration that has continued over the years and has opened the way to all sorts of fringe movements and splits. We need to do whatever we can to repair that mistake. I am trying to get the leading figures in the Muslim world who have the minds and the faith and the vision to come together to reaffirm the moderation of Islam. Islam is called *wasatiya,* which means "centralist." This is in the Quran. It is where we should be now.

MV: Don't the fundamentalists say that theirs is the real Islam?

KH: I have read the Quran time and again, and with the passage of years I have learned that very little in Islam is rigid. I don't like the term "fundamentalism" and I wish it had never come into being. But Islam is not fundamentalism. It was very open as it spread throughout the world. It made major contributions. Then, in the tenth century or so, Islam changed course and went into decline.

MV: What serious differences have you with other schools of Islam?

KH: Take the so-called fundamentalists, for example. They want to consider the Prophet a messenger who delivered the message, and that's that. Their main challenge is to destroy everything that came down through the Prophet and the Prophet's descendants. That has been their drive ever since the outset, to destroy the links of Muslims with their history. They take a very extreme attitude at the universities they sponsor, influencing the students they produce. It has produced extremism, limited mindsets and a very clear lack of vision, far from the true teachings of Islam which make it unique. Islam is suitable for every time and for every people.

MV: Do you mean by "the true teachings of Islam" the Islam that was before the close of *ijtihad?*

KH: Yes. The true teachings of Islam as they came in the Quran and as the Prophet conveyed them.

MV: Are your ideas like those of Abduh or the Mu'tazilites?

KH: I have my own way that I identify with, not with any particular school in a particular way.

MV: Would you agree that the Muslim decline can be dated from the ninth century when Islam missed the chance to become the religion of reason and moderation by crushing the Mu'tazilite movement?

KH: That is essentially correct, and we must do what we can to change that now.

MV: Whom do you regard as an appropriate teacher of Islam today?

KH: I don't think such a teacher is yet there. Unfortunately, teaching and learning in the Muslim world have declined as a result of political changes. Al-Azhar in Egypt used to be the pinnacle of reference to Muslims, at least for Sunnis, but since the Egyptian revolution there has been an erosion. Now there is an attempt to revive it, which I hope succeeds. Similarly, Najaf and Karbala, for the Shi'ites, should be centers of learning and light. But, unfortunately, changes in Iraq have caused so much persecution, so many human losses, that the hub has moved to Qom in Iran. These two centers have to return to what they were.

MV: What is the difference between Najaf and Qom?

KH: Najaf is the heart of Shi'ism. Qom represents the heart of a political ideology. Since Shi'ite theologians cannot live and study in Najaf, Qom has taken a more important position.

MV: Are there any alternatives to Al-Azhar for the Sunnis?

KH: Al-Azhar is moving but maybe not fast enough. The sheikh of Al-Azhar, Muhammad Tantawi, who seems to be a very able man and we were pleased to see him, attended the last meeting of the Aal Al-Beit Foundation. We started Aal Al-Beit University in the same spirit as the foundation. There should be more encouragement of enlightened, Muslim yet modern, institutions that hopefully will prepare people to open up and to preserve Islam.

MV: Are you thinking at Aal Al-Beit University of restoring the traditions of openness and reason of the Mu'tazilites?

KH: Yes, along with many other good universities and centers of learning, recently created or revived, that want to help bring the Muslim people together and resolve their difficulties.

MV: Do you think of yourself as an Islamic model?

KH: I would never think that I had it in me to be an Islamic model. But I have seriously thought time and again of quitting everything I'm doing to concentrate on theology. It hasn't been possible but it's often crossed my mind.

MV: Would you be willing to describe your own level of piety?

KH: I made the *hajj* many years ago. I don't drink. I say my five prayers every day. But that's something I don't talk much about. It's between me and God.

MV: If you had the opportunity, what theology would you teach?

KH: I believe the answers are there in our Quran, certainly in the overall sense. Take the question of peace, for example. There's so much in the Quran on peace, as there is on submission to one God, the attributes of God, heaven and respect for the other two monotheistic religions. These are teachings we don't much hear about, but they affect me in my political life, supporting my firm belief that I'm doing the right thing. It's along these lines that so much can be taught.

MV: What is your position on amending the *shari'a*?

KH: In fact, we tried here to base Jordan's civil law on the *shari'a*. Years ago, we got some of the best brains in Jordan and the Muslim world to sit together and bring about this civil law. We believe we succeeded and many Muslim states now copy it. It's a unique contribution that Jordan has made. Yes, there was much to preserve but also a need for changes in the *shari'a*.

MV: Do you think of yourself as an Islamic monarch?

KH: I'm an Islamic monarch in believing that Islam embraces all, that it gives people their freedom, that it does not differentiate in the way it treats people. Maybe this is a different concept from what others in this part of the world hold. But I believe I'm a Muslim in advocating tolerance, in believing very strongly that Jordanians are one people with equal rights.

MV: What is an Islamic state?

KH: An Islamic state is a state based on the morality that comes through faith and religion. We believe that Islam completed the two great Abrahamic religions, that the Quran is the most valid and clear word of God. There is no book like the Quran. It's so rich. But it must be subject to interpretation in every era to deal with the world. You can't just hold it up at any point in time and say, "That's it." Nobody has the right to do that.

MV: How about the *sunna,* the *hadith*?

KH: The *sunna* is also important but much that is in it, as you know, is not verified. The *hadith* are in some cases certain and in some cases not. Occasionally, you find a hodgepodge of ideas that make the meaning hard to grasp.

MV: You say that Islam today is misinterpreted. Is it, in some cases, being deliberately abused?

KH: The faulty teaching of Islam has left the door open to exploiters, people who have tried to use it in a non-Islamic way. Islam is not "today." Islam is an afterlife. You work throughout your life for the afterlife. And what I see is people working for today, using Islam to gain their own objectives.

MV: Don't Muslims recognize this exploitation?

KH: The problem is that Islam has not been competently taught to our young people. Often the least qualified students, unable to master other subjects, have ended up learning Islam and becoming sheikhs. The best minds should be encouraged to study Islam. That's what we are trying to do in Jordan. We want our best people to bring an Islamic revival, in the proper sense.

MV: Isn't this a futile effort, since the Arabs place so much effort on preserving Islam unchanged?

KH: Yes, but the damage has taken place over a very long time, and will take a long time to correct. We're not seeking leadership. We're seeking a collective effort to reform Islam. We are trying, and with some success.

MV: Let me ask you about some Islamic concepts. What about *bid'a,* the notion that innovation and creativity are sinful?

KH: This is totally alien to Islam, as I see it. I'm not saying there should be no limits, but if we're talking about limiting creativity, I'm against it. When *ijtihad* was closed, that was the beginning of the end. Hopefully it will be ameliorated.

MV: What is your concept of *shura?*

KH: My concept is that it is another word for democracy. It is incumbent on us as Arabs to share in shaping our future, honestly and openly in dialogue. But what we see in our part of the world is intolerance to ideas and to dialogue: "I am right and you have to accept that." That is alien to Islam and to its future. I think others are looking and listening at what we are doing here in Jordan. You can't stop the clock. It has to move ahead.

MV: Is there much controversy over drinking in Jordan?

KH: Being a Muslim, you are advised not to drink and you shouldn't drink. But it doesn't mean that you have a right to impose that on non-Muslims. Such tolerance, in fact, is our religion.

MV: How many Jordanians would you estimate would like to have a ban on alcohol or a required *hejab* in the society?

KH: I can't give you any figures, but anybody in Jordan who believes couldn't possibly subscribe to these demands, because without openness and without all working together there's no future. Some of these people are linked to ideologies or to forces within the area that would like to see the destruction of Jordan. But a lot of politicians and others underestimate the majority of Jordanians, who solidly oppose that sort of thing.

MV: Don't many Muslims regard restrictions on behavior as what Islam is?

KH: Yes, but unfortunately they are moving about on the surface, the superficial things in Islam, not the substance.

MV: Hasn't that been the problem with Islam for a long time?

KH: Yes, it has.

MV: Do you have a position on the *hejab?*

KH: My personal position is that there are certain rules that are cited in the Quran and refer only to the family of the Prophet. But, more important than the *hejab,* I am totally against the idea that a Muslim woman should not have the same opportunities as a Muslim man to learn, to open up, to work, help shape the future. To close Islam down to a sexist approach is totally intolerable and ridiculous. It's not Islam.

MV: Doesn't the Quran provide some confused guidance on women, saying they are subject to men?

KH: I think Islam reveres men and women alike. The Quran speaks very much of the rights of women and mothers. If you take the period of the Prophet and the birth of Islam, women were a very important part of it. Restrictions against women didn't exist then and there is no reason why they should exist now.

MV: Are you saying restrictions have been imposed since the early years of the Prophet?

KH: Yes, I think they have been imposed in a subsequent period. Islam brought with it the ban on killing a female baby. It brought with it enlightenment. The Prophet said in a *hadith:* "Take half your faith from Aisha," his wife. So how can Islam be belittling of women and their role? During that period they were poets. Women fought in battles. You'll find true Islam if you go back to its origins, an open and not a closed Islam.

MV: How do you read what the Quran says about polygamy, about taking four wives?

KH: I read two verses. One says four wives, but another requires you to treat them equally and says you won't be able to treat them equally. What does the Quran mean? It means that polygamy is not the right thing. No, I do not believe in polygamy.

MV: What position do you take on the imperative for *jihad?*

KH: Who has the right to call for *jihad?* The concept of *jihad* is all-encompassing. Islam requires that you improve yourself, in anything you do. It's not just battle and fight. *Jihad,* as war, should have ended with the Prophet, who alone had the right to call for it. So I believe that extremist movements in the name of *jihad* are wrong. Muslim life has a certain sanctity. If you commit suicide, no one is permitted to come to your grave and pray. So when you see suicide attempts portrayed as *jihad,* leading to heaven, I believe this is an abomination of Islam.

MV: Since all Muslims read the same texts, how do you think so many went astray? How did the suicide bombers in Jerusalem come to believe that this is what God wants them to do?

KH: I believe the impact of the extremist leaders on the young, on the unnurtured, has been almost criminal. I have read the Quran so many times, and each time I read it something becomes clearer, and with the passage of years I always find something new. When you think of idealistic young people, wanting to do so much, if you couple that with oppression and lack of opportunity, you find fertile ground for extremism. I've seen it so many times. And I've seen how people have started out and how they have ended up. Many who have the opportunity to think things out eventually mature and settle down. This, I suppose, is a part of life. What we need to do is to speak openly about Islam, and defend it and present it properly and prevent its abuse.

MV: But the Muslim Brotherhood is not a small phenomenon, and its justification of *jihad* in the name of Islam has become popular and widespread. How does it get away with that?

KH: At a certain time, Islam was considered a possible weapon in the struggle against Communism and colonialism, and it was encouraged to be such. Afghanistan is just an example. It's a shame to every Muslim that Afghanistan has ended up as it has.

MV: But *is* it a shame to every Muslim? There are so-called "Afghans" in Algeria, in Egypt, probably here in Jordan, certainly across the river in the West Bank. They are very dangerous.

KH: Yes, they are. And what sort of distorted minds they have, what sort of distorted visions! They engage in money laundering and drug trafficking and other criminal activities in the name of Islam. I don't know how. I think that a lot of people have been mentally abused, to the point where this is the result.

MV: Some of them are probably very smart people. . . .

KH: Yes, those who run these things and lead people astray. Much blame lies with them. But it also lies with Islamic governments and officials who were not watching while their schools and universities were teaching Islam in the wrong way.

MV: It is a tragedy of our time that Arab civilization, lacking dynamism and creativity, is falling increasingly behind other cultures. In this book, I ask whether Islam, in its orthodox form, is to blame. As you see it, why is Islamic civilization not moving forward?

KH: I think there are many reasons. Let me just take our prayers, five times a day. Islam imposes a ritual to recite parts of the Quran, learning them by heart without necessarily understanding what they mean. I doubt whether there are many people who have really read the whole Quran. And it's only if you do that you understand what Islam is truly about. So there is this superficial approach. To pray you have to recite verses, in many cases not knowing what they mean. But with deep understanding of the Quran, Islam becomes a dynamic movement, opening up every opportunity. It is not rigid at all.

MV: Men and women who have Islamic educations, even in Jordan, say that schoolwork is all memory, without analysis or examination.

KH: I agree with them.

MV: How are the children to learn that Islam can open up this world to them, which is what you say they must learn?

KH: That is what we are trying to deal with as best we can. Sadly, we inherited a situation that prevailed before, of memorizing rather than understanding. The absence of discussion, of debate, is among our greatest weaknesses. In Jordan we went all out on schools and universities, building everywhere, but our standards dropped considerably from the days of limited schooling. So now we are concentrating on quality, and on openness, and dialogue. But to bring all that about requires time and sustained effort and stability. It also requires peace, because without it you are not sure what any day will bring. So when we speak about peace and the need for it, it is really one of our top priorities. And anyone who fights it—and there are some in Jordan—would have us remain where we are, or sliding backward.

MV: Do you think the next generation of Jordanian children will have a different frame of mind from their fathers and grandfathers?

KH: We are trying, we are trying.

MV: But isn't there a strong Islamic component in the administration of Jordan's schools, holding back change?

KH: There was, and there probably still is, but we're trying to depoliticize the schools and teach Islam as it should be taught.

MV: In Islam, there is always a line—symbolized to me by Khomeini's *fatwa* punishing insults to the Prophet—beyond which speech and thought cannot go. Do you draw a line, and where is it?

KH: In general, I believe the judgment that we receive comes after our death, based on what we have done in this life. It has to do with the Almighty, and also with the judgment of people after we are gone. I'm not for excess in anything, including so-called freedom. But I would never appoint myself a judge, to say that because I disapprove of how someone has behaved he is no longer a Muslim. That is something that is beyond me or anyone else. Yet I don't understand how anyone in his proper mind would insult the Prophet.

MV: When you say someone is not a Muslim, doesn't it trigger the Islamic law on apostasy? Many of the great interpreters say that Islam requires putting to death anyone who would leave the religion. How would you deal with that?

KH: I have so many other problems before I ever reach that one.

MV: But many Muslims applauded Khomeini's *fatwa*, and justified the murder of Farag Foda in Egypt, on these grounds.

KH: I don't think that individual leaders have the right to determine who lives and who dies. There are many ways of examining these matters. I do not stand with much that is decreed, and sometimes followed up by action, along these lines. I've read what Rushdie has written and it was very deeply offensive and very deeply objectionable. But I would not sanction murder and wouldn't expect anyone I know to do that.

MV: So you apply your principle that God will judge Rushdie in the afterlife?

KH: Of course.

MV: Leaving aside insults to the Prophet, do you feel there is a line that can be drawn in *political* speech?

KH: No, as witnessed by what you hear and see in Jordan.

MV: Well, a Jordanian went to prison recently for what he said, though you pardoned him soon afterward. There is also a press law which, I am told, is designed to limit free speech.

KH: I don't know that it's designed to limit free speech but it is certainly designed for the judiciary to address distortions of truth and morality. I believe this would happen anywhere in the world. We opened up here in Jordan without having time to develop codes for preserving our coherence and our unity and our dialogue as they should be. So we had to look at certain—not restraints, people can write whatever they feel like writing—but if they infringe on certain areas in a blatant way . . .

MV: What areas?

KH: For example, attacking people in a manner that is incompatible with the truth, false accusations. There is no restraint. But undermining the very roots of a society is not what freedom is about. Freedom is your freedom to do whatever you like without infringing on the freedoms of others. That is precisely the line we are trying to draw. Are people in Jordan telling you there is no freedom? There is freedom. Too much at times.

MV: Shifting the subject, how would you describe the Islamic movement in Jordan?

KH: It's passing through an interesting phase, a dialogue between moderates and extremists. The extremists, who want to take us back to the distant past, are a very small number. In fact, politicized Islam is a very small percentage of Jordanians. The dialogue might heat up, but it is still essentially political.

MV: Are there really people who believe the society can go back to the *rashidun*?

KH: There may be some. That's freedom of thought.

MV: Why do Muslims find the distant past so appealing?

KH: I think it's the search to stabilize oneself. Again, my hope is that going back to the proper teaching is the answer. We Muslims can't live without faith, without our beliefs. But where do you receive them from? During the years of crisis in Jordan, things were left without the proper attention. We never thought we would have an Islamic problem. So there was not as much watchfulness as there was against other elements that were trying to undermine this country. The Islamic movement lived with the protection of the regime and then became a political movement. Now it is divided between moderates and extremists, who would like to exploit it. And the instability in the region is a factor, including lack of progress on the peace front.

MV: Do you think Jordan is endangered by the Islamic radicals?

KH: I don't think so. We will be able to talk over things and work them out in the best interests of the people of Jordan.

MV: How democratic are these Islamic parties?

KH: Their thoughts are not clearly defined, and I believe there is some danger. When we returned to parliamentary life after the long absence, I said it would probably take us about twenty years for things to jell up, and unfortunately I have been proven right. At a certain point we had twenty-three parties. If you want to have a system based on political parties, you need people who have thoughts and ideas and plans and programs that they can present to the voters. This has not yet happened. As for the Islamic parties, how they would behave if they came into power is unclear to me. We are bound by the national charter, which we've all agreed on, including the political Islamic movement. But if you take the whole spectrum of the opposition parties, which are trying to ally with the Islamic movement, it may come out to 10,000 out of 4 million-plus Jordanians. So political parties are not convincing as yet to the grass roots, because they lack experience and the ability to look forward. It will take time before we reduce to three or four parties to run in elections.

MV: What is the future of fundamentalism in the Arab world?

KH: It grows, like other movements in this part of the world, if there is no evolution, no progress toward greater freedom, greater dialogue, greater debate between people on all issues. Whenever an attempt is made to stop the clock, that is when you can expect trouble from extremist movements. If the basic social problems are dealt with, and if we have peace, then I think that the future is very bright. We will have greater moderation and Islam will be a source of strength for true Muslims.

MV: And you really believe that peace is essential for moving in this direction?

KH: I believe that peace is absolutely essential.

MV: The Arab world is historically weak at political succession. Have you taken measures in Jordan to correct that weakness?

KH: I have some thoughts on the succession. I have sought to produce a system that would be close to the true teachings of Islam while selecting the best available person. The House of the Prophet is a force for stability and continuity, and democratic monarchy is my ideal. When I was considerably younger and my first son was born, things were so turbulent here that I thought that if anything happened to me, he would not have the opportunity to take over. So I chose my youngest brother, which is probably an indication of the way I feel, to be crown prince. And he has done very, very well. I've brought him up as close to me as I could all these years. I've talked to him and others about a system to choose the best-qualified person from the line of sons and grandsons of Sharif Hussein. This would avoid subjecting someone who is young to exploitation. I hope sometime soon to present a system—I was thinking of a family council—that will provide for the line of my succession.

It was clear from listening to King Hussein that he represents a vision of Islam that is very distant from Islamic orthodoxy, and even more distant from Islamic fundamentalism. To call it modernism might do the King a disservice, since he would very likely explain that, whatever the resemblance, it is what the Hashemites have believed since the time of the Prophet. Its Meccan roots impart to the vision much more persuasive credentials than if it were of recent religious vintage, or the product of one man alone.

But, in terms of the decline of Arab civilization, what matters is not so much the history of the King's Islamic concept as its minority status within the Islamic community. The Hashemites rule over a tiny country; their influence beyond its borders is limited. The King, whatever his efforts, does not have a large following as an Islamic thinker. That the heir of the grandest of Islamic dynasties holds to these views surely makes them a valid candidate for mainstream thought. But not even a king can generate optimism that they will be widely accepted.

What King Hussein articulates to Muslims is a Hashemite option for understanding their faith. It seems to hold much promise—far more promise than the competing options—for reconciling Islam with the modern world. In the larger arena where the struggle for the soul of Islam is conducted, there is scarcely a sign that the Hashemite option will prevail. But the clear impact it appears to have made in Jordan during the so-far brief Hashemite reign suggests that Muslims may, after all, be listening.

Notes

Source references are keyed to the author's last name, with an identifying word if the bibliography cites more than one title.

Chapter 1   *Through the Damascus Gate*

1. The World Bank provides a similar story in its publication *Claiming the Future: Choosing Prosperity in the Middle East and North Africa,* Washington, 1995.

2. *Foreign Affairs,* September/October 1996, p. 24. See Chapter 7, pp. 206–8 on the Saudi bombings.

3. Bennabi, *Problème,* pp. 61–62.

4. Peters, *Children,* pp. 71–72.

5. Rahman, *Islam and Modernity,* pp. 46–47.

6. On Abduh, see Hourani, *Arabic Thought,* pp. 130–60, and Rahman, *Islam,* pp. 216–20.

7. See Al-Azm; see also article on "usul" in Gibb and Kramers, *Shorter Encyclopedia.*

8. The material on Taliban is drawn from articles in the *New York Times* by correspondent John F. Burns, published throughout 1996. Burns subsequently won the Pulitzer Prize for this work.

9. Quoted in Esposito, *Islamic Threat,* p. 157; also Esposito's account of the period of Ghannoushi's activism, pp. 153–63.

10. This quote is among several from "What We Need Is a Realistic Fundamentalism," from the periodical *Arabia,* October 1986.

Chapter 2   *The Murder of Farag Foda*

1. Excerpts published in *Women's Rights: A Quarterly Women's Human Rights Journal,* August 1996; translation by Marilyn Tadros.

2. Mitchell's study is the chief source for historical background on the Brotherhood.

3. Quoted by Sivan, p. 24.

4. The newspaper *Al-Hayat,* November 24, 1995.

Chapter 3   *The Prophet and the Book*

1. Cited by Peters, *Muhammad,* p. 23.
2. Translation of Maulawi Sher'Ali, Oriental and Religious Publishing Corporation, Rahwah, Pakistan, 1979. See also discussion under "ummi" and "Muhammad" in Gibb and Kramers, *Shorter Encyclopedia.*
3. Pickthall, p. x.
4. Quoted in Gibb, *Mohammedanism,* p. 25.
5. See article on "Kur'an" in Gibb and Kramers, *Shorter Encyclopedia.*
6. Most of my citations are from the translation of Marmaduke Pickthall. A few are from Kenneth Cragg. Both are British scholars. Pickthall, a convert to Islam, conveys the verses more literally, providing some of the flavor; Cragg, an Anglican cleric, tends to be more contemporary. Pickthall uses the Arabic *Allah* for God, holding that it "has never been applied to anything other than the unimaginable Supreme Being." Cragg prefers the English term, holding that God is God, whether worshiped in London or Mecca. I have taken the liberty of substituting other translations when one or the other is obscure. See Bibliography for a list of translations consulted.
7. See Edward Said, *Orientalism,* a celebrated study.
8. Pickthall, p. 351.
9. See Viorst, *Sandcastles,* pp. 395–96.
10. Pickthall, p. 463.
11. Mernissi, *Beyond the Veil,* Part One.
12. See Al-Awa, *Islamic Law,* pp. 49–58, 61–64. See also Foda trial in Chapter 2 and the Turabi statement in Chapter 5.
13. Quoted by Hitti, *History of the Arabs,* p. 144.

Chapter 4   *Sudan: The Islamic Experiment*

1. The best account of the *Mahdiyya,* the era of Muhammad Ahmad, is contained in Holt, *Mahdist State.*
2. See Ann Lesch, "The Destruction of Civil Society in the Sudan," chapter in Norton, *Civil Society in the Middle East.* Also Lesch's unpublished essay, "Unity vs. Separation in the Sudan," courtesy of the author.
3. My own interview is supplemented by a Turabi interview in *Islam, Democracy, the State and the West* Lowrie, Arthur L., ed., a roundtable with Dr. Hasan Turabi (World and Islam Studies, Clearwater, 1993); by a Turabi article in *Middle East Affairs Journal,* Winter 1995, pp. 17–25; and by the transcript of a hearing on Islamic fundamentalism before the House Subcommittee on Africa on May 20, 1992.

Chapter 5   *Making the* Shari'a

1. See the discussion on "shari'a" in Gibb and Kramers, *Shorter Encyclopedia.*
2. Lewis, *Arabs in History,* pp. 60–61; Peters, *Commonwealth,* pp. 87–93. See also discussion in Chapter 1, pp. 8–9.
3. Lewis, op. cit., pp. 59–79; Peters, op. cit., pp. 87–98.
4. Schacht, *Introduction.* See also Schacht in Khadduri and Liebesney, pp. 39–43, and Goldziher, pp. 38–43.
5. Schacht, pp. 28–36.

6. Schacht, in Khadduri and Liebesney, op. cit., pp. 44–47.

7. Hitti, *History of the Arabs*, pp. 305, 404–5.

8. Wiggin and Smith, *Arabian Nights*, pp. 332–39.

9. Clot describes the wedding on p. 48, the dream on p. 242. Hitti, *History of the Arabs*, also describes the wedding, p. 302.

10. Goldziher, p. 64; Clot, p. 217.

11. Hitti, *History of the Arabs*, pp. 297–316.

12. See "Mu'tazila" in Gibb and Kramers, *Shorter Encyclopedia*.

13. Peters, *Commonwealth*, p. 468; Watt, *Islamic Philosophy*, pp. 82–90; Rahman, *Islam*, pp. 91–94.

14. Khadduri, *Islamic Conception*, p. 55; see also the entry for al-Ashari in Glasse, *Concise Encyclopedia*.

15. Schacht, Chapters 2 and 3 in Khadduri and Liebesney, *Law in the Middle East*.

16. Cited by Goldziher, p. 55.

17. Coulson, *Islamic Law*, pp. 62–65; Peters, *Commonwealth*, pp. 242–43.

18. See discussion in Rahman, *Islam*, pp. 43–85; Coulson, *Conflicts*, pp. 8, 82, 124; Riyad Maydani, in Khadduri and Liebesney, *Law in the Middle East*, pp. 227–29.

19. Coulson, *Islamic Law*, pp. 80–82; Schacht, in Khadduri and Liebesney, pp. 74–75; Rahman, *Islam*, pp. 63–67; Vesey-Fitzgerald, in Khadduri and Liebesney, p. 85.

20. Al-Awa, *Punishment*, p. 52. See also discussion on the Foda assassination in Chapter 2.

21. Schacht, *Introduction*, p. 78.

22. Coulson, *Conflicts*, pp. 61–71. See "Shari'a" in Gibb and Kramers, *Shorter Encyclopedia*.

23. Goldziher, pp. 93–96.

24. For extended treatment, see Mernissi, *Beyond the Veil*, and Saadawi, *Hidden Face*.

25. Coulson, *Islamic Law*, p. 222.

26. Hourani, *Arabic Thought*, pp. 130–60; Rahman, *Islam*, pp. 216–20.

Chapter 6 *Khomeini's Triumph*

1. This quote is from Farhang Rajaee, "Islam and Modernity," in Marty and Appleby, *Fundamentalism Project*, Vol. 2, p. 113.

2. *New York Times*, September 20, 1996; *Washington Post*, December 15, 1996.

3. Quoted in Bakhash, p. 21.

4. Cottam, pp. 146–50.

5. Bakhash, pp. 22–23; Abrahamian, p. 20.

6. Bakhash, p. 23.

7. Ibid., p. 32; Keddie, *Roots of Revolution*, pp. 157–58.

8. Bakhash, pp. 33–36; Mottahedeh, pp. 245–46.

9. Quoted in Arjomand Said Amir *Turban*, pp. 98–99.

10. Quoted in Riesebrodt, p. 136.

11. Quoted in Bakhash, p. 39.

12. Arjomand, *Turban*, p. 101; Cottam, p. 137.

13. Bakhash, pp. 45–48.

14. Ibid., pp. 72–73; Arjomand, *Turban*, pp. 152–53, 160.

15. Arjomand, "Shi'ite Jurisprudence," in Marty and Appleby, *Fundamentalism Project*, Vol. 3, p. 94.

16. Bakhash, pp. 83–86.
17. Arjomand, *Turban,* p. 139.
18. The observations on the revolution's consolidation are, for the most part, from ibid., Chapter 8.
19. See Rajaee in Esposito, *Iranian Revolution,* p. 68.
20. Quoted by Ramazani in ibid., p. 48.
21. My italics of "world." Translation based on Ramazani, in ibid., p. 56, and Weatherby, p. 154.
22. Ramazani text in Esposito, *Iranian Revolution,* p. 56; Weatherby, p. 155. See also parallel discussion on the Islamic justification for the murder of Farag Foda in Chapter 2.
23. Quoted in Rajaee in Marty and Appleby, *Fundamentalism Project,* Vol. 2, p. 116.
24. See Geraldine Brooks, "Teen-Age Infidels Hanging Out," *New York Times Magazine,* April 30, 1995.

Chapter 7   *The Saudi Dilemma*

1. Helms, pp. 55–56.
2. Both the 1991 and the 1992 documents are reviewed in the *Middle East Journal* by Dekmejian, pp. 630–34.
3. Interview in *Mideast Mirror,* November 13, 1996, p. 18, and confirmed by author.
4. Helms, pp. 80–82.
5. Quoted in Hourani, *History of the Arab Peoples,* p. 180.
6. The best review of this subject is in Helms, pp. 80, 84, 94–97.
7. Holden and Johns, pp. 104–7.
8. Quoted by Helms, p. 258. See also Helms's account on the rise and fall of the Ikhwan.
9. *Washington Post,* November 14, 1996.

Chapter 8   *The Anguish of Algeria*

1. Rouadjia examines the rise of the mosque culture in *Frères.*
2. See Graham Fuller's report for the RAND Corporation.
3. Rouadjia, pp. 196–208.
4. Labat, pp. 52–53.
5. Ibid., pp. 57, 99–101.
6. Malek, pp. 30, 42.
7. Merad, *Réformisme,* pp. 80–85, 124–33.
8. Labat, pp. 64–67.
9. Interview with Rabia Bekkar in Beinin and Stork, p. 291.
10. See also Labat, pp. 75–78, 168–69.
11. Bennabi, *Vocation,* p. 85.
12. He was not alone. Among others, the modernist thinker al-Afghani, precursor of Abduh, also used it as a motto. See Rajaee in Vol. 2 of Marty and Appleby, *Fundamentalism Project,* p. 107.
13. Bennabi, *Problème,* pp. 86–91.
14. Labat, pp. 90–94; Roberts, Hugh, "The Expansion and Manipulation of Alge-

rian Islamism, 1979–1992," in Marty and Appleby, *Fundamentalism Project*, Vol. 4, p. 428.

15. Jean-Paul Mari, *Nouvel Observateur*, January 19, 1995, p. 29.

16. Labat, pp. 272–90.

Chapter 9   *The Beleaguered Muslims of France*

1. Boubakeur, p. 22.

2. Dietmer Loch, a teacher at the University of Bielefeld in Westphalia. The excerpts appeared in *Le Monde*, October 7, 1995.

3. Boubakeur, pp. 74–77, 105–7.

4. Ibid., pp. 97, 125.

5. See Huntington study.

Chapter 10   *The Hashemite Option*

1. Salibi, p. 75.

2. Husscin, pp. 7, 12, 300.

3. Ibid., p. 12.

Selected Bibliography

Translations of the Quran

Ben-Shemesh, A. *The Noble Quran*, Massada, Tel-Aviv, 1979.
Cleary, Thomas. *The Essential Koran*. Harper, San Francisco, 1993.
Cragg, Kenneth. *Readings in the Qur'an*. Collins, London, 1988.
Dawood, N. J. *The Koran*. Penguin, New York, 1974.
Pickthall, Marmaduke. *The Meaning of the Glorious Koran*. Dorset Press, New York, no date.

Bibliography

Abrahamian, Ervand. *Khomeinism*. University of California Press, Berkeley, 1990.
———. *Radical Islam: The Iranian Mojahedin*. I. B. Taurus, London, 1989.
Abu-Rabi, Ibrahim M. *Intellectual Origins of Islamic Resurgence in the Modern Arab World*. State University of New York Press, New York, 1990.
Adas, Michael. *Islamic and European Expansion*. Temple University Press, Philadelphia, 1993.
Ahmed, Leila. *Women and Gender in Islam*. Yale University Press, New Haven, 1992.
Akhavi, Shahrough. *Religion and Politics in Comtemporary Iran*. State University of New York Press, Albany, 1980.
Akhtar, Shabbir. *A Faith for all Seasons: Islam and the Challenge of the Modern World*. Ivan R. Dee, Chicago, 1991.
Alama, Mohammed. *Arabia Unified*. Hutchinson Benhan, London, 1980.
Al-Awa, Muhammad S. *On the Political System of the Islamic State*. American Trust Publications, Indianapolis, 1980.
———. *Punishment in Islamic Law*. American Trust Publications, Indianapolis, 1993.
Al-Azm, Sadiq. *South Asia Bulletin, Comparative Studies of South Asia, Africa and the Middle East*, Vol. 13, Nos. 1 and 2; Vol. 14, No. 1.
Al-Azmeh, Aziz. *Ibn Khaldun*. Routledge, New York, 1990.
Arjomand, Said Amir. *The Turban for the Crown*. Oxford University Press, New York, 1988.
———, ed. *The Political Dimensions of Religion*. State University of New York Press, Albany, 1993.

Atkins, John. *Sex in Literature.* Vol. 3, *The Medieval Experience.* John Calder, London, 1978.

Bakhash, Shaul. *The Reign of the Ayatollahs.* Basic Books, New York, 1984.

Barakat, Halim. *The Arab World.* University of California Press, Berkeley, 1993.

Barrau, Jean-Claude. *De l'Islam et du monde moderne.* Le Pré aux Clercs, Paris, 1991.

Beinin, Joel, and Joe Stork, eds. *Political Islam.* University of California Press, Berkeley, 1997.

Bennabi, Malek. *Le Problème des idées dans le monde musulman.* El Bay-yinate, Algiers, 1990 edition.

———. *Vocation de l'Islam.* Éditions du Seuil, Paris, 1954.

Berque, Jacques. *L'Islam au défi.* Gallimard, Paris, 1980.

Bill, James A. *The Eagle and the Lion: The Tragedy of American-Iranian Relations.* Yale University Press, New Haven, 1988.

Blin, Louis, et al. *Algérie: 200 hommes de pouvoir.* Indigo, Paris, 1992.

Boubakeur, Dalil. *Charte du culte musulman en France.* Éditions du Rocher, Paris, 1995.

Brooks, Geraldine. *Nine Parts of Desire.* Doubleday, New York, 1997.

Bulliet, Richard W. *Islam: The View from the Edge.* Columbia University Press, New York, 1994.

Butterworth, Charles E., ed. *The Political Aspects of Islamic Philosophy.* Harvard University Press, Cambridge, 1992.

——— and I. William Zartman, eds. "Political Islam," *The Annals of the American Academy of Political and Social Science,* November 1992.

Caspar, Robert. *"Le Renouveau Mo'tazilite,"* *Mélanges,* 4. Institut Dominicain d'Études Orientales du Caire, 1957.

Chehabi, H. E. *Iranian Politics and Religious Modernism.* Cornell University Press, Ithaca, 1990.

Chittick, William C. *Faith and Practice of Islam.* State University of New York Press, Albany, 1992.

Cleveland, William L. *Islam Against the West.* University of Texas Press, Austin, 1985.

Clot, André. *Harun al-Rashid.* New Amsterdam, New York, 1986.

Commins, David D. *Islamic Reform.* Oxford University Press, New York, 1990.

Coon, Carleton S. *Caravan: The Story of the Middle East.* Krieger Publishing Co., Huntington, NY, 1976.

Cottam, Richard W. *Nationalism in Iran.* University of Pittsburgh Press, Pittsburgh, 1964.

Coulson, Noel J. *Conflicts and Tensions in Islamic Jurisprudence.* University of Chicago Press, Chicago, 1969.

———. *A History of Islamic Law.* Edinburgh University Press, Edinburgh, 1964.

Crone, Patricia, and Michael Cook. *Hagarism: The Making of the Islamic World.* Cambridge University Press, 1979.

Dekmejian, R. Hrair. "The Rise of Political Islamism in Saudi Arabia," *Middle East Journal,* Autumn 1994.

De Seife, Rudoldphe J. A. *The Shari'a: Introduction to the Law of Islam.* Austin & Winfield, Bethesda, MD, 1993.

Dietl, Wilhelm. *Holy War.* Macmillan, New York, 1984.

Djait, Hichem. *Europe and Islam.* University of California Press, Berkeley, 1985.

Dodge, Bayard. *Al-Azhar: A Millennium of Muslim Learning.* Middle East Institute, Washington, 1974.

Eaton, Charles L. *Islam and the Destiny of Man*. State University of New York Press, Albany, 1985.

Eickelman, Dale F., and James Piscatori. *Muslim Politics*. Princeton University Press, Princeton, 1996.

Enayat, Hamid. *Modern Islamic Political Thought*. University of Texas Press, Austin, 1982.

Endress, Gerhard. *An Introduction to Islam*. Columbia University Press, New York, 1988.

Esposito, John L. *Islam: The Straight Path*. Oxford, New York, 1991.

———. *Islam and Politics*. Syracuse University Press, Syracuse, 1984.

———, ed. *The Iranian Revolution: Its Global Impact*. Florida International University Press, Miami, 1990.

———. *The Islamic Threat*. Oxford University Press, New York, 1992.

Étienne, Bruno. *La France et l'Islam*. Hachette, Paris, 1989.

Ezeldin, Ahmad Galal. *Terrorism and Political Violence*. University of Illinois, Chicago, 1987.

Foda, Farag. *Before the Fall*. Joint Publication Research Science, Washington, 1985.

Fuller, Graham E. *Algeria: The Next Fundamentalist State?* RAND, Santa Monica, CA, 1996.

Gaffney, Patrick. *The Prophet's Pulpit*. University of California, Berkeley, 1994.

Gaudefroy-Demombynes, Maurice. *Muslim Institutions*. Allen & Unwin, London, 1950.

Geertz, Clifford. *Islam Observed*. Yale University Press, New Haven, 1968.

Gerber, Haim. *State, Society and Law in Islam*. State University Press of New York, Albany, 1994

Gibb, Hamilton A. R. *Mohammedanism*. Oxford University Press, New York, 1962.

———. *Studies on the Civilization of Islam*. Princeton University Press, Princeton, 1982.

———. and J. H. Kramers. *Shorter Encyclopedia of Islam*. Cornell University Press, Ithaca, 1974.

Giffen, Lois A. *The Theory of Profane Love Among the Arabs*. New York University Press, New York, 1971.

Gilsenan, Michael. *Recognizing Islam*. Pantheon, New York, 1982.

Glassé, Cyril. *The Concise Encyclopedia of Islam*. HarperCollins, San Francisco, 1991.

Goldziher, Ignaz. *Muslim Studies*, Vol. 2. Allen & Unwin, London, 1971.

Haddad, Yvonne, et al. *The Islamic Impact*. Syracuse University Press, Syracuse, 1984.

Hanafi, M. Jamil. *Islam and the Transformation of Culture*. Asia Publishing House, New York, 1970.

Hanna, Milad. *The Seven Pillars of Egyptian Identity*. General Egyptian Book Organization, Cairo, 1989.

Hayes, John R. *The Genius of Arab Civilization: Source of Renaissance*, MIT Press, Cambridge, 1983.

Helms, Christine Moss. *The Cohesion of Saudi Arabia*. Johns Hopkins University Press, Baltimore, 1981.

Hitti, Philip K. *History of the Arabs*. St. Martins, New York, 1970.

———. *Islam: A Way of Life*. Gateway Regnery, Chicago, 1970.

Hodgson, Marshall G. S. *The Venture of Islam:* Vol. 1, *The Classical Age of Islam;* Vol. 2, *The Expansion of Islam in the Middle Periods;* Vol. 3, *The Gunpowder Empires and Modern Times*. University of Chicago Press, Chicago, 1974.

Holden, David, and Richard Johns. *The House of Saud*. Holt, New York, 1981.

Holt, P. M. *The History of Sudan*. Westview, Boulder, 1961.

———. *The Mahdist State in Sudan*. Oxford University Press, New York, 1958.

Horne, Alistair. *A Savage War of Peace: Algeria 1954–1962*. Penguin, London, 1977.

Hourani, Albert. *Arabic Thought in the Liberal Age, 1798–1939*. Cambridge University Press, Cambridge, 1983.

———. *Europe and the Middle East*. University of California Press, Berkeley, 1980.

———. *A History of the Arab Peoples,* Harvard University Press, Cambridge, 1991.

Hunter, Shireen. *Iran After Khomeini*. Praeger, New York, 1992.

Huntington, Samuel P. *The Clash of Civilizations and the Remaking of World Order*. Simon & Schuster, New York, 1996.

Hussein, King. *Uneasy Lies the Head*. Bernard Geis [no location cited], 1962.

Ibn Khaldun. *The Muqaddimah*. Princeton University Press, Princeton, 1967.

Jansen, G. H. *Militant Islam*. Harper & Row, New York, 1979.

Jansen, Johannes J. G. *The Neglected Duty*. Macmillan, NY, 1986.

Kabbani, Rana. *Europe's Myths of Orient*. Indiana University Press, Bloomington, 1986.

Karsh, Efraim, ed. *The Iran-Iraq War: Impact and Implication*. St. Martin's Press, New York, 1990.

Keddie, Nikki R. *An Islamic Response to Imperialism*. University of California Press, Berkeley, 1968.

———. *Roots of Revolution*. Yale University Press, New Haven, 1981.

———, ed. *Scholars, Saints and Sufis: Muslim Religious Institutions Since 1500*. University of California Press, Berkeley, 1972.

Kedouri, Elie. *Democracy and Arab Political Culture,* Washington Institute for Near East Policy, Washington, 1992.

———. *Islam in the Modern World*. Holt, New York, 1980.

Kelly, Marjorie, ed. *Islam: The Religious and Political Life of a World Community*. Praeger, New York, 1984.

Kennedy, Hugh. *The Early Abbasid Caliphate*. Croom Helm, Beckenham, 1981.

Kepel, Gilles. *Muslim Extremism in Egypt*. University of California, Berkeley, 1963.

———. *À l'Ouest d'Allah*. Seuil, Paris, 1994.

———. *La Revanche de Dieu*. Seuil, Paris, 1991.

———. *Le Prophète et le Pharaon*. Seuil, Paris, 1993.

———. *Les Banlieues de l'Islam*. Seuil, Paris, 1987.

Khadduri, Majid. *The Islamic Conception of Justice*. Johns Hopkins, Baltimore, 1984.

———. *Political Trends in the Arab World*. Johns Hopkins Press, Baltimore, 1979.

———. and Herbert J. Liebesny, eds. *Law in the Middle East,* Vol. 1, *Origin and Development of Islamic Law*. Middle East Institute, Washington, 1955.

Kramer, Martin, ed. *The Islamic Debate*. Dayan Center, Tel-Aviv, 1997.

Labat, Severine. *Les Islamistes algériens*. Seuil, Paris, 1995.

Labica, Georges. *Politique et religion chez Ibn Khaldoun*. SNED, Algiers, no date.

Lacey, Robert. *The Kingdom of Saudi Arabia and the House of Saud*. Harcourt, Brace, Jovanovich, New York, 1981.

Lacoste, Yves. *Ibn Khaldun*. Verso, London, 1984.

Laroui, Abdallah. *The Crisis of the Arab Intellectual.* University of California Press, Berkeley, 1976.

Lawrence, Bruce B. *Defenders of God*. Harper & Row, New York, 1989.

————, ed. *Ibn Khaldun and Islamic Ideology.* E. J. Brill, Leiden (Netherlands), 1984.

Lemaire, Jacques and Jacques Marx. *Les Intégrismes* (in the series *La Pensée et les hommes*). University of Brussels, no date.

Lewis, Bernard. *The Arabs in History.* Harper, New York, 1966.

————. *Cultures in Conflict.* Oxford University Press, New York, 1995.

————. *Islam and the West.* Oxford University Press, New York, 1993.

————. *The Muslim Discovery of Europe.* Norton, New York, 1982.

————. *The Political Language of Islam.* University of Chicago Press, Chicago, 1988.

————. *Race and Slavery in the Middle East.* Oxford University Press, New York, 1990.

————. *The Shaping of the Modern Middle East.* Oxford University Press, New York, 1994.

————, ed. *Islam,* Vol. 1, *Politics and War;* Vol. 2, *Religion and Society.* Walker and Company, New York, 1974.

Lunt, James. *Hussein of Jordan.* William Morrow, New York, 1989.

Madelung, Wilferd. *Religious Trends in Early Islamic Iran.* Persian Heritage Foundation, Albany, 1988.

Mahdi, Muhsin. *Ibn Khaldun's Philosophy of History.* University of Chicago Press, Chicago, 1971.

Makki, Hassan. *Sudan: The Christian Design.* The Islamic Foundation, Markfield, Leicester, 1989.

Malek, Redha, *Tradition et révolution: le véritable enjeu.* Bouchene, Algiers, 1991.

Malley, Robert. *The Call from Algeria.* University of California Press, Berkeley, 1996.

Marty, Martin E., and Scott Appleby. *The Fundamentalism Project,* Vol. 1, *Fundamentalisms Observed,* 1991; Vol. 2, *Fundamentalisms and Society,* 1993; Vol. 3, *Fundamentalisms and the State,* 1993; Vol. 4, *Accounting for Fundamentalisms,* 1994. University of Chicago Press, Chicago.

Massignon, Louis. *Hallaj: Mystic and Martyr.* Princeton University Press, Princeton, 1994.

Mawdudi, Abul A'La. *Towards Understanding Islam.* International Islamic Federation of Students, Kuwait, 1982.

Mehden, Fred R. von der. *Two Worlds of Islam.* University Press of Florida, Gainesville, 1993.

Merad, Ali. *Ibn Badis, commentateur du Coran.* Librairie Orientaliste, Paris, 1971.

————. *Le Réformisme musulman en Algérie de 1925 à 1940.* Mouton, Paris, 1967.

Mernissi, Fatima. *Beyond the Veil.* Indiana University Press, Bloomington, 1987.

————. *Islam and Democracy.* Addison-Wesley, Reading, 1992.

Messick, Brinkley. *The Calligraphic State.* University of California Press, Berkeley, 1993.

Metz, Helen Chapin, ed. *Saudi Arabia: a Country Study.* Library of Congress, Washington, 1993.

Milani, Mohsen M. *The Making of Iran's Islamic Revolution.* Westview, Boulder, 1994.

Miller, Judith. *God Has Ninety-nine Names.* Simon & Schuster, New York, 1996.

Mitchell, Richard P. *The Society of the Muslim Brothers.* Oxford University Press, London, 1969.

Mortimer, Edward. *Faith and Power: The Politics of Islam.* Random House, New York, 1982.

Mottahedeh, Roy. *The Mantle of the Prophet*. Penguin, New York, 1985.

Munson, Henry Jr. *Islam and Revolution in the Middle East*. Yale University Press, New Haven, 1988.

――――. *Religion and Power in Morocco*. Yale University Press, New Haven, 1993.

Musallam, B. F. *Sex and Society in Islam*. Cambridge University Press, Cambridge, 1983.

Nasr, Seyyed Hossein. *Islamic Life and Thought*. State University of New York Press, Albany, 1981.

――――. *Science and Civilization in Islam*. Barnes & Noble, New York, 1968.

Netton, I. R. *Muslim Neoplatonists*. Allen & Unwin, London, 1982.

Newby, Gordon D. *A History of the Jews of Arabia*. University of South Carolina, Columbia, 1988.

Norton, Augustus R., ed. *Civil Society in the Middle East,* Vol. 2. E. J. Brill, Leiden (Netherlands), 1996.

Patton, Walter M. *Ahmed Ibn Hanbal and the Mihna*. E. J. Brill, Leiden (Netherlands), 1897.

Payne, Robert. *The History of Islam*. Dorset Press, New York, 1959.

Peroncel-Hugoz, Jean-Pierre. *Le Radeau de Mahomet*. Flammarion, Paris, 1983.

Peretz, Don, et al. *Islam: Legacy of the Past, Challenge of the Future*. North River Press [no location cited], 1984.

Peters, F. E. *Allah's Commonwealth*. Simon & Schuster, New York, 1973.

――――. *Children of Abraham*. Princeton University Press, Princeton, 1992.

――――. *Judaism, Christianity and Islam,* Vol. 1, *From Covenant to Community;* Vol. 2, *The Word and the Law and the People of God;* Vol. 3, *The Works of the Spirit*. Princeton University Press, Princeton, 1990.

――――. *Muhammad and the Origins of Islam*. State University of New York Press, Albany, 1994.

――――. *A Reader on Classical Islam*. Princeton University Press, Princeton, 1994.

Pierre, Andrew J., and William B. Quandt. *The Algerian Crisis: Policy Options for the West*. Carnegie Endowment, Washington, 1996.

Pinault, David. *The Shi'ites*. St. Martin's Press, New York, 1992.

Pipes, Daniel. *In the Path of God*. Basic Books, New York, 1983.

Piscatori, James, ed. *Islamic Fundamentalism and the Gulf Crisis*. American Academy of Arts and Sciences, Chicago, 1991.

Powers, David S. *Studies in Quran and Hadith*. University of California Press, Berkeley, 1986.

Qutb, Sayyid. *Milestones*. American Trust Publications, Indianapolis, 1993.

Rahman, Fazlur. *Islam*. University of Chicago Press, Chicago, 1979.

――――. *Islam and Modernity*. University of Chicago Press, Chicago, 1982.

Rahnema, Ali, ed. *Pioneers of Islamic Revival*. Zed Books, London, 1994.

Ramadan, Said. *Islamic Law*. [No publisher cited], 1970.

Ramadan, Tariq. *Islam, le face à face des civilisations*. Librairie Tawhid, Lyon, 1995.

Ramazani, Rouhollah K. *The Foreign Policy of Iran, 1500–1941*. University of Virginia Press, Charlottesville, 1966.

――――, ed. *Iran's Revolution: The Search for Consensus*. Indiana University Press, Bloomington, 1990.

Reeves, Minou. *Female Warriors of Allah*. Dutton, New York, 1989.

Riesebrodt, Martin. *Pious Passion: The Emergence of Modern Fundamentalism in the United States and Iran*. University of California Press, Berkeley, 1993.

Rodinson, Maxime. *The Arabs*. University of Chicago Press, Chicago, 1981.

———. *Islam and Capitalism*. University of Texas Press, Austin, 1981.

Roff, William, ed. *Islam and the Political Economy of Meaning*. University of California Press, Berkeley, 1987.

Rosenthal, Erwin I. J. *Judaism and Islam*. Thomas Yoseloff, London, 1961.

Ronadjia, Ahmed. *Les frerès et les mosqués*. Karthala, Paris, 1990.

Roy, Olivier. *The Failure of Political Islam*. Harvard University Press, Cambridge, 1994.

Ruedy, John, ed. *Islamism and Secularism in North Africa*. St. Martin's Press, New York, 1994.

Rushdie, Salman. *The Satanic Verses*. Viking, New York, 1988.

Saadawi, Nawal El-. *The Hidden Face of Eve: Women in the Arab World*. Beacon Press, Boston, 1980.

———. *Memoirs from the Women's Prison*. University of California Press, Berkeley, 1986.

Said, Edward W. *Orientalism*. Vintage, New York, 1979.

Salibi, Kamal. *The Modern History of Jordan*. Tauris, London, 1993.

Satloff, Robert B. *From Abdullah to Hussein*. Oxford University Press, New York, 1994.

Sayeed, Khalid Bin. *Western Dominance and Political Islam*. State University of New York Press, Albany, 1995.

Schacht, Joseph. *An Introduction to Islamic Law*. Oxford University Press, London, 1964.

Schimmel, Annemarie. *Calligraphy and Islamic Culture*. New York University Press, New York, 1984.

Schmidt, Nathaniel. *Ibn Khaldun*. Columbia University Press, New York, 1930.

Sellum, Sadek. *L'Islam et les Musulmans en France*. Tougui, Paris, 1987.

Shah, Indries. *The Sufis*. Doubleday, New York, 1964.

Shaked, Haim. *Life of the Sudanese Mahdi*. Transaction, New Brunswick, 1978.

Simone, T. Abdou M. *In Whose Image?* University of Chicago Press, Chicago, 1994.

Sivan, Emmanuel. *Radical Islam*. Yale University Press, New Haven, 1985.

Smith, Wilfred Cantwell. *Islam in Modern History*. Princeton University Press, Princeton, 1977.

Sonn, Tamara. *Between Qur'an and Crown*. Westview Press, Boulder, 1990.

Sourdel, Dominique. *Medieval Islam*. Routledge & Kegan Paul, London, 1979.

Stowasser, Barbara F. *Religion and Political Development: Some Comparative Ideas on Ibn Khaldun and Machiavelli*. Center for Contemporary Arab Studies, Georgetown University, Washington, 1983.

Sylvester, Anthony. *Sudan Under Nimeiri*. Bodley Head, London, 1977.

Tamimi, Azzam, ed. *Power-Sharing Islam?* Liberty, London, 1993.

Tibawi, A. L. *Islamic Education*. Luzac, London, 1979.

Tibi, Bassam. *The Crisis of Modern Islam*. University of Utah Press, Salt Lake City, 1988.

Vaziri, Mostafa. *The Emergence of Islam*. Paragon House, New York, 1992.

Viorst, Judith. *Imperfect Control*. Simon & Schuster, New York, 1998.

Viorst, Milton. *Reaching for the Olive Branch: UNRWA and Peace in the Middle East*. Indiana University Press, Bloomington, 1989.

———. *Sandcastles: The Arabs in Search of the Modern World*. Knopf, New York, 1994.

Voll, John O., ed. *Sudan: State and Society in Crisis*. University of Indiana, Bloomington, 1991.

Watt, W. Montgomery. *Bell's Introduction to the Qur'an*. Edinburgh University Press, Edinburgh, 1970.

————. *Free Will and Predestination in Early Islam*. Luzac, London, 1948.

————. *The Influence of Islam on Medieval Europe*. Edinburgh University Press, Edinburgh, 1972.

————. *Islamic Philosophy and Theology*. Edinburgh University Press, Edinburgh, 1962.

————. *Islamic Political Thought*. Edinburgh University Press, Edinburgh, 1968.

————. *Muhammad at Mecca*. Clarendon Press, Oxford, 1953.

————. *Muhammad at Medina*. Clarendon Press, Oxford, 1956.

Weatherby, W.J. *Salman Rushdie: Sentenced to Death*. Carroll & Graf, New York, 1990.

Wensinck, A. J. *The Muslim Creed*. Oriental Books, New Delhi, 1979.

Wiggin, Kate D., and Nora A. Smith. *The Arabian Nights*. Barnes & Noble, New York, 1993.

World Bank, Claiming the Future: Choosing Prosperity in the Middle East and North Africa. Washington, 1995.

Wright, Robin. *Sacred Rage*. Simon & Schuster, New York, 1985.

Zakaria, Rafiq. *The Struggle Within Islam*. Penguin Books, New York, 1989.

Zwemer, Samuel M. *The Law of Apostasy in Islam*. Marshall Bros. Ltd., London, 1924.

Glossary

bid'a—innovation, usually in reference to orthodox belief, hence heretical.

dhimma—persons, generally Christians and Jews, whose religious practice is protected under Muslim law in return for certain legal restrictions and a special tax payment.

fatwa—a legal opinion delivered by a qualified Islamic scholar.

fitna—disorder or social strife, usually interpreted as a challenge to a ruler.

hadith—a tradition or precedent set by the Prophet, the foundation of the *sunna* and hence of Islamic law.

hudud (sing. *hadd*)—offenses for which the Quran provides fixed punishments: drinking, theft, armed robbery, illicit sex and sexual slander. The most famous *hadd* is theft, in that it requires the cutting off of the hand.

ijma—consensus of believers.

ijtihad—from *jihad*, striving, debate over the interpretation of Islamic law, often said to be "closed" since the tenth century.

imam—head of the *umma*, used by Sunnis to mean a prayer leader and by Shi'ites to mean a successor to Ali.

jahiliyya (adj. *jahili*)—the era of ignorance in Arabia that preceded the coming of Islam.

jihad—striving, used to mean both a quest for holiness and the waging of holy war.

kafir—one who refuses to see the truth, an infidel.

madrasah—a school that teaches Islamic law, more commonly an Islamic secondary school.

mujahideen—from *jihad*, striving, those who strive, commonly used to mean Islamic warriors.

rashidun—the "rightly-guided ones," referring to the first four caliphs who succeeded to the Prophet.

shari'a—"the way," the name for Islamic law.

shura—consultation, a product of tribal tradition, a process commanded in the Quran for the solution of communal problems.

sunna—tradition, the collective precedents set by the Prophet, which is the foundation of Islamic law.

taqlid—the acceptance of truth on the authority of an *imam*, the foundation of Islamic orthodoxy.

ulama (sing. *alim*)—from *ilm*, knowledge, a body of scholars recognized as authorities on Islamic law, the closest thing in Islam to a clergy.

Index

ABOUT THE AUTHOR

Milton Viorst has written about the Middle East for twenty-five years, much of them while on staff at *The New Yorker*. He is the author of a dozen books, including the critically acclaimed *Sandcastles: The Arabs in Search of the Modern World* and *Sands of Sorrow: Israel's Journey from Independence*. He lives in Washington, D.C., with his wife, Judith. They have three sons.